Neil Elliott is an adjunct faculty member in Biblical Studies at Metropolitan State University and United Theological Seminary. He is the author of *The Rhetoric of Romans* (1990; Fortress Press edition, 2006) and *Liberating Paul: The Justice of God and the Politics of the Apostle* (1994; Fortress Press edition, 2005), and a contributor to *A People's History of Christianity,* vol 1: *Christian Origins* (Fortress Press, 2005).

D1598553

THE
ARROGANCE
OF
NATIONS

PAUL IN CRITICAL CONTEXTS

*The Paul in Critical Contexts series offers cutting-edge reexaminations
of Paul through the lenses of power, gender, and ideology.*

Apostle to the Conquered: Reimagining Paul's Mission
Davina C. Lopez

The Politics of Heaven: Women, Gender, and Empire in the Study of Paul
Joseph A. Marchal

Christ's Body in Corinth: The Politics of a Metaphor
Yung Suk Kim

THE
ARROGANCE
OF
NATIONS

READING ROMANS
IN THE
SHADOW OF EMPIRE

NEIL ELLIOTT

Fortress Press
Minneapolis

THE ARROGANCE OF NATIONS
Reading Romans in the Shadow of Empire

Cover image: Roman eagle on a round base. Musée des Antiquités Nationales, Saint-Germain-en-Laye, France. Photo © Erich Lessing / Art Resource, NY
Cover design: Laurie Ingram
Book design: The HK Scriptorium, Inc.

Library of Congress Cataloging-in-Publication Data

Elliott, Neil, 1956-
The arrogance of nations : reading Romans in the shadow of empire / Neil Elliott.
p. cm.—(Paul in critical contexts)
Includes bibliographical references and indexes.
ISBN 978-0-8006-3844-3 (alk. paper)
1. Bible. N.T. Romans—Criticism, interpretation, etc. I. Title.
BS2665.52.E45 2008
227'.106—dc22   2007044118

The paper used in this publication meets the minimum requirements of American National Standard for Information Sciences—Permanence of Paper for Printed Library Materials, ANSI Z329.48-1984.

Manufactured in the U.S.A.

12 11 10 09 08 1 2 3 4 5 6 7 8 9 10

If we rightly understand ourselves, our problems are the problems of Paul: and if we be enlightened by the brightness of his answers, those answers must be ours. . . . In the past [those] who hungered and thirsted after righteousness naturally recognized that they were bound to labor with Paul. They could not remain unmoved spectators in his presence. Perhaps we too are entering upon such a time.

—Karl Barth

Only a genuine philosophy of history is capable of respecting the specificity and radical difference of the social and cultural past while disclosing the solidarity of its polemics and passions, its forms, structures, experiences, and struggles, with those of the present day. . . . Only Marxism can give us an adequate account of the essential mystery of the cultural past, which, like Tiresias drinking the blood, is momentarily returned to life and warmth and allowed once more to speak, and to deliver its long-forgotten message in surroundings utterly alien to it. This mystery can be reenacted only if the human adventure is one. . . .

—Fredric Jameson

Our nation's move toward empire is an issue for us not only as citizens of the United States but also as Christian theologians. Christian faith must articulate itself in the context of the dominance of a civil religion that is also a political theology. This political theology is remarkably similar to the political theology of Rome in the first century of the Christian era. . . . The situation for Americans today is remarkably like that of Paul. . . . Even in the churches, it is risky to state clearly that loyalty to Christ requires Christians to stand against the goal of worldly empire.

—John B. Cobb Jr. and David J. Lull

Contents

Timeline

63 B.C.E. Gnaeus Pompeius Magnus (**Pompey the Great**), having defeated Mithridates of Pontus and been hailed as a god in Asia Minor, exerts Roman control over Judea as well. Upon his return to Rome he forges an alliance with Gaius **Julius Caesar** and Crassus (the First Triumvirate) to rival the ascendant power of Marcus Tullius **Cicero** (106–43 B.C.E.).

44 **Julius Caesar** (b. 100) is assassinated; his grandnephew and adopted son Octavius, who takes the name **Octavian** (63 B.C.E.–14 C.E.), vows to avenge him.

31–27 After defeating Marc Antony's forces and compelling his suicide, Octavian returns to Rome and is hailed as "**Augustus**" by the Senate, who confer on him tribunician power for life.

Paul may have been born in the last decade B.C.E. or the first decade C.E.

14 C.E. At Augustus's death, his stepson, **Tiberius** Julius Caesar (42 B.C.E.–37 C.E.), whom he had adopted, comes to power. During his reign, Tacitus would later write, "all was quiet" in Judea (*Hist.* 5.10), the crucifixion of Jesus of Nazareth (in 30?) failing to attract the historian's interest.

31 At Tiberius's death, **Gaius** Julius Caesar Germanicus ("Caligula," 12–41 C.E.), whom Tiberius had made his son in his will, comes to power.

38–41 Roman policy exempting citizens from the poll tax in Alexandria prompts some Judeans to sue for citizenship; the resulting backlash from Greek citizens escalates into a firestorm of persecution. **Philo** (*ca.* 30 B.C.E.–45 C.E.) leads an embassy of protest to Rome, during which he and his comrades are dismayed to hear of Gaius's effort to install a statue of himself in the inner sanctuary of the Jerusalem Temple.

41 Gaius is assassinated by a conspiracy of Roman officers, who set Tiberius's nephew, Tiberius **Claudius** Nero Germanicus (10 B.C.E.–54 C.E.), in power. Claudius immediately issues a decree suppressing riots in Alexandria.

49   Claudius orders the expulsion of some Judeans from Rome, probably after disturbances in the streets.

54   Claudius dies, probably poisoned: his niece and wife, Agrippina, is suspected. Upon his accession to power, her son, and Claudius's adopted son, **Nero** Claudius Caesar (37–68), requests that the Senate confer divine honors upon Claudius.

55 or 56   (Or, possibly, one or two years later): Paul writes the letter to the Romans, whom he has been delayed from visiting by the urgency of his travel to Jerusalem with the collection. According to Acts (chaps. 21–28), that trip ends in disaster as Paul is confronted by a mob in the Temple precincts; he is subsequently hauled before a series of Roman magistrates, ending up at last in Rome.

65–68?   According to 1 Clement (6:1), Paul and Peter were put to death under Nero, who had targeted *Christiani* for persecution in the wake of the great fire in 64. Paul's own execution (by beheading, according to Eusebius, *Eccl. Hist.* 2.25) may have been the result of a formal hearing.

66–70   A series of outrages by Roman soldiers sparks revolt in Judea; after four brutal years, the Romans conquer Jerusalem and destroy the Temple.

68   Nero kills himself to avoid capture in a military coup.

Illustrations

Preface

Men anpil, chaj pa lou: the Haitian proverb declares, "with many hands, the burden is not heavy." Though writing can be a solitary enterprise, every author knows the inestimable value of the support of family, friends, and institutions. Above all, I thank Mary Ellen for her patience and encouragement over the years it has taken to bring this project to fruition. I owe thanks also to faculty colleagues at Metropolitan State University and to clergy colleagues in the Episcopal Diocese of Minnesota for the confidence they expressed in awarding research grants to support my work.

Though the interpretation of Romans I present on the following pages is distinctive, the tremendous debts I owe to the insights and labors of the "great cloud" of New Testament scholars will be obvious throughout. Given the wealth of other scholarly resources on Romans available today, notably the long-awaited and richly rewarding Hermeneia commentary by Robert Jewett (*Romans* [Minneapolis: Fortress Press, 2006]), I have made no attempt here to represent comprehensively the views of other scholars. For encouraging conversation and challenging questions, I thank especially Dick Horsley, Pamela Eisenbaum, Amy-Jill Levine, Mark D. Nanos, Christopher P. Stanley, and the members and participants in the Paul and Politics Section and the Seminar on Paul's Use of Scripture of the Society of Biblical Literature, who have helped to shape the argument here in important ways; though of course, they are not responsible for my construal of Romans. I am grateful for the confidence shown in this work by Scott Tunseth and Michael West at Fortress Press, for the capable and considerate efforts of Marshall Johnson, James Korsmo, Tim Larson, Josh Messner, Laurie Ingram, and Susan Johnson, and for the skill and talent of Leslie Rubin, Chuck John, and Jeska Horgan-Kobelski.

I studied Paul as a graduate student at Princeton Theological Seminary under the deft and passionate guidance of J. Christiaan Beker, who had drunk deeply at the spring of Karl Barth's *Sachkritik* and who had come in his own work to understand the "inner dialectic of the matter" in Romans as "the coming cosmic triumph of God." It was Chris Beker whom I first heard voice disquiet that discussions of Paul's apocalyptic thought had usually neglected the question of Roman imperial eschatology as expressed, for example, in Virgil's *Fourth Eclogue*. That question, as much as Chris's wide-ranging theological imagination, scholarly erudition, and passionate commitment to the triumph of God from which it sprang, set me on the path that has led to this book. I remember him with affection and gratitude.

Women merchants wait in line at a savings and loan office near Thiotte, Haiti. Such small business women, ti machann, *are the mainstay of Haiti's informal economy. Image ©
Gideon Mendel/CORBIS.*

INTRODUCTION

A Perennial Question

─────────── **Port-au-Prince, Haiti, August 1995** ───────────

The lunchroom of the U.S. embassy is chilled by constant air conditioning. Fluorescent light glares off the hard planes of plastic tables and the linoleum floor. Styrofoam cups of Coca-Cola and instant coffee are on offer to visitors. The spare environment conveys efficiency and reassures the visitor that the familiar sights, smells, and tastes of a prefabricated American culture can prevail even here, inside this artificial bubble, away from the noise of the teeming streets, the hot crush of laboring bodies, and the swirling aromas of charcoal, sweat, diesel exhaust, and rotting garbage. (A decade later, journalist Christian Parenti will describe a similar atmospheric cocoon inside the Green Zone in U.S.-occupied Iraq.[1])

I visit Haiti in the company of a human-rights lawyer and a Haitian-American translator. Our task: to prepare a report on the aftermath of the notorious 1991 coup d'état that removed from power a democratically elected and wildly popular president, former priest Jean-Bertrand Aristide. The coup regime that followed presided over three years of terror, during which some five thousand men, women, and children were killed (to name only the conservative estimates of human rights reports) before U.S. Marines landed in a much-celebrated "intervention" in October 1994. Our team's report will focus on the evidence for an orchestrated campaign of sexual assault and torture, carried out by police and paramilitary forces, especially in the poorer neighborhoods of Port-au-Prince. The report we write will be one of the first to focus upon state-sponsored sexual violence against women as a human rights crime.[2]

Only yesterday, we made our way on foot down the dusty, debris-strewn alleys of Pétionville to meet with a group of forty Haitian women, including frightened teenage girls and wizened old *ti machann,* the street vendors who scratch together a living peddling charcoal stubs, fruit, or chunks of sugarcane in the choking dust and exhaust of the streets. The wide difference in their ages notwithstanding, these women had all been brutally raped and beaten by organized squads of police and paramilitary thugs, members of the notorious Front for the Advancement of the Haitian People (in French, FRAPH), who had swept through their neighborhoods in waves of terror by night. Some of these women had been forced to watch their children beaten or tortured in front of

1

them; others had watched their husbands or lovers killed or abducted, never to be seen again.

In the months after those attacks, all of these women had come under the cautious, solicitous care of a team of Haitian women lawyers and therapists. After more than a year together, they had decided as a group to go before a much-anticipated "truth commission" to tell their stories.

These courageous women shared a modest lunch of soup and chicken with us, then sang a robust chorus about freedom and invited us to join in an exuberant circle dance. At last, choking back tears and anger, a few of them told us their stories. Several said they still recognized their attackers on the street from time to time, wearing the new uniform of the reorganized Haitian National Police. Although the United Nations was taking extraordinary measures to protect their identities, we asked the women if they feared reprisals even now from the men who had attacked them. "I do not care what they do to me," one woman in her sixties immediately replied, straightening her six-foot frame. "They killed my husband; they can try to kill me. *Men m'ap gen jistis!*—But I will have justice!"

Today, with her cry still ringing in our ears, we have come to the U.S. embassy with something less than optimism. Although the Clinton administration has claimed credit for ending the coup regime by sending Marines ashore in October 1994, we are only too aware how carefully the intervention was structured to protect the coup leaders from prosecution, to obscure any record of U.S. involvement in the violence of the three-year coup regime, and to circumscribe the executive powers of the newly restored president, Aristide.[3]

With such ominous precedents before us, we want to know what role the U.S. government intends to take in bringing other perpetrators, the "small fry," to justice—for accountability was, after all, what Americans were told was the goal of the 1994 U.S. invasion. We have already heard Haitian human rights leaders voice their grave suspicion that the U.S. government's default on a promise of one million dollars for the long-delayed "truth commission" indicates that the United States will undermine any genuine effort to bring the criminals to account.

The State Department attaché for human rights extends a friendly hand and offers us Cokes. A freshly scrubbed young man with an Ivy League education, looking every bit the calm and efficient young professional though (as he tells us) he is only a few weeks into his new job, he can afford to be cheerful. "U.S. policy in Haiti is the last great experiment in Wilsonian democracy," he buoyantly explains. "What the United States hopes for is another success story like El Salvador."

Our faces betray that his comment has taken us aback. I wonder whether, by naming Wilson, this earnest young man really wants to evoke the horrors perpetrated by Woodrow Wilson's Marines in the wake of the first U.S. invasion of Haiti, what a subsequent internal Marine inquiry described as the "indiscriminate killing" of perhaps 15,000 "natives," and what a Marine officer later called "hunting down" suspected rebels (meaning any who resisted or fled) "like pigs."[4] Or does the historical record simply not intrude on the imaginative world this young acolyte of U.S. policy has learned to inhabit?

The human-rights lawyer with our delegation asks what makes El Salvador a "success story." She observes that the U.S.-brokered peace accords in El Salvador bestowed immunity from prosecution upon the military and civilian architects of twelve years of repression: the engineers of approximately 70,000 civilian deaths per U.N. estimates. She wonders aloud how that result squares with U.S. government commitments, through international covenants like the U.N. Charter and the Organization of American States Convention on Human Rights, never to allow immunity from prosecution for gross human rights violations. Will it be U.S. policy to grant tacit impunity to the architects of similarly horrific crimes in Haiti?

The attaché looks us over with a flinty calculation. Perhaps, I imagine, he is trying to fathom how much we actually know about the State Department's role in recent events. At last he offers a broad, disarming smile. "Ah, that's the perennial question of the Western hemisphere, isn't it?" he asks. "Whether to seek vengeance against the 'bad guys,' or to let bygones be bygones and get on with creating a Western-style democracy."[5]

We talk for a few minutes more, but our questions get no further than that half-smirking reference to armed teams of rapists and murderers as "the bad guys," and a facile equation of accountability—the minimum threshold of justice required under international law—with irrational impulses to "vengeance."

"Blessed are those who hunger and thirst to see right prevail," Jesus declared: "they shall be satisfied" (Matt. 5:6, REB). The Haitian women we met in Pétion-ville spoke with throats parched with that thirst for justice. For at least one official carrying out U.S. policy in Port-au-Prince, on the other hand, it seems the only thirst that matters can readily be slaked with the offer of another Coca-Cola.

Posing a Perennial Question

My concern in the following pages is with the question of justice. Justice is not only the "perennial question" that haunts U.S. policy in the Western Hemisphere. Justice is the question, or better, the contest at the heart of what Marxist critic Fredric Jameson has called the "single vast unfinished plot" that is human history. That plot, which Jameson characterizes as "the collective struggle to wrest a realm of Freedom from a realm of Necessity," is the ultimate horizon of all human cultural expressions, and of their interpretation. The consequence Jameson draws is that our conventional habit of distinguishing "cultural texts that are social and political and those that are not"—religious texts, for example—is "something worse than an error." It is a symptom of the pervasive logic of capitalist culture which privatizes individual experience and insulates the individual imagination from the horizons of political change.[6]

Jameson's point is perhaps nowhere more evident than with regard to the interpretation of Paul's letter to the Romans. Contestation over justice is at the heart of
the letter, but that fact has been long obscured by the Christian dogmatic tradition.
Library shelves groan under the weight of volumes insisting that the *dikaiosynē
tou theou* of which Paul speaks is a purely theological concept, the "righteousness"
that is a transcendent attribute of God alone; or else it is, as an expression of that
righteousness, the "justification" that God imputes to human sinners, regardless
of their action for good or ill. These phenomena are so sublime, so abstract, and so
beyond analogy with mere human justice that only carefully trained theological
professionals may comprehend and interpret them accurately.

That dogmatically determined construal of the letter has been challenged, however, first by liberation theologians in Central America. In *Marxism and the Bible*
(1974), José Porfirio Miranda argued that justice between human beings was the
"revolutionary and absolutely central message" of Romans, a message "customarily
avoided by exegesis."[7] In *The Amnesty of Grace* (1991), Elsa Tamez protested the
abstraction, universalism, and individualism of the classical doctrine of justification by faith, which when applied in the abstract to the realities of Latin America,
"where the most obvious sin is structural" and where "the sins that kill are very
tangible," yielded disastrous results: "justification viewed from an abstract, individual, and generic plane is good news more for the oppressors than for the poor."
For Tamez, the consequence for responsible interpretation of Paul's thought was a
simple and straightforward commitment: "to reject every approach that favors the
rich to the detriment of the poor."[8]

Subsequently, North American scholars have argued for a *re*-politicized reading
of Romans (that is, for a reversal of previous reading practices that *de*-politicized
the letter). In *Liberating Paul* (1994), I protested the theological "mystification"
of Paul and the "Babylonian captivity of the letter to the Romans" in the powerful wake of Reformation dogmatics, developments that marginalized the political
aspects of Paul's thought.[9] In *Reading Derrida/Thinking Paul,* Theodore W. Jennings Jr. has lamented the restriction of the reading of Romans "to a confessional/
ecclesiastical ghetto of doctrinal interest"; the result, he protests, is that "Paul's
concern for the question of justice has been transformed into a question of interior
or private righteousness." As a result of this theological manhandling on the part
of the apostle's "ecclesial and dogmatic jailers," "the question of justice has been
effectively silenced, substituting in its place a doctrine of justification that absolves
the believer from the claim and call of justice."[10] In their commentary on Romans,
John B. Cobb Jr. and David J. Lull observe that "in the Roman Empire, what people today call 'religion' and 'politics' were inseparable"; they find in Romans a vision
"that sharply contradicted the political theology" of Paul's day.[11] Most recently, in
his Hermeneia commentary, Robert Jewett has declared that "the argument of
Romans revolves around the question of which rule is truly righteous and which
gospel has the power to make the world truly peaceful."[12]

But these perspectives on the letter are not yet prevalent in scholarship, or in North American Christianity. The dominant reading of Romans among Reformation churches, emphasizing justification by grace through faith alone, has often had a quiescent effect, serving to neutralize impulses toward collective action for social change. At the same time, the cultural currents that wash through more evangelical and Fundamentalist churches and, increasingly, throughout U.S. political life promote the powerful impression that the righteousness that so preoccupies the biblical God is a matter of strictly personal morality and of adherence to a strident nationalism. This understanding of "righteousness," Helmut Koester has observed, "functions as an important support for the structures of the state," calling forth proper decorum and due respect, especially from the religious. However, Koester protests that the moralistic interpretation of Paul is "impossible": Paul's God was "not interested in righteous individuals," but wanted "to create righteousness and justice for people, for communities, and for nations."[13]

The reading of Paul against which Koester protests is readily illustrated. Perhaps no biblical text is more often deployed "as an important support for the structures of the state" than the notorious exhortation to "be subject to the governing authorities" in Rom 13:1–7. A single personal anecdote may serve the point.

Hannibal, Missouri, March 2003

The weekend after George W. Bush ordered the bombing and military invasion of Iraq in what is customarily called the Second Iraq War, I walked through downtown Hannibal, Missouri, a town that relies for tourism on its fame as the home town of American author and humorist Mark Twain. Like many town centers across the United States, the Hannibal main street was decked out in U.S. flags, yellow ribbons, and placards urging passersby to "Support Our Troops." One solitary sign of dissent hung in a coffee shop window, a single typed page inviting citizens to an evening "discussion" of the war.

The woman who had posted the modest invitation told me that neighbors had already challenged her "anti-Americanism." "It's hard to question the war in Hannibal," she said. When I asked how that squared with the town's public celebration of the best known member of the Anti-Imperialist League, she answered, "that would be news here. Most people in Hannibal don't know anything about Mark Twain beyond *The Adventures of Tom Sawyer* and *Huckleberry Finn*."

A tour of the local museums bore out her point. An exhibit dedicated to Mark Twain's literary career focused almost exclusively on his humorous writings. I found two references to Twain's literary tours of Europe, but not a hint that he had spoken regularly and often in Europe, as well as in the United States, on behalf of the Anti-Imperialist League. On one wall, a turn-of-the-century newspaper cartoon depicted Twain seated upon a throne, being paid court by the "Crowned Heads of

Europe"; behind his throne, a single figure labeled "Leopold" sat dejected, his head on his fist. The museum caption described Twain's fame in Europe but offered no explanation of Leopold. No one would learn in this museum of the horrific atrocities carried out in the Congo by King Leopold of Belgium, or of Twain's fervent efforts, alongside other activists in Europe and the United States, to make those atrocities an international cause célèbre.[14]

Newspaper advertisements and hastily erected signs around town invited residents and visitors to attend "prayer services for our troops" at any of a number of local churches. In most other American cities, the signs might have been unexceptional, but they struck an ironic note in Hannibal, where every gift shop and museum store sold several different editions of Mark Twain's short, bitterly satirical essay, *War Prayer*. The essay tells of a mysterious stranger who interrupts the eloquent prayers of a local pastor on a Sunday morning and points out to the congregation that an unspoken prayer has accompanied their spoken words to heaven. Their prayer for victory is also a prayer for the God of love to blight the land and the homes of the enemy, to leave widows and orphans desolate and without hope.[15]

I saw no invitations from churches to discuss the *War Prayer*. Except for that single conversation in a coffee shop, there was no indication that anyone in Mark Twain's home town was the least troubled by invitations to join in prayers (in the phrasing of a ubiquitous bumper sticker) to "Support *Our* Troops." Indeed, the only literary allusion informing the cultural discourse of Hannibal, Missouri, accompanied one local pastor's letter in the local newspaper. He wrote, "It is the duty of all Christians to stand with their president in a time of war (Rom 13:1–7)."

If Hannibal were exceptional, I would not recount the experience. My point is that even in one town where one might have expected the flicker of a thoroughly American anti-war sentiment to be visible, discussion could be managed, and dissent largely precluded (in public as well as in the churches), by an appeal to Paul's letter to the Romans.

Reading Differently

The argument of this book is that from its very first lines, Paul's letter burns with the incendiary proclamation of God's justice, and with a searing critique of the injustice (*adikia*) of those who smother and suppress the truth (1:17–18). The themes that dominate Romans are *political* topics: the imagination of a global order achieved through the obedience of nations (see chap. 1 below); the arrogance and hypocrisy of wicked rulers who "suppress the truth" (chap. 2); the tension between justice and the pretensions to "mercy" shown by the conqueror to the vanquished (chap. 3); the serviceability of religious values and popular devotion (chap. 4); and questions of realism, hope, and the common good (chap. 5). These themes reveal how powerfully Paul and the assemblies he addressed were caught up in the swirling currents of Roman imperial culture. That culture, like all imperial cultures, ancient and modern, was preoccupied with what the late cultural critic Edward Said called "notions that certain territories and people require and beseech domination." Said's insistence that we "take empire seriously" and abandon the pretense of neutrality regarding its effects has helped to inspire the rise of postcolonial criticism in biblical studies. One of the leading figures in this development, Fernando F. Segovia, applies the principle by insisting that a fully contextualized reading of the New Testament texts must address "the reality of empire" as "an omnipresent, inescapable, and overwhelming sociopolitical reality."[16]

Taking empire seriously in biblical interpretation requires looking in two directions at once. Looking back at the ancient Roman Empire, we will attend to what Marxist historian G. E. M. de Ste. Croix has called "a massive system of exploitation of the great majority by the ruling classes," and of the myriad ways, which Ste. Croix and others have ably documented, in which imperial rule, and the ideological representation of the emperor's role in particular, served to maintain and reinforce a thoroughly "parasitic" economic system.[17] Looking simultaneously at our own context, we must be as alert to the "cultural logic of late capitalism" that informs and shapes contemporary life, including what sociologists have termed the "production of the sacred" in public religion and the academic disciplines involved in biblical studies.[18]

There are significant points of analogy between ancient Roman imperialism and the complex fabric of contemporary imperialism, by which I mean both the global military supremacy that is official U.S. policy and the globalizing capitalism that it serves.[19] There is admittedly a danger here of anachronism in comparing two very different historical contexts; but a greater danger would be a failure to take seriously the resemblance between the ways distinct ideologies serve to legitimate and naturalize the dominant social order in both ancient Roman and contemporary U.S. imperialism. In both contexts, for example, representations of benevolence, paternalism, and authority, focused in the figure of a single wise, caring, autocratic ruler, serve to mask the exploitative dynamics of the economic order. Precisely because my concern is an ancient text that continues to be invested with tremendous authority in the U.S. culture, understanding the dominant ideological functions of rhetoric in both contexts is an urgent task.[20]

Because so many of us—in the U.S. culture broadly, in American churches especially, but in academic circles as well—suffer what Said decried as the "astonishing sense of weightlessness" regarding "the gravity of history,"[21] the effort that follows, to read Paul's letter in the context of Roman imperial ideology, may at first glance appear eccentric. The less traveled path on which I embark in the following pages has seen increasing traffic in recent years, however, in the work of scholarly colleagues in the Paul and Politics section of the Society of Biblical Literature, and beyond.[22] Those colleagues will recognize my debts to their efforts to take empire seriously; others will recognize how much I owe as well, to advances in the growing fields of rhetorical criticism and postcolonial interpretation, and to the interest in "people's history" and the hidden transcripts of subordinated or marginalized groups.[23]

The greatest challenge to a political reading of Romans is the broad assumption that we already know what Romans is about. It is, we commonly assume, self-evidently a debate with Judaism, its argument directed primarily against Jewish works-righteousness (on an older, Lutheran reading), or against the Jewish ethnocentrism that mobilized a concerted Jewish opposition to Paul's intolerably inclusive gospel (according to the "New Perspective"). But the letter is explicitly addressed to *non*-Judeans, representatives of "the nations" (*ta ethnē*, commonly rendered "Gentiles": see below). In *The Rhetoric of Romans* (1990), I argued that given that clear and explicit address (see 1:5–7, 11–15; 15:14–16), the rhetoric of Romans must be read as directed to that audience. As Stanley K. Stowers later made the point in *A Rereading of Romans* (1994), the habit of importing an implied Jewish audience serves dogmatic and apologetic purposes but flouts the clear rhetorical indicators of the letter. Ben Witherington III has taken the same approach in his socio-rhetorical commentary to Romans.[24] I will presume those more extensive arguments regarding the letter's non-Judean audience in what follows.

But more is at stake in our interpretation than an accurate reading of the letter's argumentation. Too often, theological readings of Romans have relied on historically untenable stereotypes of Jews and Judaism. The not-yet universal recognition of that fact has both fueled and complicated the modern study of Paul. Conventional readings also serve—as they have served for centuries—to reinforce a distinctive *Christian* self-understanding, as if it had been the apostle's purpose to provide Gentile Christians, both ancient and modern, a sort of theological pedigree for their legitimacy. Indeed, a long train of interpreters, beginning with Krister Stendahl, have asserted that such defense or legitimation of the Gentile church was the letter's foremost purpose.[25] In this way, the force of Paul's rhetoric is deflected away from *us*—the modern, comfortable, more-or-less secularized first-world Christians who remain the primary consumers of Pauline scholarship, and for whom questions of Israel's destiny and the observance of the Jewish law are usually a matter of only moderate academic interest—onto *them,* the Jews who "failed" to accept the Pauline gospel of universalism that we presume as self-evident, and whom we can afford to regard, from a safe emotional distance, with a polite blend of curiosity and condescension.

As often as we treat Romans differently from Paul's other letters, imagining that it is not a letter of urgent exhortation as they are, we who imagine ourselves to be the modern heirs of his universalistic legacy ensure that we have nothing to fear from it. Whether we are properly tolerant Christians or appropriately liberal academics, or both, we can rest assured that Paul has nothing critical to say to *us*. Indeed, if his purpose was to defend the incipient Gentile-Christian movement—"people like us," after all—from the irrational opposition of prejudiced rivals, then we can read

Romans with a certain self-congratulatory satisfaction. His words do not touch on our privileges or presumptions; they rather commend our prerogatives.

But this is not the way we should hear Romans. To the contrary, this letter challenged, criticized, and confronted what Paul considered troubling aspects of the nascent movement of Christ-believers in his day. One goal in the following pages is to dispel some of the theological fog surrounding Romans, and thus to overcome some of "the astonishing sense of weightlessness" in Pauline studies with regard to the gravity of imperial power. If we do not immediately hear the counter-imperial aspects of Paul's letter, perhaps it is because we are predisposed, by the constricted, privatized, and domesticated contexts in which Paul's letters are most usually read, to perceive in them only a narrow bandwidth of what we consider religious discourse.[26] If one effect of this work is to challenge such notions, it shall have served an important purpose. For those of us who recognize that American imperial ambition and myths of national innocence have distorted and disrupted the witness of contemporary faith communities, and especially Christian churches, to an alternative citizenship, few messages could be more urgent.

Toward a Contemporary *Sachkritik*

If we intend to approach the letter to the Romans with the sort of theological seriousness that Karl Barth offered in the early twentieth century, we will need, like him, to read Romans alert to "the situation in which we ourselves actually are." Barth encountered in Romans "that which urgently and finally concerns the very marrow of human civilization."[27] In Romans, I contend, we see Paul's critical engagement with the claims of imperial ideology and with the corrosive effects of those claims within the Roman congregations of Christ-believers. The material realities in which we live require that a contemporary *Sachkritik,* our own effort to penetrate to "the inner dialectic of the matter," must take with utmost seriousness the ideological forces that shape our own perceptions, determine our own attitudes, and elicit our own compliance (or at least our acquiescence), as well.

No legitimate reading of Romans in our contemporary situation can remain oblivious to the effects of empire today. Precisely because of the ideological forces that constrain our perceptions, however, such a *Sachkritik* will not come easily to many of us.

Reading the signs of the times

Over the last quarter century, we who live in the global North, who are accustomed to reading the Bible in conditions of unprecedented comfort and privilege, have been faced with a new challenge: to learn to hear the biblical voices anew by attending to how our neighbors living at the periphery of imperial culture hear and experience them. If we open ourselves to them, the bearers of so-called theologies of liberation and postcolonial criticism can alert us to the sociopolitical forces at work in our own lives as well as theirs. From our global neighbors, we can learn—if we will listen—that "no theology and no institutional church can be examined in a vacuum; they must be considered in the context of the political and social reality in which they exist and act." So wrote José Comblin, a liberation theologian work-ing in Brazil, for whom "political and social reality" meant living under "American empire and . . . its farthest-reaching export—the national security state."[28] Writing in 1979, Comblin had Latin American realities particularly in view; but his com-ments apply as well to the fateful U.S. support for other national security states like the Baathist regime in Iraq through the 1980s, or the far more lethal military regime in Indonesia through the 1990s, to select but two representative cases.

Our neighbors in the global South, and a swelling chorus of prophetic voices in the North, implore us to take in a disturbing truth. The militarized empire of global capitalism, the very system that has brought so many of us unparalleled pros-perity, which so many of us even regard as sacred, continues to devastate their lives and the lives of their children. It is hard to take in that truth. It is hard, in part, because it is so much easier for us to recognize the evils of *other* systems—formerly, of Soviet expansionism, or now, of the organized terrorism aimed at U.S. Middle East policies—than the evils of the system in which we live, and from which we reap undeniable material benefits.

It is hard to take in that truth, in part, because as the martyred Jesuit academic Ignácio Ellacuría remarked, the "fundamental dynamic" of this system, its "pitiless exploitation," "intrinsic malice," and "predatory ferocity," are ordinarily visible in their true magnitude "only beyond the boundaries of the rich countries, which in numerous ways export the evils of capitalism to the exploited periphery."[29] It is pos-sible for those living at the center of imperial culture to avoid seeing the effects of empire. One must immediately add the qualification that the "exploited periphery" exists at the blighted heart of many U.S. cities as well. Three decades ago, black theologians in the United States recognized that the regime of "exploitative, profit-oriented capitalism is a way of ordering life fundamentally alien to human value in general and to black humanity in particular. Racism and capitalism have set the stage for despoliation of natural and human resources all around the world," not least in our own cities.[30] The pernicious illusion nevertheless prevails that the exploited are personally and morally culpable for the ruinous effects of their own exploitation.

It is, finally, hard to take in this unwelcome truth because omnipresent, corporate-owned electronic media surround us with the messages that our system has won because of its own inherent superiority; that the miserable have earned their misery through sloth; that the sufferings that require our most urgent action are insults to our own national pride; and that our most important preoccupation must be constant, unremitting consumption (represented to us as "our way of life").[31]

However unfamiliar and uncomfortable the perspective to which our global neighbors invite us, however, theological seriousness requires facing the material realities of our age and scrutinizing the dominant ideological representations of those realities on offer all around us. We should not imagine, with a post-modern sensibility, that attending to the themes of imperial ideology is simply one interpretive choice among others. I follow Fredric Jameson in regarding the political interpretation of literary texts like Romans "not as some supplementary method, not as an optional auxiliary to other interpretive methods current today . . . but rather as the absolute horizon of all reading and all interpretation." Holding Romans aloof from political interpretation as if it were fundamentally some other kind of writing, or as if political interpretation could not finally comprehend what was most essential to the letter, only reinforces the artificial distinction between "public" (and political) and "private" (and religious). Ultimately, insulating the interpretation of Romans from political and ideological criticism (or marginalizing political criticism as only one option among others) serves to reconfirm those ideological constraints that isolate religion from playing any meaningful role in history. "The only effective liberation from such constraint," Jameson writes, "begins with the recognition that there is nothing that is not social and historical—indeed, that everything is 'in the last analysis' political."[32] In similar terms, the theologians of liberation have called for decades for the recognition that first-world theology is as completely ideological a product as anything emerging from the periphery of empire.

An ideological-critical reading

Neither, however, may we imagine that we can stand with Paul at some transcendent point, looking down upon the plane of history as if he and we were completely free of its constraints. A *Sachkritik* attentive to the ideological forces at work in a historical situation necessarily attends to what Jameson calls the *strategies of containment* by which those forces in Paul's day, and in our own, repress certain possibilities from consciousness. Jameson argues that because of the constraining power of ideology, a text often points obliquely beyond itself to possibilities that "remain unrealized in the surface of the text." It follows that we cannot content ourselves to read the surface of a text like Romans, but must read beneath and behind it, or better, *through* it to get at the fundamental contestation of power that is inscribed in it.[33] We must read against the grain, listening for what remains unsaid (in Jameson's terms, what has been repressed) as much as what is said.[34]

That proposal is uncontroversial in the study of other writings from the early Roman period. We know that our classical sources left much unsaid that did not align with the interests of the dominant classes. Exceptions prove the rule: there were stridently anti-Roman voices raised in the first century, like the fiercely defiant British warriors Calgacus and Boudicca, for example. But we know of them only because long after they had fallen to their Roman conquerors, Tacitus attributed to them speeches that amplified his account of the expansion of Roman supremacy. We know that some Judeans of the Second Temple period protested Roman arrogance and violence, though none of our sources provide access to direct and explicit criticism of Rome. It is universally recognized that the Habakkuk Pesher from Qumran assails Romans in a bitter indictment, but they remain veiled under the label *Kittim. Fourth Maccabees* expresses hostility to Roman rule, though disguised as an encomium on the "self-control" and "philosophy" of rebels of another age.[35] Even Josephus acknowledges the eloquence of anti-Roman rebels, though he demurs from providing samples (*War* 2.348).

Paul issued no call to arms against Rome; he rallied no rebel garrison. If, however, we attend to those fissures in the text where a unified surface reading becomes impossible, we can recognize subterranean forces at work beneath Romans. Those forces are the object of our investigation. The rhetoric of Romans shows that Paul participated in a cultural transcript, drawing on the repertoires of Judean scripture and apocalyptic writings, that was inescapably in conflict with the empire's absolutizing claims on allegiance.[36]

A political reading begins from the specificity of a given text in its full historical context, grasped, Jameson proposes, "as the imaginary resolution of a real contradiction" inherent in that historical context.[37] In the case of Romans, I contend, these are the contradictions inherent in a situation in which Roman imperial ideology has come into conflict with alternative understandings of justice, order, and community among the empire's subjects. At a second, more general level, the text is apprehended as "an individual *parole* or utterance" within the broader collective and class discourses that "fight it out within the general unity of a shared code."[38] We will not arbitrarily limit the range of discourses that constitute the context of Romans by setting the letter over against contemporary Judean writings alone, then, as has been the repeated practice in past theological interpretation. Rather we will situate Paul's letter *and* the writings of his Judean and non-Judean contemporaries in a broader context of varying responses to Roman rule. An ideological-critical reading of Romans will investigate the effects in the letter of conflicting modes of production in the early Roman Empire, just as Norman Gottwald has taught us to recognize, in the Hebrew Bible, the evidence of seismic upheavals and collisions between conflicting modes of production and their corresponding ideological representations under the Persian Empire.[39]

But precisely because we are caught up in history as much as were Paul and his contemporaries; precisely because we have *not* reached the recently heralded "end of history," but find ourselves engaged, as they were, in an unfinished drama in which competing visions of history's fulfillment are pitted against one another, for this reason we recognize with Jameson that the ultimate horizon of political interpretation is the sweep of history itself. A text like Romans becomes an occasion to recognize in our own day, as in Paul's, the deep struggle through human history that is manifested, from the point of view of Marxist analysis, in conflicts between different material modes of production, but is experienced by its participants as the long-enduring struggle "to wrest a realm of Freedom from a realm of Necessity" (or as Paul phrased it, to experience "the redemption of our bodies," Rom 8:23). A fully political *Sachkritik* of Romans involves our exploration of what is "unsaid," unspeakable, and repressed in our own ideological environment as well. Postcolonial interpreters refer to the critical theological tasks of unmasking, unveiling, and uncovering the deep logic that legitimizes exploitation in our own day as well, especially where the legitimization of injustice bears the sheen of a divine patina. Ultimately, the "decolonizing" of modern biblical interpretation requires decolonizing *us* who are the first-world producers and consumers of biblical interpretation.[40]

Agreements and divergences

The project I have just described requires situating the rhetoric of Romans within a broader rhetorical context, an environment where discourse was shaped and constrained by disparities of power. In the following pages, I will not provide anything like a running commentary on Paul's letter. There are any number of valuable commentaries on Romans available, the most formidable being Robert Jewett's recent Hermeneia commentary, and I will not try to reproduce their efforts. Given the space limitations of the present work, neither will I seek to catalogue points of agreement or disagreement, or polemically to argue for the superiority of my reading or the inadequacy of others where we disagree. My goal is simply to present a coherent reading of the letter that describes both the constraints on discourse, and countervailing impulses to resist those constraints, in a particular imperial situation.

It may nevertheless be helpful at the outset to situate my reading on the landscape of current interpretations of Romans. First, I realize that proposing a political reading of the letter may seem tendentious to some. Equally, my repeated references to the deleterious effects of imperial culture may seem prejudicial to readers for whom the accomplishments of the Augustan age (or our own) are properly objects of admiration. As Karl Galinsky observes in the introduction to his monumental study *Augustan Culture,* "our interpretations of the past are much influenced by our experience with contemporary society, politics, and culture." Currents in twentieth-century European politics have played a decisive role in the perceptions of Augustus and his age,[41] and we should expect nothing different in a time when the self-declared imperial ambitions of contemporary American policymakers are also deeply controversial. Whether we should understand the rise of the Principate and the so-called *Pax Romana* primarily as a narrative of economic and political exploitation achieved through force, or as one of the most important accomplishments in the history of Western civilization—or both, on the grounds (well documented among the proponents of the Roman Empire) that genuine peace can be achieved only through force—these are judgments about which I will not try to change the reader's mind. (That Roman emperors and governors themselves described their motives as including the economic exploitation of the provinces is, of course, a simple matter of fact.)

Similarly, Augustus consolidated tremendous military, economic, political, moral, and sacred power, gaining broad acceptance for his rule on the basis of his own *auctoritas*—the "material, intellectual, and moral superiority" that provides "the ultimate power of the emperor on the moral level."[42] Whether that achievement has any lessons for our own day—when sweeping executive powers, including the exercise of personal discretion in interpreting the constitutional reach of those powers, have been claimed for the president of the world's greatest military power—is a question regarding which I will not attempt to persuade the reader, though I believe certain resemblances in the two situations are compelling.[43]

Romans is widely regarded today as addressed to a specific situation in Rome. Tensions between Judean and non-Judean members of the assemblies gathering in Christ's name threatened Paul's understanding of his own apostolic responsibility. Paul addressed that situation with rhetoric that appealed to a common fund of shared values and convictions, including both Judean scripture (which he quoted here more than in any other letter) and the traditions of the early Christ-movement. So far I am in complete agreement with an emerging consensus.

I shall argue further that Paul also invoked recognizable themes from imperial propaganda, usually in such a way as implicitly to challenge them. I take those invocations and allusions as evidence that the situation in the Roman assemblies was shaped, not primarily by tensions somehow inherent in the proximity of different ethnic groups, as current social-scientific readings have suggested, but to *perceptions* and *themes* in the broader ideology and culture of the Augustan and post-Augustan age.

As we shall see, a number of recent interpreters have alerted us to the political implications of some of Paul's vocabulary, for example "messiah" (*christos*), or "lord" (*kyrios*), or "assembly" (*ekklēsia*). Others have shown that in a highly agonistic culture such as ancient Rome, where an intense competition for honor was played out within fixed relationships of superior and inferior, Paul's exhortations to mutual respect and deference would have been dramatically countercultural. These observations are important, but they tend to portray the tension between Paul's rhetoric and imperial ideology as indirect and rather incidental. I argue, in contrast, that the argument of Romans as a whole collides *inescapably* with the claims of empire, even if that collision is never expressed in explicit terms.

In previous writings, I have described Paul's as an "anti-imperial gospel" and his theology as subversive of imperial values. Others have criticized such characterizations as imprecise and anachronistic. Elisabeth Schüssler Fiorenza has argued convincingly that labeling Paul's gospel "counter-imperial" prematurely rescues Paul for "liberationist" causes, obscures or avoids the extent to which "even resistance literature" can "re-inscribe the structures of domination against which it seeks to argue," and relieves the interpreter of the duty "to inquire as to how such inscribed imperial language functioned in the past, and still functions today."[44] Though I intend to show that some aspects of Paul's rhetoric in Romans were subversive of some of the claims of imperial propaganda, I recognize that Paul never provides a systematic or comprehensive critique of the emperor (whom he never names) or of the empire as such. The empire as such is never his direct target: his goal is to lay a claim on the allegiance of his listeners with which the rival claims of empire inevitably interfered. It is not just that his argumentation is occasionally oblique. Paul's own thinking and rhetoric also was shaped by the ideological constraints of his age. He did not float serenely above his historical situation, as an approach to his letters as "inspired scripture" implies. To borrow an apt phrase from Schüssler Fiorenza, Paul's thought was as fully *kyriarchal,* in its own way, as that of any imperial propagandist (see further chap. 1).[45]

In so far as his thought was shaped by the contestation over power that surrounded him, and in which imperial themes and tropes were dominant, Paul resembled his Judean contemporaries. In strictly historical terms, then, I consider it anachronistic to read Romans as an early specimen of Christian theology. The letter is rather one expression of the range of Judean response to the Roman Empire. What makes Romans distinct from other contemporary Judean writings is not Paul's distance from other forms of Judaism, but the peculiar—one is tempted to say, unique—situation Paul addressed, namely, the recent ascendancy of a non-Judean majority in the local Roman assemblies of what was initially a Judean messianic movement (with all that that implied vis-à-vis Roman hegemony). I read the letter not as a Christian critique of Judaism, or a defense of Gentile Christianity, but as a Judean critique of an incipient non-Judean Christianity in which the pressures of imperial ideology were a decisive factor.

Several of the terms just used, especially Gentile and Christian, are admittedly anachronistic, and I will avoid them in what follows, or use them only advisedly. That may prove disconcerting to readers who expect to learn from these pages what Paul has to say to Christians. That is all to the good. We are well warned against interpretations that privilege the voice of Paul in artificial isolation from his own historical context and that thus serve, however unintentionally, to reinforce the most baleful effects of the Pauline legacy in contemporary society.[46] Such principled warnings stand over against everything that follows. Seeking to interpret Paul in the context of Roman imperial power in his own day does not relieve us of the critical and ethical responsibilities we bear regarding imperialism in our own day. We must, at last, answer for ourselves.

A final qualification regarding my use of "Judean" to translate the Greek *Ioudaios*: Some scholars have recently proposed distinguishing between the term *Judeans,* an ethnic and geographic term for a member of the people hailing from Judea, and the term *Jews,* denoting cultural and religious adherence to the way of life of that people. Shaye Cohen has argued that it is anachronistic to speak of "Jews" before about 100 B.C.E.[47] Philip F. Esler chooses to speak of "Judeans" in Paul's day as well, as a way of conveying *both* the ethnic-geographic and the religious components of Judean identity that "both insiders and outsiders regarded as fundamental," something for which he argues our contemporary usage of "Jew" is inadequate.[48] It is in just this respect that I employ the term *Judean* in what follows, though I do not in any way mean to question or deny the historical continuity between the *Ioudaioi* who were Paul's contemporaries and the modern Jews who are mine.[49] The burden against which I press throughout this book is the weight of the centuries-long projection into Paul's day of subsequent Christian stereotypes regarding Jews and Judaism. I use *Judean* here as a way of reminding the reader and myself that we are dealing with ancient terms, *Ioudaios* and *Iudaeus,* which were used both by those who were and by others who were not *Ioudaioi* to define what being *Ioudaios* meant. My interest is in letting first-century Judeans, Paul above all, speak for themselves.

──────── **The Rhetoric of Romans and the Rhetoric of Rome** ────────

A political *Sachkritik* of Romans requires us to situate Paul's rhetoric amid surrounding discourses as precisely as possible. This, in turn, requires attending to the way disparities in power constrain discourse in a colonial situation. Unfortunately, these are tasks for which traditional rhetorical criticism has proven itself flatly incapable.

Rhetorical-critical dead ends

Because of the legacy of Christian apologetics and Reformation polemics, Romans usually has been or is read as a religious document in which the apostle Paul sets out his distinctive theological views concerning Christian identity and practice, in implicit contrast, if not direct opposition, to the Jewish religion. This approach to Romans necessarily relies upon characterizations of Jews, Judaism, and the Jewish Law as somehow deficient in comparison with Paul's "universal," "law-free" gospel. The Christian theological reading of Romans has also largely set the limits of the rhetorical-critical study of the letter. The widespread perception of the letter's double character, that is, as a letter written to non-Judeans that nonetheless is primarily concerned with Jewish themes, clearly begs rhetorical-critical investigation.[50]

But only rarely has rhetorical criticism led interpreters to question the assumptions, inherited from Reformation dogmatics, that the letter is fundamentally Paul's presentation of a doctrine of salvation, and that this doctrine is fundamentally incompatible with, and opposed to, the Judaism of his contemporaries.

The result is that for a majority of interpreters, the letter remains a theological sample by means of which Paul seeks to introduce himself or his gospel, to "show [the Romans] *in advance* what his gospel *will* be," to offer "an *example* of the kind of preaching or teaching he *will* practice when among them," "to present his gospel" to them so that they might "know more about its character and his mode of argumentation," to introduce to them "the teaching activity Paul *hopes to do* at Rome" or "the gospel *to be . . . proclaimed* [in Spain]," including sample admonitions regarding a way of life "that *would* ensure the success" of the Spanish mission; to "[provide] a sustained account of his understanding of the gospel" to "justify his message and mission" by "clarifying and defending his beliefs," to "inform the church [in Rome] about his missionary theology" so that they would "know his thinking."

These common characterizations of the letter, couched predominantly in the subjunctive mood, as a theological "position paper," a "think piece" drawn from the apostle's portfolio, have an impressive following.[51] They coincide with a perception of the letter as written under circumstances free of constraint, a perception particularly convenient for generalizations about the letter's content as Paul's "basic theological position . . . more or less completely set forth" in its "most complete and complex synthesis," "the most sustained and reflective statement of Paul's own theology"—again, views representative of a wide range of interpreters.[52] But the characterizations I have just cited have scant basis in the text itself. Paul says nothing in the letter to indicate that he is presenting his own ideas to garner his readers' approval of himself or his mission.

Unfortunately, rhetorical-critical interpretations of Romans have often done little more than glean from the classical Greek and Roman rhetorical handbooks a novel technical nomenclature for an outline of the letter that has already been established, without the benefit of rhetorical categories, in dogmatic readings. For example, the conventional identification of Romans 1:16–17 as the theme or thesis of the letter, in defiance of the formal and syntactical features of those verses, is sometimes expressed now as a rhetorical-critical insight, though without any more substantiation than an appeal to a "consensus" among interpreters.[53] Similarly, some interpreters tend to describe the letter in terms resembling the genre of the philosophical treatise or letter essay, though it bears none of the hallmarks of the ancient letter essay.[54] Others seek to identify the rhetorical genre of the letter according to the categories of the ancient rhetorical handbooks, but falter on prior assumptions regarding the letter's purpose.[55]

In contrast, I expect the ancient handbooks to be of only limited usefulness in determining the genre of Romans. The handbooks were designed, after all, for the fairly formal expectations of public oratory in the Greco-Roman world. But as scholars of classical rhetoric themselves have reminded us, many forms of speech cannot be fitted into the fairly rigid categories of the handbooks: notably, the authoritative, often spontaneous, and ecstatic speech that is characteristic of what George A. Kennedy called "religious" rhetoric.[56] Romans is persuasive rhetoric, but it is presented in terms of the *announcement* of the effective power of God (*euangelizesthai*), a mode of rhetoric that finds scant treatment in the classical handbooks. Paul's reliance on arguments from Israel's scripture and his resort to the category of divinely revealed "mystery" (11:25) point us toward what Aristotle called "inartificial" proofs.[57] Paul's invocation of sacred power—when he introduces himself as one called and set apart by God (1:1, 5, passim); when he declares that the power of God "is being revealed" in his proclamation (1:15) and that the justice and the wrath of God are likewise "being revealed" (1:16–18); his reference at the end of the letter to "what Christ has accomplished in me in the power of signs and wonders, by the power of the Holy Spirit" (15:18–19)—similarly highlight a distinctive "apodeictic" aspect of his rhetoric, that is, his evocation of the divine "proof" or "manifestation" (*apodeixis*) of heavenly power. Paul explicitly characterizes his rhetoric to the Corinthian assembly in just these terms, as a "demonstration [*apodeixis*] of spirit and power" rather than reliance on "persuasive (words) of wisdom" (1 Cor 2:4).[58] A similar rhetoric characterizes Romans. The exigence, the perceived need calling forth this letter, is God's active purpose in calling Paul to bring about "faithful obedience among the nations" (1:5).[59]

Because the classical handbooks presumed the power relationships of the established civic order, they provide no categories for describing rhetoric in tension with that order. Judicial rhetoric was the rhetoric of the law court, where the interests of the propertied class were inevitably served. Deliberative rhetoric was appropriate to the public assembly, from which those without property were excluded. Shame and honor, the themes of epideictic or ceremonial oratory, similarly were defined by the ruling class, as Mark Reasoner and Robert Jewett have observed.[60] Indeed, the handbooks assume that persuasive speech was a possibility only among the "civilized." From the perspective of a master rhetorician like Cicero, the only language the rabble understood was force;[61] and the casual air with which Aristotle discussed the speaker's options regarding testimony torn from slaves under torture, to which he attributed no inherent evidentiary value whatsoever, similarly speaks volumes regarding the relation the handbooks assume to exist between persuasion and coercion.[62] We should not assume such resources will be of direct or uncomplicated assistance for our understanding of an "invasive" or disruptive rhetoric such as Paul's in Romans, a rhetoric that announces the revelation of "God's wrath . . . against the impiety and injustice of those who by their injustice suppress the truth," who although claiming to be wise, have been made fools by God's "darkening" of their minds (Rom 1:18, 21–22).

Romans as exhortation

Finally, although the ancient rhetoricians occasionally recognized the phenomenon of exhortation by letter, it played no role in their discussions of formal public discourse. The hard-and-fast distinction made in the handbooks between epideictic rhetoric (ceremonial rhetoric, concerned with praise and blame) and deliberative (concerning advantageous and disadvantageous action) simply breaks down with regard to the genre of the hortatory or paraenetic letter.[63] But that is exactly what Romans is. It is no coincidence that appeals to the handbooks often serve characterizations of the letter as a last will and testament, a think-piece, or a theological self-introduction. These readings necessarily minimize explicit statements of the letter's purpose in 1:11-15 and 15:14-16, and fail to recognize that Paul's diplomatic language in just those passages employs a well-known convention in Greco-Roman moral exhortation (see further chap. 1).

Further, as Victor P. Furnish showed a generation ago, exhortation is not limited to a "paraenetic section" at the end of Romans, but gives structure to the argumentation of the whole letter.[64] The appeal in Romans 12 called hearers "to a new life exactly opposite" the life Paul had described in 1:18–32. That appeal was based on and recapitulated the language in Romans 6, where Paul's explicit subject was baptism into Christ.[65] The whole of the letter, Furnish concluded, was structured by a form of exhortation that was common in the early churches, a form that Rudolf Bultmann characterized as the "formerly . . . but now" scheme, which emphasized the change brought about by baptism from a former life to a new life.[66]

Most scholars concede that the letter explicitly addresses its recipients as from "the nations" (*ta ethnē*: 1:6, 13; see 15:14–16). A minority of scholars have insisted, rightly, that the letter's argument must be read as directed to the *explicitly named* audience rather than by importing a supposed Judean opposition into the letter, however congenial such a maneuver may seem to Christian apologetics.[67] The goal of rhetorical-critical interpretation of Romans should be to understand how the argumentation of the whole letter would have functioned to achieve the adherence of the explicitly named non-Judean audience. I have argued that case at length in an earlier work and will presume aspects of that argument here.[68]

Scholars generally concede that the argumentation of Romans reaches an emotional climax in Romans 9–11, but often fail to follow through with the consequences of that observation. Nils Dahl demonstrated decades ago that the sorts of epistolary features that normally help us recognize the purpose of any other of Paul's letters are more evident in Romans 9–11 than in chapters 1–8. "Attention to such details," Dahl concluded, "shows that in Romans 9–11 Paul not only unfolds the theological theme of the letter as a whole, but also addresses the epistolary situation more directly than in most parts of Romans 1–8."[69] Instead, then, of reading the letter as a series of proofs of a thesis in 1:16-17, we should recognize the overall structure of the letter as exhortation that reaches a climax in chapters 9–11 and is elaborated in chapters 12–15. It follows that chapters 1–8 should not be read as the doctrinal core of the letter, but as an argumentative preparation for the appeal in the later chapters that reaches its rhetorical climax in 9–11. Ben Witherington rightly describes the earlier chapters as constituting an extensive *insinuatio,* the "subtle or indirect approach" recommended by the ancient rhetoricians in situations in which the speaker's case was expected to be controversial or unpopular. It is not until Romans 9, Witherington remarks, that "Paul has finally arrived at what has concerned him the most about the theological misunderstanding in Rome."[70]

More precisely, Witherington declares that Romans provides "a *refutatio* of Gentile misunderstandings about Jews and Jewish Christians." I hold (with Witherington) that those "Gentile misunderstandings" constitute not just one aspect of the situation addressed by Romans, but the primary exigence of the letter. Although the majority of scholars continue to insist that at least one dominant purpose of the letter is to rebuke an inappropriate Jewish "boast," represented either by Judeans among the Roman assemblies or by hostile Judean outsiders (in Rome, Jerusalem, or elsewhere), I observe that Paul never addresses himself to actual Judeans in the course of the letter (see chap. 3 on the function of the diatribe in 2:17-24). To the contrary, Paul explicitly directs the climactic warning in 11:13-34 to non-Judeans (*hymin de legō tois ethnesin*).

The "theological misunderstanding" to which Witherington refers has been described by other interpreters as "arrogance" (J. Paul Sampley), "nascent anti-Judaism among the Roman Gentile Christians" (William S. Campbell), or a "local anti-Jewish sentiment" tending toward "proto-Marcionism" (N. T. Wright).[71] There is significant consensus that Romans addresses a specific situation, in the aftermath of Claudius's expulsion of Judeans from Rome in 49 and Nero's presumed rescript of that edict in 54, in which an ascendant majority of non-Judeans in the assemblies were in a position to look down on returning Judean exiles. Interpreting the evidence for this expulsion and its consequences will occupy part of chapter 3, where I also question to what extent this anti-Jewish animus is rooted in a distinctly *Christian* theological perception. I suggest that the letter confronts both the "boast" of supremacy over Israel and, by necessity, the attitudes in the wider cultural environment that nourished that boast.[72]

Here I point out that this consensus, and the attitude that it attributes to Paul's non-Judean hearers, militates against the common generalization that in Romans Paul seeks to legitimate the "Gentile church."[73] The non-Judeans addressed in Romans 11 are decidedly *not* individuals anxious about their standing before God and hungering for Paul's apostolic legitimation. We should resist the common presupposition that Romans involves a defense of the Gentile church against presumed Judean opposition; more, we should question why that presupposition remains so prevalent in the absence of any corroborative evidence in the letter.

Reading "voice under domination"

A rhetorical-critical approach to Romans that takes empire seriously requires first that we situate the rhetoric of Romans in a complex field of discourses in which the themes and tropes of imperial ideology were both abundant and powerful, and second, that we take account of the constraints imposed on discourse by disparities in power.

To the first point: we must investigate rhetorical themes (or *topoi*). *Topos*-investigation has a recognized place in rhetorical criticism, but it previously was applied to Romans only along conventional theological lines by comparing Paul's view of the law to a supposedly antithetical view of the law in Judaism.[74] We are now in a position to take a much broader approach to topos investigation. Important studies have described the dominant themes in Roman imperial ideology and propaganda, as evidenced in contemporary poetry and panegyric speeches, official inscriptions, monuments, and the ubiquitous imagery of civic worship. These insights have been the focus of recent efforts to situate Paul in the context of empire, though not yet in the disciplined terms of a systematic topos criticism.[75]

To the second point: given the disparities of power inherent in an imperial or colonial situation, political scientist James C. Scott insists that discourse in the public sphere can rarely be taken as a straightforward indication of what subordinates truly believe; it can be presumed only to represent the values of the dominant. Most of the political life of subordinate groups is to be found "neither in overt collective defiance of power holders, nor in complete hegemonic compliance, but in the vast territory between these two polar opposites."[76] Ordinarily, "the public performance of the subordinate will, out of prudence, fear, and the desire to curry favor, be shaped to appeal to the expectations of the powerful."[77] Similarly, the public transcript as often as not conceals the actual intentions of the powerful, which find complete expression only in a sequestered social space. However sophisticated the social science models at our disposal, Scott suggests, if we focus only on the official or formal relations between the powerful and weak, we have attended only to the public transcript and ignored the informal, "off-stage" or "hidden transcripts" of both groups.[78] We should consequently regard the surviving expressions of the dominant class with suspicion, because they provide only one, very partisan perspective on social reality.

Scott's method is of more than academic concern in a day in which officials of the world's most powerful government dissemble about their true motives and intentions[79] and regard the public disclosure of their hidden transcripts as acts of betrayal, or treason.[80] But the point is made routinely now regarding our sources from the early Roman Empire as well. For example, historian Martin Goodman observes that most of the surviving evidence regarding the character of the Roman Empire "was produced by those who cooperated with imperial rule," and therefore "modern understanding of the Roman world depends on appreciation not just of what was said but of what was left unstated from fear or from calculation." Usually "it did no good *to the rulers or to the ruled* for either of them to admit that the empire was controlled by terror."[81] Similarly, Michael Parenti remarks that because the Roman order depended on "a coercive, fear-inspiring dominion" achieved through military conquest and enslavement, interpreters attempting a "people's history" of the early Republic must reconstruct the experience and perceptions of the underclass by reading "against the grain" of elite sources.[82] These programmatic statements are consistent with Fredric Jameson's more general observation that class discourse is "essentially *dialogical* in its character," and that "the normal form of the dialogue is essentially an *antagonistic* one." It follows that "the illusion or appearance of isolation or autonomy which a printed text projects"—as when it is regarded, for example, as sacred scripture—must be "systematically undermined" in the course of interpretation.[83]

It might be objected that it is illegitimate to apply the results of Scott's cross-cultural studies of contemporary peasant communities in colonial situations to a single text from the ancient Roman world. Surely the sorts of controls employed in a contemporary ethnographic study are not available when we pick up an ancient text from a context no longer available to us. Further, applying Scott's categories of hidden and public transcript to Romans would seem to require assigning Paul rather arbitrarily to one or another social location, a move that we might presume would say more about the interpreter's prejudices than about Paul himself or his assemblies.[84]

Those objections are important; they are also readily answered. First, Scott's primary attention is on the public transcript: he is able to identify and discuss alternative, partially hidden transcripts when multiple contemporary texts may be compared, allowing him to distinguish different social sites and their respective transcripts. Rather than assign Paul a priori to the ranks of the empire's acolytes, or conjure a romantic picture of subversive Pauline assemblies meeting furtively by night, we are in a position to identify characteristics of public and hidden transcripts in Paul's day by comparing contemporary texts, and by attending to the clear descriptions in contemporary sources to the constraining effect of power on discourse (see chap. 1).

Second, although recent scholarship has produced wide recognition that some of Paul's phrases actually have political connotations, a clear example being the identification of an imperial slogan in the phrase "peace and security" (1 Thess 5:3), that recognition hardly justifies an indiscriminate hunt for political connotations throughout his letters. There are, nevertheless, criteria for establishing, to a greater or lesser degree of probability, what Richard B. Hays has called "intertextual echo" in Paul's letters; and though Hays's considerable efforts have been directed to identifying Paul's allusions to Israel's scripture, the same criteria are readily applicable to identifying echoes of Roman imperial themes.

My intention in each of the following chapters is to explore Paul's sustained interaction with imperial topoi throughout the rhetoric of Romans. I do not mean to suggest that although Paul *thought* he was speaking theologically in this letter, he was really, though unwittingly, speaking politically. We need not impose a crude dichotomy between theological or political interpretation, or arbitrarily assign primacy to one or the other. An ideological-critical approach to the argument of Romans allows us to recognize at once both the pressure of ideological forces in Paul's environment to limit or impose closure on the imagination of the possible, and the countervailing impulses to transcend that pressure that emerge from the collective imagination. To account for these impulses, Fredric Jameson speaks of a collective "political unconscious" into which aspirations toward freedom are again and again repressed by one or another form of domination. For his part, Paul speaks in this letter of the "groaning" that the Spirit generates, in "sighs too deep for words," among those who anticipate the "glorious liberation of the children of God," their "adoption" and the "redemption" of their bodies (8:18-27). An ideological-critical approach allows us to read Romans attuned to that groaning.

Augustus in military dress. Marble figure from the Prima Porta (Vatican Museums; photo © Erich Lessing / Art Resource, N.Y.).

CHAPTER ONE

IMPERIVM

Empire and the "Obedience of Faith"

The arrogance of powerful nations blinds them to the impossibility of achieving through force the willing consent of peoples whose labor and resources they would claim for their own. This impossibility generates tremendous tension within an empire's ideological system, a contradiction so threatening that it must be suppressed through ideological mechanisms that Fredric Jameson has termed "strategies of containment."[1] The ideology of the Roman Empire, no less than contemporary imperial ideology, was preoccupied with the challenge of "winning the hearts and minds" of conquered peoples.

Examining this constellation of rhetorical *topoi* offers a necessary lens for reading Romans. Paul declared that he was charged by God with securing "faithful obedience among the nations" (1:5, my trans.). That statement is a guide to the purpose of the letter and an indication of the political dimension of Paul's rhetoric. Because the obedience of nations was the prerogative claimed by the Roman emperor, we must situate Paul's rhetoric in a wider field of discourses, across different social locations, in which coercion and consent, obedience and subjection were aligned or opposed to each other.

The tension within Paul's letter between willing obedience and subjection has its roots in the ideological contradictions of the Roman imperial system. Romans shows that Paul's own thinking was constrained by the ideological pressures of his age. These pressures are not dissimilar to our own.

The Battle for Hearts and Minds

The consent of weaker peoples is of paramount importance to the ways in which the powerful seek to represent their rule to themselves and to their subjects. For that reason, the doctrinal system of an empire can ordinarily comprehend the refusal of the ruled to submit willingly to the benign intentions of their rulers as due only to some inherent fault that renders them unworthy, uncomprehending, and ungrateful. Thus, Edward Said observed, imperial cultures must rely on notions of bringing civilization to primitive or barbaric peoples and of the disturbingly

25

familiar ideas about flogging, death, or extended punishment being required when "they" misbehaved or became rebellious, because they mainly understood force or violence best; they were not like "us" and for that reason, deserved to be ruled.[2]

At its most generous, imperial ideology may sublimate this fault into a defect on the part of human society, understood generically. So the Christian Realism that served as the unofficial theology for much of the American Cold War establishment expounded on "the inescapable taint of sin on all historical achievements."[3] With regard to past endeavors, where historical hindsight is improved, similar generosity leads the architects of imperial policy belatedly to admit "the power of nationalism to motivate a people," as it did the Vietnamese through the middle decades of the twentieth century, "to fight and die for their beliefs and values." This was one of the "lessons learned" from the Vietnam War, according to former U.S. Secretary of Defense Robert McNamara; yet it did not impede the determination of the would-be-conqueror nation, in McNamara's words, to win "the hearts and minds of people from a totally different culture" through the application of force.[4]

That phrase gained currency during the Vietnam War, as architects of U. S. military policy sought to win the hearts and minds of the Vietnamese people through what was meant to be an irresistibly persuasive combination of carpet bombing, the covert assassinations of perhaps 100,000 civil leaders (Operation Phoenix), and the forced resettlement of whole villages. A similar strategy (though with the bombing of civilian areas on a more limited scale) was applied throughout Central America in the 1980s, with comparable results: hundreds of thousands of people killed; civil society and infrastructure destroyed; at most, ambiguous success for the United States in achieving its political goals in the region; but nothing that could be confused with widespread popular approval or consent for U.S. hegemony. Predictably, policymakers found the fault not in U.S. policy, but in the inadequacies of peoples not yet "ready for democracy."

Today, the government of the militarily most powerful nation on earth has arrogated to itself the right—or, in the preferred vocabulary of U.S. policymakers, has accepted the "unparalleled responsibilities"—of conforming other nations to its own vision of a global order. The corollary, commonly regarded in the United States as regrettable but unavoidable necessity, is that this noble vision can be attained only through the application of spectacular force.[5] Within imperial culture, the necessity and legitimacy of bending the peoples of other nations to the will of American empire is routinely seen as self-evident. As journalist Thomas L. Friedman explains, every "global order" needs "an enforcer." That is "America's new burden," Friedman declares, though without explaining either what is new about the role or exactly to whom it is a burden (surely not to policymakers or the interests they represent, as Friedman also makes clear).[6] Within this mindset, the notion that force can achieve the willing consent of those who are its targets is uncontroversial; indeed it is a matter of explicit military strategy.[7] It is even possible to imagine that the perceptions of force among the subjugated can be modified through better marketing, as by "branding" the Iraq War.[8]

The U.S. occupation of Iraq is widely regarded as a test case for winning hearts and minds by eliciting both fear and goodwill. After the devastating U.S. bombardment of Fallujah in November 2004, in which untold hundreds of civilians were killed, military officers and mainstream newspaper columnists alike regarded the campaign as a necessary and appropriate means to persuade the survivors to vote in an upcoming election in ways congenial to American interests. By producing "the spectacle of the subjugated city," a *Washington Post* commentator wrote, U.S. bombardment would generate sufficient fear among the "ordinary people" of Fallujah to "clear the way" to favorable election results. Drawing out the implications of such statements, peace activist Jonathan Schell wondered whether the U.S. military had abandoned the classic formula, "hearts and minds," from the days of the Vietnam War. Faced with the spectacle of heavy civilian casualties at the Fallujah general hospital, one of the U.S. military's first targets, he wrote:

> the reaction of the heart could only be pity, disgust, and indignation. Thus, only the "minds" of "the townspeople" could draw the necessary conclusions, as they survey the corpse-strewn wreckage of their city. In short, the people of Iraq will be stricken with fear, or, to use another word that's very popular these days, terror. Then they'll be ready to vote.[9]

But Schell's misgivings were not shared by the military, for whom it still seemed possible to win *both* Iraqi hearts and minds if only the global news media would give up their irrational hostility toward the United States.[10]

The theoretical relation of violence and persuasion is a central topic in the so-called New Rhetoric.[11] The relation of force and opinion has been at the heart of analyses of modern imperial ideology and discussions of postcolonial theory as well.[12] But the architects and advocates of Roman imperial policy in Paul's day proved themselves equally articulate on the subject.

Winning Hearts and Minds in Ancient Rome

Admittedly, the coercive aspect of the empire that Rome built is a delicate subject for some. In his study of "imperial ideology and provincial loyalty in the Roman Empire," classicist Clifford Ando objects that reading class conflict into the ancient sources springs in part from "illusory and deceptive continuities between the ancient and modern worlds," and from "contemporary desires to view Rome with twentieth-century eyes." For Ando, only an "anachronistic cynicism," an "arrogance born of luxury," permits contemporary interpreters to read the literary remains of the ancient Roman elite with suspicion and to "patronize subject populations" in the ancient world "with deterministic ideologies of rebellion."[13] Unfortunately, Ando does not suggest how we might avoid reading with our own twentieth- or twenty-first-century eyes. Nor has he evidently avoided the danger himself; in his buoyant enthusiasm for the "manifest success" of the Roman Empire, one detects no noticeable deviation from the reigning ideology of contemporary empire. In his explanation of the Roman Empire's cohesion across the centuries, Ando minimizes the role of violence, insisting to the contrary that "propaganda is not necessarily rendered persuasive through the exercise of coercive force."

That is a truism that we may observe readily illustrated, for example, in U.S.-occupied Iraq today. But that hardly means that we should resume the innocence of imperial propaganda. The same example shows that empires routinely and deliberately seek to join force to persuasion. "The manifest success of Rome in and of itself gave propaganda considerable empirical validity," Ando declares—another truism, if we take it to include Rome's manifest success in enslaving or destroying whole cities (Corinth, for example, in 146 B.C.E.). But Ando means instead only "the seductive power exercised by material prosperity," evident in Roman achievements in "adorning cities with marble" and "leading clean water from distant hills." He pleads at last for the "sincerity" of the elite texts at our disposal, asking, "what is the 'topos' if not the expression, however banal, of a great truth?"[14]

The obvious answer is that the *topoi* of imperial propaganda are the ideologically necessary instruments for representing actual power relationships in the public transcript. With ancient Rome particularly in mind, historian Richard Gordon observes that imperial themes provide an "unconscious veil distorting the image of social reality within [a] class and sublimating its interest basis" in such a way as to represent "a social fact—that is, imperialism"—in "the guise of fate and piety."[15] Because an empire relies upon coercion, it is by its very nature, in Walter Wink's phrase, "a system in a permanent crisis of legitimation,"[16] requiring a rhetorical arsenal of themes of inevitability, beneficence, and consent. These were the principal stuff of Roman imperial propaganda.[17]

The contours of Roman imperial ideology

An agrarian tributary empire, particularly one as parasitic as Rome's, had specific ideological requirements.[18] In his discussion of "class struggle on the ideological plane" in the Greco-Roman world, G. E. M. de Ste. Croix discussed the effective combination of "terror and propaganda" in Roman imperialism. He amply documented what he termed "the simplest form of psychological propaganda" that merely teaches the governed "that they have no real option but to submit. This tends to be intellectually uninteresting, however effective it may have been in practice, and consists merely of the threat of force. It was particularly common, of course, in its application to slaves,"[19] but was inadequate by itself. Also necessary, and of more interest to Ste. Croix, was "a more sophisticated form of ideological class struggle," "the attempt of the dominant classes to persuade those they exploited to accept their oppressed condition without protest; if possible, even to rejoice in it. . . . The most common form of the type of propaganda we are considering is that which seeks to persuade the poor that they really are not fitted to rule and that this is much better left to their 'betters.'"[20] Edward Said had modern empires in mind when he observed that "the rhetoric of power all too easily produces an illusion of benevolence when deployed in an imperial setting."[21] But the ideology of benefaction and patronage was just as pervasive, if not more so, in the Roman Empire. The codes of patronage effectively masked the deeply exploitive nature of the tribute- and slave-based economy by simultaneously concealing the rapacity of the ruling class and naturalizing fundamentally unequal relationships through routines of highly theatrical reciprocity.[22]

The Roman ideological system proved remarkably adaptive. When, in the first century B.C.E., a devastating contest between two rival warlords threatened to lay bare the true nature of the system, the Senate moved swiftly to represent the emerging victor, Octavian, as a sacred figure (Augustus), whose efforts had secured not debilitating war (as the evidence might otherwise have indicated), but supreme peace throughout the empire, the *pax Romana*. The establishment of the principate was thus "the completion of a pyramid of power and patronage, involving the placing of a coping stone, admittedly a very large and heavy one, on top of the whole oppressive edifice."[23] The quickly developed ideology of the principate held that the *princeps* (the "first man") was the refuge and champion of the masses against the avarice of the Senate, a claim belied by the evidence.[24] Upon Octavian's return to Rome, the Senate promptly awarded him a ceremonial golden shield, the *clupeus aureus,* celebrating him as the very embodiment of valor (*virtus*: in Greek, *aretē*), mercy (*clementia*: *epeikeia*), justice (*iustitia*: *dikaiosynē*), and dutiful devotion to the gods, his ancestors, and his posterity (*pietas*: *eusebeia*). Through the emperor, on his own account, "a large number of . . . nations experienced the good faith of the Roman people" (that is, their *fides*; in Greek, *pistis*), and through him, the Roman people themselves came into their divinely ordained destiny, to rule the world.[25]

When catastrophic transitions (especially the coups d'état following the assassination of Gaius and the apparent murder of Claudius) threatened to demonstrate that emperors were, after all, interchangeable instruments of ruling class domination,[26] imperial ideology assured the public of continuity and stability through the legal fiction of dynastic succession (that is, familial, including adoptive, descent from Augustus: see the Timeline at the beginning of the book); by senatorial acclamation of the successor; and in the case of Claudius—one year before Romans was written—as of Tiberius and Augustus before him, by the grant to the predecessor of divine honors as one ascended into Olympian heaven. Finally, the increasing expansion of the Roman economy through the conquest and enslavement of subject peoples was effectively represented as the inevitable, divinely ordained, and indeed salutary destiny of the Roman people. As Virgil put it in the *Aeneid*, it was the destiny of Aeneas's descendants to "crush proud nations," to "rule the world . . .

to crown peace with justice, to spare the vanquished and to crush the proud."[27] The self-evident corollary was that conquered nations were inherently inferior, destined to be ruled, as Cicero had labeled Judeans and Syrians "peoples born for slavery."[28]

The reading of Romans presented here depends on recognizing that these themes were perceived and treated differently in different social locations. Seeking to gain a measure of "the impact of domination on public discourse,"[29] James C. Scott distinguishes between what he calls the public transcript, that is, the zone of direct interaction between dominant and subordinate classes, and the "hidden transcripts" of the subordinate, on one hand, and the "hidden transcript of the dominant," on the other (see Fig. 1.1).

Fig. 1.1. Hidden and Public Transcripts as described by James C. Scott

Hidden transcript of the dominant	Public transcript (with roles and expectations for subordinate and dominant classes)	Hidden transcript of the subordinate
Distinct from the perceptions attributed to the powerful in the public transcript; hidden because constrained by prevalent ideology.	Expressed in the public sphere as this is defined by the dominant classes, the public transcript includes roles assigned to the weak and the dominant, the powerless and the powerful alike; yet these are under constant negotiation in "the most vital arena for ordinary conflict, for everyday forms of class struggle."	Distinct from the perceptions attributed to the subordinate in the public transcript; hidden because constrained by coercive force.

The hidden transcript of the powerful: The inevitability of rule by force

The hidden transcript of the dominant is "an artifact of the exercise of power. It contains that discourse—gestures, speech, practices—which is excluded from the public transcript by the ideological limits within which domination is cast." The powerful can speak with candor when they know they are alone among their peers "and can let their hair down." Such hidden transcripts are of particular value because the full public transcript offers only occasional, accidental glimpses into the actual motives of the powerful; as Scott observes, "dominant groups often have much to conceal, and typically also have the wherewithal to conceal what they wish."[30]

It is precisely the difference between the solemn assurances the elite gave their subjects regarding their altruism and benevolence, and the candor with which they admitted their rapacity to one another in private, that enables us to distinguish the hidden transcript of the powerful from the public transcript.[31] The powerful frankly admitted the profit motive, especially when attributing it one-sidedly to their rivals.[32] The costs of conquest were normally borne by the imperial treasury (meaning, by the slaves, peasants, and laborers who actually produced the wealth Rome appropriated through taxation), whereas the profits accrued to a small circle of wealthy and powerful individuals.[33] (The phenomenon has precise contemporary parallels, as Michael Parenti observes.)[34] The rich occasionally commented on the miserable diet to which peasants were reduced after their crops had been confiscated for export, through taxation or sheer extortion.[35] On occasion, they could admit the causal connection between the misery of the poor and the "insatiate avarice" of their own class.[36] And no less an advocate of empire than Nero's advisor Seneca could comment to a peer that "we Romans are excessively haughty, cruel, and insulting" to slaves.[37]

Two ancient authors allow us to "listen in" on the hidden transcript of the powerful as the emperor Tiberius discusses the practices through which the Roman elite set about "plundering the provinces on a vast scale."[38] On one occasion, Tiberius admonished an overly rapacious prefect in Egypt, "I want my sheep shorn, not shaved." By shearing he apparently meant an appropriate, that is, politically sustainable level of exploitation (though we should not expect official tax edicts to have been phrased in that manner).[39] Neither did tax collectors likely present themselves to the peasants from whom they made their exactions as "blood-suckers," though according to Josephus, Tiberius used that metaphor to explain why he replaced his governors only infrequently.[40] Decades later, Juvenal advised those preparing for a provincial governorship to moderate their greed, since due to the exactions of their predecessors, the poor provincials' "very bones have been sucked dry of marrow."[41] For his part, Nero honed the principle to a fine point, as Suetonius reports: "His invariable formula, when he appointed a magistrate, was: 'You know my needs! Let us see to it that nobody is left with anything!'"[42]

Among themselves, the Roman ruling class acknowledged quite candidly that their rule could never rely on popular support alone. Good public order required the application or threat of force, not least because it was all subordinates could understand. When one slave murdered his master in 61 c.e., a lawyer rose in the Senate to support the traditional punitive executions of 400 of the slave's fellows by insisting, "you will not restrain that scum except by terror."[43] The actual brutality of the slave system was projected onto the "scum" themselves, and the actual vulnerability of slave bodies was internalized, by a curious imaginative inversion, by their masters: "you see how many dangers, insults, and mockeries we are liable to," complained Pliny. "No master can be safe because he is indulgent and kindly, for masters perish not by the exercise of their slaves' reasoning faculty but because of their wickedness."[44]

The same necessity applied to the masses. Cicero insisted that foolishly appealing to the consent of the governed risked putting civic order in the hands of the unruly mob, the people's assembly whose salient characteristic was "irresponsibility," "that monster which falsely assumes the name and appearance of a people."

Only "the best men" could be motivated by a "sense of shame." For lesser classes, the threat of punishment was necessary. It followed, naturally enough, that oligarchy and dictatorship were not only the most efficient, but also the most salutary forms of government, since "dominion has been granted by Nature to everything that is best, to the great advantage of what is weak."[45]

In Cicero's day, the theme was already ancient, for Aristotle had assumed it. It also would prove long-lived, for centuries after both Aristotle and Cicero, intellectuals in the provinces would unselfconsciously describe Roman imperial rule as "established according to reason, for it is a law of nature, one common to all men . . . that the strong shall always rule over the weak" (Dionysius of Halicarnassus). Josephus put a similar argument into the mouth of Herod Agrippa as he sought to persuade the rebels of Jerusalem to surrender to the Romans; on his account, he himself made an impassioned appeal to the rebels to honor the "established law, 'yield to the stronger.'"[46]

Roman imperialists like Cicero simply "did not concede that their subjects or dependents had any right to be free of Roman rule. Liberty was the privilege of the imperial people" alone.[47] A contemporary of Augustus, the historian Livy, declared it common knowledge that from the beginning, the "first" and "noblest men" in various cities across the Mediterranean had welcomed Roman hegemony, but that "the common mass and those displeased with their circumstances desired a revolution." Of necessity, then, Roman hegemony relied upon a judicious combination of persuasion (for the elite) and force (for everyone else).[48] According to Cicero, both shame and fear were necessary to instill public decorum in two classes of people, respectively: those who accepted proper standards of honor (and thus could feel and respond to shame) and the lower classes, who responded only to force and terror.[49] Closer to Paul's time, the historian Velleius Paterculus used the same *topos* to explain that in the wake of a particular crisis, "all citizens have either been impressed with the wish to do right, or have been forced to do so by necessity."[50] Later, the provincial Plutarch found it telling that the Romans built countless altars to Fortune, the god who had given triumphs into their hands, but that "they have no shrine of Wisdom or Prudence" as do peoples who value persuasion; clearly military prowess had proven the more serviceable virtue for their empire.[51]

What Ando termed the "seduction" of the provincial elite in fact relied on the frank calculation of what resistance would cost. Susan E. Alcock has documented the material hardship created by "the *de facto* subjugation of the Greek cities" by Rome long before 27 B.C.E., which entailed both military destruction of whole cities, the consequent collapse of others, and the severe disruption of "the lives of thousands of individuals" in communities affected by the economic, political, and military imposition of Roman control even in cities that survived.[52] G. E. M. de Ste. Croix similarly observed that "Rome made sure that Greece was kept 'quiet' and friendly to her by ensuring that the cities were controlled by the wealthy class, which now had mainly given up any idea of resistance to Roman rule and in fact seems to have welcomed it for the most part, as an insurance against popular movements from below."[53]

The same dynamic is evident today, of course, as journalist Thomas Friedman observes: "once a country makes the leap into the system of globalization, its elites begin to internalize this perspective of integration, and always try to locate themselves in a global context" instead, say, of seeking to advance the interests of the majorities of their own people.[54] The process seems quite natural to Friedman; we must look to other contemporary observers, for example, psychologists in French-occupied Algeria (Franz Fanon) or El Salvador under U.S. domination (Ignácio Martín-Baró), for a less buoyant discussion of the effects of "national security" measures on the masses.[55]

The hidden transcript of the subordinate: Imperial violence seen from below

It is not surprising that the empire's subjects agreed with their superiors that force was indispensable to Roman hegemony. After all, they bore its brunt. Their response to Roman greed, lust, and violence was often unalloyed hatred. So much we can gather from the limited sources available to us. By definition, Scott observes, "the hidden transcript of many historically important subordinate groups is irrecoverable for all practical purposes. What is often available, however, is what they have been able to introduce in muted or veiled form into the public transcript."[56] "The first *open* statement of a hidden transcript, a declaration that breaches the etiquette of power relations, that breaks an apparently calm surface of silence and consent, carries the force of a symbolic declaration of war."[57]

Expressions of outright defiance of Roman rule were rare, desperate, and doomed. Tellingly, the few "declarations of war" against Rome available to us have been passed on by Roman historians after the ungrateful wretches had been put to death; the posthumous recitals illustrate the erstwhile ferocity of the vanquished and thus magnify the glory of the conquerors. Tacitus attributes a defiant speech to the war chief Calgacus, challenging his fellow Britons to resist the arrogant Romans, who could not be appeased by even the most restrained obedience of their subjects.[58] Tacitus also quotes the rallying cry of another Briton, the rebel Boudicca, from her war chariot, in which she stood with her two daughters who had, like her, been violated by Roman soldiers. Tacitus, himself a Roman aristocrat, passes these speeches along without any qualm regarding the justice of Roman conquest.[59]

There are a few other examples of overt defiance of Rome.[60] Among Judeans, we gain a few oblique glimpses of anti-Roman rhetoric from Josephus, who writes for his own apologetic purposes decades after the disastrous revolt of 66–70 C.E. His agenda in presenting anti-Roman attitudes as a "Fourth Philosophy," an improper deviation from the three authentic "philosophies" of Judaism (those of the Pharisees,

Saduccees, and Essenes), is well known.[61] Josephus acknowledges (through the voice of Agrippa, seeking to calm the populace of Jerusalem) that "there are many who wax eloquent on the insolence of the procurators and pronounce pompous panegyrics on liberty." Unlike Tacitus, however, Josephus declines to provide specimens of this "eloquence," preferring to give space instead to his own oratorical talents in the cause of submission.[62]

Currents of protest

The paucity of direct first-hand evidence is precisely what we should expect on Scott's analysis of the effects of domination upon discourse. Unable to express their resistance openly, subordinate groups must ordinarily rely on strategies of indirection and disguise, or else seek the safety of anonymity. There is abundant indirect evidence for "a permanent current of hostility" on the part of the masses in Rome to "senatorial misrule and exploitation," from the time of the Republic on.[63] The occasional surprise expressed by the elite when a gesture of courage sparked an explosion of popular unrest suggests that the common people more usually were constrained to suppress their dissatisfaction.[64] Defiance surfaced in strategies of anonymity that Scott calls the "everyday forms of class struggle."[65] Strategies of "political disguise" included graffiti, effigies anonymously erected in public,[66] and spontaneous street demonstrations (termed "riots" by the elite).[67] The alternatives available to subordinate groups are more complex, then, than a naked choice between silence and defiance. What Scott calls the "strategic uses of anonymity," including collective action and the anonymity of the crowd, reflects "a popular tactical wisdom developed in conscious response to the political constraints realistically faced," that is, the constant threat of violent suppression.[68]

In the years of Nero's reign alone, we notice the threat of slave insurrection smoldering in Tacitus's comment that one of Agrippina's aristocratic rivals was condemned for "disturbing the peace of Italy by failing to keep her Calabrian slave-gangs in order"; in his reference to "riots, with stone-throwing and threats of arson," provoked by official corruption in nearby Puteoli; and in the account of an angry mob surrounding the Senate house, armed with stones and torches, when the Senate condemned four hundred slaves to death in retaliation for the murder of their master.[69]

There was plenty to protest, not the least in Nero's day, despite his wide reputation among modern scholars as an improvement over his predecessors. While the lower classes often regarded the emperors, rightly or wrongly, as "a restraint on the rapacity of the Senate, and for themselves a refuge,"[70] many were perfectly aware that Nero, in particular, was neither. His heavy-handed exactions "exhausted the provinces" and eventually sparked revolts in Britain and Judea.[71] When the people of Rome itself pressed for relief from the "excessive greed" of duty collectors, Nero proclaimed

*Colossal head of the emperor Nero. Ca.
65 C.E. Marble. Staatliche Antiken-
sammlung, Munich. Photo © Alfredo Dagli
Orti; Bildarchiv Preussischer Kulturbesitz/
Art Resource, N.Y.*

himself the people's champion, but initiated "reforms" that streamlined the collection system and lowered only selected duties that cut too deeply, in his view, into the
profits of the wealthy (two of whom he personally acquitted of charges of embezzle-
ment and abuse in Africa).[72] Nero eliminated public banquets; perhaps he saw them
as an extravagance wasted on the masses, who (after all!) already enjoyed the monthly
grain distribution—the *frumentatio,* which for more than a century had been necessary to maintain a fifth of the population of Rome at the subsistence level (if it
did that much). Even this was not safe from the emperor's avarice: Tacitus reports
that Nero appropriated a large part of the grain supply for his own financial specu-
lation.[73] The emperor's astounding extravagance—including ostentatious building
projects and constant ceremonial self-indulgence, as well as the incredible largesse
he bestowed on his personal clients—strengthened the impression that his rule had
brought tremendous wealth to Rome. However, it also brought him to such personal
financial straits that he eventually turned, Suetonius declares, to "robbery and black-
mail," imposing arbitrary penalties and confiscation of the estates of his richest political enemies (including the six men who, in the elder Pliny's words, "owned half of
Africa"[74]). He appropriated sacred property from temples in Rome. The lower classes
shrewdly perceived such recklessness as a direct threat to their interests, as when the
rumor spread that the latest ship from Alexandria carried in its hold not grain, to ease
the price of bread in Rome, but sand for the imperial wrestlers.[75]

Forms of anonymous protest—anonymous jokes circulating through the capital
and graffiti appearing on public walls overnight—mocked the key claims of imperial propaganda, ridiculing Nero's extravagant building projects, mocking his claim
to be descended from the ancient Trojan hero Aeneas, and after 59 C.E., taunting

him as his mother's murderer as well,[76] despite his calculated efforts in the theater (ably discussed by Edward Champlin) to identify that act as the embodiment of mythic themes of justified matricide.[77]

It is customary in classical and biblical studies to accept the view that many of Nero's abuses emerged only later in his rule, after earlier years that provided "an exemplary form of government and law enforcement, despite the profligate personal habits of Nero himself." At the time Paul wrote Romans, after all, Nero had not yet ordered his own mother's execution.[78] In his monograph on the emperor, Edward Champlin warns against accepting the later Christian demonization of Nero as monster and points out that long after his suicide, he enjoyed an impressive career as a figure in the popular imagination.[79] But Nero's "posthumous popularity" as an avenging angel (or devil) hardly means that, as Champlin puts it, he was remembered as "a good man and a good ruler" during his lifetime. Rather it shows simply that he was remembered as one capable of spectacular violence, and (as Champlin points out) of a theatrically performed disdain for the sensibilities of the ruling class, which endeared him to theatrical audiences without actually upsetting the disparity in power.[80] Conventional references in modern scholarship to "five good years" at the beginning of Nero's reign depend on a much-later comment by Trajan (emperor from 98 to 117 C.E.) that the building projects of all the other emperors had been surpassed by "five years of Nero." But other contemporaries could grudgingly acknowledge the splendor of his buildings and still recognize the moral disaster of his reign: "What is worse than Nero?" quipped Martial, "What is better than Nero's baths?"[81]

My point is not to mount a referendum on Nero's rule, but to observe the fact, amply documented for his rule and those of his predecessors with impressive consistency, of chronic resentment on the part of the lower classes toward what they clearly perceived as a plutocracy hostile to their interests.

The Dialectic of Defiance and Caution

Scott's analysis explains why the ancient sources upon which we must depend for a history "from below" offer only indirect testimony. "The frontier between the public and hidden transcripts," he writes, "is a zone of constant struggle between dominant and subordinate—not a solid wall. The capacity of dominant groups to prevail—though never totally—in defining and constituting what counts as the public transcript and what as offstage is . . . no small measure of their power. The unremitting struggle over such boundaries is perhaps the most vital arena for ordinary conflict, for everyday forms of class struggle."[82]

His insight is hardly a modern discovery. No less erudite an observer than Philo of Alexandria provided an analysis very similar to Scott's when he contrasted the "untimely frankness" (*parrhēsian akairon*) of those who resisted Rome openly, but at an inopportune time, with the caution (*eulabeia*) that is more usually appropriate to the public square. "When the times are right," Philo explains, "it is good to set ourselves against the violence of our enemies and subdue it; but when the circumstances do not present themselves"—as is usually the case in history, Scott suggests—"the safe course is to stay quiet."[83] "Staying quiet" clearly implies the self-restraint that keeps an oppositional transcript hidden.

The two sets of circumstances that Philo described did not inhere in two fixed and segregated social zones, but were possibilities precisely in the public sphere. The public transcript reproduces the dominant values of the ruling class but also serves the purposes of the subordinate by allowing them to veil or cloak their resentment or defiance. Philo's phrase, "when the times are right," points to *circumstances* allowing the irruption of a previously hidden transcript into the public transcript. What Philo describes in Roman Alexandria Scott calls the "unremitting struggle" to define what may and may not be said about power relations in public. As Philo also makes clear, the "right time," that is, the circumstances in which defiance may be openly expressed, are determined by force, or its relative absence. His complaint about those who speak with "untimely frankness" is not just that they have misjudged circumstances but that their brazen miscalculation has brought brutal and catastrophic reprisals against their own people and their own families—an apparent reference to the awful events of 38–41 C.E. in Alexandria.

The public transcript: Contesting the relation of coercion and consent

The reciprocal roles assigned in the public transcript of the Roman imperial order were clear enough, and recently have been the subject of important studies.

On one side, one could see inscribed on every public surface, hear in official panegyric, and in civic ceremonial be swept up into the open and official representation of the glory and beneficence of the empire.[84] Just as in our own day the *National Security Strategy of the United States* extols the happy "union of our values and our national interests" in the expansion of U.S. hegemony, so the Roman ruling class regarded the expansion of the empire through military conquest, enslavement, and systematic economic exploitation as the marvelous coincidence of self-interest and benevolence. So Cicero, writing a century before Paul:[85]

> Wisdom urges us to increase our resources, to multiply our wealth, to extend our boundaries. . . . Wisdom urges us also to rule over as many subjects as possible, to enjoy pleasures, to become rich, to be rulers and masters; Justice, on the other hand, instructs us to spare all men, to consider the interests of the whole human race, to give everyone his due, and not to touch sacred or public property, or that which belongs to others.[86]

In the public transcript, the elite described rule over others as springing naturally from the benign consideration of the needs of inferiors. The historian Appian
considered it common sense that the Greeks had invited Roman domination by
their shameful infighting, which proved their incapacity for self-rule; Herodian
called their warring "an ancient condition," a flaw that required the discipline of an
outside power.[87] P. A. Brunt observes that the elite regarded even nations beyond
Rome's reach "as rightfully their subjects." Lands and peoples already conquered
were described as enjoying the "friendship" of Rome, even when in actuality they
were "expected to behave as vassals," for example, by offering their children as
hostages to prevent wholesale destruction. Where Roman exertions to subjugate
peoples (that is, to "restore peace") were successful, loyalists perceived that Rome's
hegemony was beyond dispute or protest, being founded on a superior capacity for
ruling, a natural right to demand submission from all others.[88] Wherever they met
resistance, they saw only the bad faith of insubordinate peoples.[89]

The quintessential expression for the reciprocal responsibility between conqueror and conquered was *fides,* "faithfulness" (Greek *pistis*), "a cardinal, shared
Roman value and an essential concept for Rome's *imperium." Fides* was routinely
illustrated on coins, for example, by the portrait of the Roman conqueror extending one hand in alliance, holding a spear in the other—to be wielded in protection
of Rome's allies, of course.[90] Cicero hailed justice (*ius*) and faithfulness (*fides*) as
the hallmarks of beneficent Roman rule. *Fides* and *amicitia,* "friendship," were the
potent euphemisms by means of which Rome represented to subject peoples—in
rhetoric, inscriptions, and monuments—that their subjection and willing obedience would be rewarded by the protective care of their conquerors.

In the eyes of the elite, these virtues were self-evidently compatible with the exertion of force. Early in the Republic, the dictator Sulla boasted that "from the beginnings of their empire the Roman people have preferred to acquire friends rather
than slaves, thinking it safer to rule by good will rather than by force," the historical record notwithstanding.[91] When ambassadors from Rhodes came to Rome to
offer their submission, they sued to become clients of Rome as their patron and
asked to be protected by the bond of *fides.*[92] Cato the Elder accused a political rival
of humiliating Rome's "allies" (in this case, client princes) and thereby violating
Roman *fides*; arguably, the violation also demonstrated its true nature.[93] *Fides* was
a watchword of the Augustan age, along with "Peace, Honor, old-fashioned Shame,
and Valor, which had been neglected" previously: so Horace.[94] Augustus used
"friendship" and "faithfulness" interchangeably with the language of conquest and
subjection in the *Res gestae,* the "Acts of the Divine Augustus," reciting how he had
"subjected the whole world to the sovereignty [*imperium*] of the Roman people."
He had, through warfare, "reduced to a state of peace" the lands of the Gauls, Spain,
Germany, and the Alps and compelled the Parthians and other peoples to "seek as
suppliants the friendship [*amicitia*] of the Roman people." Such statements indicate the close relationship in the imperial mentality between "peace" and conquest,

"friendship" and subjection. Rome's friendship sometimes required the surrender of the children of a royal house as hostages, as in the case of Parthia. "A large number of other nations," Augustus summarizes at length, had "experienced the good faith of the Roman people," that is, their *fides*.[95]

On the other side, however, the public transcript also included rehearsals of the servile deference required of the subordinate in the elaborate rituals of respect and subjection observed in the city streets, no less than in public assembly. The most abject expressions of deference were called forth from the powerless, as exemplified (to take but one of a number of available texts) in an Egyptian papyrus letter written by the peasants of what historian Ramsey MacMullen called "a 'monopolized' village":

> We wish you to know, Lord, that . . . we have never handed over our bodies—rather, year in and year out, that we have completed our due services but surrender ourselves to no one. . . . But if any should come for the best of our young fellows, we would not say you nay. Do whatever seems best to you to do.[96]

Note here both the lingering hint of pride ("we have never handed over our bodies") and the abject humiliation, all the more pathetic by contrast, of a village ready to surrender their sons to the magistrate for his own (unnamed) purposes. All this was accomplished, we must remember, by force. MacMullen remarks on the recurrent references in the Egyptian papyri to "physical outrage, . . . beatings, maulings, and murders" through which the Romans and their tax farmers "wrung ultimately from the provincial peasants all that could be economically extracted."[97] We do not know the outcome of the petition of this village, or of countless others to be read from the papyri. Clifford Ando finds in them an occasion to marvel at the confidence provincials put in the Roman legal system.[98] I note instead the deference required even of those seeking the vindication of their rights and the redress of injury in that system.

Coercion and consent may have appeared complementary to the imperial mind, but the subjects of the empire could readily distinguish and even oppose the two. Philo, who could hint broadly at the brutality of Roman magistrates, in general, and of Gaius (Caligula) in particular, presented Moses by way of contrast as the world's premier lawgiver. In his laws, Moses "suggests and admonishes rather than commands," in laws written "in order to exhort rather than to enforce."[99] Josephus, whose politics were far more accommodationist toward the Romans than Philo's,[100] nevertheless similarly could acknowledge that Roman governors could be "intolerably harsh." He, too, identified the superiority of the Judean constitution in Moses' decision to create a theocracy, overseen by priests "preeminently gifted with persuasive eloquence and discretion," rather than a monarchy or an oligarchy based on compulsion. Moses recognized that "issuing orders without words of exhortation, as though to slaves instead of free men, savored of tyranny and despotism."[101] These two Judean voices, writing as apologists for the Judean cause, relied on the current Roman *topos* but inverted it: coercion and consent were incompatible, and the former was unworthy of free people.

Typically, expressions of protest or resistance in the Judean literature that has come down to us are couched in veiled or muted terms. They offer glimpses into what we may presume, following Scott's argument, was a deeper, richer hidden transcript of resentment, the subterranean resistance that ultimately erupted in rebellion. Such, for example, was the oblique invective of the first-century B.C.E. *Psalms of Solomon*, where the arrogance of Pompeii was condemned without naming him except as "the sinner" (*ho hamartōlos*) and his troops as "foreign nations" (*ethnē*); or again, the esoteric biblical interpretation of the Habakkuk Pesher from Qumran, which condemned the violence and arrogance of the Romans as those who "eat up all the peoples like an insatiable vulture," but only under the symbolic name *Kittim*. Philo offered allegorical interpretations of Scripture, reading biblical characters as figures of tyranny (the sons of Cheth in Gen 23:7; Joseph himself in Genesis 37).[102] When he complained elsewhere of the breathtaking sadism of Roman taxgatherers in Egypt, he did so in carefully vague or even evasive language, referring to "a person" (*tis*) who was put in charge of tax gathering "a little time ago."[103] Following the Roman destruction of Jerusalem, we find the same bitter condemnation of Rome in the veiled allegorical symbolism of the apocalypses.[104]

───────────── **The Public Transcript in Nero's Rome** ─────────────

The phenomena Scott discusses as "hidden" and "public transcripts" are not aspects inhering in texts as such, so that if only we spent sufficient time staring at a text (such as Romans) through the right methodological lens, we could confirm its character as one or the other. No ancient text spontaneously reveals itself as a hidden transcript. As Cynthia Briggs Kittredge rightly warns, to apply Scott's work to biblical studies, we necessarily depend on a historical reconstruction of a particular historical context, and of the way in which power constrained the discourse of social groups in that context.[105]

Edward Champlin's recent study of Nero enables us to say a great deal about the cultural environment in the city to which Paul wrote. Champlin emphasizes the rich repertoire of statuary, monument, inscription, and (of special relevance with regard to this emperor) theater, all conveying a single, powerful message regarding the inevitability and rightness of the imperial regime. This cultural repertoire surrounded the observer with highly charged images of the gods and of illustrious heroes of the past, images displayed in every public corner of the city of Augustus, replicated in private works of art, and elaborated by the poets, orators, and historians of the day. ... [D]aily life was permeated by such examples from the past, all dedicated to comment on the present. It was customary to present Rome's leaders wrapped in the deeds and virtues of figures from myth and legend, and the Roman people were thoroughly accustomed to read and appreciate the messages they bore.[106]

If the public transcript was a zone of contestation, one voice in that contest was clear and powerful. Nero (or rather, his speechwriter, Seneca) provides one of the most vivid expressions of the imperial understanding of the necessity of rule. Looking out over "this vast throng—discordant, factious, and unruly, ready to run riot alike for the destruction of itself and others if it should break its yoke"—the emperor realizes that without his benevolent leadership, "no part of the wide world can prosper."

> Just as the body depends upon the governance of the mind, in the same way this vast throng, encircling the life of one man, is ruled by his spirit, guided by his reason, and would crush and cripple itself with its own power if it were not upheld by wisdom. ... For he is the bond by which the commonwealth is united, the breath of life, which these many thousands draw, who in their own strength would be only a burden to themselves and the prey of others if the great mind of the empire should be withdrawn. ... Such a calamity would be the destruction of the Roman peace, such a calamity will force the fortune of a mighty people to its downfall. Just so long will this people be free from that danger as it shall know how to submit to the rein; but if ever it shall tear away the rein, ... the end of this city's rule will be one with the end of her obedience.[107]

And what of other voices? That a deranged eighteen-year-old could be described as the "mind of the empire" says something about the tone of public deliberation in Nero's day. Champlin's observations about the constricted sphere of public discourse in Rome bear out Scott's argument regarding the constraints of power in the public transcript. In the mid-first century B.C.E., Cicero had recognized only three public zones in which the Roman people could speak their mind: public assemblies, elections, and the games and gladiator shows. After the accelerated consolidation of power in the single figure of the emperor, the marginalization of the first two zones, public meetings and elections, meant that by the mid-first century C.E., "the outlet provided by the games became even more important." The games and the theater were the remaining public venues where the Roman people could take advantage of large numbers and individual anonymity to proclaim their views about current public issues, loudly and directly, to their leaders. It was generally understood that things could be said within the special confines of a theater, circus, or arena which could not be said elsewhere. . . . This outlet provided by the games became even more important under the principate, as one-man rule stifled republican politics, and the institutions of debate (the public meetings) and voting (the assemblies) faded away.[108]

Perhaps this "outlet" was allowed to continue precisely because the role assigned to the people had become so tightly circumscribed: in Champlin's words, "the games lent themselves to a ritualized dialogue between the emperor and his people."[109] In this "ritualized dialogue," Nero presented himself as the champion of the people; attentive, at least theatrically, to their voices.[110] (The feigned populism of fantastically wealthy leaders, whose policies in fact serve the interests of their own class, is a phenomenon familiar enough in our own day as well.) But the constraints imposed on the public transcript meant that direct dissent was suppressed.

In the last public site where the people's voice was still heard, albeit in a highly stylized fashion, Champlin speaks of an "abundance of evidence," from the late Republic onward, "that Roman theatrical audiences were extraordinarily quick to hear the words spoken and to see the actions presented on stage as offering pointed commentary on contemporary life."[111] Playwrights and actors alike changed or read lines so as to produce a subversive double entendre; equally important, audiences occasionally responded to double entendres even if these had not been intended. Champlin concludes that

This remarkable sensitivity on the part of the audience underscores the heightening of awareness within a Roman theater: audiences *expected* to find contemporary relevance in the productions; performers *expected* to have their pointed remarks and actions caught, interpreted, and appreciated. . . . In short, the Roman people were accustomed to seeing their rulers everywhere presented as figures of well-known myths, and they were accustomed to performances on stage that commented directly on their own contemporary concerns. . . . Rome by Nero's day was a city thoroughly accustomed to the widespread, programmatic representation of myth in public life, and to the deep implication of the audience in theatrical performance.[112]

Champlin's observations point to an important aspect of the immediate environment in which Paul's letter was read, or rather performed,[113] in Rome. Given the constraints operative in the public transcript, we might expect *direct* political commentary at odds with the prevailing order to be either rare or nonexistent there; yet for that very reason, the "remarkable sensitivity" of the Roman populace to *oblique* commentary on current events is all the more important.

But on what basis might we identify anything Paul says as bearing, however indirectly, on contemporary events?

In his landmark discussion of "intertextual echo" in Paul's letters, Richard B. Hays identified seven "tests" for reasonably identifying allusions in one text (like Romans) to another (like Isaiah or the Psalms).[114] These tests are just as applicable to the themes of myth and ideology that so charged the air of the imperial capital.

1. Under the rubric *availability*, Hays asks, "Was the proposed source of the echo available to the author and/or original readers?" We can have no doubt that through mass dissemination by means of imagery, ceremonial, and panegyric, themes of imperial propaganda saturated the cities of the Roman Empire. Indeed, recognizing the overwhelming "availability" of imperial themes in Paul's environment, we may wonder whether the energy devoted to determining how conversant Paul's non-Judean hearers were with the Septuagint might better be directed to another symbolic repertoire with which they were *undoubtedly* more familiar. (Hays himself regards just this question as "intriguing" and worthy of further investigation.[115])

2. Under *historical plausibility*, Hays asks, "Could Paul have intended the alleged meaning effect? Could his readers have understood it?" Just here Champlin's observations about the "remarkable sensitivity" of Roman audiences to irony, double entendre, and other forms of indirect commentary must be an important consideration.

3. Under *volume*, Hays is concerned with "the degree of explicit repetition of words or syntactical patterns, but other factors may also be relevant: how distinctive or prominent is the precursor text?" Here the case with regard to themes from imperial ideology is necessarily much murkier, because Paul neither quotes nor cites imperial declarations (though the contemporary recognition of an allusion to official propaganda in 1 Thess 5:3 bears note), nor does he quote from recognizable Roman works like the *Aeneid*. Hays's reference to "other factors" is therefore all the more important. Themes that loom large in Romans—justice, mercy, piety, and virtue—were *overwhelmingly* "distinctive and prominent" in Roman imperial ideology as well.

4. Hays considers another criterion, the *history of interpretation*, "one of the least reliable guides for interpretation" precisely because the interpretation of Paul's letters has been so long dominated by theological agendas. We are nevertheless at a turning point in the history of interpretation in which political themes and allusions in Paul's writings are increasingly recognized.[116]

Other criteria named by Hays—*recurrence, thematic coherence*, and *satisfaction*—are more subjective criteria involving the interpreter's sense of Paul's theology as a whole.

There is at least a prima facie case for reading Romans with the same "remarkable sensitivity" to political connotations that was evident in the Roman theater. Indeed, given that Paul's letter would have been read in a much less surveilled social site, we may suppose that the sort of expectations that Champlin describes for the theater might have been heightened there.

──────── **Winning Hearts and Minds in Romans** ────────

A call for obedience

At the beginning of Romans, Paul declares that he writes to include his hearers in the "faithful obedience among all the nations" that is his sacred duty to secure (1:5). He has long desired to come to the Romans, he writes, "so that I might reap some harvest among you, as among the rest of the nations. For I am obligated both to Greeks and barbarians, to the educated and the unlettered—therefore I am eager to proclaim God's imminent triumph to you also who are in Rome" (1:14-15).

These statements of purpose are as clear as they are politically evocative. Yet for most of Christian history, to the present day, interpreters have studiously read them in innocuously religious ways, failing to take seriously either Paul's avowed purpose or its political connotations.

The observation is now commonplace that some of Paul's most theologically significant phrases would have resonated with imperial overtones. His titles for Christ ("lord," *kyrios,* and "son of God," *huios tou theou*), for example, were titles that the Caesars also claimed.[117] The terms normally translated "gospel" or "good news" (*euangelion*) and "preach the gospel" (*euangelizesthai*) were readily employed in Paul's world as an element of imperial propaganda, referring to announcements of the emperor's victories and accession.[118] Attention to the imperial context of Romans must go beyond the observation of verbal parallels, however, to ask about the rhetorical thrust of the letter.

In the politeness of Paul's language when he expresses mutuality ("that is, that we may be mutually encouraged . . . you and me," 1:12), and his postponement until the end of the letter of his future travel plans to Rome and beyond it, to Spain (compare 1:11 with 15:28-29), interpreters like Ernst Käsemann have found indications of Paul's "insecurity," "fear," "uncertainty," and "embarrassment" before his hearers. Similarly, the expression of confidence in 15:14-16 has convinced many that whatever Paul means to accomplish in this letter, he does *not* wish to be perceived as holding his hearers to account (as his use of the word "admonish" in 15:14 might otherwise imply):[119]

> But I myself am quite confident about you, my brothers and sisters, concerning you that you yourselves are full of goodness, filled with all knowledge, and capable of admonishing [*nouthetein*] one another. But I have rather boldly written to you, in part, as if reminding you, on account of the grace given to me by God so that [*eis*] I be a minister of Christ Jesus to the nations, doing holy service to the proclamation of God's triumph, in order that [*hina*] the offering of the nations may be pleasing, sanctified in holy spirit.

Paul's courteous speech should not distract us from the force of his rhetoric, however. It should point us rather to the letter's hortatory function, since diplomatic language was one mode, in Paul's day a preferred mode, for issuing commands. The courteous tone should not mislead us, then, into assigning Romans to the genre of the "ambassadorial letter."[120] Likewise, his use of expressions of confidence is what we should expect in a hortatory letter.[121] Paul writes to elicit a definite response from the Romans. True, in the beginning of the letter, Paul mentions a prospect for a *future* visit that he names at last as the purpose of a letter now completed. This is not because the Romans themselves never really were the object of Paul's concern, however, but because Paul expects the letter *itself* to have achieved what he earlier said he would have wanted to achieve, but from which he had been prevented in a personal visit.[122] As J. P. Sampley puts it, Romans is not *about* "Paul's gospel." It *is itself* Paul's effective proclamation of an alternative lordship, at work as the Romans hear it.[123]

The letter is directed toward a clear end. However courteous Paul's tone, he speaks as the duly commissioned representative of a lord who is to be obeyed, and he writes to secure "faithful obedience among the nations" to that lord. As Victor Paul Furnish observed, the letter evokes the disobedience of unjust human beings in 1:18-32; poses slavish obedience to sin and injustice against willing obedience to God in 6:12-23; and calls the Romans to a willing obedience that is their "spiritual worship" to God (12:1-2). Their positive response to the letter will incorporate them into the fulfillment of prophecies about the nations joining in praise with Israel (15:7-13) and will ensure the sanctity of "the offerings of the nations" that it is Paul's priestly service to present (15:14-16).

His exhortation has an international horizon, as the "programmatic" phrase "faithful obedience among the nations" indicates.[124] The Christian interpretive tradition has long translated *hypakoēn pisteōs* with "the obedience of *faith*" (so NRSV), language that implies that Paul meant primarily the trusting *assent* of his listeners to his message (his gospel) or their *acceptance* of his theological propositions about the way God saves. This translation has proven serviceable to a tradition eager to contrast salvation by faith in Jesus with the works-righteousness it has attributed, wrongly, to Judaism; but it is dubious on several grounds. Lexically, *pistis* normally had the sense, even in Israel's scriptures, not of "belief" but of faithfulness, involving loyalty and steadfastness. (Correspondingly, in Rom 3:3, the NRSV rightly translates *pistis tou theou* with "the faithfulness of God," not "God's faith"; at 1 Thess 1:8-9, Paul could tell the Thessalonians that their *pistis* meant, not simply that they had ceased to *believe* in idols, but that they had turned "to *serve* [*douleuein*] a living and true God.") Indeed, the semantic range of *pistis* overlaps with that of *hypakoē*, "obedience," so that Paul can use the terms almost interchangeably in Romans.[125] Grammatically, the genitive phrase "obedience of faithfulness" functions to specify what *kind* of obedience is meant: *faithful* obedience (as contrasted with some other kind).[126] Rhetorically, the phrase "faithful obedience" helps to establish the tone (and in fact the genre) of Romans as a letter of exhortation.[127]

The specification "faithful obedience *among all the nations*" evokes a horizon beyond the Romans. Their positive response to the letter will catch them up in a larger drama, the obedience of nations that Paul has helped to bring about "from Jerusalem and as far around as Illyricum" (15:18–19). The phrase signals the eschatological announcement of God's triumph over a rebellious world.[128] It evokes a scriptural vision in which the establishment of God's dominion over the earth included the subduing of hostile and oppressive nations. The obedience to which Paul calls his hearers incorporates them into the "offerings of the nations," his collection for the "poor" in Jerusalem, to which Macedonia and Achaia have contributed (15:25-27).[129]

The NRSV translates the phrase "the offering of the Gentiles," just as in 1:5, it renders "the obedience of faith among all the Gentiles." In everyday Greek and in the Greek of the Septuagint, however, *ta ethnē* meant "the nations," roughly parallel to *hoi laoi,* "the peoples." The singular, *to ethnos,* referred not to a Gentile individual, but to a nation: thus, significantly, Paul never uses the term. (When he speaks of individuals, he uses *Ioudaios,* Judean or Jew, and *Hellēn,* Greek. Despite the subsequent title given to his letter, Paul never speaks of Romans, but of "God's beloved in Rome," 1:7.) Historical considerations, too, militate against the translation *Gentiles* as an anachronism. Although many New Testament scholars follow the NRSV in using the translation (with a capital "G," suggesting a distinct ethnic identity equivalent but opposite to Jews), the notion that non-Judeans in the Roman congregations would have thought of themselves as Gentiles is unsustainable. The Greek *ethnē* was a convenient term by which Judeans might refer to all non-Judeans. But Christopher P. Stanley rightly observes that "in social terms, *there was simply no such thing as a Gentile in the ancient world.*" Non-Judeans would naturally "have defined themselves as 'Greeks,' 'Romans,' 'Phrygians,' 'Galatians,' 'Cappadocians,' and members of various other ethnic populations." Thus, "to speak of 'Jewish-*Gentile* conflicts' in antiquity is to confuse social analysis with ideology."[130] The unfortunate proliferation of Gentiles in recent translations is a lexically and exegetically dubious practice and one to be resisted.[131]

It follows that we should not think of Paul as some sort of religious entrepreneur, offering a new message of personal salvation to individuals who happened not to be ethnically Judean. Rather, Paul "thinks in nations" (Johannes Munck); he saw himself as the apostle "to the peoples of this earth at large" (Dieter Georgi).[132] His scenario of the nations turning in faithful obedience to Israel's Messiah was a peculiarly Israelite vision, informed by Israel's scriptures. Those scriptures explicitly identified the Messiah as the one "who rises to rule the nations" (Isa 11:10), an irreducibly political phrase that Paul quotes at the climax of the chain of scriptures in Rom 15:7-13. His vision of the nations united under a single ruler echoed, and was probably shaped in response to, the imperial ideology of universal rule (*oikoumenē*) that surrounded him. When Paul recounted the nations already caught up in his apostolic work, he showed that his understanding of the universality of God's rule involved a clearly territorial dimension, the physical specificity of which resembled the boundaries of the Roman Empire.[133] When he called upon the Romans to support "the offerings of the nations" which it was his priestly duty to gather and deliver in Jerusalem, he posed himself as the agent who would fulfill ancient scriptural visions of the nations bringing tribute to Israel (Isa 60:5-7; 66:20). But this language also *usurped an imperial prerogative*. It was the *Caesar* who rightly received "the gifts of the peoples" (*dona populorum*) as a matter of divine right, seated, in Virgil's eschatological fantasy, upon the throne of Apollo himself.[134]

Beyond Ethnic Tensions

Paul's apostolic work was in inevitable conflict with the Augustan vision of the obedience of nations.[135] We miss that tension if we persist in reading Romans on strictly ethnic terms, as Paul's effort to smooth tensions arising between ethnic groups, Jews (or "Judeans") and Gentiles, and to promote a tolerant universalism between those groups. That reading enjoys tremendous popularity, especially in the so-called "New Perspective on Paul,"[136] and in two recent attempts to set the ethnic reading of Paul on firmer ground by appeal to social-scientific models. That reading does not do justice to Paul's rhetoric, however, and the social-scientific models of "ethnicity" are at best unconvincing.

In their *Social-Scientific Commentary on the Letters of Paul*, Bruce J. Malina and John J. Pilch contend that Paul's phrase "Judean and Greek" marks "a general binary division of the house of Israel." They read "Greek" not as an ethnic term ("there really were no Greek ethnics in the first century," they contend) but as referring to "a social status" meaning civilized, "the opposite of barbarian." On this account, there were two kinds of Israelites in the first century: *Judeans,* those who lived in Judea and its environs (or "people who followed the ancestral customs of Israel as practiced in Judea; emigré Judeans"), and *Greeks,* Israelites living anywhere else and participating in Hellenistic culture.[137] Malina and Pilch contend that "Paul's phrase 'Judeans and Greeks' . . . actually means 'barbarian (or Judean) Israelite and civilized Israelite.'"[138] The result is a neat alignment of categories:

Judeans = barbarians	Greeks = *ethnē*
(uncivilized Israelites, living	(Greek-speaking, civilized
in or around Judea)	Israelites, living outside Judea)

According to Malina and Pilch, Paul identified as a Greek Israelite (as opposed to a barbarian Judean). His gospel of a raised Messiah and of an imminent "Israelite theocracy" testify to his own "Israelite ethnocentrism," which limited his mission to Greek-speaking Israelites, living outside of Judea, people like himself.[139] They deny that Paul's mission involved the inclusion of Gentiles (or non-Israelites); rather, Paul anticipated that non-Israelites would recognize God's vindication of Israelites and honor God ("because of what God does for his people, not for the Gentiles").[140]

Though Malina and Pilch are to be commended for emphasizing Paul's ethnic identity as an Israelite, their proclivity to binary oppositions leads them to draw other, unlikely conclusions. Against their restriction of Paul's mission to Israelites, we need only point to the explicit address of *ethnesin* as the audience of Romans (11:13).[141] Their unfortunate equation of Judean and barbarian is based on a mistaken conflation of two phrases. Paul means something very specific by "barbarian," as we will see below.

Philip F. Esler offers a very different social-science reading of Romans, according to which Paul seeks to offer rival ethnic groups an alternative "Christian identity" that transcends their ethnic differences. In contrast to Malina and Pilch, Esler (like most interpreters) recognizes that the Roman assembly includes both Judeans (whom he identifies readily with Israelites) and non-Judeans (*ethnē*). In order to attribute tensions to two rival ethnic groups, however, Esler must account for Paul's repeated use of the term *ethnē*, which he recognizes was a Judean term for outsiders, but which he also recognizes was not a term that any group in the ancient world used to identify themselves. He suggests that by *ethnē*, Paul simply meant Greeks, which (in contrast to Malina and Pilch) he shows was in fact an ethnic self-description. The substitution allows him to read Romans as another example of the long-standing tensions between Judeans and Greeks in other places. He explains these tensions, by appeal to social-science models of ethnicity, as arising inevitably from the social dynamics of group formation,[142] so that the simple proximity of Judeans and Greeks in Rome would inevitably have developed mutual competition, antagonism, and friction.[143] Like Malina and Pilch, Esler discounts the explicit address of Paul's letter to *ethnesin*, "(representatives of) the nations," but he does so to emphasize the importance of *both* Judean and Greek ethnic blocs in Roman house-churches.[144] Like them, he also conflates Paul's phrases "the Judean (first) and also the Greek" (1:16; 2:9-10; 3:9; 10:12), with "Greeks and barbarians" (1:15)—though he holds back from equating barbarians and Judeans.[145]

Despite the sophistication of the models Esler discusses, his discussion fails to take adequate account of the political context in which ethnic identities are constructed. The problem is endemic to many New Perspective studies on Paul. Too often, rich and complex discussions of political pressures on Jewish identity in the Roman world do not carry over to the interpretation of Paul; instead the apostle is simply posed over against Judaism in religious terms.[146] Part of the explanation is the lingering dominance of a liberal Christian theological agenda that poses Paul as the champion of an "intercultural," "universalistic" religion, Christianity, over against an ethnically specific and chauvinistic religion, Judaism. As Denise Kimber Buell and Caroline Johnson Hodge make the point, interpreting Christian universalism as non-ethnic enables Christian anti-Judaism by defining a positive attribute of Christianity (universalism) at the expense of Judaism. Judaism is portrayed as everything Christianity is not: legalistic, ethnic, particular, limited, and so on. Often, they observe, Paul is positioned in such interpretation "as the evolutionary link between an ethnic and a non-ethnic, universal kind of religion. He is understood to be 'ethnically' a *Ioudaios*," but at the same time he is read as either denying the significance of identity as a *Ioudaios* or as splitting the category *Ioudaios* "into a hierarchical pair," the spiritual, inner, "true" *Ioudaios* (i.e., the Christian) being superior to the fleshly, outer, "false" *Ioudaios* (i.e., the Jew).[147] To the same point, Pamela Eisenbaum describes a tendency in New Perspective scholarship to read Paul as *ethnically* or *culturally* Jewish, a Jew *kata sarka* ("according to the flesh"), but theologically or religiously Christian.[148]

I discuss Esler's work because he represents the best motives of the New Perspective research. He seeks to avoid anti-Judaism in his interpretation of Paul. Indeed, he admits that Paul himself shared in the Judean "ethnocentrism" of his age.[149] But this only means that when Esler moves on, in ways quite familiar from traditional Christian theology, to *oppose* Paul to the ethnic presumption on which "Israel was built" and to the Jerusalem apostles who failed to transcend it, his work becomes something of the exception that proves the rule.[150] The problem is not just that the "ethnic" reading common in the New Perspective of Romans potentially "enables anti-Judaism" by trading in stereotypes about "ethnocentric" Judaism. It also represents a culture-transcending, ethnically uninflected "universalism" as an ideal, which the contemporary interpreter can occupy alongside "Paul," over against the problematic ethnicity of others. Tat-Siong Benny Liew points out that discourse about "ethnicity" is often an only slightly more refined way of talking about race in Western societies: "it is often a label for groups who are not in power." Liew calls for a postcolonial critique of such discourse, especially as it appears in biblical studies, that will "read race/ethnicity in a wider, international nexus of socio-cultural and colonial politics."[151]

Esler is by no means the chief example of the sort of ethnic reading that Liew criticizes. To the contrary, at a general level Esler himself offers important insights toward a politically and historically contextualized reading of ethnicity. He recognizes that ethnic conflict has often arisen "in the colonial experience of indigenous peoples," not surprisingly, "given that colonial policy helped" again and again to aggravate group distinctions arbitrarily and to set peoples against each other on the basis of those distinctions.[152] He also recognizes that racial theories "pretend that divisions between people that are socially constructed, nearly always to allow one group to subjugate another, have some biological basis," but that in this pretense they are revealed to be "a form of pseudo-science."[153] But Esler does not extend these insights to discuss Roman policy toward Judeans;[154] instead he proceeds to discuss "ethnicity in the ancient Mediterranean world" in broadly general and essentialist terms.[155] When he does turn to one specific episode in Roman policy—the edict of Claudius which expelled (at least some) Judeans from Rome—he minimizes its significance as "unnecessary" to the interpretation of Romans, apparently because in his view, the ethnic tensions in Rome may be satisfactorily explained as arising solely from "mutual hostility between Judeans and Greeks"—a hostility for which he offers no historical explanation.[156] The predominance of the category of ethnicity means that other interpretive categories, notably the political, are minimized.

Esler also draws attention because he explicitly acknowledges the ideological import of his work. He finds in Paul an important resource for facing concerns in the world today: "The contemporary issue driving the current study of Romans is the nature of Christian identity—that is, the question of what it means to be a Christian—in a world rent by violent, often murderous conflict between groups, *in particular those of an ethnic kind.*"[157] Esler declares that ethnic conflict is "one of the most pressing evils in our world," and cites in illustration "the breakup of Yugoslavia during the years 1991–1994," the 1994 massacre of Tutsis by Hutus in Rwanda, the Palestinian-Israeli conflict, tensions between India and Pakistan over Kashmir, and conflict between Protestants and Catholics in Northern Ireland.[158] His concerns are commendable.

But we might well ask why we should focus attention on conflicts "in particular … of an ethnic kind." Indeed, we might well ask why ethnicity should be the primary category for understanding the specific conflicts Esler has named—or others, including the misery in occupied Iraq, routinely interpreted in Western media as the result of ethnic or sectarian strife. *Political,* and particularly *imperial,* forces influenced the construction of ethnic identity and exacerbated tensions between ethnic groups in the ancient Roman world. But just as surely, imperial powers shape and exacerbate ethnic conflicts today, just as they use ethnicity to mask the deeper economic and political realities of conflicts around the world—realities that these powers would likely rather not have examined.[159] It is not self-evident that we should construe conflicts in either era narrowly in terms of ethnicity and ethnic tension; nor that we should seek a solution in a supposed multicultural or universalist perspective that goes no further. To the contrary, any number of voices today call us to go on to ask "embarrassing questions" about the true nature of power relations in the "new world order" of actually existing capitalism. For example, Mamood Mamdani points out that the Western construction of "good" and "bad Muslims" masks "a refusal to address our own failure to make a political analysis of our times," specifically an analysis that will take account of the dynamics of actually existing imperial and power structures. The point finds echoes around the world.[160]

Ideological Constraints in Romans

The rhetoric that begins Romans itself points beyond ethnicity to the imperial construction of identity. Paul declares that he is "obligated both to Greeks and barbarians, to the educated and the unlettered" (1:14-15). It is a mistake to conflate these phrases (as do Malina and Pilch, Esler, and many others) with "Jew" and "Greek" or with "Israel" and "the nations." The phrase "Greeks and barbarians" also has been read as a summary description of the non-Judean world.[161] But it is more to the point to observe that the phrase routinely is found on the lips of Romans (and Judeans under Roman rule) as they describe *the world's peoples as Rome's subjects.*[162] Paul is not inviting different members of his audience to identify with one or another ethnic group. He is defying the imperial construction of peoples, and so he amplifies the phrase "Greeks and barbarians" with another phrase that we might fairly translate "the more and less civilized." He evokes imperial categories—categories that will not appear again in this letter—precisely to show that his own obligation does not fall along the line of Rome's "civilizing" mission.

The same defiance rings in his assertion that he is "not ashamed of the proclamation of God's triumph, for it is God's power" (1:16). We know better now than to hear this declaration as an expression of Paul's insecurity, "uncertainty and embarrassment." Robert Jewett writes that Paul here is refusing the shame that Roman culture would have attributed to him as the apostle of a crucified man.[163] Paul's sharply ironic language regarding the "shame of the cross" in 1 Cor 1:18-31 shows that he rejected the definitions of honor and shame current among the Roman elite.[164] But we can say more. Honor and shame are always acutely contested in a colonial situation.[165] The refusal to be "put to shame" is the defiance of the social and political order in which shame is constructed; thus, for example, Socrates refused to admit "shame" before his Athenian accusers.[166] The Roman aristocracy shared a powerful sense of national honor, *gloria,* in the expansion of the Roman Empire, but attributed shame to the enemies of Rome.[167] The author of *4 Maccabees* responded by putting into the mouths of the Jewish martyrs under Antiochus IV the refusal to put themselves, the Torah, or their ancestors to shame; they refused the tyrant's definition of what was reasonable, just, merciful—or shameful.[168] As Luise Schottroff observed, the protest of having nothing to be ashamed of was a requisite element in the genre of later Christian martyrologies as well.[169]

Paul was "not ashamed of the proclamation of God's triumph" simply because in it, *real* justice was seen, "the justice of God." This was powerful, saving justice, experienced as genuine faithfulness between a faithful God and those who act in trusting obedience; it was the justice that Israel expected God to enact through the Messiah (Psalm 72).

Others have observed that Paul's language about "faithful obedience among the nations" closely resembled the Hellenistic vision of nations united by a common enlightened civilization,[170] or closer to Paul's own time, the Augustan vision of nations brought together in obedience to a single lord.[171] But noticing such verbal and conceptual similarities must not obscure the fundamental difference. Paul states his clear purpose to bring the nations under obedience *to the God of Israel and his Messiah.* Recognizing the echoes of imperial *topoi* allows us to see that the contrast with the claims of empire is hardly incidental.

The burden of this chapter is to situate the rhetoric of Romans within the wider context of Roman discussions of coercion and consent, force and friendship, as the yoked instruments of imperial rule. The material dynamics of exploitation in the Roman Empire generated a fundamental ideological tension between the *order*

Rome achieved through force, and the claim of *justice* that Rome raised in order to win the hearts and minds of its subjects. Rome's use of force achieved peace for all, and so, within the imperial imagination, it made sense to erect the Altar of Augustan Peace on the field of Mars, the god of war who had brought Rome victory. Similarly it made sense, given imperial premises, for Augustus to boast that during his principate the Senate thrice ordered the gates of the temple of Janus closed, offering ritual demonstration that through warfare, war had been brought to an end. (Nero would copy the gesture, though with much less warrant.)[172]

The same ideological tension, between *order* (*taxis*) and *justice* (*dikaiosynē*), shapes Romans. Paul shares with many of his contemporaries in the ideologically constructed horror of social disorder. Philo had earlier declared that the rumors of Caligula's having fallen ill filled the world with dread of "the many great evils which spring from anarchy."[173] Paul, too, held civil strife (*eritheia*) in great dread (Rom 2:8), and considered well-deserved the condemnation of any who "resisted authority" (13:2).[174] We might imagine that both these Judeans had seen enough of the terrible costs of civil unrest, as borne by the vulnerable Judean populations in both Alexandria and Rome. After all, Paul was not simply indulging a lyrical inclination when he wrote of "hardship, distress, persecution, famine, nakedness, peril, and sword" (8:35). But we also must recognize the thoroughly kyriarchal texture of his rhetoric in Romans as the effect of the ideological constraints of Roman imperialism.

Paul could not have joined Plutarch in exulting, with cheerful defiance of the historical record, in the "true freedom of the inhabitants of the Roman Empire." For Plutarch, the Roman Empire was different from all other empires in that "the Romans govern free men, not slaves."[175] For Paul, the world has been "subjected to futility" and "bondage to decay" (Rom 8:20-21). God's Spirit militates against that subjection through the "groaning," as of a woman in labor, in a creation yearning for its liberation. The Spirit also agitates among those who wait for "the glorious liberation of the children of God" and "the redemption of our bodies" (8:22-23).

But, if for Paul, God is the source of the world's coming liberation, *God is also the one who has imposed the present subjection* (8:20). Here we see the constraining power of kyriarchal ideology upon Paul's thought. At least implicitly, he opposes the reigning kyriarchy of Rome, and can speak with fervor of a coming liberation from it. But he seems incapable of imagining the end of Roman kyriarchy without describing the ascendancy of a new and better kyriarchy, that of the Messiah, the *kyrios,* who will subdue and rule, *archein,* over the nations with justice. He cannot describe the steps the elect might take toward the day of liberation; theirs is only to "wait for it with patience" (8:25). He does not dwell on the social characteristics of a redeemed world, and never describes the "glorious liberation" of the children of God as a realm of absolute freedom. A world without kyriarchy is for Paul *almost* unutterable.

Throughout the letter, Paul sets a *willing and consenting* obedience over against its opposite, an obedience *characterized by compulsion and submission.* Thus the "faithful obedience of the nations" of which Paul speaks is described as a joining with Israel in joyful concert (15:9-13). The depraved obedience to dishonorable passions (1:21-26) stands in marked contrast with the willing obedience of renewed minds, not conformed to this world (12:1-2), and the exhortations that follow highlight the *willing* character of their obedience (12:3-9).

Disobedience is more than a failure to obey God. It is choosing to obey forces hostile to God, surrendering oneself to another, rival dominion, living under the compulsion of sin (*hyph' hamartian*, 3:9). Those who have through baptism left the dominion (*kyrieuein*) of death behind (6:9) are no longer to live as if "enslaved to sin" (*douleuein*, 6:6); they are no longer to let sin "reign" in their mortal bodies (*basileuein*) so that they obey (*hypakouein*) its passions (6:12-13). They have been "freed" from sin.

But this freedom is only possible because they have been *redeemed,* a metaphor from the slave market that retains its connotations for Paul. Thus, in baptism, they "were made slaves to justice" (*edoulōthēte tē dikaiosynē*, 6:12-23). They must "present" or "surrender" (*paristanein*) their members to God as the "war trophies" (*hopla*) of justice, becoming "obedient from the heart" (compare 12:1-2).

Thus, Paul does not imagine a realm of absolute freedom from constraint. Everyone is "accountable to God" (3:19); no human being enjoys absolute autonomy, but must inevitably serve (as a slave: *douleuein*) one reign (*basileuein*) or another. Adam's disobedience (*paraptōma*) provided the occasion for the introduction of the "reign" of sin and death (*basileuein*, 5:17, 21); Christ's obedience, literally his doing "what was right" (*dikaiōma*), ushered in the opposing "reign" (*basileuein*) of grace through justice (5:20). Freedom from obligation to the law—being no longer "under law" (*hypo nomou*, 6:15, cf. 3:19)—is not license to do sin, that is, to disobey God. This freedom is only possible to those who have died to the dominion that previously held them captive, that is, to the flesh (7:6), just as a widow is no longer bound by law to her deceased husband (7:1–5).[176] But no one enjoys absolute freedom from obligation. To the contrary, the law that once functioned as a "law of sin and death" now functions as "the law of the spirit of life in Christ Jesus" (8:2), and those who are in Christ are now enabled (and obligated) to fulfill its just requirement (*dikaiōma*, 8:4).

The tensions in this letter go far beyond the tensions within the exhortation to be subject to governing authorities (Rom 13:1-7) and the tensions between that passage and its epistolary context. The whole of the letter is riven by *ideological* tensions. Paul contrasts life in the flesh and life in the Spirit by saying that "the mind that is set on the flesh is hostile to God; it does not submit to God's law" (*ouch hypotassetai*, 8:7-8). The implication is that the life of the Spirit *does* "submit" to God. But moments later Paul declares that the Spirit (that is, *of* God) groans *against* subjection—the subjection of creation to corruption, which he then states, paradoxically, is subjection *to* God. Similarly, he declares that some fellow Judeans, though having a zeal for God, have sought to establish their own justice and thus failed "to submit to God's justice" (10:3). The contrast established elsewhere in the letter between willing obedience (*hypakoē*) and submission (*hypotassesthai*) here breaks down, as it does in Paul's assertion that God has "imprisoned everyone" in disobedience (11:32).

Fredric Jameson's proposal for ideological analysis allows us to recognize in this tension, which Paul fails to resolve, the effects of a greater ideological tension in the Roman order. The language of liberation in Romans 8 arises from a collective aspiration. For Paul, however, the thought of unfettered freedom remains a matter of "inward groaning," expressible only in "sighs too deep for words." It is, in the terms of Jameson's analysis, an *unutterable* thought, a thought that has been *repressed* into the collective "political unconscious" by the constraints of imperial ideology—yet irrupting here, if only for a moment, onto the surface of the text. The tensions evident on the surface of Romans point to the "strategies of containment" that function as ideological constraints in the Roman world, as Fig. 1.2 indicates.

Jameson adapts A. Greimas's use of a "semiotic square" to map the indications of *ideological closure* within a text that are evident in the ways the text seeks to resolve "a dilemma, an aporia, . . . a concrete social contradiction."[177] I identify the fundamental tension in *Roman imperial ideology,* and (as an inevitable consequence) in *Paul's letter to the Romans* as well, as the tension between *order,* perceived as a necessity to be imposed by force, and *justice,* the claim that such force is right and legitimate. Jameson holds that the tensions at work in an ideological situation produce a "restless" effort to produce new terms to "ultimately 'solve' the dilemma at hand," first by projecting the opposites of the terms in tension in an imaginative "what if . . ." exercise. Thus, the social contradiction between order and justice projects the question, *What alternatives are there to justice, or to order, as presently experienced?*[178] In other words, is there any way to imagine justice being realized, apart from the present order, that is not simply the chaos of anarchy? Is there any imaginable social order, apart from the present pretension to justice, that is not simply another unjust imposition of power?

Fig. 1.2. Ideological tensions in the Roman Empire

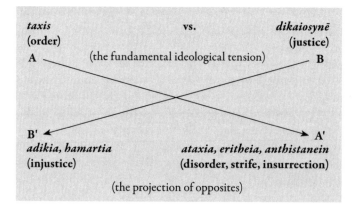

Texts are generated, Jameson argues, at the point at which the collective energy that he calls the "political unconscious" seeks release from the ideological constraints of a situation "by projecting combinations" of the possible projected values. Thus, Fig. 1.3 represents, surrounding the values in tension (order, justice) and the projected countervalues (injustice, disorder), four possible resolutions.

Fig. 1.3. Ideological closure in Romans

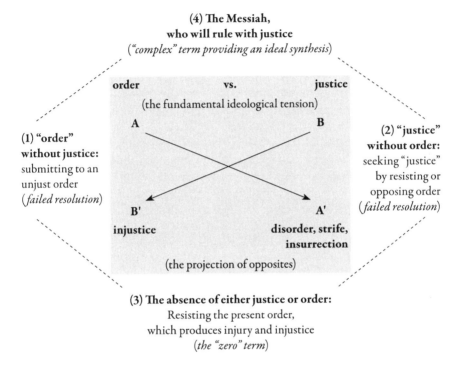

As indicated in this diagram, two conceivable combinations, in Paul's thinking, are unacceptable; that is, they are *failed solutions* to the ideological dilemma: (1) the premature acceptance of (Roman) order in the absence of justice, in terms of what historians of Judeans in the Roman world have called "accommodation"; and (2) the premature effort to achieve justice by a rejection of (Roman) order, as manifested in rebellion. It bears emphasizing that these are not theological judgments, made in the abstract or according to a priori principles. *They are possibilities projected and foreclosed by Paul's historical experience—and the experience of many of his Judean contemporaries—of the material environment in which he and they lived.*

A third term (3) Jameson calls the "neutral" or "zero" term, the "union of purely negative or privative terms" in the initial contradiction. In the case of Romans, the imaginative question, *What if there were neither order nor justice?* is represented in just the intolerable situation that many scholars have suggested Paul anticipated in

Rome itself: namely, that his non-Judean hearers might take part in civil disturbances protesting Nero's tax policies, and thus put the embattled Judean community at even greater risk.[179]

According to Jameson, the "complex term" (4) provides the "ideal synthesis"
that is imagined to resolve the contradiction at the heart of the text. In the case
of Romans, this "ideal synthesis" subsumes the initially contradictory terms,
order vs. *justice,* in a new unity—the ideal order to be imposed by a truly just lord,
the Messiah.

The benefit of adapting Jameson's work in this way is that it allows us to recognize some of Paul's judgments as the effects of *ideological constraints* in his
situation. What is repressed from this system is, first, any notion of unrestricted
freedom. The *kyriarchal* constraint on Paul's thought effectively distances Paul
from many of his modern readers for whom democracy, equality, and the rights
of the individual are sacrosanct; but it places him squarely alongside others of his
contemporaries. For Paul, there is no realm of pure freedom; in its place, for Paul,
is the dread of anarchy.

The diagram also helps us to interpret Paul's statements about *obedience as subjection,* including subjection to the present governing authorities. No other imagined conceptuality seemed capable of resolving the fundamental tension in Paul's
situation: neither accommodation nor rebellion, nor the dread prospect of *eritheia,*
self-interested and socially destructive lawlessness. This is due to *specific* historical
and ideological circumstances I shall have occasion to explore further below. Paul
was therefore compelled to imagine that endurance and subjection were, *for the
present,* appropriate. (I note that endurance, *hypomonē,* which appears throughout
the letter, was a hallmark virtue in the apocalypses as well, beginning with Daniel.[180]) Paul could imagine subjection to the governing authorities as coinciding
with obedience to God, because he imagined that the governing authorities themselves had been subjected to God ("they have been set in order under God," *hypo
theou tetagmenai eisin,* 13:1). But he did not recount any narrative in which that
subjection had taken place. Nor did he propose to examine whether actual Roman
magistrates were aware of their responsibility, or whether they had carried out their
obligations in the course of carrying out their duties. The point is one of *ideological
necessity,* given the constraints just described. It is inconceivable, "unutterable," for
Paul that God might *not* be in control—even of the governing authorities that he
could describe in 1 Corinthians 2 as being hostile to God.

But this means that Paul did not intend to enjoin subordination or subjection
as a *permanent state of affairs.* Paul could not imagine that the Roman order should
long endure (see Rom 13:11-14). That Roman power should remain the decisive
political reality for the indefinite future and that the subjection to Rome that he
recommended should mean continued subjection to an unjust, exploitative, and
violent order—this possibility, too, was intolerable for Paul, and thus repressed
from consideration in Romans 13.

As the catastrophe recorded in Acts 21–28 makes abundantly clear, Paul did not know the future. To read his exhortations as if he were responding to a universe in which the Romans, or some other conqueror, naturally held dominion in perpetuity, is thoroughly anachronistic and reveals more about the contemporary interpreter's assumptions than about Paul's.[181] But neither do we, on an ideological reading, have the luxury of retreating into theological abstractions, attributing Paul's messianism either to his privileged supra-historical insight (revelation) or to his religious genius. *Like other Judeans of his time,* Paul embraced a messianic and apocalyptic viewpoint, informed by Israel's scriptures, as a way of perceiving the material and ideological realities of Roman imperialism. But that historical observation simply extends the question to take in many of Paul's contemporaries as well.

Jameson's discussion of the "political unconscious" allows a different perspective on Romans. The more interesting question, from the perspective of ideological criticism, is not *Why did Paul enjoin subjection to Rome?* but *What enabled Paul to speak, in the same letter, of an alternative?* To invoke the Spirit of God as a force striving against the bondage of the present order, to try to articulate the Spirit's unutterable yearnings for liberation—these aspects of Romans should give us pause. As James C. Scott poses the larger question, "how is it that subordinate groups . . . have so often believed and acted as if their situations were *not* inevitable when a more judicious historical reading would have concluded that it was?" Scott's own answer is that "if the elite-dominated public transcript tends to naturalize domination, it would seem that *some countervailing influence* manages often to *denaturalize* domination."[182]

Scott offers no further explanation of that "countervailing influence." In Romans 8, Paul names it the Holy Spirit. We would be hard-pressed to describe the groans of the Spirit in terms of the rhetorical handbooks, or by reference to the *topoi* of imperial ideology as these were engaged in the public transcript. The groans of the Spirit, "as of a woman in labor," clearly have a decisive place in the letter, nonetheless. An attentive reading must give account of those groans as much as of the ideological constraints against which they were—and are—exerted.

A coin minted only weeks after the death of the emperor Claudius in 54 C.E., depicts his successor, Nero, and his widow, Nero's mother Agrippina, facing each other. Both were suspected of complicity in Claudius's death. Gold; British Museum, London; photo © Werner Forman / Art Resource, N.Y.

CHAPTER TWO

IVSTITIA

Justice and the ᴄArrogance of Nations

Throughout the 1990s and into the new millennium, human rights reports on organized state terror among U.S. client states (among others)—from El Salvador and Haiti to Afghanistan and Indonesia—routinely spoke of a "crisis of impunity" to describe the systematic disintegration of the civil and legal fabric by which criminals and terrorists might be held to account. It seems that imperial influence has everywhere had a corrosive effect on international standards and the mechanisms of criminal accountability.[1] In an age in which the message of empire to the world is "we decide, you obey,"[2] the steep gradient of power distorts and deflects the requirements of justice. Those who suffer the exertions of imperial force have no real recourse. They can raise no effective counter-claim against imperial power. Their voices—if they survive to speak—are not heard.

Imperial authorities rarely can afford the unalloyed candor that invokes brute force alone; some semblance of morality must be maintained for ideological purposes, though it must not be allowed to impede the smooth functioning of the empire's operations. Routinely, in the ancient Roman Empire and in today's imperial situation, morality is represented as but one dimension of the authority enjoyed by those with the power to dominate others.

Paul contests that representation from the beginning of Romans.

———————— **Empire and the Crisis of Impunity** ————————

In 2003, the most important result of President George W. Bush's diplomatic tour of what he once referred to as "the country of Africa" was to exact from various national governments, on peril of economic sanctions, pledges that U.S. citizens would be exempt from prosecution for violations of international law, for example, crimes against humanity. The consistent message of imperial policy in the so-called new world order is clear: accountability is for others. The poor have no inalienable right to relief from the predations of the powerful. The sovereign right of empire to do whatever it wants must not be challenged or compromised.[3]

59

It is easy enough for those of us who are U.S. citizens to recognize the arrogant presumption of impunity when it appears at a distance, but not when it is voiced close to home.[4] We live in a culture of deep denial in which it is apparently impossible to recall where figures like Panama's Noriega, Somalia's Siad Barre, Indonesia's Suharto, Haiti's Cedras, Al Qaeda's Bin Laden, or Iraq's Saddam Hussein found eager and essential support early in their brutal careers. Blinded by a mythology of American innocence[5] that had abundant parallels in the Roman imperial imagination, we simply cannot remember any historical reasons why men and women in other countries should resent the imposition, often through military force, of U.S. economic and political will. We have allowed ourselves to be convinced that the citizens of Somalia, Afghanistan, or Iraq should feel nothing but gratitude for U.S. intervention. That some of them do not, and that their misery and their resentment continue in tandem, only confirms our impression that they are irrational, infantile, incapable of the lofty morality to which we hold, and therefore both fundamentally inferior to us and in need of our tutelage. The world is a terrible and tragic place where inscrutable evil persists, we tell ourselves, despite the best efforts of our benevolent government.

In May 2004, as the White House argued before the Supreme Court that the President had the "inherent" authority to detain "enemy combatants" without legal constraint, Jonathan Schell observed that the constraints of the U.S. Constitution presented "a stumbling block" to empire:

> The republic requires a single standard, to which all are subject—the law. But the empire requires a double standard—one set of regulations for others, and another set, or none, for the imperial ruler. In the imperial conception, "law" is a set of rules dictated by the ruler for everyone else to obey.[6]

The logic is ancient. The apostle Paul lived in a similar world, where Roman law was applied according to a pernicious but reliable double standard: "there was one law for the rich and another for the poor."[7] The impression that Rome ruled subject populations with respect and fairness was a carefully manufactured façade: "rights which pertained to Rome might not be conceded to others."[8] That certainly would not have surprised the "others," of course. "By intention their only thought is to do evil," declared the author of the Habakkuk Pesher, who found the true character of Roman treachery plainly laid out in the scroll of that prophet.

> In deceit and trickery they conduct themselves with all the peoples. . . .
> [They] trample the land with [their] horses and with their beasts. From far
> away they come, from the seacoasts, to eat up all the peoples like an insatiable
> vulture. In anger and [hostility] and in wrath and arrogance they speak with
> all [the peoples . . .]. They sneer at leaders and deride the nobility; they jeer at
> kings and princes, and ridicule a throng of people. . . . [They] enter the land

by the advice of a family of criminals: each in his turn, [their] rulers come, one after the other, to devastate the la[nd....] [They] added to their wealth by all their plunder.... [They] sacrifice to their standards, and...their weapons are what they worship.... [They] impose the yoke of their taxes...on all the peoples yearly, thus ruining many lands.... [They] destroy many people with the sword, including boys, the weak, old men, women, and children. Even on the child in the womb they have no mercy.[9]

The Roman strategy of rule through compliant local aristocracies inevitably aggravated tensions between the few rich and the abundant poor, the powerful and the masses of the powerless. The Judean rebellion against Rome (66–73 C.E.) provides one spectacular example of what could happen when Roman policy failed to gain popular acceptance for its client regimes.[10] The fault, of course, as the empire's wisest men solemnly explained, was to be found in the inability of the ruled to accept the necessary governance of their superiors, not in the way that governance was imposed.

A "Declaration of War" in Romans

"The Epistle to the Romans is a political theology, a *political* declaration of war on the Caesar." So political philosopher Jacob Taubes declared in a spirited series of lectures given only days before his death in 1987.[11] Other scholars have offered similarly flamboyant characterizations of the letter. I described it, for example, in *Liberating Paul* (1994), as an "ideological intifada" against Roman imperial thought.[12] But if Paul's gospel was "opposed to the Roman Empire," as others have flatly put it,[13] we should expect Romans, which contains the most extensive theological argument in any of his letters, to confront the claims of imperial propaganda. Given that, beginning with Augustus, imperial propaganda focused on the person of the Caesar himself as the embodiment of divine justice,[14] we should further expect a letter from a supposedly anti-imperial figure, especially a letter centrally concerned with the "justice of God" (*dikaiosynē tou theou*, 1:17; 3:21-26), to offer a straightforward critique of that propaganda.

Romans offers no direct critique of empire, however. When Paul opposes the justice of God with the injustice of mortals, Christian interpreters especially are used to perceiving an argument about how the injustice or "wickedness" of souls (as the NRSV translates *adikia* at 1:18) is overcome by God's justifying action. The letter is a treatise about soteriology after all, it would seem, and if there is a polemical edge to Paul's argument, it is aimed at "the Jew," who presumably expects God to justify wicked human beings in some manner that gives Jews an advantage. A host of interpreters read Rom 1:18-32 as a piece of theological bait: Paul seeks to lure the unsuspecting Jew into a trap by evoking a heavily stereotyped characterization of Gentile sinfulness. The trap is sprung at 2:1: "Therefore you have no excuse, whoever you are, when you judge others," an indictment that (at least in the eyes of many interpreters) is clearly aimed at the arrogantly self-confident Jew.

This reading, to which Christians have become habituated in part because it is so congenial to their own self-understanding, is mistaken. Romans does offer a political declaration of war, and we can recognize in it a critique of the claims of imperial propaganda, if we attend carefully to the sorts of oblique references and implied contrasts to which the considerations in chapter one point us. The letter is not a treatise on how wicked human beings can be saved; to the contrary, as we shall see, it begins by driving a rhetorical wedge between the justice of God and the false claims of mortals who pretend at justice, but deserve God's wrath instead.

The argumentative aspect of Romans 1:3-4

Taubes's characterization of Rom. 1:1-4 as "a *political* declaration of war on the Caesar" may seem an inexcusable exaggeration. After all, nothing in these opening lines sounds particularly incendiary:

> Paul, slave of the Messiah Jesus, called as an apostle set apart to the proclamation of God's triumph, which he proclaimed beforehand through his prophets in holy scriptures, concerning his son, the descendant of the seed of David according to flesh, appointed God's son in power according to the spirit of holiness by resurrection from the dead: Jesus the Messiah, our Lord ... (1:1-4)

Biblical and theological scholarship has accustomed us to read these words as religious, rather than political, language, and specifically as a rather innocuous invocation of an early Christian confession. Yet (without offering any further explanation) Taubes juxtaposed these same lines with an infamous series of events just prior to the letter's composition: the death—Taubes called it murder—of the emperor Claudius in 54 C.E., the accession of Nero, and the Senate's consecration of Claudius at Nero's request.

Contemporary with Taubes (and in a lecture given at his invitation), New Testament scholar Dieter Georgi raised the same comparison in a series of provocative questions:

> Paul's use of terminology drawn from the law of royal succession in Rom 1:3-4 shows that he is making more than a religious claim. . . . Is Paul using the traditional formula in order to support an alternative theory concerning true rulership and the legitimate *princeps*? Is he offering an alternative

to the social utopia of Caesarism, with its promise of universal reconcilia-
tion and peace as the prerequisite for undreamed of achievements resulting
in unimagined prosperity? . . . Is it Paul's intention to measure King Jesus and
his program by this yardstick?[15]

Phrased as questions, Georgi's suggestions were provocative, but hardly conclu-
sive.[16] In more recent years, Georgi's characterization of these lines as "a critical
counterpart to the central institution of the Roman Empire" has been taken up
by a few others, though they have not offered any further substantiation.[17] I cited
Georgi myself in an earlier work in speaking of "an intense 'realized eschatology'"
in the Augustan age, "through which Rome taught its subjects to celebrate the
Roman order as the coming of a golden age of peace and security, the Pax Augusta,"
but I was frankly mystified by Georgi's juxtaposition of this Roman ideology with
Romans 1.[18] Perhaps N. T. Wright has gone furthest to pursue the point, though
(as I did earlier) only in general terms. Wright has argued that for Paul, *christos*
meant fully *messiah,* the anointed king of Israel's scripture who was destined to
rule not only Israel but the whole world.[19] *Kyrios* was also the title claimed by successive Caesars as a divine prerogative: in official inscriptions each is *Kyrios Kai-*
saros, "*Lord* Caesar." Thus, Wright argued, Paul's use of the terms always poses a
strong *implicit* challenge to the lordship of Caesar: his gospel is "a royal proclamation aimed at challenging other royal proclamations," at once fulfilling the prophecies of Israel's scripture and "subverting the imperial gospel of Caesar."[20]

But because Paul does not *say* any of this explicitly—nothing here directly contests imperial claims regarding the Caesars—any subversion of the imperial gospel
remains so implicit as to seem invisible. Yes, now we can recognize that much of
Paul's language carries political connotations. The sender formula resonates with
the weight of Roman diplomatic vocabulary. Paul's self-identification as slave and
apostle echoes the prophets of Israel's scriptures but also finds analogies in the diplomatic rhetoric by which imperial officials announced themselves.[21] I have translated Paul's description of his commission, *eis euangelion theou,* as a commission
to "the proclamation of the triumph of God" to convey the contemporary political connotations of *euangelion.*[22] Given the public and political resonance, we may
imagine that the opening lines of the letter have heightened, rather than deflected,
any expectations among his audience that this discourse might include the sort of
commentary or critique of current events to which they were accustomed even in
less favorable public settings (see chap. 1). But the political resonance seems incidental to Paul's purpose in Romans, at least as we have usually understood it.

    We continue to read these lines according to older theological habits. For example,
Robert Jewett cites Georgi when he characterizes Romans as Paul's criticism of "the
official system of honor achieved through piety on which the empire after Augustus
rested," but Jewett's own analysis of Rom 1:3-4 has no connection with Georgi's discussion.[23] Like most modern commentators, Jewett is more impressed by what he
sees as the theologically uncharacteristic things Paul says here *about* Christ. Nowhere

else does Paul show any interest in Jesus' descent from David, speak of Christ's resurrection as the specific demonstration of his exaltation as "Son of God," or speak of the "spirit of holiness."[24] At first glance, these might appear minor details, but the differences have convinced many scholars that Paul is not offering his own formulations here but is trading on earlier liturgical or creedal traditions that he assumes his audience will find familiar. Surprised by what they take to be the "adoptionist" implications of Paul's language (i.e., that Jesus "became" Son of God only at his resurrection), these interpreters have stipulated that Paul is quoting a "primitive" Palestinian Jewish-Christian tradition, and that he does so to ingratiate himself with potential Jewish-Christian opponents in Rome.[25] Read in these terms, the opening lines of the letter bear only the vaguest political significance.

Jewett himself offers a remarkably specific history of no less than three layers to this creed. First is a Palestinian Jewish-Christian original, then a Hellenistic-Christian adaptation, and finally Paul's creative adaptation of both prior layers. According to Jewett, Paul combines sentence fragments from two different stages of a developing creed as a means of signaling to rival Jewish-Christian and Gentile-Christian groups in Rome his "intent to find common ground" with both. In effect, Jewett suggests that Paul's hearers would have heard his opening words as alternating signals to subgroups among them:

Fig. 2.1. Robert Jewett's reconstruction of Rom. 1:3-4

"Primitive Jewish-Christian creed"	"Hellenistic-Christian adaptation"	Paul's insertions and additions
born from David's seed	according to the flesh,	
appointed God's son		by power
	according to a spirit	of holiness
by resurrection from the dead,		
		Jesus Christ our Lord

Jewett's scheme suggests that Paul has juxtaposed sentence fragments as slogans to demonstrate that he simultaneously wears the theological colors of rival groups in Rome. This requires us to imagine that different members of the Roman church would have heard intermittent words and sentence fragments as representing their viewpoint, and heard alternating words and phrases as the slogans of others. But this is a remarkably unlikely scenario. Here, the intricacies of form-critical and tradition-critical method fail to deliver a convincing rhetorical understanding of the opening of the letter.

These lines were not written to offer an answer to the anachronistic question of later christological debates, "When did Jesus become Son of God?" Pursuing the contrast between Paul's "preexistent" Christology and a presumed earlier "adoptionist" Christology is therefore a false trail. We are on firmer ground when we seek "to take into account not only the choice of data but also the way in which they are interpreted, the meaning attributed to them" (the "heart of argumentation," according to Chaim Perelman and L. Olbrechts-Tyteca).[26] To understand the argumentative burden of these phrases, we must distinguish what Paul presumes his audience will accept as fact—namely, the resurrection of Jesus, which he clearly is not announcing to the Romans for the first time—from the interpretation of that fact that will shape his hearers' perceptions of the argument to follow.

Paul does not represent the resurrection here as a significant event in itself; rather it is significant as the event in which Jesus Christ was "appointed Son of God in power." In these phrases, Paul invokes for his audience a rich alternative transcript—an Israelite transcript, "proclaimed beforehand" through Israel's scriptures—according to which God's purposes for creation will be fulfilled through a scion of the line of David.

But we can say more. Relying on James C. Scott's discussion of "voice under domination," we can compare samples of the public and hidden transcripts in the immediate context of Romans. This comparison confirms the rather impressionistic characterizations of the Augustan age offered by Taubes and Georgi (and others) and shows that the opening lines of Romans are indeed an "engagement with power."

Rome, 54 C.E.

Late in the afternoon of October 13, the aging Tiberius Claudius Drusus was enjoying one of his favorite entertainments, watching a troupe of comic actors, when he suddenly doubled over in pain. Never a healthy man, the emperor of the Roman world routinely suffered gastric and intestinal distress. One reason was his prodigious gluttony. According to the historian Suetonius, "it was seldom that Claudius left a dining-hall except gorged and sodden; he would then go to bed and sleep supine with his mouth wide open—thus allowing a feather to be put down his throat, which would bring up the superfluous food and drink as vomit." He consequently suffered "violent stomach-aches which often, he said, made him think of suicide" (*Claudius* 33).

But this time it was worse. Claudius was taken back to his palace, where a lavish family banquet had been prepared. His wife Agrippina offered him a plate of cooked mushrooms. Soon afterwards, he lapsed into unconsciousness. Agrippina summoned her personal physician, but despite his best efforts, the emperor died during the night.

Or, perhaps, *because of* his efforts: Agrippina's physician may not have worked in vain. Writing decades after the death, Suetonius reported that "most people think that Claudius was poisoned; but when, and by whom, is disputed." The prime suspect was Agrippina herself, with the complicity of that same physician (so also Tacitus,

Ann. 12.65–66). We should perhaps not presume judgment of Agrippina, or of her son, the ascendant emperor Nero, on the basis of rumor, however widespread.[27] My interest, however, is not in opening a belated inquest into Claudius's death, but in gaining a sense of the public perception of that death and the events that followed it.

It was obvious who stood to benefit from Claudius's demise, and this surely determined which of the rumors caught fire immediately. Years earlier, Agrippina's own brother, the emperor Gaius (Caligula), had exiled her on suspicion of conspiring against him. After Gaius's assassination, when the army seized upon the unlikely Claudius, Agrippina's uncle, and acclaimed him as emperor, Agrippina returned to Rome and maneuvered herself, through gestures that Suetonius suggests were far more than familial, into Claudius's affections. Their marriage was her second, his fourth; it required an act of the Senate decriminalizing a union between an uncle and his niece. On her part, Agrippina required that her new husband adopt her son, Tiberius Claudius Nero, as his own, and promise his own daughter Octavia to Nero in marriage. Those acts should have secured Nero's place as rightful heir, even ahead of Claudius's own son, Britannicus, who was four years Nero's junior. Claudius continued to hint that he preferred Britannicus, however, and soon rumors swirled that Agrippina again was scheming against an emperor—this time, her own husband.

Now Claudius was dead, and Nero ruled in his place. (Britannicus, Claudius's favorite, would follow a year later—as would Agrippina herself in the fifth year of Nero's rule, both executed on the young emperor's express orders.) Claudius's death was kept quiet until a stately funeral could be arranged. At that ceremony, the seventeen-year-old Nero gave his stepfather's funeral oration and convinced the Senate to accord the late emperor divine honors. Thus "the burden of the massive Roman state" was laid upon Nero's slender shoulders, and he became, like the Augusti before him, *divi filius,* "Son of God."[28]

Nero's succession in the public transcript

Reciting these events gives us a sense of the wider ideological and cultural context in which Paul wrote Romans. How were events of the magnitude of the death (or, quite possibly, the assassination) of one emperor, and the accession to power of another, perceived in different social settings?

When the contemporary poet Calpurnius Siculus touched on Claudius's deification, he straightforwardly accepted the official claim. In his first *Eclogue,* he depicts two wandering cowherds who discover on the trunk of a tree a freshly carved oracle, praising the dead emperor's ascent to heaven and the accession of his stepson as an auspicious occasion of solemn joy:

> Assuredly a very god [i.e., Nero] shall take in his strong arms the burden of the massive Roman state so unshaken, that the world will pass to a new ruler

without the crash of reverberating thunder, and that Rome will not regard the dead as deified in accord with merit ere the dawn of one reign can look back on the setting of the last.[29]

Note the acceptance of the official story that Claudius was now deified "in accord with merit"; note as well the implicit contrast of the new emperor, Nero, with his ancestor Augustus, who had come to power after a catastrophic civil war (of which he had been a primary cause).[30] In accordance with what would become a stock element of court propaganda, Nero is described here as surpassing even his divine ancestor in taking up the "burden of the massive Roman state" without a troubling hint of thunder.[31]

Similarly, the anonymous contemporary *Eclogue* (discovered in a tenth-century manuscript at Einsiedeln, Germany) declares that "temples reek of wine; the hollow drums resound to the hands," the populace joining together in sacred celebration of Nero's accession. "Surely the blockish herd denies not to these times the realms of gold? The days of Saturn have returned with Justice the Maid: the age has returned in safety to the olden ways." No enemy troubles the Neronian peace; war is a distant memory (again, Nero's propagandists contrast his accession with Augustus's rise to power).[32]

A third text sounds similar themes from the public transcript—but mixed with other, discordant themes. Writing within months of Claudius's death and deification, Nero's longtime tutor and now counselor, Lucius Annaeus Seneca, offered the court his satire of the deification, titled the *Apocolocyntosis,* or "The Pumpkinification" of Claudius. Through the narrator of the *Apocolocyntosis,* Seneca affirms the divine vocation of his patron, Nero, who has inaugurated "our present period of prosperity" (*Apoc.* 1). The text describes the council of the gods who fix the end of Claudius's life and Nero's succession. Mercury endorses the death of Claudius, declaring that Nero "best deserves [to] reign."[33] Apollo takes a hand, alongside the Fates, in spinning the thread of life for the youth Nero, using not "cheap wool" but "a mass of gold" as befitting "the Ages of Gold" about to dawn. Apollo waxes particularly eloquent on the "gentle radiance" of the young emperor, whose face and voice are equal to his own.[34]

None of this is surprising; themes of the arrival of the Golden Age are as old as the *Aeneid* (1.286–90; 6.789–90)[35] and were subsequently extended to each new emperor in succession. In decreeing that Claudius had ascended to heaven, the Senate was similarly following a well-worn path. Long before Nero's accession, his hallowed ancestors Julius Caesar and Augustus had been depicted ascending into heaven or reclining there in blessed peace (see Figs. 2.1, 2.2).[36] Nero was only too eager to exploit his own connection with that sacred scheme. In an otherwise routine political speech given a year before Claudius's death, he had reminded his audience of his own purported descent from Aeneas (Tacitus, *Ann.* 12.58).

The apotheosis of two Caesars. Left: *The "Grande Camée de France," a gem cut in Rome around 20 C.E., depicts a nude Tiberius at the center, surrounded by his mother, Livia, and other family members; above him, the divine Augustus watches from heaven. In the lowest register sit barbarian families.* Right: *Claudius is depicted in the guise of Jupiter, nude and enthroned, receiving a wreath of victory; the eagle is also Jupiter's symbol. This gem was carved in 54 C.E., soon after Claudius's death. Cabinet des Medailles, Bibliothèque Nationale, Paris. Photos © Erich Lessing/Art Resource, N.Y.*

Nero's succession in the hidden transcript of the powerful

Other judgments on Nero's accession found expression among the elite, however. Because hints of an incestuous relationship between mother and son were "notorious,"[37] we may imagine (for his contemporaries certainly did) that Nero knew he had won his position through his mother's murderous machinations. In any case, the decreed deification of Claudius was obviously in Nero's own interest, not least because it distanced him in the public eye from any perceived crime. To some, nevertheless, the ceremony appeared a transparently cynical act. Tacitus later observed that Claudius's will was suppressed, and declared Nero's public sorrow "duly counterfeited." "Agrippina and Nero made a show of mourning for their victim and they elevated to heaven the man they'd carried out from the banquet in a litter," Dio Cassius would later write. Cassius quoted another Roman magistrate's gruesome quip that Claudius had been "hauled into heaven on a hook," after the manner of publicly executed criminals whose bodies were subsequently dragged to the Forum. This was L. Junius Gallio, the proconsul of Achaia who had earlier dismissed accusations against Paul in Corinth (Acts 18:12)—and Seneca's brother.[38]

In the *Apocolocyntosis,* Seneca surpassed even that barb. Eager to ingratiate himself with the new emperor, whose tutor he had been for years, and to avenge himself on the deceased Claudius, who had been a political enemy, Seneca roundly mocked the dead emperor's faltering gait and his speech impediment and even made sport of the dying man's incontinence.

Those are hardly daring moves in such a clearly sycophantic text. But Seneca went further, taking the surprising political risk of frankly admitting that "deification" is always a shrewdly calculated bit of political theater. Here is the narrator of the *Apocolocyntosis*:

If the reader asks for my sources, in the first place I will refuse to answer. . . . But if it is necessary to reveal my source, you should ask the man who saw Drusilla's ascent into heaven. . . .

The reference, which was undoubtedly intended to elicit wicked laughter from its audience, is to an actual event in the reign of the emperor Gaius (Caligula). After Gaius had killed his own sister and paramour, Julia Drusilla, a senator had been handsomely bribed to swear that he had seen the victim swept up into heaven. The suborned senator's testimony may have provided Gaius with a convenient cover story, or at least distracted public attention from the circumstances of Drusilla's death, at an inconvenient moment in his career.[39] Now, Seneca declares that it is this same unscrupulous senator, unnamed, who

. . . will claim he saw Claudius making the same journey, though "with unequal steps." . . . [He is] in charge of the Appian Way, the way by which, as you know, both the Divine Augustus and Tiberius Caesar joined the company of the gods. If you ask him, he'll tell you in private. He'll never say a word to more than one. Ever since he swore in the senate that he'd seen Drusilla going up to heaven and, for all that marvelous news, no one believed him, he has solemnly sworn that he personally will never reveal what he's seen, even if it's a murder in the middle of the Forum.[40]

Here, in a few astonishing lines, two of the most solemn events in Roman public memory—the funerals and deification of Augustus and Tiberius[41]—were evoked in crude farce. By making a notorious confessed perjurer the chief witness guaranteeing the veracity of *all* these official ascents into heaven, Seneca implicitly equated them. He thus risked what had been one of the most valuable symbolic currencies of the Principate. He exposed as fraudulent the sacred aura that had legitimated previous transitions of power, including that occasioned by the death of Augustus himself, and offered in its place a frank reference to brute force ("even if it's a murder in the middle of the Forum"). The *Apocolocyntosis* goes on to render the heavenly court of the Roman gods as a crude parody of the Senate, riddled with petty self-interest. Tellingly, it also presents the gods, in particular the deified Augustus, protesting that the elevation of Claudius has cheapened the status of deification altogether.[42]

Such irreverent jesting might have served to minimize the sacred aura of Nero's ancestor Augustus. As we have seen, Nero's court was eager to manage the comparison to Nero's advantage. Such candor about the declining currency of *apotheosis* is obviously meant for the amusement of a knowing elite; it was no doubt encouraged by the emperor's own crude joke that mushrooms were "the food of the gods" (since Claudius had become a god by eating one).[43] But these ribaldries were not for public consumption. "As Nero's claim to power rested partly on his relation to Claudius, he could hardly discredit him in public without weakening his own position." Seneca's *Apocolocyntosis* may have provided Nero and his friends "a release of feeling against Claudius in private, but the policy proclaimed on accession was maintained" throughout his reign.[44] The satire's intended audience would have regarded the notion that Claudius and Augustus alike had come to reside in heaven—however ludicrous they may find it privately—as a useful fiction to offer those who are to be ruled. For the masses, the celebration of Claudius's deification should remain the official story.[45]

We may recognize in Seneca's frankness an example of what James C. Scott calls "the hidden transcript of the dominant." As we saw in chap. 1, the surviving sources occasionally allow us to "listen in" on the conversation of the privileged when they intended to speak only to one another. Seneca's bitter satire allows us a particularly candid glimpse into the hidden transcript of the powerful within Nero's inner circle.

An alternative offstage transcript: The view from Romans

Of course, neither Paul nor any of the members of the tenement assemblies in Rome would have had access to the sort of closed conversation among the elite just described. But several considerations justify comparing the opening lines of Romans with both the public transcript and the elite transcript just discussed as these bear on the deification of Claudius and the succession of Nero.

As observed earlier, Paul is not *announcing* the resurrection of Jesus, he is *invoking* it as the event in which Jesus Christ was "appointed Son of God in power." From the start of the letter, Paul opens up a rich alternative transcript—an *Israelite messianic* transcript, "proclaimed beforehand" through Israel's scriptures—according to which God's purposes for creation will be fulfilled through a king other than Caesar. The resurrection of Jesus constitutes divine confirmation that this messianic transcript is the *real* transcript revealing the future of the world.

Given the heated ideological atmosphere we have just reviewed, and (as we saw in chap. 1) the readiness of Roman audiences to respond to even the subtlest allusions to political realities, the subversive undertone in these lines would have been unmistakable. Paul's phrases presented a conspicuous contrast with Nero's claims to legitimacy, as these appeared in numerous official inscriptions, namely, his genealogy and his sonship to the now deified Claudius:

Fig. 2.2. Rival claims to divine sonship

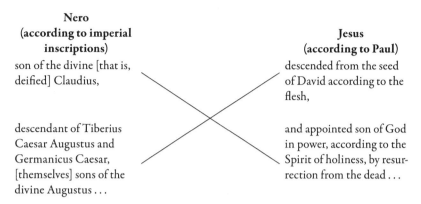

Nero (according to imperial inscriptions)		Jesus (according to Paul)
son of the divine [that is, deified] Claudius,		descended from the seed of David according to the flesh,
descendant of Tiberius Caesar Augustus and Germanicus Caesar, [themselves] sons of the divine Augustus ...		and appointed son of God in power, according to the Spirit of holiness, by resurrection from the dead ...

Here Jesus is *huios autou* (= *theou*), "son of God"; Nero, too, is *theou ... huios* by virtue of the decreed deification of his adoptive father, Claudius. Jesus is "descended from" (*genomenou ek*) David; in cognate terms, Nero is a descendant of (*eggonos = ekgonos*) Germanicus, his maternal grandfather and of Tiberius, whose adoption of Germanicus established Nero's place in the Julian lineage. As Miriam Griffin observes, the double claim made in numerous inscriptions reflects an ideological tension at the heart of Nero's succession. His claim to power "rested partly on his relation to Claudius," for whom he held barely disguised contempt; but "in reality," his selection by the army and the Senate also depended upon "his family connection with the ruling [Julian] house."[46] No such vulnerability appears in Paul's description of Jesus, however. The genuineness of his royal lineage is assumed. In place of a senatorial decree of *consecratio*, Paul declares him "appointed" (or "decreed": *horisthentos*) as son of God "in power, according to a spirit of holiness, by resurrection from the dead."[47]

Along with the reference to Israel's scriptures, these qualifiers go beyond presenting an alternative set of credentials for Jesus. They emphasize the reality of Jesus' messianic identity, as confirmed by sacred writing, royal lineage, and the power of God, and thus offer an implicit contrast with the ubiquitous, but in Paul's view unreal, claims of the imperial house. Declaring Jesus "son of God, descended from the seed of David according to flesh," implicitly distinguishes him from anyone who could not legitimately claim such a lineage (or whose claims depended upon the vagaries of revised wills or the maneuvers of ruthless mothers). To emphasize that Jesus had been "appointed" son of God, "in power ... by resurrection from the dead," invites comparison with merely procedural declarations of deification. That this happened "according to a Spirit of holiness" presents a marked contrast with those to whom holiness could be attributed only by posthumous legal fiat—especially if the honors had been requested by those suspected of murdering the candidate for deification!

Interpreting these lines from Romans against a supposed history of intramural Christian creeds and seeking to distinguish which phrases do or do not represent Paul's own christological beliefs sets artificial limits on the context of the letter.

After we attend to the broader context of political discourse, we can recognize these lines as a cohesive expression of a richer alternative transcript, maintained "offstage" among a subordinate group in Rome. As I observed in the Introduction, identifying aspects of a hidden transcript in Romans does not require a precise determination of the relative poverty or social standing of Paul or the Roman congregants—although, as I also observed, recent studies suggest that they were in fact materially poor. Rather, James C. Scott's discussion of "voice under domination" allows us to recognize the constraints that power imposed on what could and could not be said in different social locations. The comparisons just made allow us to recognize that in Romans, Paul engaged aspects of imperial ideology as surely as did Seneca's satire or the eclogues of Calpurnius Siculus—but to very different effect.

Fig. 2.3. Hidden and public transcripts regarding deification

Hidden transcript of the dominant	Public transcript	Hidden transcript in Romans
Deification is a politically useful fraud. (Seneca)	Deification is the genuine destiny of the Caesars. (Calpurnius Siculus; the Einsiedeln *Eclogue*; inscriptions)	The true son of God is the heir of David; his deification alone is genuine. (Rom 1:3-4)

Comparing the opening lines of Romans with these samples allows us to fill in the contrast at which Jacob Taubes and Dieter Georgi hinted. If Rom 1:3-4 does not provide an explicit "political declaration of war against the Caesar," as Taubes suggested, it at least offers an oblique, but unmistakable shot across the bow of imperial propaganda. But to what purpose?

———— Interpreting Paul's Gospel: Choosing Sides ————

In a letter intended to further the "obedience of nations," the implicit contrast between Christ and Caesar hardly can be incidental. Official claims that Claudius was now seated beside Augustus in heaven were expressions, not of Nero's personal self-aggrandizement, but of ideological necessity. Stability, "in the sense of the dominance of the Roman propertied classes,"[48] required representing that dominance as inevitable and appropriate. By necessity, the one person to whom the Senate had given absolute power was portrayed in the public transcript as perfectly embodying the qualities of honor, clemency, justice, and piety (*virtus, clementia, iustitia, pietas*).[49] The murder of one emperor was reframed as a divine act guaranteeing the continuity of the Julio-Claudian dynasty. His successor was portrayed as the very advent of divine justice, willing selflessly to take on the burden of ruling the empire.

In his monumental commentary on Romans, Robert Jewett declares, "The argument of Romans revolves around the question of which rule is truly righteous"—Christ's or Caesar's—"and which gospel has the power to make the world truly peaceful."⁵⁰ This important insight has long been blunted, if not completely obscured, by the tendency of Christian interpretation to read Romans 1–3 in terms of a universal human "plight" that requires divine salvation, available only through belief in the gospel, as its solution. As one commentary succinctly put it at the turn of the twentieth century, in 1:16-17, Paul "stated what the Gospel is"; in 1:18—3:20 he "goes on to show the necessity for such a Gospel. The world is lost without it."⁵¹

But when Paul juxtaposes divine justice (*dikaiosynē... theou*) and human injustice (*adikian anthrōpōn*, 1:17-18), he is not describing plight and solution. He is contrasting two contemporary dominions, two regimes, that stand fundamentally opposed to each other, the relationship between them characterized by implacable divine wrath (1:18-32). While Paul will go on in the letter to speak of divine mercy, forbearance of sins, and the setting-right of the impious, he will say nothing in this letter to reduce the opposition stated here between divine justice and human injustice; nothing, that is, to suggest that the human beings who in their injustice suppress the truth (1:18) will ultimately be set right before God. *Their redemption is not Paul's concern.*

In the Introduction, I mentioned Victor P. Furnish's indispensable demonstration that the rhetorical burden of Romans is exhortation. Note the pivotal language used in Romans 6: justice and injustice (or sin) are powers that can "exercise rule" (*basileuein, kyrieuein*), and to which people can yield obedience, or offer service as slaves, or succumb as prisoners of war, yielding their bodies up as captured "weapons" (*hopla*). Paul expressly rejects the notion (God forbid!) that those who have been baptized into Christ may continue in the service of sin or injustice, presuming on the indulgence of divine mercy (6:1-2, 15). Romans 6 is not an aside or a detour; it is a rhetorical fulcrum on which the letter moves from the description of injustice and impiety in 1:18–32 to the exhortation that begins in 12:1-2, where Paul calls his hearers away from the *schēma* of the (Roman) world to a "reasonable worship" characterized by justice.

Ernst Käsemann established the apocalyptic background of Paul's language, showing that the phrase *dikaiosynē theou* "speaks of the God who brings back the fallen world into the sphere of his legitimate claim."⁵² Robert Jewett is right, then, to understand gospel (*euangelion*) for Paul as "God's means of restoring righteous control over a disobedient creation," and right to observe that Paul presents himself "as the ambassador of the 'power of God,' extending the sovereign's cosmic foreign policy through the preaching of the gospel."⁵³

The analogy is appropriate and should be pressed further than Protestant scholarship usually has allowed. For Paul, as for Roman political and diplomatic rhetoric, the *euangelion* is the *announcement* of a sovereign's impending triumph and, necessarily, the establishment of the sovereign's claim on obedience. *But in neither case is the scope of the sovereign's dominion exhausted in the event of proclamation or collapsed into it.* In contrast, a Protestant emphasis on *euangelion* as the event of proclamation often has meant that "the justice of God," that is, the attribution of "righteousness," is conveyed by and communicated in "the Word" that is "the gospel." Günther Bornkamm exemplifies this tendency when he writes of the gospel as *"making present* the event of salvation" which is *"actualized* in the spread of the gospel." When Paul says (1:17) that the justice of God is "revealed in" the gospel, Bornkamm understands what is "revealed" to be nothing other than *"the message itself* as an eschatological salvation-event. It is . . . the word in which God's will is accomplished in the present."[54]

But Paul means more than this. The revelation of the justice of God is an occasion of power, a power that empowers his defiant refusal to be "put to shame." Because shame is a social reality, we should regard the revelation of God's justice that empowers Paul's "shamelessness," too, as a social, indeed (to point the issue) a public reality. But this means that the revelation of God's wrath that manifests God's justice also must be a public revelation—not (as much Protestant theology would have it) a private matter of the convicted heart. Note the chain of subordinating conjunctions (*gar*):

> *for* I am not ashamed to announce God's imminent triumph;
> *for* this proclamation is the power of God for salvation to all who are faithful,
>   to the Jew first and also to the Greek;
> *for* in it the justice of God is revealed, through faithfulness, to faithfulness; as
>   it is written, "The one who is just will live by faithfulness,"
> *for* the wrath of God is revealed from heaven against all impiety and injustice
>   of those who by their injustice suppress the truth. . . . (Rom 1:16-18)

The power of the sovereign whose triumph Paul announces is *manifest,* he declares, not merely asserted in a homiletical appeal to the willing heart.

We must turn to Latin American theologians to find the clear perception that the justice of God that Paul invokes is none other than the justice to which the prophets of Israel continually called their nation.[55] In the Psalms, for example, the king's exercise of God's justice is manifest in securing the welfare of the poor and helpless. In Paul's letter to the Romans, it is manifest in the revelation of God's wrath against human injustice, as the syntactic construction of these verses makes clear. I have italicized the repeated use of a subordinating conjunction *gar*, which connects Paul's statement of purpose regarding the Romans (1:13-15) to his declaration of confidence in God's saving justice (1:16-17), which in turn is connected to the manifestation of God's wrath (1:18).

We should be astonished how regularly these connections are broken in commentaries, in Bible translations, and even in critical editions of the Greek text of the letter, where 1:16-17 are torn free of their context and isolated as a self-contained unit. This grammatically indefensible procedure is useful, of course, to a particular theological reading of the letter, for it makes these phrases resemble the statement of a theme, namely, justification by faith, which Protestant dogmatics regards as the distinctive core of Paul's gospel. But these are interpretive missteps. Admittedly, in Paul's day, philosophers and students of rhetoric *did* compose "theme essays," but these always bore the marks of their genre, for example, a title introducing the subject (consider Seneca's treatise *De clementia,* "Concerning Clemency") and a self-conscious description of one's method in preparing the essay.[56] Because no such signs exist to justify bracketing a theme in Romans, we are left to read the letter according to the clear epistolary signs it bears.

Neither is the crucial distinction between so-called "justification by faith" and "justification by works" in view here, though its central importance for Lutheran theology would seem to require it. As Douglas Harink argues convincingly, the traditional emphasis on justification not only misunderstands it as an inner and individual matter, but also gives the theme "a more important place in Paul than it actually has."[57] Rather, Paul's explicit concern at the beginning of Romans is to contrast the justice of God with the injustice of those human beings who "through their injustice suppress the truth," against whom God's wrath now "has been revealed."

The justice of God

I am translating *hē dikaiosynē tou theou* as "the justice of God," rather than "righteousness," for several reasons. First, the word *righteousness* retains very little of the power and range of connotation that it had in its native sixteenth century. Second, the Greek word *dikaiosynē* routinely meant justice when people in Paul's world used it, whether they were hearing imperial claims that Caesar personified justice on earth, or (in a very different context) reading Psalm 72, calling for God to give justice to "the king."

Third, and perhaps most importantly, I am convinced that the point Paul seeks to make here has been obscured by the modern theological preoccupation with "justification by faith" (or "righteousing," or "right-wising"). To be sure, recent scholarship has made important progress in understanding the phrase *hē dikaiosynē tou theou*. Even Ernst Käsemann, who most strongly resisted dislocating the theme of justification from its central role in the Lutheran reading of the letter, insisted that more is at stake here than a reference to God's chosen means of transacting salvation; that is, the "justice of God" is not a cipher for "justification by faith." The apostle means to evoke a rich biblical context in which the God of Israel was described as acting powerfully, out of God's own integrity and faithfulness to God's own ancient promises to save; which also means, acting to claim the obedience of human beings as properly God's own.[58]

Alas, that important theological insight has not gone hand-in-hand with a fundamental rethinking of the letter to the Romans. Instead, the letter continues to be widely regarded as a sort of theological position paper on justification by faith. More than a century and a half ago, F. C. Baur protested that dogmatic interests predetermined much of the interpretation of the letter in his day, precluding a genuinely historical understanding. Contemporary scholars have echoed that complaint.[59] Stanley K. Stowers has argued strenuously for freeing the historical interpretation of Romans from its theological constraints.[60] Now Douglas Harink has pressed the insights of recent scholarship even further for the cause of theological interpretation by posing the succinct proposition: "Paul does not take a message of 'faith, not works' to the nations."[61] Despite the force of arguments such as these, however, any attempt at rereading the letter in the context of the cultural currents of first-century Rome still faces an uphill struggle.

The crucial question raised in Romans 1 is, How is God's justice revealed through the revelation of God's wrath? If, as Protestant dogmatics seems to require, Paul were speaking of primarily juridical realities—that is, of God's verdict of "not guilty" pronounced, in Christ, on the unworthy, and a guilty verdict (God's "wrath") pronounced against sin (and, by implication, against those who remain outside of Christ)—then the logical connection made by Paul's conjunctions ("for . . . for . . .") would remain nonsensical.[62] Of course, just that sort of dogmatic interpretation has remained vitally important for a theological tradition eager to emphasize its distance from, and superiority over, Judaism (those "outside of Christ"), and later, Roman Catholicism (where Luther found a contemporary equivalent of the "works-righteousness" Paul opposed). But this interpretation has difficulty making sense of what Paul actually says.

How, exactly, are the justice and wrath of God both "manifest" (*ephanerōthē*, 1:16, 18)? One suggestion has been that Paul is simply referring to two aspects of one reality, the content of his own proclamation. That is, his preaching of Christ simultaneously announces *both* God's wrath against sin *and* the justification God offers. In this view, Paul does not really mean what his language implies, that there is some public manifestation of divine justice and of wrath; he means only to assert them dogmatically.[63] Another suggestion, made famously by C. H. Dodd but almost universally rejected, holds that by the revelation of God's wrath Paul means to refer to "an inevitable process of cause and effect in a moral universe"—though, of course, on this view God's wrath is "revealed" only to those who discern that process at work.[64]

The plain sense of Paul's language, however, is that he is not ashamed to proclaim God's triumph because in it God's justice is being demonstrated—made publicly manifest—now. This is not a matter of Paul's personal opinion; it is evident to all, in the demonstration of God's wrath against the wicked and unjust. Just here we stumble over the interpretation of Paul's letter because we do not share Paul's perception of the manifest wrath of God against the unjust. But that is because we have not yet grasped what he writes next.

A critique of imperial injustice

Paul continues (and note that at this point, at Rom 1:18, we are still in the middle of a single complex sentence!) with a description of the "impiety and injustice" against which God's wrath is revealed (1:18-32). Two important and interconnected questions are urgent: First, whom is Paul describing? Second, what purpose is this description meant to serve in the larger sweep of Paul's rhetoric?

Unfortunately, here again, dogmatic assumptions about Paul's purpose in the letter have predetermined answers to both questions. On the assumption that in Romans, the apostle is setting out a "doctrine of salvation," these verses are made to bear the burden of summarizing the universal "plight" of all human beings who stand (by virtue of their humanity) under the power of sin. Nothing less than an "indictment of humankind" in the sin of Adam is supposedly in view.[65] Paul does not mention Adam here, however. The sequence he does describe, from ingratitude (1:21) to idolatry (1:22-23) to bodily degradation (1:24-27) to rampant, inexcusable iniquity (1:28-32), defies alignment with either Adam's or Israel's story.[66] Further, Paul does not seem to be setting up a depiction of a (human) plight awaiting a (divine) solution. Rather, the spiral of degradation he describes is already the direct result of divine action. *God handed them over,* abandoning these rebels to utter iniquity. *That* is the "revelation of God's wrath" that demonstrates God's justice.

As a depiction of human beings in general (*anthrōpōn,* 1:18), this would seem to be an unacceptably harsh exaggeration.[67] Consequently, a broad majority of interpreters prefer to break Rom 1:18—3:20 into a two-part indictment, finding here a description, not of humanity in general, but of the "*Gentile*" world as seen from the perspective of Hellenistic Judaism. On this view, Paul turns to a separate indictment of "the Jew" either at 2:1 or at 2:17. Proponents of this view note that Hellenistic Jews often perceived idolatry and sexual immorality as characteristic signs of the "Gentile" world.[68] A number of early Jewish texts described the "decline" of the Gentile world at some mythic point in the past, either because of human folly and ignorance (the Wisdom of Solomon; Jubilees) or because of the deluding influence of fallen heavenly beings (the "sons of God" in *1 Enoch).*[69]

We must return in the next chapter to examine the widespread view that this broad depiction of moral corruption is but a rhetorical feint, bait in a trap Paul means to set for an implied Jewish hearer. A few observations must suffice now regarding the character, tone, and thrust of Paul's argument here.

First, as Stanley K. Stowers has rightly observed, narratives of moral decline were common throughout the Greek and Roman world, beyond Hellenistic Judaism, from the Greek Hesiod to the Roman Virgil.[70] Especially in the Principate, we find extended play on the mythic theme that a golden age had arrived with the accession of one or another Caesar; references to previous declines in the human race are now being reversed, thanks to the intervention of the gods, in the radiant destiny of the Roman people. Virgil rhapsodized that with Octavian's triumph, "wars cease and the rough ages soften. . . . The gates of war, grim with iron and close-fitting bars, shall be closed" (*Aen.* 1.291–96). Paul's Roman contemporaries extolled the "second birth" of a golden age with the accession of Nero.[71]

What none of these supposed parallels provide, however, is the notion that is the very engine of Paul's argument here: that outrageous and destructive sexual indulgence and, ultimately, the utter depravity described in 1:28-32 are evident to all as God's punishment on idolaters. This is not a decline narrative like the other examples adduced by scholars, nor is Paul describing a previous immoral age that now gives way to a golden age of justice and peace. This is not an etiology narrative either, offering a traditional Jewish explanation of "how the 'Gentile' world came to its present immoral state," in need of God's intervention. This is Paul's announcement that God has already intervened, demonstrating divine justice precisely by executing divine wrath against those who practice spectacular wickedness.

For the same reason, the heated attention these verses currently receive in tortured church debates over the place of homosexuals, the ordination of gays and lesbians, and the appropriateness of blessing same-sex relationships appears grossly misplaced. Paul is not offering a theological perspective on homosexuality, on homosexual desire, or on gay and lesbian persons. A number of official documents from different denominations state, solemnly but often with genuine sympathy, that from the biblical viewpoint, homosexual desire illustrates the effects of sinful humanity's fallen state, in a way that heterosexual desire does not.[72] But this is not Paul's point. It is now well established that the classical world did not conceive of what we today call homosexual orientation, a natural erotic preference for others of the same gender, as distinct from heterosexual orientation. Paul's contemporaries perceived a single reality, sexual desire, which could attach to people of either gender. How much less likely is it that Paul would feel constrained to offer an explanation of homosexual desire!

Paul is not offering an explanation. Nor can we tell, from these lines, where Paul thinks homosexual acts, in general, come from, because homosexual acts, *in general*, simply are not in view.[73] Instead, he refers to shameful acts, including homosexual acts among others, that are the result of a specific, terrible drama in which God has abandoned specific people—active idolaters—to degrading sexual desires. As a result of this divine action, these people have been made to "burn" with desire for others of the same sex—desires "beyond what is natural"—and have acted out these desires in shameful and destructive ways, on their way to ever greater wickedness.[74] Paul is not talking about homosexuals in general any more than he is talking about "gentiles" in general or human beings in general. His field of vision is narrowly focused on people who refused to honor God, embraced idolatry instead, and were abandoned by God to degrading sexual acts and profound wickedness.[75]

More to the point: these are people whose fate is so apparent to all that Paul can appeal to it as evidence that God's "justice" is now being revealed (1:17-18). Who are these people?

My answer is that Paul intends his hearers to recognize definite allusions to none other than *the Caesars themselves*. No others could serve Paul's argument so effectively by offering, in their own persons, a fitting lesson on the inevitability with which divine punishment follows horrendous crimes.[76]

It is surely relevant that a similar perception was common among Paul's near-contemporaries. Consider, for example, how Suetonius structured his review of the life of Gaius (Caligula). After describing omens accompanying Gaius's birth and glimpses, already in the child, of "the natural brutality and viciousness" that would characterize the man (*Gaius* 11), Suetonius reports allegations, which he is ready to believe, that Gaius had his predecessor (and adoptive grandfather) Tiberius murdered (12). The new emperor's reign began hopefully, "like a dream come true" (13); but after narrating some actions and policies of which he approves, Suetonius turns to address Gaius "the Monster" (22). First come the titles the emperor claimed for himself: "pious," and "best and greatest of Caesars"; then an anecdote in which, at dinner with visiting potentates, he toys with the title "king." Only when his courtiers talk him out of such an ill-judged move (however frank a recognition of his actual power it might have been) does Gaius settle on the title "god." He then began to encourage worship of himself as a god, altering statuary of the Greek and Roman pantheons to bear his own likeness and establishing a shrine to himself (22). His arrogance led him to treat his own grandparents with contempt; he forced his father-in-law to commit suicide (23).

Suetonius then reports Gaius's sexual outrages. "It was his habit to commit incest with each of his sisters" and to humiliate his wife publicly with the fact (24). As to his marriage, Suetonius summarizes: "it would be hard to say whether the way he got married, the way he dissolved his marriages, or the way he behaved as a husband was the most disgraceful." He reports a series of women whom Gaius forcibly humiliated, under the coarse disguise of marriage (25). As to other relatives, Suetonius declares, "it would be trivial and pointless" to record the cruelty with which Gaius led them to their deaths, at least compared with his weightier crimes; Suetonius treats similar maltreatment of senators and discrete executions of political enemies just as dismissively (26). Gaius's brutality toward the lower orders was notable only for its capriciousness and sadism (26–27).

Suetonius connects the emperor's "savage crimes"—the cataloguing of which continues for some while—with the astounding arrogance from which it sprang. Gaius claimed to possess the virtue of "inflexibility," by which, Suetonius quips, "he must have meant 'brazen impudence'" (29). "Everything that he said and did was marked with equal cruelty" (32), a cruelty indulged and accelerated, if not caused, by the unchallenged power he was allowed to wield. "In his insolent pride and destructiveness he made malicious attacks on men of every epoch," attempting to murder memory itself (34).

At last Suetonius returns to the "far-fetched extravagances" in which Gaius indulged, beginning with the sexual. "He had not the slightest regard for chastity, either his own or others," as yet another list of predations indicates. Suetonius mentions passive and active homosexual encounters with celebrities, aristocrats, and "various foreign hostages," as well as lechery expressed "toward almost every woman of rank in Rome," including occasional rapes of women pulled from the dinner table and humiliated (36). Gaius was as abusive of Rome's wealth (37–40). These vices converged when the emperor opened a public brothel as a fundraiser, staffed (by coercion) with women and youths from aristocratic families (41).

After quickly reviewing Gaius's inconsequential conduct of military affairs (43–49), Suetonius refers to some apparent neurological disorder that might have explained his behavior (50). Suetonius believes this disorder accounted for both the emperor's overconfidence and fearfulness. "Here was a man who despised the gods, yet shut his eyes and buried his head beneath the bedclothes at the most distant sound of thunder" (51). At length Suetonius reports several conspiracies to assassinate Gaius (56), and narrates the one that succeeded. Officers who had suffered repeated humiliations ambushed the emperor at the theater and stabbed him to death, "including sword-thrusts through the genitals"—brutally obvious acts of vengeance (56–58).

It would be difficult to imagine a career that better illustrated the precise sequence that Paul describes:

arrogant refusal to honor the divine creator;
the turn to idolatry and worship of the creature;
a descent into defiling sexual lust;
and finally an expansive catalogue of cruelty and outrage.

The match between Paul and Suetonius is admittedly inexact. Suetonius speaks not only of the arrogance and insolence of Gaius, but of a "brain sickness" that drove some of his behavior. Paul offers no such organic explanation for the arrogant whom God punishes. And Suetonius is more interested in variant accounts of the plot to assassinate Gaius and the details of its execution. On the other hand, Suetonius also details portents on the days leading up to the deed, implying that the gods sanctioned Gaius's death.

Paul's more theological perspective resembles that of another contemporary Judean. Philo of Alexandria speaks at one point of "the supremely evil vices of infidelity [*apistia*] and ingratitude [*acharistia*] to the Benefactor of the whole world, who through His power bestows blessings poured in unstinted abundance" on all people. This is not just a text combining similar concepts to Paul's: this is Philo's characterization of Gaius, specifically of his decision to promote worship of himself as a god. Philo, like Suetonius, speaks of Gaius's extravagance and "incontinence" (*akrasia*), his insatiable "appetites still unsatisfied when the cavities were stuffed full," and his "lasciviousness venting itself on boys and women." He ridicules the pretensions to divinity on the part of one so demonstrably ungod-like—full of "insatiable and quenchless" lusts, "utterly ignoble, brimful of cowardice," and stripping cities of all good and turning them into hellholes of misery. Surrounding himself with murderous sycophants, the emperor revealed himself "a master avid for slaughter and thirsting for human blood." That bloodthirstiness, Philo declares, would eventually have decimated every city in the empire "had not his death *at the hands of justice*" prevented him.[77]

Philo offers a similar verdict on the fate of Flaccus, the governor of Alexandria whom Gaius recalled to Rome in the wake of the pogrom there (see chapter 3). It was "the justice [*dikē*] which watches over human affairs" that destroyed Flaccus. Further, as his erstwhile victims, the Judeans of Alexandria, declare—as they give thanks to God upon hearing in their ghetto of Flaccus's arrest—God brought low "the common enemy of the nation," "not when he was afar off, . . . but just here close at hand, almost before the eyes of the wronged, to give them a clearer picture of the swift and unhoped-for visitation." It was the *public, visible punishment* of the Roman enemy that offered the manifestation of God's justice.[78]

Both Philo and Paul provide theological perspectives on the divine punishment of the wicked. Gross ingratitude to God leads to insatiable lust, which leads to violence and outrage worthy of death. Philo calls the final punishment at God's hands justice; Paul speaks of the wrath of God, in which divine justice, *dikaiosynē*, is revealed (Rom 1:17-18). Philo refers explicitly to Gaius; Paul speaks more generally of "human beings who through their injustice suppress the truth."

Fig. 2.4. The end of notorious evildoers in Suetonius, Philo, and Paul

Suetonius (*Gaius*)	Philo (*Embassy to Gaius*; *Flaccus*)	Paul (**Romans 1**)
describes the arrogance and brutality of Gaius,	describes the arrogance and brutality of Gaius (and of Flaccus),	describes the injustice, impiety, arrogance, and brutality of "human beings who suppress the truth . . ."
possibly resulting from "a brain sickness";	the result of his refusal to honor God;	as the result of their refusal to honor God;
attributes his death to a conspiracy (but names portents implying the consent of the gods)	attributes his death to the manifestation of God's justice (emphasized in the case of Flaccus)	attributes their punishment to the manifestation of God's wrath (justice)

I wish my point to be clear. We cannot say with certainty that Paul intended his audience to think specifically of Gaius. Certainly, the subsequent emperors also provided, by their conduct, ample justification for the sort of language Paul uses. To take but one example much closer to the writing of Romans: Claudius's "cruelty and bloodthirstiness" were notorious, according to Suetonius, who reports that among the scores of the emperor's victims from the equestrian order was his own father-in-law (*Claudius* 29; 34). For his part, Nero—who had begun to reign as emperor only a year or two before Paul wrote this letter—had in his youth given evidence of "insolent, lustful, extravagant, greedy, cruel" behavior, which Suetonius later would have excused had it not been amplified after Nero came to enjoy extraordinary power, as emperor, to act with impunity. The caprice of Nero's brutality and his practice of "every kind of obscenity," including the rape of a woman consecrated as a Vestal virgin and incest with his own mother, appalled the historian, who nevertheless steeled himself to recount a few other particularly horrible practices (*Nero* 26–29). As previously mentioned, Nero's financial profligacy led him to desecrate temples, relieving them of any sacred objects made of gold or silver, which he promptly had melted down for his own profit (32). Suetonius recounts the most notorious murders, especially of Nero's own mother and aunt; "there was no family relationship which Nero did not criminally abuse" (35). For his part, Tacitus reports that in the year after the murder of Claudius and the execution of Britannicus, Nero organized violent gangs for nightly rampages through the city streets, to the point that Rome "by night came to resemble a conquered city" (*Ann.* 13.20).

The point, then, is not to identify a specific emperor as the narrowly delimited reference of Paul's language in Rom 1:18-32. I mean only to suggest that his hearers, living in the very city where the savagery of one emperor after another was notorious, would easily have heard his phrases as allusions to the imperial house. (Recall that U.S. citizens quite easily decoded the campaign promise of one candidate in the 2000 presidential elections to "restore the dignity of the White House," on its surface ambiguous enough, as a clear reference to specific misdeeds of his predecessor.) The specific sequence Paul describes—refusal to honor God; descent into idolatry; sexual debauchery and degradation; unrestrained ruthlessness—seems an almost clinical recital of the conduct of these men. Instead of imputing to Paul a heated, irrational exaggeration as he describes general human sinfulness or an equally stereotyped Judean prejudice regarding the rampant idolatry and immorality of the non-Judean world, we can read every phrase in this passage as an accurate catalog of misdeeds of one or another recent member of the Julio-Claudian dynasty.

More important is the rhetorical force of Paul's argument here. The revelation of divine justice that grounds Paul's confidence toward his Roman hearers (1:15-17) is evident in the revelation of divine wrath against wickedness, which he describes in some detail. His claim has rhetorical force only insofar as the phenomenon he describes, God "handing over" the evildoers to depravity, is immediately recognizable. To be sure, there are biblical precedents to this concept: for example, God's "hardening" of Pharaoh's heart (Exod 9:16; recalled in Rom 9:17-18) or God's reducing the Babylonian king Nebuchadnezzar to living like an ox in the field (Dan 4:28-33). Paul's language of the wrath of God "being revealed" (*apokalyptetai*) simply invites his hearers to recognize a more contemporary parallel, in the spectacular deaths of one emperor by assassination and another by presumed murder. Here it is important to recall the theme that Philo set over his extended account of Gaius's rise and fall: "divine providence for human affairs."[79]

Most important, Paul's rhetoric impels his hearers to choose between the justice he represents and the rampant injustice that already stands under the wrath of God. This rhetoric implies an imminent "day of reckoning," to which Paul refers in 13:12 as simply "the day." Paul here invokes a shared, apocalyptically tinged transcript even as he asks his hearers to distance themselves from the sordid iniquity of the imperial house. This is an apparent minority transcript. It is an anomaly compared to the sources that come down to us from participants in Rome's imperial ideology or the accommodationist writings of some of Paul's Jewish contemporaries.[80]

Justice and the Crisis of Impunity

The rhetorical effect of the indictment just discussed is achieved in Rom 2:1:

> Therefore you are without excuse, O mortal, every one who judges: for in that by which you judge another, you condemn yourself, for you, who judge, do the same things.

We must resist a prevalent misreadings of this passage, according to which Paul has set an elaborate trap for his Judean listener, which he now springs. The Judean has judged the immorality and viciousness that Paul has just (on this reading) attributed to the pagan world; now Paul wheels on that Judean listener to condemn the very moralism that he himself has just expressed.[81]

Stanley K. Stowers has done us a great service in his efforts to dismantle this flawed interpretation. Stowers shows that Paul takes part here in a much longer cultural discussion regarding moral accountability. The larger unit 1:18—2:16 "may be seen as a protreptic or missionary sermon to an imaginary gentile": it is *not* a trap for the Judean, for as Stowers rightly points out, Paul does not address a Judean rhetorically until 2:17 (see chapter 3, below).[82]

In 2:16,

> Paul . . . speaks to an imaginary gentile . . . warning him of his precarious situation in the present historical moment (2:1-5) and promising him that God will judge both Jews and Greeks as an impartial judge by the standards of the law and Paul's gospel (2:6-16). God has mercifully delayed punishing the gentiles in order to provide time for repentance (2:4-5).[83]

The technique of speech-in-character (*prosōpopoieia*) was routinely used in the diatribe as a part of moral exhortation. A teacher would suddenly turn on an

imaginary interlocutor in an accusation, in the second person, intended to have a
hortatory effect on the audience.

> The real objects of the admonition or rebuke, however, are people in the
> audience whose behavior corresponds to the vices or behavior typified in the
> characterization of the interlocutor. Paul's characterization in 2:1-5 is clearly
> recognizable as the "pretentious person" (*ho alazōn*); the one who hypocriti-
> cally pretends to moral virtue and arrogantly criticizes others even though he
> does the same kinds of things.[84]

It is crucially important to recognize that Paul is here indicting the attitude of
hypocrisy, not of moral judgment as such (which Protestant scholarship has been
too quick to attribute to "the self-righteous Jew"). The element required to read
2:1-16 as a trap for the Judean is missing, namely, any indication in the text that
the litany of injustice and impiety in 1:18-32 came from a Judean other than Paul
himself. Reading the self-righteous Jew as Paul's target requires just what is missing here: some indication of a rhetorical distance between the speaker in 1:18-32
and 2:1-16. In the absence of such a textual dislocation, reading 2:1-16 as a trap for
the Jew is logically incoherent and exegetically baseless. Indeed, it would have been
rank hypocrisy on Paul's part first to have presented the litany in 1:18–32 and then
to have rounded on his audience to condemn them for sharing the same moral
revulsion to which he himself had just given expression. Such a move—especially
so early in the letter—would have wiped away any moral credibility on his part and
rendered him a thoroughly untrustworthy speaker.[85]

But this is *not* a trap for those who hold a high standard of morality; it is a warning against hypocrisy, against holding oneself aloof from the crimes just named at
the same time one is complicit in similar attitudes or actions. Its hortatory effect is
intended for the non-Judean audience of the letter, warning them against wrongful,
hypocritical judgment. Wayne A. Meeks observed decades ago that the language in
this diatribe-like address is picked up again later, in Romans 14, where, however, it
is aimed in explicit warnings at "the strong" not to hold their "weaker" neighbors
in contempt.[86] But the rhetorical function of such a speech-in-character, following
on a livid depiction of the crimes of the imperial house, is much broader.

This speech begins as Paul introduces himself as apostle of a *true* "son of God" in
1:3-4, and continues as he invokes the revelation of God's wrath against the notoriously impious and unjust, then warns his audience, through a speech-in-character
apostrophe, against hypocrisy in 2:1-16. The argumentative effect of this rhetoric
is to open up a distinction between reality and appearance. This is an example of
argument by dissociation, a strategy that characterizes much of the letter's rhetoric.
As rhetoricians C. Perelman and L. Olbrechts-Tyteca explain, such argumentation
works by distinguishing appearance from reality—or more precisely, by distinguishing those appearances that accurately reflect reality from those that do not.
Such arguments seek to show that an accepted link between two elements does not,

in fact, exist; it thus remodels conceptions of reality so as to prevent false connections or conclusions from being drawn.[87]

As we have seen, Paul's implicit argument dissociates the claims of the imperial house—to embody wisdom, justice, and the approval of the gods—from actuality.

It is Jesus the Messiah who *truly* enjoys God's favor, having been descended from an authentic royal line, prophesied in Israel's scriptures, and confirmed by God's raising him from the dead.

Paul's charge to announce God's dawning sovereignty in the person of this Messiah (that is, to "evangelize") embodies God's power and thus does not put Paul to shame. This claim implies a dissociation of imperial claims to embody honor, glory, and power from what is in fact true.

That dissociation is quickly followed by another that Paul develops at length in 1:18-32: those who claim to be wise are in fact foolish; their claims to recognize divinity are disastrously mistaken. And, by implication, the claim that one ruler follows another in an unbroken sacred succession is exploded, for the demise of one or another member of the imperial house is nothing less than the public manifestation of the power of God—the God Paul serves—to execute wrath on the defiant.

The lesson for Paul's audience is an implicit warning, again cast in terms of an argumentative dissociation: *Appearances can be deceiving.* What seems to be a just order is nothing of the kind. The presumption that those who continue to prosper in such an order do so by the favor of heaven is a fatal mistake. God is not mocked. Divine mercy has but one goal: not to indulge impudence, but to compel the repentance of the wicked. Any who presume they stand on firm ground within this order as they look down upon the fallen are in grave danger.

As we shall see, that lesson has very specific ramifications for Paul's audience in Rome.

The emperor Augustus is depicted showing mercy to captured barbarians, who clutch their children. Silver cup from a villa in Boscoreale. First century C.E. Photo © Erich Lessing/Art Resource; reconstruction, based on an earlier photograph taken before the cup was damaged, by Michah Thompson of Augsburg Fortress.

CHAPTER THREE

CLEMENTIA

Mercy and the Prerogatives of Power

Within the dictates of imperial ideology, the sovereign's occasional exercise of mercy, like the executive pardon, is not a recognition that the rights of the pardoned have been violated, or that any external rule of justice or of law has been outraged. Rather, it redounds to the personal glory of the sovereign, demonstrating his power and beneficence.

This imperial logic drove the slanderous representation of Judeans among their neighbors in first-century Rome. "We are blasphemed," Paul protested (3:8); but as we shall see, this was a slander with precise historical contours.

Upon Nero's accession, one of the ways he exercised his own personal prerogative as emperor was to extend clemency to those who had suffered punishment or exile at the hands of his stepfather. These very likely included Judeans whom Claudius had expelled from Rome, under circumstances that (as we shall see) tell us more about Roman policy than about the character or conduct of the city's Judean population. Almost all commentators on Romans today cite this expulsion as part of the background for Paul's letter. Normally this has meant explaining why the non-Judeans in the Roman churches would have had reason to look down on their Judean neighbors. When some interpreters go further, however, to attribute failure or malfeasance to these neighbors, they imply that the Judeans had deserved Claudius's severe response. Such characterizations of the Judean population perpetuate ancient perceptions on the part of hostile Romans in Paul's own day, implying that Judeans were undeserving of the mercy Nero had deigned to show them.

It is just this perception that Paul already opposes in this letter. Relying on familiar techniques appropriate to the diatribe, he elicits from a fictitious Judean character the strident denial of any presumption on divine mercy. But if Judeans, who have been given tremendous privileges by God, cannot presume on these privileges to exempt them from accountability before God, how much less can others! To presume that divine punishment long withheld is evidence of God's indulgence would be a disastrous mistake, and one that Paul seeks to prevent the Roman assemblies from making.

The Prerogatives of Power

As discussed in chapter two, imperial ideology normally requires that an empire's crimes are suppressed in the public transcript or else glossed as regrettable necessities, inflicted when mischievous subordinates require stern discipline. On the other hand, any temporary reprieve from the suffering inflicted is readily represented in the public transcript as evidence of the generosity and compassion of the ruler. Mercy is the prerogative of the powerful, appropriate only when the object of mercy is truly powerless and submissive, as Slavoj Žižek explains (reflecting on Western portrayals of worthy and unworthy victims in the former Yugoslavia).[1] The logic is both hypocritical and one-sided. The imperial elite claim a monopoly on humanism, expecting the rest of the world to sympathize above all with their own suffering, as Gilbert Achcar observes (reflecting on the relative moral weight accorded in the U.S. to hundreds of thousands of Iraqis killed under U.S. sanctions in the ten years before Sept. 11, 2001). Sympathy is due "only for people like themselves." Because empires subsist from the domination of other peoples, imperial mercy can be expressed only along a clear "dividing line between those who must live and those who must die."[2]

Other recent examples illustrate the force of this dual presumption, of national innocence and of benevolence. In 1999, when tremendous international pressure compelled President Bill Clinton to reverse a 25-year policy of U.S. support for the spectacularly violent Indonesian occupation of East Timor, the moment was celebrated in the American press as the dawn of a "noble phase" in U.S. diplomacy in which "principles and values" would determine the new "norms of humanitarian intervention." But Clinton had not offered "humanitarian intervention": he had simply ceased (however temporarily) to provide the opposite, massive military support for a brutal and illegal occupation.[3] Again, when U.S. Secretary of State Colin Powell traveled to Halabja, Iraq, in March 2003 to commemorate thousands of Kurds murdered by Saddam Hussein during two days of bombing and a poison gas attack more than fifteen years earlier, the U.S. press solemnly reported his declaration to the survivors that "the world should have acted sooner," and his reassurances that "what happened here in 1988 is never going to happen again." But Powell, and a compliant press, failed to observe that "the world"—or at least the Reagan Administration, which Powell had served as National Security Advisor in 1988—had in fact acted quickly and decisively at the time, reassuring Hussein of continued support. (Hussein did not become a monster, in official U.S. eyes at least, until he imperiled the oil fields of Kuwait in August 1990.)[4]

We see, then, that within the logic of empire, "mercy" is not something due to others under any obligation that might present a restraint on the exertion of power. In a secret February 7, 2002, memorandum, U.S. President George W. Bush determined that none of the provisions of the Geneva Conventions applied to how U.S. military and intelligence forces at Guantánamo Bay would treat persons captured in Afghanistan "or elsewhere throughout the world." He declared that he had "the authority under the Constitution to suspend Geneva as between the United States and Afghanistan," but went on to "decline to exercise that authority at this time." The implication was clear: if forces under the President's command declined to use torture against someone in their custody, it would *not* be because they were deterred by the standards of international law or by any recognition of the fundamental human rights of their captive. Given the logic of imperial power, only the personal discretion of the President might legitimately prevail on the detainee's behalf.[5]

The point is to observe the workings of the dominant ideological system in an imperial situation. The massive suffering of thousands upon thousands of human beings does not rise to the level of an impediment to policy. The dignity of the victims as human beings is not acknowledged, *except* when such acknowledgment redounds to the glorious benevolence of the rulers. The moral gravity expressed at Halabja in 2003 is the prerogative of an unassailable sovereign power; but that power does not thereby admit to any constraint to which it might be held to account in the future.

To similar effect, in Paul's day, Roman imperial ideology construed mercy as the sole prerogative of those who enjoyed absolute power. Understanding how that theme was at play in the immediate historical context of Romans is vital to understanding the letter.

The mercy of the Augusti

Mercy was a vital theme in the ideology of Roman imperialism. If for Cicero it was self-evident that the Romans were destined to "multiply our wealth, to extend our boundaries . . . to rule over as many subjects as possible," it was equally incumbent upon them to "spare all men, to consider the interests of the whole human race, to give everyone his due, and not to touch sacred or public property, or that which belongs to others." Similarly Virgil described the peculiar "arts" of the Roman people as *parcere subiectis et debellare superbos*, "to spare the vanquished and to crush the proud."[6] There was no contradiction, since mercy was by definition the right of the conqueror over those who submitted, just as the insolent who dared to resist earned their chosen fate. Clemency was the practice of "moderation toward a defeated enemy, provided the latter was not recalcitrant or heinous . . . but submissive to the *pax Romana*."[7] Given the options of destruction and subjection, the vanquished would naturally be grateful to be spared (an ancient expectation with contemporary parallels).[8]

Clementia was "the operative principle after ongoing conquests and submission of other peoples," Karl Galinsky observes. It was particularly associated with Octavian, who promised the Senate that he would conduct himself "in a mild and humane way," after the manner of his gentle father, Julius Caesar. (Galinsky goes on to note, that was "not the way things turned out to be," at least until Octavian had destroyed his chief rival.)[9] *Clementia* was one of the virtues celebrated on the golden shield which the Senate subsequently donated to Augustus and one of the chief virtues of which the emperor boasted in the *Res gestae*:

> I undertook many civil and foreign wars by land and sea throughout the world, and as victor I spared the lives of all citizens who asked for mercy. When foreign peoples could safely be pardoned I preferred to preserve rather than to exterminate them. (3.1–2)

Note the criterion of imperial mercy. Paradoxically, the architects of empire may feel less safe the more control they exert over the lives of others. As P. A. Brunt observes, Rome's "reactions to the possibility of a threat resembled those of a nervous tiger, disturbed when feeding."[10] For Cicero and Caesar alike, even a potential rival to Roman power required elimination. The Romans already knew well the doctrine of pre-emptive war. In the Roman case, anxiety was bred of avarice. Rome's wars were never motivated by self-interest, so far as the public transcript went, but by concern to help neighbors who requested Roman intervention,[11] or by the need for self-defense.[12] The last could simply mean that another people had resisted conquest. The "mortal sin of self-defense" (Noam Chomsky's phrase for Nicaragua in the 1980s)[13] is a contagion that threatens to spread, and must be eliminated. The reasoning was (and is) one-sided: "Rights which pertained to Rome might not be conceded to others."[14]

The sovereign's prerogative to exercise mercy (*clementia*) is well illustrated on one of two silver cups from a Roman estate in Boscoreale, buried when Mt. Vesuvius erupted in 79 C.E. (see p. 86). Copied, during Augustus's lifetime, from monumental reliefs in Rome, the cup on one side depicts Mars, the god of war, leading a train of conquered nations to the seated emperor, who receives a globe from Venus and winged Victory. On the opposite side, Augustus is depicted seated, surrounded by his victorious officers, extending a hand in mercy to "spare the conquered"— bearded old men in barbarian dress who prostrate themselves before him, clutching small children in their arms.[15] The central figure in the image is Augustus. His act of mercy confirms his virtue; it owes nothing to the rights of his subjects but is a matter of his own serene prerogative.

After Augustus, *clementia* became a standard claim on the part of his successors. When a Parthian delegation came to beg Claudius to give them as king a hostage who had been trained in the Roman art of government, the emperor agreed, then proceeded to give the hostage king one last lecture. He should exercise mercy and justice among his new subjects, "virtues all the more welcome" because (Claudius presumed) the Parthians would have had no experience of either before tasting Roman magnaminity.[16]

Upon Claudius's death (likely at the hands of Nero's mother), Nero promised the Senate he would reign with a mercy surpassing any of his predecessors except

Augustus (in proof of which he proceeded to lavish wealth upon veterans and
Senators).[17] The speech that Seneca wrote for the young Nero one or two years
before Romans was written, "On Mercy" (*De clementia*), is widely credited with
having had a moderating effect on the young emperor. (It also might simply have
been the case that Nero's excesses grew to be far more obvious after he required
his advisor to commit suicide, causing the early years to appear milder in comparison.) *De clementia* combines lofty rhetoric with abject flattery and cold political
calculation. It addresses Nero as embodying "the great mind of the empire," calm
and benevolent, without whom the great irrational herd, who are the people of
Rome, would quickly fling themselves to destruction. He surpasses all his ancestors, including the divine Augustus, by having come to power without shedding
a drop of blood (no mention of Claudius's fate darkens the mood). Nero will be
the most beloved of Caesars if he continues to present himself to the people as
the most blameless; the quickest way to the people's hearts is through the application of clemency.[18] But mercy must be dispensed in moderation. Seneca is swift to
admit the common wisdom that "mercy upholds the worst class of men, since it is
superfluous unless there has been some crime," it being self-evident that Roman
justice sufficed to preserve the innocent. "An indiscriminate and general mercy"
will undermine public morality. The people must be kept under the rein. Seneca
recognizes the usefulness of terror, expressed in the slogan "Let them hate, if
only they fear." But he played on Nero's "desire for popularity, and his fear and
insecurity," in urging the sovereign to seek a balance of terror and mercy, love and
fear, mixed together.[19]

Clementia was, then, the indulgence shown by a sovereign to his unworthy subjects, an undeserved favor that highlighted his moral superiority to them. Two particular occasions on which imperial clemency was proclaimed bear directly on the
occasion of Romans. One is Claudius's order suppressing civil unrest in Alexandria
in 41 C.E. The other is Nero's order, probably in 54 C.E., rescinding his stepfather's
expulsion of Judeans from the city of Rome. To understand these events, and their
role in shaping the rhetoric of Romans, we must bear in mind the fundamentally
parasitic nature of the Roman imperial economy.

─────────────── **Death and Taxes** ───────────────

"The Romans wrung ultimately from the provincial peasants all that could be economically extracted." So historian Ramsay MacMullen summarized a wealth of
evidence, painstakingly gathered, for first-century Roman Egypt. He painted an
intimate and detailed portrait of the "predatory arrogance long latent in the pax
Romana," giving particular attention to the violence of tax gatherers as attested by
the protests and petitions that have survived on papyri.[20]

Nero's advisor, the philosopher Seneca. Terracotta bust made after a Greek original; a bronze bust found at Pompeii was made after the same original. Height 34 cm. The Louvre, Paris. Photo © Erich Lessing/Art Resource, N.Y.

Violence, for example, such as that experienced by an old farmer with only one eye, who protested that after he had been subjected to constant harassment and plundered by avaricious neighbors, he was assailed by the local tax gatherer's assistant, who "held me in contempt because of my infirmity." The peasant complains that the deputy

> first publicly abused me and my mother, after maltreating her with numerous blows and demolishing all four doors of mine with an ax so that our house is wide open and accessible to every malefactor—although we owed nothing to the *fiscus*. . . .[21]

Again, MacMullen quotes a petition (quoted in chapter 2) from the village of Euhemerus to their Roman "master and patron," apparently indicating that in order to meet an unsustainable tax burden, they were willing to sacrifice some of their young men; to precisely what fate is not clear.[22] Summarizing some seventy such pleas for justice, MacMullen emphasizes "the recurrence of physical outrage, the beatings, mauling, and murders. They may accompany a robbery (thefts being frequent) or play a part in intimidation. The plaintiff may allege an attempt to drive him clean out of the village; his enemies want his land, or access to water, which was scarce."[23] This everyday brutality was not the result of rogue officials or a few bad apples, in the everyday parlance of empires seeking to minimize levels of destruction and misery that cannot simply be attributed to the unworthiness of the wretched souls they govern. The policy was systematic; its rapacity was cheerfully admitted, indeed celebrated, by its architects. Recall the instructions of Nero to a newly appointed provincial governor, around the time Romans was written: "You know my needs. See to it no one is left with anything!"

"At the very outset of their rule over Egypt," MacMullen observes, "the emperors raised village officials to a position directly responsible for their local taxes and corvées." He describes a "common pattern of desperation":

> First, initial conquest by the Romans; next, the rapid confiscation of all hidden weapons; then, the assessment by the conquerors of what they have gained so as to exploit its riches methodically; the consternation of the censured; and thereafter recurrent spasms of protest against the weight of tribute harshly calculated and still more harshly exacted,

spasms including often "suicidal" attempts by peasants who withdrew from their fields, or mounted the futile tax revolts that punctuated the first century.[24]

MacMullen cites a third description of the brutality of tax gatherers in Roman Egypt. Writing during the reign of Gaius (Caligula), Philo of Alexandria called on "rulers of cities" to "cease from racking them with taxes and tolls as heavy as they are constant." He objected not only to the injustice of the taxes, but to the violence by which they were collected. The Romans had intentionally appointed as tax-gatherers "the most ruthless of men, brimful of inhumanity, and put into their hands resources for overreaching." Their own "natural brutality" was compounded by "the immunity they gain from their masters' instructions." The results were appalling. The tax agents sought to extract impossible burdens from the wretchedly poor through mass kidnappings, public torture and executions of family members, even holding for ransom the bodies of murdered relatives on threat of mutilating them savagely. Philo does not wonder that whole villages were depopulated by the terror.[25] Such evidence belies the equanimity with which some modern interpreters continue to regard Roman taxation as a fundamentally benign, if unpleasant burden.

Alexandria, 38–41 C.E.

The catastrophe that befell the Judean population of Alexandria—perhaps the largest concentration of Judeans in the Roman world—less than twenty years before Paul wrote Romans shows us much about the central role Roman policy, including tax policy, played in tensions between Greeks and Judeans (and others) and in the construction of ethnicity in Paul's world. As John G. Gager points out, after Octavian's defeat of Antony in 31 B.C.E., "Roman power was the basic fact for all inhabitants of the Mediterranean basin." It was Roman power "that created the conditions in which Alexandrian anti-Semitism came to life."[26]

The general outline of events is well known.[27] Soon after Octavian, the future Augustus, defeated Marc Antony and annexed Egypt (in 31 B.C.E.), he imposed a new tax on non-citizens, the *laographia*, that exempted only the Greek citizens of Alexandria. Though they were long-time residents of the city, the majority of Judeans in the city were not citizens and thus were subject to the tax, along with the non-Greek Egyptian masses. Some, at least, of the Judeans sought to parlay the generally sympathetic attitude of the Caesars into a grant of citizenship.

Upon Gaius's accession in 37 C.E., simmering tensions regarding taxation reached a boiling point. The Roman governor of Alexandria, Flaccus, had been an outspoken supporter of Gaius's rivals, and feared the new emperor's retaliation. This made him vulnerable to the manipulations of powerful local figures who were vocal opponents both of Rome and of the Judeans, who had long enjoyed privileges under the Caesars. A tour by Rome's recently named client prince in Galilee, Agrippa I, inflamed both anti-Roman and anti-Judean sentiment in Alexandria. The anti-Judean lobby seized the moment to press their cause. They cajoled Flaccus into enacting severe anti-Judean policies in exchange for not denouncing him before the emperor. The governor ordered the seizure of synagogue property, issued a decree that Judeans were "strangers and aliens" in Alexandria, forced their relocation to the first known ghetto in the world, and initiated the arrests, humiliation, and scourging of elders of the Judean *gerousia*. Flaccus then gave his Alexandrian rivals a free hand as they set their gangs loose in the streets for a weeks-long orgy of pillage, beatings, torture, and murder.[28]

The emperor Gaius used force to suppress the unrest and had Flaccus brought to Rome to face charges (he was subsequently condemned and executed). In the months that followed, rival delegations from Alexandria went to Rome to plead their case: one from the Greek elite, led by the academician Apion, and another from the Judean community, including Philo. The audiences were a farce. The emperor tormented the Judeans, accusing them of being "god-haters" because they refused to recognize his divinity, and taunting them with absurd questions about their customs. The Greeks, we may surmise, raised the sort of vicious accusations against the Judeans that were already common enough in Egypt at the time: their origin in a mass expulsion of polluted persons from Egypt; their hatred of outsiders; and their impiety, evidenced in their destruction of their neighbors' temples, the name of their capital city, *Hierosyla* ("Sacrilege"), and their refusal to worship at the statues of the emperors. The Judean delegation's despondency only deepened when they were informed that Gaius had ordered a statue of himself erected in the Jerusalem Temple.[29]

That catastrophe was postponed by the hesitation of Petronius, Gaius's governor of Syria, and at last averted by Gaius's assassination. Josephus tells us that on news of the emperor's death, Judeans in Alexandria rose up in arms against their neighbors. (As Gager points out, these "would surely have represented groups and interests different from those of Philo and his social class."[30])

Gaius's successor, Claudius, moved swiftly to put down the violence. Two of the Greek leaders who had been most outspoken in their antagonism to Rome were brought to trial and sentenced to death. Claudius's decree to the antagonists in Alexandria is widely read as favorable to the Judean cause—although it falls short of granting them citizenship—because Josephus has transmitted a version of the decree that obscures the civic status assigned to the Judeans.[31] The more likely authentic text is less favorable to the Judeans and speaks volumes about the imperial perception of the trouble:[32]

> With regard to the responsibility for the disturbances and rioting, or rather, to speak the truth, the war against the Jews . . . I have not wished to make an exact inquiry, but I harbor within me a store of immutable indignation against those who renewed the conflict. . . .

An "exact inquiry" might have identified those responsible for massacre and mayhem and held them to account, something about which the emperor apparently could not be further troubled. His "immutable indignation" is directed against "those who *renewed* the conflict," that is, the Judeans, but nothing is said here about the individuals who began it, or the Roman governor's dereliction of duty, or the previous emperor's willful aggravation of the situation.[33] So far as Claudius was concerned, the root cause of all the violence was the "mutual enmity" of two ethnic groups. Its solution, plainly enough, was mutual tolerance, enforced by the threat that an ordinarily benign and merciful emperor might resort to force:

> I merely say that, unless you stop this destructive and obstinate mutual enmity, I shall be forced to show what a benevolent ruler can be when he is turned to righteous indignation.

Claudius warned the Alexandrians "to behave gently and kindly toward the Judeans who have inhabited the same city for many years," and not to dishonor their religious customs. But he warned the Judeans "not to aim at more than they have previously had"—that is, not again to pursue citizenship—"and not in the future to send two embassies as if they lived in two cities, a thing which has never been done before"—an unseemly gesture that had proved just what outsiders they were to the city.

> Nor are they to bring in or invite Judeans coming from Syria or Egypt, or I shall be forced to conceive graver suspicions. If they disobey, I shall proceed against them in every way as fomenting a common plague for the whole world.

This episode and its dénouement are instructive, first in regard to the malleability of "ethnicity" during this period. If, in the provinces, participation in the imperial cult held out for the ambitious the prospect of "becoming Roman, staying Greek,"[34] some at least of Philo's contemporaries sought to "become Alexandrian, staying Judean." That should not surprise us, since as Shaye J. D. Cohen observes, Judeans in the Diaspora were not immediately distinguishable from their neighbors. "Jews looked like everyone else, dressed like everyone else, spoke like everyone else, had names and occupations like those of everyone else, and in general closely resembled their gentile neighbors."[35] The Judeans of Alexandria thought it reasonable to seek recognition as both Alexandrian citizens and members of the Judean *politeia*.

Some of their neighbors disagreed, for reasons that sprang as much from their antipathy toward the Caesars and their jealousy of citizenship—"the primary irritant"[36]—as from any hostility toward the Judeans themselves. They posed their opposition in terms of the Judeans' unsuitability to participate in the Roman order. Their supposed origins as lower-class Egyptians and their contempt for the rites of others showed that the Judeans could never take their place among enlightened peoples who accepted the Roman gods alongside their own. It is not enough, then, to read the catastrophe in Alexandria as an episode of ethnic tension between Greeks and Judeans: this was a case of rivalry among colonized peoples jockeying against each other for the favor of the colonial power.

Also notable is the imperial construal of the situation. Claudius knew better than to accept the Alexandrians' posing of the issues. Far from a squabble between ethnic groups, the anti-Judean bloc had stirred up trouble in clear defiance of Roman policy, attempting to triangulate with Flaccus against the Judeans. Claudius rejected the strategy and condemned its architects.[37] But he also warned the Judeans not to import troublemaking compatriots from Syria, indicating that from the Roman point of view, Judeans were, just like the Alexandrians, potentially troublesome residents of the Eastern provinces who must learn their place in the Roman order.

Note, finally, the emperor's claim of unparalleled benevolence. Regardless of the effects of Roman policy, regardless of whatever miseries and injustices were left without redress, it was to be understood that he had Alexandria's best interests at heart. Claudius would hear no more of the rival groups' claims on imperial justice; by definition, the settlement he imposed was final and merciful.

Rome, 49 c.e.

We do not know whether, or to what extent, the violence in Alexandria was felt among the Judeans of Rome. We may well imagine they were quite aware of what had happened, and felt the blows of Gaius's capriciousness just as keenly as did Philo and his delegation to the emperor.

We know a deep current of anti-Judean antagonism ran through the Roman aristocracy, going back at least to Cicero who had described them as a people "born to servitude." We know that in 19 C.E., Tiberius had deported four thousand Judeans to Sardinia to fight pirates and expelled the rest of the Judean community from Rome; Josephus explains that this was an overreaction to a notorious scandal in which a few Judeans had swindled an aristocrat's wife out of a great deal of money by posing as agents of the Jerusalem Temple.[38] Philo attributed Tiberius's hostility to the overweening influence of his wickedly anti-Judean advisor Sejanus, who wished "to root out the people."[39] But the expulsion was also a routine imperial reaction to unrest. There were riots that year protesting grain shortages, and Tiberius may simply have struck at a convenient target, a minority population both conspicuous and vulnerable, to make an example of them and thus restore law and order in the streets.[40]

We know that the anti-Judean slanders that Philo's opponents, Apion and Chaemeron, brought into Gaius's court thrived among the Roman aristocracy for decades. Chaemeron, after all, later tutored the emperor Nero; and decades later, Josephus was compelled to address his apology for the Judean people to their chief literary adversary in his work *Against Apion*.

Of Claudius's policy toward the Judeans in Rome, we know only of the expulsion in 49 C.E. that many scholars consider a catalyst for the situation addressed in Romans. The event, the differing accounts in ancient sources, and its consequences for the Roman churches have been the subject of extensive research. Suetonius offers a single brief report that has been subjected to repeated examination. In Latin, it reads: "*Iudaeos impulsore Chresto assidue tumultuantes Roma expulit*" (*Claudius* 25.4). The customary translation is, "Since the Jews constantly made disturbances at the instigation of Chrestus, he [Claudius] expelled them from Rome" (LCL). Just what the "instigation of Chrestus" means, however, is a matter of considerable controversy. Two studies have proven particularly illuminating on the question.

As H. Dixon Slingerland shows, a "Christianizing interpretation" has read Claudius's edict as the imperial response to civic unrest among the Jews of Rome, *provoked by a turbulent Jewish rejection of Christianity*.[41] On this widely accepted reading, "Chrestus" is Suetonius's misspelling of "Christus," that is, (Jesus) Christ. The Jewish "disturbances" (sometimes read as "riots") were caused by the Jewish rejection either of Christian preaching,[42] or of specific Christian practice involving shared table fellowship of Jews and "gentiles."[43] To the question, how could synagogue debates over the proclamation of Jesus as Messiah have prompted such massive imperial reaction as an expulsion of a great number of Judeans, the implicit answer on this interpretation is the intensity of Jewish intolerance for the Christian message. Thus, James C. Walters declares that "the implications of the Christian message for Jewish self-definition and the threat it represented to the boundaries of Judaism were quite capable of stirring violent opposition. . . . Christians were a threat to the integrity of Judaism in Rome."[44]

The problems with this Christianizing interpretation are, first, that it reads the expulsion in narrowly religious terms as an episode in the rise of Christianity and its separation from Judaism in Rome, rather than more broadly as an episode in the history of Roman policy toward the Judeans and other subject peoples.[45] But the penchant among Christian interpreters for assuming, on the basis of Acts 18:2, that Jewish Christianity was at issue[46] is anachronistic and unnecessary. More likely Prisca and Aquila were simply caught up in a general action against Judeans as such.[47]

Second, the Christianizing interpretation gives undue emphasis to arguments from silence regarding the identity of Chrestus. Slingerland's meticulous study results in a more persuasive alternative. Suetonius was familiar enough with the names *Christiani* and *Christus* (see *Nero* 16.2). His use of Chrestus was probably not a mistaken reference to Jesus Christ, but a reference to an otherwise unidentified Roman that he expected his audience to recognize.[48] His reference to the Judeans of Rome as *tumultuantes* was the sort of prejudicial characterization on which Suetonius often relied in his history; thus the search to identify a specific cause for a discrete episode of Jewish rioting is misplaced. Further, after comparing the syntax of the phrase *impulsore Chresto* with similar adverbial phrases throughout Suetonius's *Lives of the Caesars*, Slingerland concludes that the phrase functions to explain not why Jews caused disturbances, but why Claudius expelled them. That is, he did so *impulsore Chresto,* at the urging of Chrestus (just as Philo attributes Tiberius's actions against Judeans to the influence of Sejanus). Slingerland thus translates Suetonius's report, "Chrestus caused Claudius to expel the continuously rebelling Jews."[49]

Third, Slingerland points out that interpreters often hold the Judeans themselves "responsible for the hostile attitudes and actions which they faced" by trading in generalizations about "the problems presented by the Jewish people" and "the rigidity of the Jewish faith," "the inflexible temper of Judaism," the nature of Jews as a "turbulence-prone" and "troublesome" group with a "tendency to disturb the public order," their "general inability to compromise," their "sense of their own self-importance," and so on.[50] A Christianizing interpretation of the edict blames the disturbances that provoked it specifically on Jewish inability to tolerate the Christian message.

A preferable explanation for the expulsion is to be found, not in specific Jewish actions that require explanation in terms of putative Jewish characteristics, but in Roman policy. Claudius continued his predecessors' policy of seeking to control Judeans and adherents to other foreign "superstitions" in the city. As Leonard Victor Rutgers has shown, the impulse behind this imperial policy was not a religious concern but a political one. "It was quite common for the Roman authorities to expel easily identifiable groups from Rome in times of political turmoil. Such expulsions were ordered not for religious reasons, but rather to maintain law and order." This is why the expulsions under Tiberius and Claudius were limited to the Judean population of Rome, and not empire-wide or even region-wide actions. It is not unlikely that some Judeans, in fact, were involved in civic disturbances, but we cannot say why. "Rome intervened because there were disturbances and not because it wanted to meddle in the internal affairs of the Jewish community," or any other community, in Rome. Indeed, Rutgers offers, the Judeans may have been "just a convenient group whose expulsion could serve as an example to re-establish peace and quiet among the city populace at large." Different Roman emperors or magistrates held anti-Judean views, but Rutgers argues that

> at best, a dislike for Judaism served to justify on a subconscious level decisions that had essentially been reached on the basis of administrative and legal considerations. . . . Rome's measures concerning the Jews had straightforward political causes.[51]

Rome, 54 C.E.

There is wide agreement that Romans was written, at least in part, to address a specific situation in the Roman assemblies. When Judeans who had been expelled from the city by Claudius in 49 were allowed to return by Nero, soon after his accession, they returned to a city in which much of the community life they had previously known was in disarray.[52] In an influential 1970 article, Wolfgang Wiefel catalogued the expressions of contempt leveled against Judeans by their Roman neighbors in the latter half of the first century C.E. They were scorned as beggars and fortune tellers infesting the public parks; they scraped by on a miserable diet, apparently without adequate access to decent kosher food.[53] They were derided as "the weak" in the city.[54] Although there is no reason to attribute these characterizations to the effect of the expulsion under Claudius alone, we may reasonably assume that that event, and the subsequent return of former exiles, made a lasting impression. Although Judeans officially still enjoyed the emperor's favor, Nero's own advisor, Seneca, complained that noxious Judean practices had spread among the non-Judean populace, a development he found doubly offensive since "the conquered [*victi*] have given their laws to the conquerors [*victores*]."[55] Given that the assemblies to which Paul wrote were "surrounded by a society marked by its aversion and rejection of everything Jewish," Wiefel found it understandable that in Romans, Paul should strive to instill a different attitude toward Israel among his audience.

But we are in a position to say more about the attitudes Paul struggled against in this letter. As we have seen, in 41 C.E. Claudius portrayed his severe posture toward the Judeans of Alexandria as milder than they deserved, due to his benevolence. Upon Claudius's death in 54 C.E., Nero set himself to conspicuous reversals of his stepfather's policies as a way of demonstrating his superior clemency. One of these gestures, we may safely presume, was to allow the exiled Judeans to return to Rome.[56]

Given all that we have seen regarding the representation of imperial clemency in official imagery and propaganda, we may hazard an informed guess regarding the perception of this action among the Judeans' neighbors. First, we know nothing of any efforts on Nero's part to exonerate these exiles of any accusations, formal or informal, that Claudius had raised against them, or to increase the esteem in which generally they were held. He allowed them to return, after all, not to improve their lot, but to enhance his own prestige as a benevolent and merciful ruler. But Seneca himself had reminded Nero that in the common view, "mercy upholds the worst class of men," and that "an indiscriminate and general mercy" would undermine Nero's credibility.[57] We can imagine that non-Judeans in Rome would have looked upon these returning exiles not only as the wretched and broken people that they appeared, but as the undeserving beneficiaries of imperial largesse, troublemakers who had escaped being held accountable for their misdeeds. They would have appeared, in Seneca's phrase, "the worst class of men," being upheld by misdirected mercy.

Paul's stylized conversation with a Judean in Romans 2–3 is a rhetorical device aimed precisely at combating this prejudicial conclusion on the part of his non-Judean audience. "We are blasphemed," Paul protests: we are judged as sinners and slandered as wishing to do evil, yet to reap rewards from it (Rom 3:7-8). His address to a Judean contemplates the possibility that "the name of God is blasphemed among the nations" on account of Judean malfeasance (2:24). That rhetorical possibility helps us to understand the role of this dialogue within the letter's argumentation, as the following discussion will make clear.

—— **A Warning against Presuming on Mercy (Romans 2–3)** ——

As we have seen in chapter 2, one effect of Paul's rhetoric in the beginning of Romans is to drive a wedge between his hearers and the sort of arrogant presumption that characterized the imperial house (1:18-32). In a stylized second-person address to a fictitious interlocutor, Paul then warns against a self-deluding hypocrisy that presumes upon God's mercy as an escape from accountability to God. *All* are accountable to God and will be judged according to their works (2:1-16). It becomes clear as the letter progresses that this fictitious address has a very real hortatory burden: Paul warns his Roman audience against misconstruing their status "in Christ" as a presumption on God's mercy. The "expiation" achieved in Christ's blood is not an expression of divine forbearance, but an *end* to God's forbearance of *previous* sins that were "passed over" but will be no longer (3:21-26). Now, God justifies—sets persons right—out of the faithfulness of Christ in which they have been made to participate; this demonstrates God's justice in a way that previous divine forbearance did not, as the clauses in 3:25-26 make clear.[58] To similar effect, Paul contrasts two christological schemes in Romans 5:12-21 to emphasize that what God achieved in Christ was *more than* relief from the penalty of trespasses; it was the dawn of a new dominion, the "reign" of grace (5:21).[59] The consequences he draws out in 6:1-23 are specifically relevant to those who have been baptized into Christ: they are not to misconstrue the grace they received as an opportunity to presume on divine mercy, to "continue in sin that grace may abound."

Here we may compare Paul's rhetoric with the way Roman imperial propaganda presented the clemency of the Augusti. Imperial mercy was the exercise of a sovereign's prerogative toward the undeserving in such a way as to redound to his own glory. Paul speaks similarly of God's mercy as the sheer, unilateral initiative of a sovereign toward those who do not deserve mercy (3:23-24; 5:6-8). But where Seneca advised the emperor to be judicious in his granting of amnesty, out of concern that too-great leniency would undermine the public perception of the emperor's power, Paul insists that God's "kindness and forbearance" are themselves the expression of God's power. God's mercy produces repentance, faithfulness, and obedience: therefore, it cannot compromise God's justice. To the contrary, God's mercy is the public manifestation of God's justice—insofar as those who have received mercy are thereby moved to respond in obedience.

Another comparison is even more central to the larger purpose of the letter. We may set the perception of the emperor's clemency shown toward Judeans—the undeserving *victi*, in the view of imperial ideology—over against the conversation Paul stages with a Judean in 2:17—3:20.

Paul's dialogue with a Judean

When Romans has been read as a treatise on salvation, this apostrophe has been read as an indictment of "the Jew," intended to show both that the Jew needs Paul's gospel as much as "the Gentile" and that the Jew is in greater danger of resisting the gospel because of a false presumption. This "characteristic Jewish boast" must be "demolished" by proving that the Jew is just as guilty of disobedience as the sinners described in 1:18-32.[60] Although virtually all interpreters have read the larger purpose in 1:18—3:20 as establishing the universal accountability described in 3:19 ("so that the whole world may be accountable to God"), many have seen Paul's particular target as the boastful and arrogant Jew. "What is argued [in 1:18—3:20] is the equal status of Jew and Gentile under sin," J. Christiaan Beker wrote; but "what is *presumed* is the self-evident character of the Gentile under sin. . . . If it can be shown that the catena of Scripture in 3:11-18 applies to the Jews, *then* it is self-evident that the whole world is accountable to God as well, for Gentiles are by nature sinners."[61] But this reading, based in part on a mistranslation of 3:19, misses the point of Paul's argument. It is hard to imagine the Jew who would have been surprised by Paul's point, as he cites Jewish scripture to argue for Jewish accountability to Israel's God. Paul's point—addressed to a non-Judean audience—is that Jewish scriptures establish God's claim on the whole world, *not* just upon Judeans. All the world—not just Judeans—is accountable to God.[62]

Paul's stylized address to a Judean in 2:17—3:9 is meant not to indict the Jews or to criticize Judaism, but to enlist a fellow Judean as a witness to make an important point to his non-Judean audience. Here it is crucially important that we understand how Paul's use of diatribe-like techniques functions.[63]

No one has done more to help us understand Paul's use of diatribe-like techniques in Romans 2–3 than Stanley K. Stowers. In his 1981 study, *The Diatribe and Paul's Letter to the Romans*, Stowers reviewed and offered corrections of previous work on the social setting, hortatory and instructive purposes, and rhetorical techniques of the diatribe. In *A Rereading of Romans* (1994), he applied these and other insights to a full-scale reading of the letter. As we saw in chapter 2, Stowers ably demonstrated that the sudden rhetorical turn to second-person-singular address at Rom 2:1 ("you are without excuse, whoever you are, O mortal, when you judge") was not a rhetorical trap for the Jew, but fit a broad pattern of moral exhortation in which speech-in-character was used as "a personal indictment of any of the audience to whom it might apply. . . . The address in 2:1ff. reaches out to sharply indict those who have pretensions of being on a different plane morally." Stowers consequently declared it "anachronistic and completely unwarranted to think that Paul has only the Jew in mind in 2:1–5 or that he characterizes the typical Jew."[64]

In contrast, in 2:17-24 Paul clearly has the Jew in mind, and just here many interpreters have found the exegetical smoking gun confirming that part, at least, of Paul's purpose in the letter is to come against a distinctly Jewish boastfulness and presumption on God's mercy. Here again, however, Stowers's insights into the function of diatribe-like techniques suffices to establish, to the contrary:

- that the use of direct address with a fictitious person, including speech-in-character, did *not* mean that the actual audience of the letter was now in view. Paul is not addressing the attitudes of actual Judean opponents in his Roman audience;
- that the interpreter's task was to understand what the use of this technique was meant to accomplish with the explicit non-Judean audience of the letter; and
- that Paul's target was not "Judaism in general"; therefore "it is grossly misleading to generalize this fictitious address to a critique of Judaism."[65] Stowers rightly explodes the common description of this passage as an "indictment" or "concrete attack" on Jews, or as an attempted "demonstration" that Jews in general are as much under the power of sin as "Gentiles."[66]

In order to understand what Paul's target was, Stowers insisted we must understand how diatribe-like techniques functioned in moral or instructional address. He rightly identifies different diatribe-like techniques among Hellenistic and Roman moralists:

- the use of *objections,* indicated, for example, by expressions such as *phēsi* ("he says") or *tis erei* ("someone will say") or *sy ereis* ("you will say": compare the clear objection in Rom. 9:19, which is clearly rebuked at 9:20, or the objection in 1 Cor. 15:35, rebuked in 15:36);
- rhetorical questions, imperatives, or accusations intended to convict the fictitious interlocutor of wrong thinking or hypocrisy (*elenchos*-rhetoric), sometimes indicated by a negative term of address such as *mataie* ("O you misguided person"), *infelix* ("you unhappy person"), or *aphrōn* ("fool," 1 Cor. 15:36);
- rhetorical questions leading to false conclusions, often indicated by an invitation to consider consequences: for example *ti oun* ("what then?"), *kai ti* ("and so, what?"), or the particle *mē* ("not [this, surely?]").

All of these forms are clearly evident in Romans. Just here, however, some categorical confusion distorts Stowers's reading of diatribe-like elements in the letter. Unfortunately, Stowers does not carefully maintain the distinctions between the diatribe-like techniques that he has identified. The result is a confused reading of the diatribe-like address in Romans 2–3 that fundamentally misunderstands Paul's purpose in this section and in the letter as a whole.

Diatribe in the apostrophe to the Judean (2:17-24)

Stowers reads Rom 2:17-24 as a series of "indicting rhetorical questions." The picture the apostle paints, according to Stowers, is

> not just of the pretentious person but of the pretentious moral and religious leader and teacher. The "Jew" here pretends to have a special relationship with God. He boasts . . . of his relation to God. . . . Bragging about what he does not truly possess is the chief mark of the pretentious person. He also boasts in the law while breaking it. This person pretends to have great ethical knowledge, knowledge of the law and of God's will. Finally, he pretends to be a teacher and moral guide to others, although he does not embody what he teaches.[67]

But (against Stowers) the person Paul addresses is *not* "bragging about what [he] does not truly possess." To the contrary, Paul is clear that the Judean *does* possess these things (see Rom 9:4-5).[68] Neither do we hear Paul's Judean interlocutor admit that he has broken the law; indeed, Paul has so structured the dialogue at this point that the interlocutor has no opportunity to respond. Stowers insists (and I agree) that the apostrophe is not meant as Paul's characterization of Jews as such. But to the question, just what is Paul's purpose, then? Stowers has given different answers: either Paul is simply showing off, providing the Roman church a sample of his rhetorical skill by showing the sort of diatribe-like technique of which he is capable;[69] or else he is hurling a long-distance invective at perceived Judean opponents in Jerusalem.[70]

These judgments fail to follow through with Stowers's own insights into the function of diatribe in Paul's environment. The use of speech-in-character and of rhetorical questions to a fictitious interlocutor was normally "didactic," Stowers observed.

> In using the methods of indictment and protreptic the teacher employs objections directed toward the various types of students, would-be students, auditors, and philosophers who characteristically make up his audience and for whom the style has been shaped. . . . All of the apostrophes in Romans indict pretentious and arrogant persons. Rather than indicating a polemic against the Jew, the apostrophes in Romans censure Jews, Gentiles, and Gentile Christians alike. None are excluded from the censure of the pretentious.[71]

These conclusions follow naturally from Stowers's discussion of the normal didactic or hortatory effect of diatribe-like techniques. Indeed, Stowers concludes from Rom 15:14-16 that "what Paul plans to do in Rome he is already doing in this letter, that is, *euangelisasthai.*"[72] But Stowers does not follow through on these observations to ask how the apostrophe to the Jew in 2:17-24 is integrated with the larger rhetorical purpose of challenging arrogant attitudes *among Paul's predominantly non-Judean audience* in a fundamentally hortatory letter.

We gain a clearer understanding of the apostrophe in 2:17-24 if we apply to Romans Stowers's description of how leading questions functioned in diatribe-like rhetoric. The contrast with 2:1-6 bears notice. There, Paul levels an accusation against a hypothetical interlocutor, using indicative statements:

> Therefore you are without excuse, O mortal, everyone who judges, for in that by which you judge another you condemn yourself, *for you who judge do the same things.*

In 2:17-24, in contrast, Paul asks his hypothetical Judean interlocutor a series of questions:

> . . . Do you not teach yourself? . . . Do you steal? . . . Do you commit adultery? . . . Do you rob temples? . . . By transgressing the law, do you dishonor God?

But he does not wait for an answer and so cannot deliver a guilty verdict comparable to 2:1.[73] The apostrophe here remains conditional: *if* you steal, commit adultery, and rob temples, *then* you dishonor God; *then,* the verdict of Scripture would apply: "the name of God is blasphemed among the nations because of you!" (2:24). *Then* your circumcision would avail you nothing (2:25). The apostrophe imaginatively embodies the assertion Paul has already made in 2:12-13: "as many as have sinned in the law will be judged by the law."

It would be hard to imagine a self-respecting Judean arguing *against* Paul here: which of his contemporaries would have protested that being a Judean in fact gave one a license to sin? But Paul's Judean contemporaries are not his target. The non-Judeans in Rome are. It is *they* who need to hear that Judeans do not, in fact, presume on God's grace and mercy to indulge their sins.

Diatribe in the Judean's response (3:1-9)

That is just what the audience hears when Paul's Judean interlocutor at last gets a chance to talk back, in 3:1-9. Here again, Stowers's insights into diatribe style are keys to interpretation; here again, however, Stowers has failed to follow through with these insights. He showed that in general, teachers employing diatribe-like style would use leading questions and false conclusions to move their fictitious hearer to the right conclusion. Puzzlingly, however, in his 1981 study, Stowers read the rhetorical questions in 3:1, 3, 5, 7, 8, and 9 not as Paul's leading questions but as *objections* from the Jewish interlocutor. (In 1994 he modified this outline, but continued to read 3:1 and 3:9 as objections.) This way of construing the dialogue puts the Jew on the defensive, recoiling from Paul's earlier questions in 2:17-24. To read the question, "then what advantage does the Jew have?" as the Judean's protest implies that the Judean had previously assumed that his "advantage" was precisely the license to get away with theft, adultery, and the robbing of temples. But this is scarcely credible even as a fictitious dialogue. To the contrary: as I argued in *The Rhetoric of Romans* (1990), on the basis of Stowers's own discussion of diatribe-like technique, we should read the questions in 3:1-9 not as objections from the interlocutor, but as *Paul's* leading questions, and the answers as his dialogue partner's appropriate drawing of right conclusions and rejection of wrong conclusions.[74]

The conversation thus runs as follows:

3:1	*Paul's leading question*	Then what advantage has the Judean? Or what is the value of circumcision?
3:2	*Interlocutor's response*	Much in every way. For in the first place, the Judeans were entrusted with the oracles of God.
3:3	*Paul*	What if some were unfaithful? Will their faithlessness nullify the faithfulness of God?
3:4	*Interlocutor*	By no means! Although everyone is a liar, let God be proved true....
3:5	*Paul*	But if our injustice serves to confirm the justice of God, what should we say? That God is unjust to inflict wrath on us? (I speak in a human way.)

3:6	*Interlocutor*	By no means! For then how could God judge the world?
3:7, 8	*Paul*	But if through my falsehood, God's truthfulness abounds to his glory, why am I still being condemned as a sinner? And why not say (as some people slander us by saying that we say), "Let us do evil so that good may come"?
	Interlocutor	Their condemnation is deserved!
3:9a	*Paul*	What then? Do we have any defense (against God's judgment)?
3:9b	*Interlocutor*	No, not at all; for we have already charged that all, both Judeans and Greeks, are under the power of sin. . . .

This way of reading the diatribe conforms more naturally to Stowers's insights about the way teachers could use leading questions in fictitious dialogues to shape the perceptions and attitudes of their audiences. But it fundamentally changes our perception of Paul's purpose. He is not *indicting* a Judean who recoils in self-protection and protest; rather he is *enlisting* a Judean colleague who heartily endorses his conclusion. *Yes,* says his witness, *if* I have committed the sins you describe, I most assuredly deserve judgment! To expect otherwise would be to dishonor God—and to justify the reprehensible allegations raised against my people by the nations, that we imagine we may "do evil that good may come." Far better for me to be judged than for God's honor to be impugned!

The Judean interlocutor is not concerned to protect his privilege over against God's claim; to the contrary, he enthusiastically agrees with Paul that Judeans enjoy no defense against God's judgment. The question in 3:9 has often been read as a repetition of 3:1, the unusual Greek form *proechometha* taken either as an active middle ("are we any better off?" NRSV) or a passive ("are we at a disadvantage?" NRSV note). But the verb is a genuine middle, meaning "raise a defense for oneself" or "put up a defense." When the Judean is asked whether he shares the presumption of being exempt from God's judgment that was criticized in 2:1-6, he immediately gives an exemplary response: "Not at all!"[75]

The non-Judean audience overhearing this conversation is meant to learn an important lesson about Judeans. Regardless of the emperor's claims to magnanimity; regardless of the more scurrilous generalizations likely to be heard in the Roman street about the returning exiles as unworthy beneficiaries of Nero's clemency; regardless of the offense given by the displaced and probably disreputable individuals asking for help in the city parks and alleys; regardless of the quasi-official view that their people were in decline, broken, and destined to be subjugated, present circumstances in Rome had little to do with genuine mercy or with the justice of God.

Here again we are in touch with the character of Paul's argumentation as the dissociation of concepts.[76] The fundamental dissociation toward which Paul's rhetoric drives is *the distinction of appearance from reality,* which in Romans means also *the distinction of the present from the future*; or more precisely, the dissociation of the present *as the failed realization of God's purposes in history* from the future *as the complete realization of those purposes.* The full revelation of God's justice is yet to come. That will be a day of judgment: of glory and honor for those who have endured in doing right, but wrath and punishment for all who have done evil (2:6-11). In place of the present regime of arrogance and pretension, corruption and contempt for the truth, *that* day will bring a universal and inescapable judgment according to works. Until now, the world has seen signature examples of God's wrath being revealed (1:18-32); but until now, history has more usually been the arena of God's forbearance of sins (3:25). God's kindness and mercy have provided a temporary reprieve, allowing time to repent; but that time is drawing quickly to an end.

To read the present disposition of power and privilege as the climax of history would be a grave mistake. To join in the delusion that the exercise of imperial prerogative constitutes genuine mercy, and that justice means no more than brokering favor regardless of desert, would be morally disastrous.

The Manifestation of Mercy in History

Paul's stylized conversation with a Judean in chapters 2–3 thus anticipates the argument of chapters 9–11. There, too, the relation of God's mercy to the present moment in history is at the theological heart of the issue. Understanding divine mercy aright is necessary to discerning the will of God, "the good and acceptable and perfect," but given imperial realities, it also sets one inevitably at odds with the mentality of the present age (12:1-2).

Israel's "stumbling"

As we have seen, H. Dixon Slingerland described an *interpretatio christiana* of Suetonius's report. That interpretation attributed Claudius's edict of expulsion to a violent reaction in Roman synagogues to Jewish-Christian agitation. That Christianizing reading of Suetonius aids and abets a corresponding Christianizing reading of the situation that provoked Romans. On this reading, Claudius's edict had its most intense effect in causing, or accelerating, the separation of Gentile Christians from the synagogue. Caught in the middle upon their return to Rome after Nero's accession, Jewish Christians found themselves a minority within churches dominated by Gentile Christians. That intramural situation in the Christ assemblies created tensions that Paul sought to relieve in this letter. His concern in chaps. 9–11 goes beyond addressing interpersonal tensions; he wrestles with theological questions arising from the perception—a perception he shares with his audience—that the people Israel have "stumbled." His concern is to insist nevertheless that they have *not* stumbled "so as to fall" (11:11).

What was this "stumbling"? In Romans 9–11 many interpreters find Paul defending a gospel that was "poignantly, even agonizingly, challenged . . . by the refusal of his own people to accept it." A number of scholars have seen behind these chapters Paul's previous failure in Galatia, Jewish opposition in Jerusalem, and tensions between Judeans and non-Judeans in the Roman *ekklēsia*; but most of all, it was "the failure of the mission to the Jews," Israel's rejection of the gospel, that evoked his concern.[77] So E. Elizabeth Johnson has declared, without further explanation, that "the apparent failure of the Jewish mission is undeniably one of the factors that prompt Romans 9–11."[78]

But just *when* did this "failure of the Jewish mission" become apparent? At what point did the refusal of a certain percentage of Judeans to accept the message about Christ come to constitute the failure of *Israel as a people*? And—given Paul's clarity that Israel may have stumbled, but *not* so as to fall (11:11)—was this "failure" a premise Paul shared with his audience, or a false conclusion on their part that he sought to oppose?

In his 1970 article, Wolfgang Wiefel sought a connection between Claudius's edict and Paul's letter. Wiefel attributed to the expulsion "the end of the first Christian congregation in Rome," which previously had "consisted of Jewish Christians." Romans was written to "a new congregation" constituted after that edict, he wrote, a congregation dominated by Gentile Christians who stood outside the synagogue and were probably "influenced by Paul's gospel of freedom from the law." The Jewish Christians who returned under Nero's rescript entered that predominantly Gentile-Christian congregation and found themselves socially and ritually marginalized. This much of Wiefel's reconstruction of the situation has become familiar now in more recent discussions as well.[79] But it bears notice that Wiefel attributed the contempt shown by the non-Judean majority to *anti-Judean currents in the wider society*, currents that would have had nothing to do with the question of Judean rejection of "the gospel."[80] As we saw earlier in this chapter, the brute facts of the expulsion of 49 c.e., framed as it was (at least subsequently, by Suetonius) by a disparagement of Judeans as such, and the framing of the return of the exiles in terms of the emperor's exercise of his prerogative to show mercy, would have been sufficient to explain contemptuous attitudes toward Judeans in general, and Judeans in the Christ assemblies in particular, among Paul's audience.

A Christianizing reading perceives in Romans 9–11 Paul's anguish that more of his fellow Judeans are not, like he is, believers in Christ. But this anguish is imported into the text. Nothing Paul says here requires us to imagine that he sees the paucity of Jewish Christians within the *ekklēsia* as a failure on the part of his people to have "believed the gospel." Yes, Paul referred earlier to the *apistia* of "some" Judeans in

3:1-9: "What if some [Judeans] were unfaithful?" (*ti gar ei ēpistēsan tines?*). But the context refers not to a rejection of Paul's (or any other) gospel, but to theft, adultery, robbing idols, and breaking the law in general (2:21-24). *Apistia* evidently means not "unbelief" (in Christ) but *unfaithfulness or disobedience to God.* Here in 9:1–4, Paul expresses his concern for his fellow Israelites who have not yet entered into the glory and "sonship," *huiothesia,* that are rightly theirs. But neither have the members of the Roman *ekklēsia*: for although the Spirit testifies that they are God's children (8:14-17), that is an inheritance for which they wait, with the rest of creation, in eager longing (8:18-25). The cause of Paul's anguish is evidently not something that the *ekklēsia* possesses but Israel does not; rather it is a future vindication that appears hopelessly delayed. It is not self-evident that Paul worries because some of his fellow Judeans stand outside the church.

He is grieved for his fellow Israelites and wishes he could be cut off from Christ if it would benefit them (9:1-5), but he never says that they have cut themselves off from God, or that God has rejected them ("By no means!" 11:1). Paul is concerned—naturally enough, given recent history in Alexandria, Rome, and Judea itself—that his people are "blasphemed" among the nations (2:24; 3:8). He has just spoken of the "sufferings of the present age" (5:3; 8:18), and of tribulation, distress, persecution, famine, nakedness, peril, sword, and of "being killed all the day long" for the name of God, "regarded like sheep to be slaughtered" (8:35-36). Those, as we have seen, were real enough perils, and his appeal to the Roman church to sympathize with those who face them is the emotional climax of the letter. But Paul nowhere expresses concern that more Judeans are not flocking to church services.

Despite their zeal in pursuing God's justice, they have failed to recognize that the Christ is the end, that is, the goal of the Torah (9:30—10:4). But Paul does not say they have consciously rejected Christ out of a preference for Torah. He declares that "they have not all obeyed the *euangelion*" (10:16), which on a Christianizing interpretation evokes occasions of failed apostolic preaching such as those narrated in the book of Acts. But Paul does not refer to any such occasion. Rather, he cites Moses and Isaiah, suggesting that the words that have "gone out to the ends of the earth" (10:18) are the words of Jewish scripture. If we set aside the anachronistic Christian assumption that *euangelion* must mean a gospel about Christ requiring *pistis,* "belief" (see chap. 1), we may understand this language on Judean premises. Given present circumstances, which seem to offer no evidence that the final triumph of God's justice is at hand, some Judeans have pursued their own vindication, *tēn idian dikaiosynēn,* rather than awaiting with faithfulness the vindication promised in their own Scripture. It is the Roman assembly, *not Paul,* who have linked Israel's "stumbling" with their own standing in Christ and concluded that they have supplanted a fallen Israel.

Paul speaks of a "remnant," and he names a remnant of one: himself, which he considers enough to make his point that God has not rejected his people (11:1-5). He speaks of "some branches" being "broken off," but says nothing to suggest that "breaking off" involved a rejection of the proclamation of Christ. Paul is not

concerned that Israel has stumbled so as to fall. To the contrary, he is quite sure
that "the gifts and the call of God are irrevocable" (11:29). For these reasons, interpreting chapters 9–11 as Paul's agonized wrestling with Israel's ultimate destiny,
as if his Christian gospel had somehow cast a shadow over their future—or as if
the refusal of other Judeans to share his belief were somehow a threat to his own
confidence—strikes a false and anachronistic note.

These chapters, and indeed the whole of the letter, often have been read as
driven by the problem of theodicy. As J. Christiaan Beker posed the problem, the
"profound issue" at the heart of Romans is "the role of Israel in salvation-history.
. . . If [God] has ceased to be faithful to Israel's promises, how can he be trusted by
the Gentiles?"[81] Richard B. Hays adopts the same perspective: the "driving" question in Romans is, "how can we trust in this allegedly gracious God if he abandons
his promise to Israel?"[82] And E. Elizabeth Johnson finds in Romans 9–11 Paul's
answer to a theological problem posed by the demographic shift in the *ekklēsiai*:
"the Church [is] full of Gentiles and Jews are staying away in droves":

> The danger is twofold: either God has ceased to keep promises to Israel and
> thus cannot be trusted to keep promises to the Church, or God has become
> partial to Gentiles, since it is they who believe Paul's gospel, in which case
> God is neither impartial nor faithful.[83]

But for whom, we should ask, is the first possibility a "danger"? Not for the non-
Judean congregation in Rome; they are apparently cheerful enough about what
they see as the demise of Israel and their replacement of them. They are not anxious about the faithfulness of God; rather they arrogantly presume upon it for
themselves. Neither can we understand Paul as driven here to wrestle with premises he does not share—namely, that Israel has stumbled in any way that threatens
the faithfulness of God. The second suggestion—that "God has become partial
to Gentiles" in neglect of the covenant people—is clearly not a "danger" for Paul,
either, because it is simply impossible for him.

The driving argument in these chapters is not to defend or explain the faithfulness of God against evidence that compromises it but to *assert* God's faithfulness to
God's own purposes against the arrogance of the non-Judeans in the Roman *ekklēsia*.
It is the non-Judean church—not Paul—that announced the "falling" of Israel and
conflated that "theological fact" with their own ascendancy as believers in Christ,
speaking of themselves being "grafted in" to replace the branches that were "broken
off." That ecclesial arrogance is not grounded in any theological perception of Israel
that Paul shares with his audience.

Rather it is the reflex, within the Christ assemblies, of the arrogance of empire,
which regards the imperial disposition of the destinies of peoples as the climax of
history. The Roman church had begun to absorb a poisonous imperial doctrine: that
the empirical hierarchy of rulers and ruled reflected the heavenly determination of

elect and accursed peoples. The mercy of the gods could be read from the surface of history. Paul disagreed.

The typological reading of Romans 9–11

Through much of history, Christian interpreters have read Romans 9–11 as a theological account of the failure of Israel and the ascendancy of the Gentile church. The result is a typological reading of these chapters that divides "true" Israel from "false," and identifies the first with the church and the second with "unbelieving" Judaism. This interpretation is false. It perpetuates the very error Paul sought to combat among his audience in the Roman *ekklēsia*.

E. Elizabeth Johnson rightly criticizes this typological reading. She protests the widespread assumption among interpreters that the questions Paul asks in 9:6, 9:30, and 11:1 are synonymous, and that each asks, in a different way, "why the Jewish majority is not Christian." On this assumption,

- 9:6-29 asks "whether or not God's word of election to Israel has been abrogated," and answers that the exclusion of "part of ethnic Israel . . . from the elect is a function of God's sovereign freedom to redefine community boundaries," namely by redefining "Israel" in non-ethnic terms. Thus, Paul seems to set up a set of oppositions, beginning earlier in the letter:

the "true" Jew	vs.	the external, physical Jew (2:28)
inward, "spiritual" circumcision	vs.	physical circumcision (2:29)
the one who works for wages	vs.	the one who trusts (4:5)
those who seek "righteousness," that is, justification before God, through faith	vs.	those who seek it through law (4:13-15)

Paul (on this interpretation) makes the distinction explicit in a schematic way in 9:6-8:

those who "truly belong to Israel"	vs.	other Israelites who do not "truly" belong (9:6)
"Abraham's true descendants"	vs.	Abraham's other children (9:7)
"the children of the promise"	vs.	"the children of flesh" (9:8)

On this reading, Paul then shows that this distinction was God's pattern throughout biblical history. Interpreters often comment on Paul's "scandalous" alignment of "unbelieving" Israel with Ishmael (9:7), Esau, and Pharaoh,[84]

Jacob the beloved	vs.	Esau the hated (9:13)
the redeemed Israelites of the Exodus	vs.	Pharaoh (9:17)

and read Paul as driven by a fundamental distinction,

those on whom God has mercy	vs.	those on whom God does not (9:14-16),

which is grounded in God's sovereignty, as that of a potter:

a vessel made for beauty	vs.	a vessel for menial use (9:20-21)

This allows Paul to distinguish typologically:

"vessels of mercy" (meaning "us," the church of Judeans and non-Judeans)	vs.	"vessels of wrath" (meaning unbelieving Israel, 9:22-24)
"my people"	vs.	"not my people" (9:25-26)
the remnant of Israel who ["only"] will be saved	vs.	those of Israel who, by implication, will not (9:27-29)

Note that this interpretation requires inserting the word "only" into the text of 9:27 to restrict salvation to the remnant alone (as in NRSV).[85] Paul's argument, on this interpretation, is (as Philip F. Esler states it succinctly) that "most Israelites" who have not "converted to Christ . . . are not Israel or God's people but that, without any injustice on God's part, that status has passed to (the small number of) Israelites and non-Israelites, the sons of God, who have achieved righteousness by faith."[86]

• On this typological interpretation, 9:30—10:21 asks "why Israel's election has in fact been rescinded," and answers that "Israel is nevertheless responsible for its own fate because it refuses to convert to Christianity."[87] The nations and Israel are explicitly contrasted:

those who attained "righteousness," that is, justification before God: the nations	vs.	those who did not attain righteousness, although they strove for it: Israel (9:30-31)
those who submit to God's way of justification	vs.	zealous but unenlightened Israel, who seek their own righteousness (10:1-3)

On this reading, the nations, meaning Gentile Christians, who accepted righteousness by faith, are contrasted with Jews who stubbornly sought righteousness through the law (the Greek particle *de* is taken in an adversative sense, "but"):

"the righteousness that comes from faith," that is, believing	vs.	"the righteousness that comes from law," that is, from "doing" (10:5-17)

The distinction between those who accept God's way of justifying *versus* those who do not is based on how people respond to the gospel of Christ:

| those who hear and respond to the gospel | vs. | Israel, who has heard but has not believed; |
| those who have found God without seeking | vs. | Israel, who have shown themselves to be a disobedient and contrary people (10:20-21) |

- This typological interpretation reads 11:1-27 as asking "whether or not God might have rejected Israel permanently."[88] Paul's eventual reference to the salvation of "all Israel" (11:25-26) is read by many scholars as an exuberant afterthought, the vestige of his own Judean ethnocentrism.[89] The salvation of "all Israel" is regarded as inconsistent with the more substantial answer, in Romans 9 and 10, that God's mercy has brought about a clear division within "ethnic" Israel and that God's faithfulness is adequately demonstrated in the salvation of a remnant:

| a remnant (of Israel), "the elect" chosen by grace | vs. | the rest of Israel (11:1-10) |
| the "some" whom Paul can save | vs. | "the rest" (11:14) whom "God did not spare" (11:21) |

On this dichotomizing reading, the "kindness" of God manifests God's sovereign right to show favor to some, but not to others:

| the "kindness" of God "toward you," meaning the believers from the nations | vs. | the "severity" of God toward the fallen, meaning unbelieving Israel (11:22) |

Elizabeth Johnson rightly observes that "so long as all three questions are understood to address the same phenomenon—Jewish unbelief," and to do so with the goal of rescuing God's honor, "then the chapters take on the incoherent character of three unrelated and mutually exclusive answers to the same question"[90]—mutually exclusive, of course, only for those who, like Johnson, read 11:25-26 as expressing Paul's genuine belief that "*all* Israel" (not just a remnant) will be saved.

But this typological reading, with its assumption that Paul seeks to establish a division between "saved" or "elect" Israel (restricted to those who "believe" in Christ) and "the rest" (those who do not), fundamentally misconstrues his argument. As Johnson shows, Paul's concern is *not* to establish "who is in the family and who is out, but who is in charge and to what purposes."[91] His argument is directed to his non-Judean audience to correct their misapprehension of historical circumstances.[92] His argumentation is an example, like earlier parts of the letter, of what modern rhetoricians describe as the *dissociation of concepts*.[93] Specifically, Paul systematically distinguishes a *mistaken* apprehension of the present as the fulfillment of God's purposes—that is, reading present circumstances as if they exhaust God's mercy—from a *true* apprehension of the present as a period during which God's purposes are not yet fulfilled, but are still held in suspense. In what follows I present an alternative way of construing the oppositions in Romans 9–11.

———— The Present, the Future, and the Mercy of God ————

Already in Romans 8, Paul seeks to drive a wedge between the present and the future that will inform his argument in chaps. 9–11. In the present, members of the *ekklēsia* enjoy the gift of the Spirit and cry out in ecstatic celebration of their new status as children of God. Yet that status as children of God (*huioi, tekna*) is also their status as "heirs" (*klēronomoi*) of an inheritance they have not yet fully received. The Spirit who assures them of what they possess also comes to voice among them in groans of anticipation—like those of a woman in childbirth—of a greater event yet to come. The contrast is between present and future:[94]

the sufferings of the present age	vs.	the glory about to be revealed (8:18)
creation's present subjection to futility and corruption	vs.	creation's imminent liberation (8:18–25)
our possession of the "first fruits"	vs.	the redemption of our bodies (8:23)
what is seen	vs.	what is hoped for (8:24-25)

This contrast is also the point of Paul's lyrical assurance that "nothing can separate us from the love of God":

the potential power of hardship, distress, persecution, famine, sword, and so on as *present* powers arrayed against the elect	vs.	the absolute power of God to redeem "the elect" *in the future* (8:31-39)

Paul's abrupt turn in 9:1-5 to speaking of his anguish regarding his fellow Israelites gains much of its pathos from the lyricism of the preceding verses. Thematic connections across the artificial chapter break at 9:1 confirm that this is a single rhetorical unit.[95] The logical force of this sudden turn is the contrast between the present assurance of God's love enjoyed by those living "in the Spirit" and the present appearances regarding Israel:

the Spirit bears witness in the *ekklēsia* that "we are *huioi* of God" (8:15-17);	yet	the Spirit bears witness to Paul on behalf of those to whom *huiothesia* rightly belongs (9:1-5).

The point of the contrast is not that one group has been chosen to enter upon "sonship" and the other has not. The point is rather that one group *now* enjoys, but only by anticipation, what it is the rightful destiny of the other to achieve as well.

The tension is not between "who is in and who is out," but between who is in *now,* and who is destined to be in *soon.* That tension might be mistaken, if one judged from the false premise that present circumstances were the index of God's power to carry out divine purposes. Just that was the misjudgment of the non-Judeans in Rome (and of numerous Christian interpreters since). But Paul expressly states to the contrary that "it is not as though the word of God has failed." This is a dissociative argument distinguishing appearance from reality:

> the *appearance* that God's word   vs.   the *reality* that it has not (9:6)
>   has failed

Everything that follows should be read according to the same dissociative scheme. The typological reading discussed above sees Paul driving a wedge between "true" Israel and merely "ethnic" Israel in 9:6b: "not all Israelites truly belong to Israel" (NRSV). But this is a peculiar translation, not least because it omits the near demonstrative pronoun *houtoi.* The Greek, *ou gar pantes hoi ex Israēl houtoi Israēl,* is better translated "*these* Israel are not all of those who are from Israel." The phrase is awkward and early on prompted the substitution *Israēlitai* in some manuscripts: "these Israelites." But the sense appears clearly enough to be a distinction between a specific subgroup, "these," and "all Israel." Given the argument of preceding chapters regarding the significance of misconduct ("disobedience": *apistia*) on the part of "some" Judeans (3:3), the most likely referent of the pronoun is "these Israelites who *have* actually 'stumbled.'" Paul concedes—as he implicitly asked his Judean interlocutor to concede in 2:17-29 and 3:1-9—that some Judeans have scandalously embarrassed their people by their misconduct. He may have the Alexandrian rioters of 41 C.E. in mind, or those who were involved in disturbances in 49 C.E. But their identification is beside the point. His reticence about just who "these" are follows from his argument: whoever they are, whatever their actions, they do not determine the destiny of all Israel.

Paul declares that "not all the children are seed of Abraham," and distinguishes "children of flesh" from "children of promise" (9:7-8), leading the majority of Christian interpreters to conclude that his point is a fundamental opposition between "ethnic" Israel and "true," spiritual Israel (present in the church). But the point seems rather to be a contrast between the existing children of Abraham at a particular moment (initially, Ishmael), and those who God promises Abraham will be his heirs (through Isaac). Again, the contrast is present versus future:

> Israel's apparent demise, *if* God's   vs.   Israel's secure future, *since* it has
>   children are only those in exis-   always been a matter of promise
>   tence now, to be judged on pres-   (9:8-13)
>   ent circumstances

I will return in chapter 4 to the question of "works" (*erga*) in Romans. Here I simply observe that Paul's contrast between the calling of God and the consequences of human effort (*ex ergōn,* 9:12) does not involve a characterization of Judaism as such but functions as part of a dissociation of present appearances and future reality:

Israel's apparent demise, *if*	vs.	Israel's secure future, *since* des-
destiny were evident in present		tiny is the result of God's grace
achievement (*ex ergōn*)		(9:16-18)

As we have seen, Paul's introduction of the language of hardening and his meta-phor of the potter's sovereign authority to decide what sort of vessel to create, and to what end (9:20-23), is surprising in its dramatic intensity. God has hardened Israel! This language is also widely misunderstood, however, when the hardening of one group (Israel) is correlated with the language of fashioning "vessels of wrath," destined for destruction. The resulting equation of Israel with "vessels of wrath" is mistaken, however prevalent. Just as earlier in the letter Paul described God mercifully "passing over previous sins" *until now,* when God's justice will at last be revealed (3:25-26), so here Paul describes God mercifully bearing with vessels of wrath that are destined for destruction (9:22)—by implication, *until now*—so that God's wrath and power could be demonstrated—by implication, *imminently.* The vessels of wrath are the unrepentant wicked. The "vessels of mercy" that have been prepared for glory (9:24) are explicitly identified as "also us, not only from the Judeans but also from the nations" (9:24), but Paul has already identified those to whom "the glory" belongs *as Israel* (9:4). His point is not to dispossess Israel by claiming Israel's privileges for the church. Rather, the dissociation of concepts continues:

Israel's apparent demise, *if* the	vs.	Israel's secure future, *since*
present hardening of "vessels of		"hardening" is in the power of a
mercy" (that is, Israel) reflected		sovereign God who works for his
God's final rejection, and the		own glory, and will ultimately
endurance of "vessels of wrath"		bring to fruition the destined
(that is, sinners being tolerated)		destruction of some vessels and
reflected God's final election:		the destined glorification of oth-
but they do not;		ers (9:22-25)

Paul cites prophetic texts, first to show God's primordial purpose to make a people, *Israel,* out of nothing (see Hos 2:25; 1:9—2:1 LXX). Then he cites Isaiah to show, not that God's original purpose has collapsed into the preservation of a mere remnant, but that God has consistently preserved a remnant (*de* in 9:27 is con-junctive, not adversative). The NRSV insertion of "only" is gratuitous and wrong. Johnson rightly observes:

Isa. 10:22 and 1:9 function for Paul to compare Israel favorably with the rest of the world by pointing to God's continual rescue of the people. Without God's preemptive mercy, Israel's peculiar relationship to the Lord of Hosts would indeed have been lost many times over and Israel would have fared no better than Sodom and Gomorrah. This means that in chap. 9 Paul is looking at God's *past* faithfulness to Israel rather than predicting the future. That will remain for chap. 11. . . .[96]

—though the answer given in chapter 11 is already foreshadowed here in Paul's observance of God's faithfulness to Israel in the past.

A thrown race

"What then shall we say?" (9:30). If we read these chapters according to the common Christian typology, we would conclude that God has finally sorted humanity into the doomed and the elect, and that in this new dispensation the previous covenant with Israel has fallen on hard times. The Judeans have had their chance, and have blown it by their stubborn unbelief. But Paul says, to the contrary, that the present circumstances of Israel *are God's doing.* *God* has "hardened" Israel, for God's own purpose; *God* has interfered with a footrace in which Israel was clearly ahead, causing Israel to stumble and allowing "the nations"—who did not know they were pursuing a goal—to surpass Israel (9:30-31). It is therefore "silly or perverse," Stowers rightly remarks, "to ask, 'How could Israel have run the race so as to have won?'"[97]

Nevertheless, Paul gestures toward an explanation, and given the apologetic and polemical needs of the Christian tradition over history, it is perhaps not surprising that his statements here have been the object of tremendous scrutiny in efforts to describe Paul's "critique of Judaism." The impediment to Israel, the "stumbling stone" (9:33), is the Torah, which Paul says has been misapprehended by Israel. They have pursued it "as through works" (9:32). Though having zeal toward God, they have not acted from enlightenment. Being ignorant of God's justice they have failed to "submit" to it, and instead have sought to establish their own (10:3). Presumably they have not recognized that the Messiah is the goal of the Torah (10:4).

I will return in chapter 4 to the vexing question of "works" that complicates Paul's argument here and in other parts of the letter. Here it must suffice to point out that the same dissociative argumentation we traced in 9:6-29 is at work here as well. The fault of Israel, if one may call it that, is one of zealous impatience. Not knowing God's timetable, Israel has tried prematurely to bring about the conditions of the messianic age; they have "pursued their own justice." Far from referring to a chimerical "works-righteousness," whereby individual Judeans might seek to secure their own standing before God (a posture that Paul's Judean interlocutor in 2:17—3:9 explicitly repudiated), this phrase more likely describes Judean efforts to achieve the vindication before the nations that was promised in their own Scriptures.

But the Roman Empire also promised justice to peoples who accepted the "good faith of the Roman people." The mistake made by some Judeans in Alexandria in 38 c.e.—a mistake obvious to everyone in Paul's day—was to take imperial pretensions to justice at face value and to sue for equal rights under law. They were violently rebuffed. We do not know the causes of whatever disturbances provoked Claudius's edict in 49 c.e.; they may have involved similar agitation for the civic recognition of Judean rights that was so precious a prize for Josephus's apologetic writings. Whatever the aspirations on the part of the Judeans of Rome, they, too, apparently met severe refusal. A Judean like Josephus might have drawn from these episodes the lesson that Judeans must re-exert themselves and must try even harder to make the case for their belonging in the Roman world. Paul drew a very different lesson: it was ultimately futile to try to usher in the conditions of the messianic age through historical effort, that is, to "bring Messiah down" (Rom 9:6).

But Paul's chief concern is not to diagnose the inadequacy in Israel's thinking. His more urgent objective is to guide his non-Judean audience to a correct perception of Israel's present circumstances. God has been found by those who did not seek God—the nations (10:20, quoting Isa 65:1), but God has also stretched out his hands to an untrusting people, Israel (10:21, quoting Isa 65:2). This is—again—not a final determination of "who is in and who is out," but a description of God's persistent efforts to bring *both* Israel and the nations to salvation (the *de* in 10:21 is conjunctive, not adversative). God has not abandoned his people (11:1).

Paul offers himself (alone!) as evidence. The argument is, again, a dissociation of appearances from reality. His reference to himself alone makes the comparison with Elijah all the more poignant:

Elijah's mistaken *perception* that he alone was left	vs.	the *reality* (seven thousand who have not bowed the knee to Baal)
the mistaken *perception* that Paul alone, or with other Judean believers in Christ, constituted the total number of Israel to be saved	vs.	the *reality*: "at the present time" God has preserved a remnant, showing God's unwavering faithfulness to Israel (11:1-6)

Israel's stumbling does not cause the nations to "win," it only sets them in a position of advantage that will inspire jealousy on the part of Israel. This is not simply the message of Israel's scriptures, but Paul's own motivation as apostle to the nations (11:13–14). He may "save some of" his fellow Judeans, but the restoration of Israel as a whole is the ultimate horizon of his apostolic work (11:15). (Note that reference, in the aorist, to the "fullness of the nations" coming in [11:25] implies a set number: the whole of Israel implies no such limit.) Again, the argumentative dissociation of present versus future is at work: the sanctity of the "first fruits" implies that of the whole, as that of the root implies that of the branches (11:13).

The apparent stumbling of Israel and the surpassing of Israel by the nations	vs.	God's purpose: to make Israel jealous through the nations, thus to restore Israel alongside the nations (11:13-15)
the holiness of first-fruits	vs.	the holiness of the whole;
the holiness of the root	vs.	the holiness of the branches (11:16)

Already implied here is the warning allegory of the olive tree in 11:17–24. The same dissociative logic applies there as well:

the present *appearance* of "dead branches" (some of Israel) and of the nations being "grafted in"	vs.	the future *reality*: God has the power to graft on the dead branches, who being native to a cultivated tree will again become vital and fruitbearing; this is God's power to bring life from the dead. The nations, however, being grafted from wild plantings, can be removed from the tree without hope of being restored a second time (11:17-24)

Present circumstances are a guide to the future only if one knows the deep logic, the "mystery," which Paul reveals. Without it, the non-Judeans in Rome are able to draw only the conclusions to which the cold logic of imperial ideology leads them: those who appear in the streets as the *victi* of imperial power, the losers of history's proud march, are in fact God-forsaken. That conclusion, Paul warns, is a fatal mistake for it attributes to the empire the power to determine the future, and that power is God's alone.

The mercy of God must be construed aright. Nero's court claimed that the humble circumstances of Judeans in the streets of Rome were as much as the wretched of the earth could hope to receive from imperial mercy, and far more than they deserved. Against that claim, Paul contemplates a dramatic reversal that constitutes a repudiation of imperial logic. History's course has *not* reached its climax in the mercy of the emperor. Rather those who now *appear* to be enemies, *persona non grata* in the imperial dispensation, in fact suffer their present ignominy "for your sake." In reality, they are the elect, beloved "for the sake of the ancestors" (11:28):

the *appearance* that Israel's suffering is their due as "enemies"	vs.	the *reality*: Israel's present circumstances are "for your sake" (*di' hymas*); in fact Israel is "the elect, the beloved for the sake of the ancestors" (11:28)

This is the mystery Paul reveals to the Roman *ekklēsia*. History has not yet run its course. Rather, we stand at the very brink of the fulfillment of God's purposes. It is *God* who has brought upon Israel a temporary hardening, to achieve a broader redemption than anyone could anticipate, when God will have mercy on all. Until that moment, it is *God* who has "imprisoned all in disobedience" (11:31-32), just as it is God who has subjected the world to futility and corruption (8:20-21). It is an imperial boast—not a Judean one—that provokes the apostle's rebuttal.

*Abraham, depicted in a fresco from the syna-
gogue at Dura-Europos, ca. 239. Photo © Art
Resource, N.Y.*

CHAPTER FOUR

PIETAS

Piety and the Scandal of an Irreligious Race

"What then shall we say: have we found Abraham to be our forefather according to the flesh?"[1]

In recent scholarship Paul's invocation of Abraham "our forefather" in Rom 4:1 has usually been read as a rebuke to Judean notions of ethnic superiority and privilege. That interpretation more usually has been presumed than argued, however. It is hard to imagine any of Paul's Judean contemporaries answering that question, phrased just that way, in the affirmative. The search to substantiate a supposed ethnic chauvinism grounded in Abraham has yielded meager results.

Questions of ancestry, destiny, and piety coalesce in the figure of Abraham. But in a letter explicitly addressed to a *non-Judean* audience, we should be alert to the rhetorical question, *How does the figure of Abraham function in the argumentation of this letter?* We should be suspicious of the assumption that Paul can only have meant to target *Judean* presumption by invoking him. In fact, another pervasive ideology on Paul's landscape combined themes of ancestry, piety, and the destiny of peoples.

—— Ancestry, Destiny, and Piety in Roman Perspective ——

We cannot explain the cohesiveness and stability of the Roman Empire by appeal to the coercive force of Rome's military might alone. Rome was successful in winning the hearts and minds of at least some of its subjects.[2] Provincial elite expressed their loyalty especially through participation in the imperial cult, which was as enthusiastically promoted locally as it was imposed from without. Through the imperial cult, "the Greeks were able to represent to themselves otherwise unmanageable power."[3] The elite who actively cultivated honors for the gods of Rome thereby enhanced their own prestige as benefactors and thus reinforced their dominance over subordinate classes. Generosity—ritualized in the provision of games, feasts, civic buildings, and the distribution of food—proved "one of the most subtle means of maintaining lasting asymmetrical relationships between social unequals." Thus imperial cult and patronage went hand-in-hand.[4] The spread of civic cult to the Roman gods and the genius of the Caesars institutionalized a new religion, "the religion of the Empire taken very broadly," across disparate cultures in a new hybrid culture of the Roman Empire.[5] It was the premier means by which the provincials "Romanized themselves" and thus came to participate in the great vocation of the Roman people to civilize the world.[6]

The primary medium of the imperial cult was a widely disseminated, but remarkably consistent iconography. Images of the pious Augustus occupied the public squares of cities from Spain to Egypt. This imagery condensed a powerful cultural myth, carefully elaborated in propaganda and literature. That myth, most fully elaborated in Virgil's *Aeneid,* depicted Augustus as the conduit through which ancient promises given by the gods to Aeneas, his ancestor, would be fulfilled. The destiny of the Roman people would extend to embrace the peoples of the world. Thus piety and ancestry were caught up in a vision of the empire's vocation to civilize the nations. That was a vision Paul pointedly did not share.

Appropriating the iconography of pietas

That the all-devouring reach of empire was inherently *just* was self-evident to the ruling class.[7] It nevertheless required repeated public affirmation. Everyone knew that brute force had brought Octavian to power, force that remained a constant factor in the political configuration. That unprecedented power required legitimation. It was urgently necessary to obscure what had so dramatically been laid bare, the fundamental dynamics of a social structure in which men powerful enough to muster huge armies warred against each other for control of the whole, amassing tremendous capacity to exploit and terrorize whole peoples.

Augustan propaganda and the mass production of imperial imagery (in statues, coins, and architecture) successfully presented that power as just and holy. Order, peace, and security had been restored, not only through the military force that had destroyed Antony's navy and driven him and Cleopatra to suicide, but through Octavian's ceremonial renunciation of the power he had seized—and the Senate's immediate grant to him of even greater power as a reward for his magnanimity. Augustus recited this evidence of his own humility at length in the *Res gestae.*

Thus the tremendous power of a voracious ruling class was consolidated in the single figure of the "Augustus," veiled as the embodiment of unparalleled justice, mercy, and reverence for the gods. Appropriately, the new stability of the *Pax Augusta*—"stability, in the sense of the dominance of the Roman propertied classes"—required not military statuary, but the representation of the emperor as the very soul of austere Roman piety.[8] One image, more than any other, would have won instant recognition from people living in any city in the Roman Empire in the mid-first century. That image, one of three standard types of statuary copied and distributed throughout the empire, was the most widely reproduced image of Augustus. Whereas earlier images had shown him in armor, emphasizing his military prowess, or even dared to depict him with the nude torso of a god, this preferred image depicted him in a long, voluminous toga, its hem pulled up over his head in the instantly recognizable Roman gesture of sacrifice. This was Augustus as the embodiment of piety.[9]

In his study of *The Power of Images in the Age of Augustus,* Paul Zanker related this image to Augustus's self-description in the *Res gestae*: "I was *pontifex maximus, augur,* a member of the fifteen commissioners for performing sacred rites [*viri sacris faciundis*] and one of the seven for sacred feasts [*viri epulonum*], an arval brother, a *sodalis Titius,* a fetial priest."[10] Zanker comments that from the 20s B.C.E. onward, Augustus clearly wished to be depicted in his toga, "at sacrifice or prayer"; his purpose was to make it clear "that he considered the performance of his religious duties his greatest responsibility and highest honor."[11] But more was at stake than the representation of the emperor as a man of deep private devotion.

Augustus the pious, his toga pulled over his head in the universal Roman gesture of sacrifice. Marble. First century C.E. From the Via Labicana. Museo Nazionale Romano (Terme di Diocleziano), Rome. Photo © Art Resource, N.Y.

The image of Augustus the pious "obviated entirely the delicate question of Augustus's power and the problem of its visual expression."[12] Indeed—paradoxically—his piety became the preferred explanation for his military defeat of his rivals and his acceptance of unprecedented political powers,[13] a phenomenon with contemporary parallels.

In the *Res gestae,* Augustus detailed not only the sacred duties he personally accepted, but his efforts to revive Rome's traditional religion. All these efforts had transparently political implications. By restoring the city's most ancient shrines (not necessarily its most popular), he evoked Rome's legendary founder, Numa, who was regarded as having embodied that characteristically Roman devotion to the gods that justified the Roman people's hegemony over other nations.[14] Augustus's consolidation of priestly colleges achieved the same effect as his elimination of ceremonial triumphs: it provided him a monopoly on the "symbolic capital" of Roman religion.[15] To whatever extent Augustus's own personal morality might have informed his legislative "reforms" regarding marriage and morals, these also gave the state an unprecedented role in what had previously been a private moral sphere. They allowed Augustus to enfold his unprecedented hold on power in a cloak of moral conservatism that would appeal to the older nobility on whose support he depended. Aimed particularly at the upper classes, these laws served to reinforce a common ideological theme as well, representing the rule of the powerful as rule by those who were the moral and spiritual superiors of the conquered.[16]

It was a mainstay of imperial court propaganda that since the advent of Augustus, the world had been awash in the rhythms of worship.[17] But the point of the ubiquitous imagery of Augustus as sacrificer was not the proliferation of sacrifice as such; it was the identity of the *one offering sacrifice,* the emperor. The *Ara Pacis,* the Altar of Augustan Peace, erected in the Field of Mars by the Senate from 13 to 9 B.C.E. makes the point clear. The reliefs that run across the (original) south side of the enclosure wall depict a host of Roman senators and dignitaries in togas, all following in procession behind Augustus, his family, and the chief priests of the Roman colleges on the way to sacrifice. The image was not intended as an object of memorialization. As Richard Gordon observes, imperial representations of the emperor at sacrifice do not depict an actual moment in the ritual process; rather the point is to identify the person of the emperor as the supreme officiant in sacrifice.[18]

Further, as Gordon, Paul Zanker, and S. R. F. Price have pointed out in separate studies, the proliferation of the Roman imperial cult, with the iconography of the pious Augustus at its center, made it possible for provincials to represent themselves as benefactors of their communities. By ritually emulating the piety and patronage of the emperor, they participated in the web of Roman power. "The institution of sacrifice was one of the key means whereby some kind of synthesis was effected between the religion of Rome, in the narrow sense, and the religion of the Empire taken very broadly. It became a sort of code for membership."[19]

The pietas *of Aeneas*

But more is going on in the carved reliefs of the *Ara Pacis*. The juxtaposition of the imagery of the sacrificing emperor with another sacrificing figure condensed a more complex mythical narrative. In a frieze on the west side of the enclosing wall, the Trojan hero Aeneas is depicted offering sacrifice to his father's gods upon reaching land in Italy. The juxtaposition of Aeneas and Augustus, both offering holy sacrifice to the gods of Rome with their togas pulled over their heads in prayer, conveys their relationship as ancestor and descendant.[20] But whereas Aeneas stands in primitive austerity, attended by two servants, Augustus leads a splendid "modern" procession of Rome's ruling class. The juxtaposition highlights the sacred power of the present order in which ancient promises given to Aeneas that he would be the ancestor of a great race, who would rule the world, have been abundantly fulfilled.

Left: *The Sacrifice of Aeneas; note the shrine to his father's gods.* Right: *A procession of priests and the imperial family, led by Augustus's ally and expected successor, Marcus Agrippa, accompany Augustus on his way to sacrifice. Reliefs from the* Ara Pacis *(the Altar of Augustan Peace). Museum of the Ara Pacis, Rome. Photo © Alinari / Art Resource, N.Y.*

The Aeneas frieze on the *Ara Pacis* depicts a small shrine in the background, presumably representing the ancestral gods that Aeneas rescued from the burning Troy.[21] The reference is to the act that sealed Aeneas's role as ancestor of Rome, narrated in the *Aeneid*. Surrounded by the blazing walls of a doomed city, Aeneas had listened to his father declare his willingness to die rather than survive capture by the Greeks. Tormented and without hope, Aeneas prepared to throw himself against the Greeks in a desperate act of vengeance; his wife pleaded with him to take her and their child with him so that they might die together, the last of the

Trojans. Just then, his father Anchises "turned his eyes to the stars and raised his palms to heaven," pleading with all-powerful Jupiter that "if our *pietas* earn it, give us your aid."

> Scarcely had the aged man thus spoken, when with sudden crash there was thunder on the left and a star shot from heaven, gliding through the darkness, and drawing a fiery trail amid a flood of light. We watch it glide over the palace roof and bury in Ida's forest the splendour that marked its path; then the long-drawn furrow shines, and far and wide all about reeks with sulphur. At this, indeed, my father was overcome and, rising to his feet, salutes the gods, and worships the holy star.[22]

The omen convinced Anchises of the gods' protection for the legacy of Troy. Aeneas lifted his frail father, who clutched the household gods, up onto his shoulders, scrupulous to avoid touching the gods himself since he had just come from bloody combat. Taking his son's hand, he bade his wife follow at a safe distance behind him and headed out into the blazing city. When next he looked back, Creusa, his wife, was no longer behind him; he never saw her again. But he successfully rescued his father, his father's gods, and his son from the sack of Troy and brought them at length, under the watchful eye of Venus, to the shores of Italy.

The Senate's juxtaposition of Aeneas and Augustus on the *Ara Pacis* was hardly an innovation. The motif of Aeneas carrying his father and son from burning Troy—itself a popular artistic motif for centuries—had already adorned a coin issued under Augustus's adoptive father, Julius Caesar. Of more decisive significance, Virgil had made the comparison to Augustus explicit in the *Aeneid*.

Aeneas had been a secondary figure in Homer's *Iliad*, characterized by tremendous piety toward the gods and destined, Poseidon declared, to rule over his

Aeneas carries Anchises and his household gods from burning Troy; depicted on a denarius issued under Julius Caesar, 69 B.C.E. Münzkabinett, Staatliche Museen zu Berlin. Photo © Bildarchiv Preussischer Kulturbesitz/ Art Resource, N.Y.

people.[23] As "the one Trojan hero who has a definite future before him," his legend was elaborated until, in the wake of Rome's conquest of Greece, Romans sought a founder for themselves "in the cycle of Greek legend, but among the enemies of Greece."[24] Virgil provided the epic poem, centered on Aeneas and the "great struggle to establish the Roman people," as a founding myth for the Principate, "Rome's first, greatest, and only lasting salvation history."[25]

Publius Vergilius Maro had been 29 years old when, in 41 B.C.E., Octavian confiscated his father's lands to help pay off his veterans (and thus settle suddenly unemployed mercenaries as his own clients). Whatever loss Virgil had sustained, his father's wealth and equestrian status had already secured him the education and social connections that would enable him to launch a successful literary career.[26] He was drawn into the charmed circle of Maecenas, something of an informal minister of culture to Octavian even before he was made Augustus. That circle was responsible for producing the ideology of a golden age in the making.[27] Virgil stamped all his art with the confidence of an aristocracy that had weathered war and economic loss, but anticipated restoration. The exuberant proclamation of a golden age in his fourth *Eclogue* celebrated the rise of a new social order with the accession of a new consul in 40 B.C.E.[28] Later, under the indirect patronage of Augustus, his writings took on a more soberly, industrious tone. As Karl Galinsky observes, the golden age of Virgil's *Georgics* and the *Aeneid* was not a paradisal age of leisure. For Virgil, the golden age "implies both a social order and an ongoing effort": it is "the result of *labor*," of "unrelenting toil." "The *Aeneid* does not celebrate fruition . . . but stresses the ongoing process that ultimately will lead to the accomplishment of a lasting, civilized order,"[29] a heady promise for the aspiring elite in the provinces.

The figure of Aeneas is the sacred type of whom Augustus is the antitype. The typology is at work from the very start of the *Aeneid,* when Neptune calms a great storm at sea that had threatened to destroy Aeneas and his Trojan band. The effect is compared with the power of a single great man, "honored for noble character and service," to calm the enraged masses and bring social peace; Virgil's readers inevitably would have thought of Augustus.[30] Later references to Augustus are explicit. After his father's death, Aeneas journeys to the underworld, where Anchises shows him the glories to come: there is Augustus, the "son of a god," who will again establish a golden age in Latium and expand the empire of Aeneas's descendants.[31] Still later, Vulcan equips Aeneas for battle with a glorious shield on which he has embossed scenes of future victories, including Octavian's defeat of Marc Antony at Actium (in a scene that echoes Aeneas's own trials at sea) and his triumphant entry into Rome.[32] The typology explains even the otherwise baffling brutality of the *Aeneid*'s closing scene, in which Aeneas, overcome with fury, dispatches his Italian enemy Turnus. The violence to which the pious Aeneas is driven in order to avenge his comrades and secure his posterity's reign is "a reflection in advance" of the extreme to which the pious Augustus would be pressed to avenge his own father and to put down the worldwide enemies of Roman peace. "The motive for revenge is the same for both, the press-ing claims of *pietas*."[33]

This is a particularly potent representation of piety. It sanctifies the violence necessary to order the world, the warfare that achieves peace. (From the impe-rial point of view, there was nothing incongruous about the Altar of Augustan Peace being erected on the Field of Mars, god of war.) This piety, embodied in the person of Augustus, is the eschatologically necessary condition for the dawning of the golden age, in which ancient prophecies entrusted to the ancestor Aeneas would at last be fulfilled. And this piety made it possible for others to be incor-porated in that glorious fulfillment, their participation in ritual and patronage guaranteeing their place in the great extended household of which Augustus was himself the father.

--------------------- Abraham "Our Forefather" ---------------------

In Romans 4, Paul offers a strikingly different narrative, featuring a rival ances-tor for the nations: Abraham. Thanks to Richard B. Hays's careful work on inter-textual echo in Paul's letters, we recognize that an earlier tradition of Christian interpretation, which read Abraham as the prototype of justification by faith ver-sus justification by works, was mistaken. That "Lutheran" reading had already been profoundly shaken by E. P. Sanders's demonstration that the traditional caricature of Jewish works-righteousness was a historically groundless caricature, driven by a dogmatic and polemical agenda. Hays showed that Paul asks about Abraham, "not because Paul wants to refute the view that Abraham was justified by a 'work' (circumcision) but because Paul regards Abraham as a representative figure whose destiny contains the destiny of others," as "the father of Gentiles as well as Jews." Abraham is not merely an "archetype for Gentile believers," he is their *ancestor* (4:11-12, 16-21). Paul makes the point himself: faithfulness was reckoned to Abra-ham for right-standing *"so that* he might be the father of all who are faithful . . ." (*eis to einai auton patera pantōn tōn pisteuontōn*, 4:11). Abraham's paternity is not a metaphor; Paul means it quite literally.[34]

The urgent rhetorical-critical question at Rom 4:1 is, Why does Paul discuss Abraham's ancestry in a letter addressed to non-Judean believers in Rome? Here, unfortunately, the answers given by Hays and by various advocates of the "New Perspective" are less than satisfying.

Hays rightly protests that Paul is *not* "expounding a message that stands in an antithetical relation to Judaism"; he is *not* "playing Christianity off against Judaism or the gospel against the Old Testament."[35] To the contrary, Paul is "speaking from *within* the Jewish tradition." Paul wants to argue that Judaism itself, *rightly understood,* claims its relation to Abraham not by virtue of physical descent from him (*kata sarka*) but by virtue of sharing his trust in the God who made the promises.

So far, so good. But who needs to hear this reassertion of a fundamentally Jewish message? Hays points in the direction of the advocates of an inferior form of Judaism:

> *Only a narrowly ethnocentric form of Judaism,* Paul insists, would claim that God is the God of the Jews only or that Abraham is the progenitor of God's people "according to the flesh," that is, by virtue of natural physical descent. For the purposes of his argument, Paul associates these (evidently false) notions with the (disputed) claim that Gentile Christians must come under the Law.[36]

But this imports an artificial construct into the text. Paul "insists" nothing of the sort. He says nothing about "a narrowly ethnocentric form of Judaism"; nor, for that matter, does anything in Romans indicate that pressures on non-Judeans to judaize are at work in Rome. Hays reads Romans 4 "juxtaposed to an ethnocentric misreading" of Abraham, presumably meaning a reading actually current within "a narrowly ethnocentric form of Judaism," but does not bother to substantiate the hypothesis.

Because many of the scriptures that Paul quotes in Romans are concerned with God's vindication, Hays argues that the larger theme of the letter, into which Paul's discussion of Abraham is integrated, is "an argument about theodicy." "The driving question in Romans is not, 'How can I find a gracious God?' but, 'How can we trust in this allegedly gracious God if he abandons his promises to Israel?'"[37] However, Hays does not elaborate further on just where that "driving question" comes from. As we saw in chapter 3, the burden of theodicy that Paul takes up in Romans 9–11 was unlikely to have come from the non-Judeans in Rome. They must, to the contrary, be warned not to "boast" about having replaced Israel (11:13-25); they seem capable enough of trusting a "gracious" God who has left Israel in the dust!

Hays seems unconcerned to coordinate Paul's argument in Romans with a particular audience in Rome, because he reads the letter as something of an intense theological soliloquy on the part of the apostles: "This text is most fruitfully understood when it is read as *an intertextual conversation between Paul and the voice of Scripture* . . . Scripture broods over this letter. . . ." Hays admits that presumably the letter is somehow addressed to a contingently historical situation, but he is not concerned to describe it: "Paul tells us little about that situation," at any rate. "Once the conversation begins"—meaning, the conversation between Paul and Scripture, which the Roman audience is allowed to overhear, for reasons after which Hays does not inquire—"the addressees recede curiously into the background, and Paul finds himself engaged with an older and more compelling partner," that is, Scripture.[38]

But from the start, this is to surrender the question of the letter's rhetorical coherence, in order to read it as an internal theological meditation on the justice of God. In contrast, an adequate rhetorical approach to the letter must ask what the discussion of Abraham does to advance an argument to the letter's explicit address-ees—those whom Paul has identified as "the nations" (*ta ethnē*).

Abraham's ancestry from a Judean perspective

Hays offers that Paul is

> laboring to refute the charge—whether rhetorical or historical—that *he,* as the promulgator of a startling new teaching incorporating uncircumcised Gentiles into the people of God, has abandoned the ways of the God of Israel. His anxiety on this score is betrayed by his uncertainty whether his offering (and his message?) will be acceptable to the Jewish Christians in Jerusalem. ... (Rom 15:31)[39]

—but again, Paul says nothing to indicate that he is laboring to refute a charge regarding his "startling new teaching," or indeed that any such charge has been made. (As we have seen in chapter 3, the rhetorical questions that sometimes read as "objections" from Judean opponents are, in fact, Paul's use of leading questions according to the conventions of a diatribe.) Hays bases his suggestion regarding Paul's "ethnocentric" opponents on Rom 15:31. But Paul says nothing there to indicate that the "unpersuaded [*apeithountes*] in Judea" are specifically opposed to his inclusion of non-Judeans in his *ekklēsiai,* and Paul has said nothing earlier in Romans to indicate that he has written this letter with those unpersuaded Judeans particularly in view.

Despite his claims to read Romans inductively,[40] Hays introduces a hypothesis regarding the letter's purpose that relies on circular reasoning. Romans is Paul's defense against the champions of an "ethnocentric" form of Judaism who have accused him of apostasy; there must have been such opposition—for why else would Paul oppose them in this letter?

Two other problems beset Hays's discussion (which I take to be representative of the best of New Perspective scholarship). First is the question of historical veri-similitude. Although the supposition is common in contemporary scholarship, we should not imagine that Judean opposition to Paul's inclusion of non-Judeans in his assemblies would have been likely. To the contrary, Paula Fredriksen points out that the inclusion of non-Judeans alongside Judeans in the eschatological com-munity would *not* have been a "startling new teaching" for many of Paul's Judean contemporaries. The notion that non-Judeans would join Judeans in worship of Israel's God was a common theme in the prophets and Jewish tradition. Furthermore, "Jews could and did eat with Gentiles," Fredriksen points out, as the Mishnah amply illustrates. "The Law-free Gospel to the Gentiles was not Paul's original contribution to early Christianity"; the Jerusalem apostles accepted it (Gal 2:1-10),[41] and if other Jews (the "circumcision party") later sought "to consolidate the community within Judaism" by pressing for "Gentile *conversions*," it was because they perceived a failure of the eschatological "timetable" initially shared between Paul and the Jerusalem apostles—not because they were involved in an "ethnocentric misreading" of Torah.[42]

Further, it is anachronistic to imagine that first-century Judeans would have held to the "narrowly ethnocentric" misreading of Abraham in Genesis that Hays postulates as the target of Romans. Pamela Eisenbaum observes that in patrilineal cultures, such as first-century Judaism, "social constructs are required for the establishment of paternity." Physical childbirth was regarded in many cultures as an occasion of pollution that could only be removed by sacrificial action performed by a man. Relying on Nancy Jay's study of genealogy and sacrificial rituals, Eisenbaum observes that "sacrifice generally makes possible the stripping away of the limits of biology and mortality (associated with women) so that one can enjoy membership in an eternal social order." All kinship is fictive; "*biology is not the determinative factor of kinship structures.*" More to the point with regard to Romans, "*As a Hellenistic Jew* Paul knows implicitly that one's genealogy is not coterminous with biology."[43] In rabbinic Judaism, it was the rite of circumcision that "constitute[d] the boy as a legitimate descendant of Abraham." Hellenistic Jewish culture, like Greek and Roman cultures, was patrilineal in that members "trace[d] their ancestry back to a single male ancestor, designed to provide society with a coherent social identity." Abraham was a clear example, but there are abundant parallels in Greek and Roman communities as well.[44]

Eisenbaum agrees with Hays that Paul invokes Abraham as an *ancestor,* not as an exemplar of a particular way of being religious. But, she observes, that ancestral connection "is only the beginning of [Paul's] argument, not its culmination." Paul's argument resembled "the common Hellenistic Jewish tradition that Abraham was the first proselyte, a reasonable interpretive deduction" from Genesis. "Therefore the descendants of Abraham cannot be exclusively Jewish," *on the grounds of Jewish scripture itself.*[45] Hellenistic Judaism already emphasized Abraham's status as "the first proselyte" from idolatry. Thus, no Judean would have imagined that the descendants of Abraham were exclusively Judean.[46] Paul's juxtaposition in Rom 9:8 of "children of the flesh" and "children of promise" means "that biological descent and ordinary human reproduction do not, cannot, will not bestow genealogical status requisite to being a member of God's family"—but Paul's contemporary Jewish interpreters already affirmed that. Abraham, they knew, was "the father of multiple nations."[47]

These observations make it even more difficult to imagine that Paul's argument is directed against a supposed "ethnocentric form of Judaism." "Contrary to popular belief," Eisenbaum notes,

> Paul does not think Jews are Abraham's biological descendants (*kata sarka*, to use Paul's language), while Gentiles become descendants by "adoption" (*hyiothesia*). He uses the term *hyiothesia* explicitly of Jews in Rom 9:4.

No Judean—neither Paul nor any reasonably competent reader of Scripture among his fellows—would have imagined that descent from Abraham was a matter of physical descent. To the question, "Have we found Abraham to be our forefather according to the flesh?", the Judean would have answered, resoundingly, "By no means!"

Using Abraham to think ethnicity

Another problem with Hays's reading of Romans 4 is its troubling construction of ethnicity, meaning Judean ethnicity, in general, and Paul's ethnicity, in particular. Here again, Hays's presentation deserves scrutiny because it represents a wider pattern in much contemporary scholarship. Paul is read as representing Judaism "rightly understood," a "universal" or "inclusive" perspective *"within the Jewish tradition,"* over against a "narrowly ethnocentric" Judaism that "misreads" Torah. The problem with this pattern is that despite Hays's effort to avoid setting Christianity in opposition to Judaism, he implicitly aligns Judaism "rightly understood" with Paul, over against the Judaism practiced (so far as Hays indicates) by all other Judeans. One possible implication is that contemporary Jews are the inheritors of an "ethnocentric misreading" of Torah on the part of Paul's Judean contemporaries.

Judaism "rightly understood"	vs.	a "narrowly ethnocentric" Jewish "misreading" of Scripture,
"universalism" and the inclusion of non-Judeans	vs.	exclusivist Jewish "ethnocentrism"
Paul (Christianity)	vs.	unspecified Jewish opponents (Judaism)

I hasten to point out that Hays himself is careful not to make the last opposition. But the implication remains a troubling consequence of a broader trend in contemporary scholarship. As we have seen in chapter 1, Denise Kimber Buell and Caroline Johnson Hodge observe that Paul often is read as a pivotal figure in the transition between Judaism and Christianity, "the evolutionary link between an ethnic and a non-ethnic, universal kind of religion":

He is understood to be "ethnically" a *Ioudaios* yet seen either to eliminate its soteriological significance or to subdivide the category of *Ioudaios* into a hierarchical pair: spirit/flesh, privileging the spiritual component but rejecting the relevance of the fleshly. This kind of distinction most often conveys a negative view of Judaism because Christianity's universalism is defined as an improvement on the particularity of Judaism: Christianity is here correlated with the spiritual and Judaism with the "flesh." . . . [48]

Pauline Christianity is depicted as "a universal, voluntary movement that specifically rejected the significance of ethnoracial identification for membership and thereby 'broke' from its Jewish roots." This necessarily implies a contrast with Judaism as an "involuntary and particular" form of community. Buell and Hodge continue: "Interpreting Christian universalism as non-ethnic enables Christian anti-Judaism by defining a positive attribute of Christianity (universalism) at the expense of Judaism. Judaism as portrayed is everything Christianity is not: legalistic, ethnic, particular, limited, and so on."[49]

To be sure, an interpreter like Hays might protest—quite rightly—that he has *not* set Paul over against Judaism; to the contrary he has been careful to insist that Paul writes from "*within* Jewish tradition."[50] But Hays has not identified any other representatives among Paul's contemporaries of the class "Judaism rightly understood." Indeed, he takes Paul's insights to be unique (he refers to the apostle's "startling new teaching").

Buell and Hodge are on target in their criticism of New Perspective interpreters when they point out that even when Paul is discussed in terms of "differences among Judeans" (as when Hays places Paul "*within* the Jewish tradition"), interpretation may fail "to overcome . . . anti-Jewish implications." Pamela Eisenbaum observes the same tendency, even among scholars identified with the New Perspective who have "tried in earnest to take Paul's Jewish identity seriously." Too often they fail to do so "in as thoroughgoing a manner as is often claimed": they tend instead to understand Paul as "Jewish *kata sarka,* that is, he was ethnically Jewish," but "no longer religiously Jewish." For those Eisenbaum terms the "*kata sarka* scholars," Paul was "so radically transformed by his experience of Christ that he moved outside the bounds of Judaism, or at least he moved so far to the margins that he ventured into something no longer recognizably Jewish."[51] (Hays might object that it was not Paul's "experience of Christ" *alone,* but the interaction of his experience of Christ with his now transformed encounter with Scripture, that led him to the limits of Jewish thought.) Indeed, we should hardly expect anything else, given Eisenbaum's acute observation that "the study of Paul—more than the study of Jesus—continues to be the arena of discourse where Christians (and recently some Jews) work out their religious identity." Contemporary debates about Paul's Jewish identity "are emblematic of the ongoing attempt by Christians to define their religious identity vis-à-vis Judaism."[52]

As I noted in chapter 1, we continue to use Paul—and Paul's reading of Abraham—to think with. The interpretive move to oppose Paul's transcendence of ethnicity to "a narrowly ethnocentric"—but nonetheless characteristic?—form of Judaism implicitly positions the interpreter above the limits of ethnicity that mark *others*. The liberal ideal of establishing universal values that transcend ethnic difference—and ethnic particularity—is tremendously powerful in Western society; but that liberal ideal also marks the limits of discourse as constrained by capitalist ideology. *Ethnic* differences may be perceived and "transcended" in a vision of multicultural harmony; but differences in *power* and *class* may thus be elided from view.[53]

The destiny of an "impious" people

But if Paul is not targeting a supposed ethnocentric form of Judaism, what *is* the purpose of his invocation of Abraham?

The solution lies in the rhetorical question that precedes 4:1: "Or is God the God of Judeans alone? Not also of the nations? Yes, also of the nations, if God is one . . . !" (3:29-30). The question is echoed in Paul's affirmations regarding Abraham's ancestry, not of those descended from circumcision alone but also those who follow in Abraham's footsteps, though uncircumcised (4:11-12). The point is clearly that Abraham is ancestor of the nations, including the non-Judean members of Paul's audience in Rome. But this affirmation is not aimed polemically against some ethnocentric Judean boast. Far from being a *challenge* to Jewish sensibilities, these questions embody that most central of Jewish affirmations, the *Shema*.[54] As Mark D. Nanos has observed, the oneness of God *necessarily* means, on Jewish premises, that God is God of the nations as well, for "if [God] is not the One God of all outside Israel who believe in him, then he is not the One God of Israel; he is not the One God at all."[55] Eisenbaum sums up the logic of Paul's argument this way: "Now, if a Jew's status before God does not depend on biological lineage, then surely such lineage is not required for Gentiles either."[56] But she also shows that every Judean would have shared that premise.

The target of Paul's argument is the non-Judean, who is explicitly addressed in the letter and whose boasting over a supposedly fallen Israel is Paul's principal target (11:13-25). It is *their* misunderstanding of Judaism to regard Abraham's ancestry as limited to the (vanquished) Judeans. Expressed more pointedly, Paul addresses an audience whom he expects is tempted to think of genealogy in a deterministic way, and of Abraham's ancestry, in particular, as unworthy.

We have seen in chapter three that the perception of Judeans against which Paul strives in this letter was not simply the result of fewer of them being present in the Roman *ekklēsia*. The material conditions in which Rome's Judeans lived, especially after the expulsion of 49 C.E., were evidence, *from the standpoint of imperial ideology,* that they were a people "born to servitude." Paul argued against the

presumption that the Judeans whom Nero characterized as the unworthy beneficiaries of his own mercy presumed upon the mercy of God as well.

But as we saw above, imperial ideology also explained that the power and privilege enjoyed by the Roman people was the result of their piety that was concentrated in the figure of the Augustus. Piety and destiny were indissolubly linked.
Pietas had drawn to Aeneas the favor of the gods, guaranteeing the glorious destiny
of his descendants. *Pietas* had ensouled the divine Augustus, enabling him to bring
to fulfillment the ancient promises given to Aeneas. And *pietas*—enacted in public
benefactions and sacrifice as these were combined in the imperial cult—characterized the loyal participants in the blessings that Augustus had provided.

The obvious corollary was that the vanquished had earned their place through
their lack of piety. The Alexandrian delegation to the emperor Gaius had made
that express charge regarding the Judeans who dared to intrude on the gymnasium:
they were *anosioi Ioudaioi*, "impious Judeans." Gaius had indulged the accusation,
for only an atheistic people could have failed to recognize his divinity. Jews were
decidedly *not* pious, from the perspective of the empire. They despised the gods;
they preferred to worship an empty chamber (or worse) within the Jerusalem Temple, demonstrating that they were in fact atheists; they preferred their own peculiar
and superstitious customs. Their faith repelled a cultured Roman like Seneca not
only because it was irrational and offensive, but because it was the religion of a
defeated people (*victi*).

Piety and impiety, *eusebeia* and *asebeia,* were hotly contested terms in the
Judeans' long campaign to win acceptance on the civic landscape of the Roman
Empire. Shortly after the catastrophe of Alexandria, and perhaps not long before
Paul wrote Romans, a Hellenistic Judean penned a treatise on reason that exalted
the Judeans martyred by Antiochus Epiphanes. When the tyrant had required that
the Judeans disobey God by sacrificing to an idol and eating pork, taunting the
aged Eleazar that he could not be a philosopher and observe so inferior a religion,
the old man replied that the Judeans could hardly betray their reputation for piety,
to which the law commanded them. He returned the insult: "You may tyrannize
the impious," he declared, "but you shall not dominate my religious principles,
either by words or through deeds" (*4 Macc.* 5:38). The last phrase foreshadowed
the torture that would follow. One after another, the narrator declares, the aged
Eleazar, seven young brothers, and their mother defied the tyrant, who appealed
to them to abandon their ignoble superstition; one after another, they proclaimed
their own piety (*eusebeia*) and in the judgment of the author, demonstrated it by
accepting martyrdom rather than yielding. One after another, they proved they
were true sons of Abraham.[57]

God vindicates those who are faithful, Paul declares uncontroversially. But he
continues: to those who, though not working, trust the one who vindicates the
impious, their faithfulness is reckoned for their vindication (4:5). This, surely, is
scandalous. But we must interpret the scandal carefully. Paul did not mean everything that the Lutheran doctrine of the "justification of the ungodly" requires

him to mean. After all, he described impiety (*asebeia*) earlier, in 1:18-32, without suggesting that it could be redeemed; to the contrary, God's wrath was revealed against those who in their impiety and injustice suppressed the truth (see chapter 2). Neither is it apparent that Paul expects his midrash on Genesis here to demonstrate that Abraham himself was objectively "ungodly" or impious before he had received circumcision. If his purpose here were by midrashic maneuver to construct an "ungodly Abraham" in order to explode a characteristic Judean boast, the argument would be so idiosyncratic as to be rhetorically nonsensical. But Paul does not oppose Abraham the faithful, uncircumcised non-worker to Abraham the poster child for an imaginary Jewish works-righteousness *or* a Jewish ethnic chauvinism.[58]

As Pamela Eisenbaum has suggested, Paul referred to Abraham as *asebēs* to indicate his origins among the idolatrous Chaldeans.[59] If there was a Judean boast in the figure of Abraham, it was neither a legalistic nor an ethnocentric boast, but a *theological* one. Paul's contemporaries, whether Judean or non-Judean, would have known that Abraham came from Ur and that he had left his city, his country, and the gods of his family behind in order to obey God's call. In the *Liber antiquitatum biblicarum* 6 he refused to cooperate in the idolatrous construction of the Tower of Babel. In *Jubilees* 11–12, he recognized that idolatry was empty and astrology was futile; his zeal in obedience to God even led him to destroy the local shrine of the Chaldean gods. Philo hailed him as a wandering hero who rejected the foolishness of worshiping stones as gods (*Virt.* 218–19); Josephus's portrait of Abraham was similar (*Ant.* 1.154–57).[60]

These antecedents suggest that in 4:5, Paul uses the term *asebēs* ironically. He invokes Abraham precisely as the ancestor of those who *appear* impious because they have left Rome's gods behind; but they are in fact *faithful,* as Abraham was, because they have turned to the living and true God—the God capable of bringing life from the dead (4:19-21). He means thus to urge the non-Judeans in the Roman *ekklēsia* to own their descent from Abraham, alongside the beleaguered Judean community. Refusing the imperial identification of piety with power and privilege, they should accept their own status as *impii* in the eyes of Rome and lift their own eyes to the horizon of the future, just as Abraham did. This will constitute their "reasonable worship" (12:1-2), which is the reverse of the actual *asebeia* described in 1:18-32.

Abraham as Aeneas's Rival

"Paul and Abraham share a calling," Eisenbaum declares, in that both are called by God "to a purpose that benefits not only them and their families, but also the rest of humanity." Most important, both are involved in the conversion of the nations from idolatry: Abraham as the prototypical proselyte, Paul as the apostle charged with securing the faithful obedience of the nations. Eisenbaum presses the comparison further, arguing that "Paul positions himself as a new kind of patriarch, capable of unifying the multitude of nations who are already potentially related to one another through Abraham." He "creates Abrahamic descendants," not through biological reproduction "but through his preaching and teaching. He is a verbal progenitor." Paul saw himself, she concludes, as "a new Abraham."[61]

This captures the connection between Paul's apostolic work and the generative role of Abraham as "father of many nations." But posing Paul as a "new Abraham" obscures precisely the unique generative role of Abraham. As Eisenbaum herself notes, Paul "creates *Abrahamic* descendants"—not his own. Regarding Paul as a "new Abraham" also risks obscuring the unique role of Christ's sacrifice as the event that makes it possible for new members to be incorporated into the community of Abraham's descendants.[62]

We come closer to understanding the role of Abraham, the faithful but "impious" ancestor, in Romans if we take into account the pressure of imperial ideology on the situation to which Paul wrote. That pressure was characterized in part by a particular way of attributing the destinies of peoples to the meritorious piety of their ancestors. We may compare the respective roles of two ancestral figures in their respective salvation histories: Aeneas, the pious ancestor of the Roman people, represented above all in the *Aeneid* but also in the ubiquitous imagery and ritual of the Roman imperial cult; and Abraham, the "impious" ancestor—not of the Judeans alone, but of the nations as well, as Paul argues in Romans 4:

Fig. 4.1. Rival ancestries for those destined to inherit the world

Aeneas the pious, who in response to a heavenly omen carried his father, his son, and his ancestral gods away from the burning Troy, bringing them safely to Ilium;

Abraham the impious, who abandoned heavenly omens and left his father's gods behind to follow God in trust that he would receive a new posterity;

Augustus the pious, whose vengeance against his father's murderers secured peace for all who share ritually in his sacrifice;

Christ, whose death made possible the incorporation of "many nations" as Abraham's descendants;

the local officiants in the imperial cult, who through sacrifice extend the benefactions of the Augusti

Paul, whose priestly duty it is to present the "offering of the nations" in Jerusalem

Of course, Paul never mentions Aeneas or Augustus. All of the explicit "intertextual echoes" in Romans are to Israel's scriptures. But bear in mind the tremendous prevalence of cues linking Aeneas, Augustus, and the fates of the peoples in imperial statuary and ritual, on coins and in public and private art celebrating the Aeneas myth, and in the ubiquity of the *Aeneid* itself. Bear in mind the tremendous importance accorded these links in imperial ideology. And bear in mind the saturation of these themes in the popular culture, so much so that theater audiences in Rome could be expected immediately to recognize even brief quotations from the *Aeneid* written into a play,[63] and it appears we should consider another form of intertextual allusion to have been at work when Paul's audience heard Romans 4. We should expect that the rhetorical question, "have we found Abraham to be our forefather according to the flesh?" would have struck at least some in his audience as peculiar, since they would have been thoroughly accustomed to think of *Aeneas* as the ancestor of the family of nations, and Abraham—if they thought of him at all—as the ancestor of the Judeans alone. But that is precisely the perception Paul is laboring explicitly to counteract.

Piety and "vindication through works"

This comparison illuminates the vexing question of the "works of the law" in Romans. That theme runs like a scarlet thread throughout the letter. Paul has insisted that "apart from law God's justice has been revealed" (3:21), and that boasting before God is excluded, not by a law of works but by a law of faithfulness (3:27-28). He framed his discussion of Abraham in terms of a contrast between the one who works for a due reward and the one who does not work, but "is faithful to the one who sets right the impious" (4:4–5). Later he declares that although Israel pursued a "law of vindication" (or of justice: *nomon dikaiosynēs*), they failed to reach that law, because they strove "not out of faithfulness but as if out of works" (9:31-32). It has seemed clear to countless generations of interpreters, influenced by the Christian theological tradition, that the fundamental opposition in Paul's letter is between "justification by works" and "justification by faith," and that these align fairly naturally with the practice of Judaism that has led to Israel's stumbling and rejection of the Messiah, and to the emergence of a believing church of non-Judeans, respectively.

justification by works	vs.	justification by faith
law	vs.	grace
(Judaism)	vs.	(Paul and Christianity)

One problem with this neat picture is that we cannot substantiate the premise it requires: namely, that Paul's Judean contemporaries thought of "works of the law" as a means of achieving saving merit before God. To the contrary, E. P. Sanders's demonstration that such "works-righteousness" was not evident in any Second Temple Jewish writings (except, arguably, for the anomaly of *4 Ezra*, which is later than Paul anyway) provoked the crisis in Pauline interpretation that the New Perspective seeks to resolve. While Judean writings certainly abound with references to the tremendous importance of obeying God by doing "the works of law" or "works of justice," and with assurances that such obedience will be rewarded in the final judgment,[64] it is impossible to distinguish those affirmations from what Paul himself declares in Rom 2:6-16.[65] What, then, does Paul oppose when he contrasts vindication through faithfulness with vindication through works of law?

James D. G. Dunn launched the New Perspective with his proposal that the phrase referred not to a legalistic attitude but to the deeds that the law required of Israel, which had come over time to be understood as reinforcing "the sense of Israel's privilege, . . . the law as marking out this people in its set-apartness to God, . . . protecting Israel's privileged status and restricted prerogative." Especially, then, the term referred to practices like circumcision, Sabbath, and diet that distinguished Jews from their neighbors.[66] However, the phrase is not used that way outside of Paul's letters; in fact the language of being "justified" by "works of law" only occurs elsewhere in the curious document 4QMMT, where it refers to particular rulings on Temple rituals that separated one Jerusalem sect from another. The document says nothing of distinguishing Judeans from non-Judeans, and in fact is of little help for our question.[67]

Lloyd Gaston observes that the language of seeking vindication (or "justification") by "works of law" occurs only in letters in which Paul addressed non-Judean audiences. It functions in Galatians as part of the apostle's polemic against the inclination of non-Judeans to judaize (which for Gaston and John G. Gager means not conversion to Judaism, but a partial, selective adoption of signal Judean practices).[68] While this is a helpful corrective to the mistaken theological habit of presuming that "works of law" language always refers to Judaism as such, it is not as helpful in Romans, where judaizing practices are not evidently in view. In Romans, Paul says the members of Israel have mistakenly tried to pursue "their own vindication," striving "not out of faithfulness but as if out of works" (9:31-32).

It is of the utmost importance for interpreting this phrase to keep in mind the wider political situation of the Judean communities under Roman rule. Jacob Taubes focuses the issue brilliantly when he writes that the concept of *nomos* in Romans takes up a formula for "compromise" on the part of various peoples, incorporated with their various ethnic customs and national laws, into the Roman Empire.

> All of these different religious groups, especially the most difficult one, the Jews, who of course did not participate in the cult of the emperor but were nevertheless *religio licita* . . . represented a threat to Roman rule. But there was an aura, a general Hellenistic aura, an apotheosis of *nomos*. One could sing it to a Gentile tune, this apotheosis . . . one could sing it in Roman, and one could sing it in a Jewish way.

Taubes cites Philo and Josephus as examples of "singing" the hypostatized understanding of *nomos* "in a Jewish way."[69] The phenomenon is familiar to historians of

Judaism in the Hellenistic age. John J. Collins describes it as "the common ethic" among Diaspora Jews:

> Jewish apologists like Philo and Josephus could boast of the extent of Moses' fame but were also extended in their efforts to remove the scandal of his laws and reconcile them with Hellenistic culture. In fact, while the Mosaic law always retained an authoritative position in Jewish life in the Diaspora, its role was by no means a simple one. It could be treated selectively, by highlighting some laws and neglecting others, and it could be buttressed with philosophical and religious foundations, which were remote from the original Torah. The variety of Diaspora Judaism and its peculiar character can be appreciated in the light of the ways in which it adapted the traditional laws.[70]

If we may speak of a Judean effort to seek vindication through "works of law," that phrase appears more appropriately to refer to a widespread campaign on the part of Hellenistic Judeans to interpret and to practice their law in ways that harmonized with the Hellenistic ideal of a common *politeia*. If Hellenistic culture had promulgated an intense and pervasive ideology of works—that is, of *eu-ergeia*, benefaction[71]—Roman imperial ideology had appropriated that ideology for portraying the emperor as the supreme benefactor. The *Aeneid* extolled the importance of hard work in bringing in the golden age (and in so doing obscured the role of military conquest, exploitation, and forced labor). Augustus portrayed himself as the consummate practitioner of "works-righteousness" in the widely disseminated account of his own "works" (*praxeis*), the *Res gestae*. It was a Roman theology of vindication through "works of law" that pervaded the environment of the Roman congregations and those congregations themselves.

It was a Roman theology of "works" that had led some Judeans in Alexandria to attempt to secure their rights in terms of Roman law, no doubt exhibiting their own achievements and capacity for future benefactions to the city. They had been decisively rebuffed. So had their careful diplomatic appeal to Gaius. More assertive mass protests in Judea had forestalled the erection of Gaius's statue in the Temple, but only until the emperor's death removed the threat. Claudius had expelled some number of Judeans: there is no indication in our sources that any figment of due process was observed, or any consideration given of the rights of Judean individuals or of the community as a whole. Perhaps Paul seeks to draw the lesson of recent history when he declares that "Israel pursuing a law of vindication did not attain to law—because [they exerted themselves] not out of faithfulness [to God] but as if from works" (9:31-32).

Their error had nothing to do with a flaw inherent to their religion or their culture. To the question, "What is wrong with Judaism?" Romans provides no answer. The error of some Judeans—the characteristic error of Israel under Roman rule, as Paul generalizes it—had everything to do with the options available in an imperial situation. The Judeans had gambled on the trustworthiness of Roman law, hoping to find in the civic recognition of their faithfulness to their own laws that Roman law was indeed a "law of justice" (*nomos dikaiosynēs*). That, Paul says, they did not find.

Justice, he asserts, comes from God alone. Because everyone is "under sin," no one should expect to be vindicated out of works of law (3:20, 28). That is, the appropriate posture in a world subjected to futility is rather the hope for coming glory, which is manifested in endurance in the face of present affliction (5:1-5). If some stand in God's good favor it is because of the faithfulness of Jesus the Messiah, in which they share (3:21, 30-31). This faithfulness involves waiting patiently, expectantly, on the God who can reverse present circumstances—who can even raise the dead. Of those who show such faithfulness, Abraham is the genuine ancestor.

The expectation that haunts Romans is not aggressive pressure from the synagogue to judaize; it is the arrogant presumption of Roman imperial culture that any who wish to be respected will demonstrate their worth by conforming to the regime of benefaction and patronage. Paul calls his audience to abandon that expectation and instead to hold to the hope that "does not put to shame" (5:5).

IUDAEA CAPTA: *A coin struck under the emperor Vespasian celebrates the destruction of Jerusalem in 70 c.e., depicting Judea as a disconsolate woman seated beneath a palm tree. Israel Museum (IDAM), Jerusalem. Photo © ArtResource, N.Y.*

CHAPTER FIVE

VIRTVS

Virtue and the Fortunes of Peoples

It is a tendency of imperial ideology to portray the present disposition of power and privilege as the culmination of the human story, to collapse the great unrequited struggle of history into a simple contrast of before and now. But in order to represent the status quo as just and equitable, imperial ideology must account for disparities of power in terms of disparities of worth, according to an at least implicit hierarchy of peoples.

Roman imperial ideology promulgated just such a hierarchy, with the descendants of Aeneas at the top and unworthy peoples—including the Judeans—beneath them (see chapter four). The rhetoric in Romans is set against this implicit hierarchy, yet Paul cannot mount an argument "based in the structure of reality" because, from Paul's point of view, present circumstances provide only meager and misleading data.[1] The exhortations in Romans 12–15 are grounded in an "apodeictic" rhetoric of demonstration that appeals beyond the present, indeed that seals off the present from contact with the genuine destiny of peoples. This ideological closure is achieved through the gestures of Judean apocalypticism.

Virtue at the End of History

Soon after he arrived in Rome in the late first century C.E., the socially ambitious provincial Plutarch sought to ingratiate himself to prospective friends with a fawning piece of panegyric, *On the Fortune of the Romans*. In this speech, Plutarch posed the rhetorical question whether Rome's supremacy was due more to Virtue (*Aretē*) or to Fortune (*Tychē*). Plutarch suffered no illusion that virtue was its own reward. However admirable, and however well represented in the host of Rome's past worthies, Virtue had a reputation for failure to crown its brightest adherents with success. Fortune, on the other hand, was widely regarded as unreliable, even capricious. "Virtue's labors, they say, are fruitless, Fortune's gifts untrustworthy." To which should the pride of Rome's sovereignty be ascribed?

143

Plutarch answered, unsurprisingly, *both*. "By joining forces," Virtue and Fortune "co-operated in completing this most beautiful of human works," the Roman
Empire. Thus he claimed to vindicate Virtue as "most profitable" because she had
"done such good to good men," and Fortune as "a thing most steadfast" because
"she has already preserved for so long a time" Rome's marvelous, beneficent power.
It could not have happened any other way; this, Plutarch declared, was divine destiny. Rather than abandoning the human race to the "swell and drift" of history,
the "shifting conditions of human affairs," Chronos had chosen to bless with Fortune the one people in whom Virtue "in every form was inborn"—the Romans.[2]

Some years earlier, another provincial, the Judean Joseph ben Mattathias (Josephus), had expressed similar ideas as he implored his fellow Judeans to abandon
their defense of besieged Jerusalem. The practical argument was obvious: "the
might of the Romans was irresistible," as other nations had already discovered.
"An established law" of brute force governed human affairs: "Yield to the stronger," since "the mastery [*to kratein*] is for those pre-eminent in arms." But Josephus
offered another, more palatably theological argument. Fortune (*Tychē*) had passed
over to the Romans. "God who went the round of the nations, bringing to each
in turn the rod of empire, now rested over Italy." The Romans had already shown
their moral superiority by holding themselves back from destroying the Temple,
while the rebels risked its destruction by defying Rome from its walls. The Romans,
he pleaded, were "naturally lenient in victory," and indeed were the Judeans' "own
true allies." Yet the Romans had been drawn to Judea to oppose "the impiety of
the land's inhabitants," that is, the partisan strife of the Hasmonean dynasty, and
so God had "subjected to the Romans those who were unworthy of liberty." How
much worse, Josephus cried, were the rebels.[3]

Neither Plutarch nor Josephus can be described as intellectually adventurous in
these passages. Both expressed the banal realism of those who imagine they stand
at "the end of history," confident that the future will be only a continuation of
the present and that such a future will be, for them at least, satisfactory. The final
and proper disposition of the wretched of the earth was accomplished. That the
world's peoples were ultimately better off under the stern but necessary discipline
of empire was, for both men, a foregone conclusion. Their perspective must have
seemed obvious to countless subjects of Roman imperialism, who could readily
draw the appropriate lesson from the face of history. As Terry Eagleton observes,
the ideological strategies of empire serve to naturalize hegemony and to make present power relations appear inevitable.[4]

Virgil, a much subtler mind than either Plutarch or Josephus, could allow the
voice of dissent to ring in his epic; but the *Aeneid* is the exception that proves the
rule. As Aeneas and his Trojan horde march against the capital of the kingdom
they have invaded, royal Juno addressed the council of Olympian gods to protest
their aggression. "Did any man or god constrain Aeneas to seek war and advance as
a foe" upon the kingdom of the Latins, or to "stir up peaceful peoples?" She admitted the Trojans had been wronged, their city destroyed. But

what about the fact that the Trojans are attacking the Latins with smoking torches, that they are overrunning the fields of other men and are driving off the booty? What about laying claim to a father-in-law and leading an espoused maiden away from the arms of her lover, begging peace with their hands while mounting weapons on their ships?[5]

Good questions, these, which aroused murmurs of agreement from the assembled gods, and might have caused a momentary cloud of doubt to pass over the mind of a good Roman reader. But Jupiter answered them with a thundering equanimity. He would not take sides:

> Whatever fortune everyone enjoys today, whatever hope each one . . . entertains, I will regard with no distinction, whether it is by the destiny of the Italians that the camp is besieged, or by some unfortunate error of Troy or some unsound advice. . . . Each one's beginnings will bring labor and fortune. Jupiter is the same king for all men. Fate will find a way.[6]

The protest of innocence is disingenuous, given Jupiter's decisive intervention throughout the preceding narrative. But it bore home an ideological truth as important for Virgil as for Plutarch and Josephus. The eventual triumph of the Roman people was the inevitable result alike of fate and of their own virtue. They had won the "labor and fortune" of world domination. We see at work in the *Aeneid* the force of ideology as what Fredric Jameson has called a "strategy of containment," accommodating and neutralizing the possibility of dissent from Roman domination.[7] The peoples, the narrative implies, had had their chance, in a history governed by an impartial heaven. One people had emerged victorious, and to them the future rightly belonged. The thought that the others might still play a role in shaping their own history was repressed: for Nero, into the stuff of nightmares, as Suetonius relates.[8]

In our own day, an official of the U.S. State Department has announced our arrival at "the end of history" after the fall of the Berlin Wall and with it, the perceived collapse of any alternative to the liberal democratic order and the selective economic freedoms of global capitalism.[9] There appear no imaginable futures other than the inevitable unfolding of the "free market," as we have learned to call the global economic order that is imposed by a deft combination of military, diplomatic, and economic force. That *ideologically asserted* free market daily assimilates more and more of the world's *actually existing* free markets into the stern and arbitrary discipline of "structural adjustment."[10]

In the powerful West, the initial exuberance of standing at the "end of history" has faded somewhat after the terrible blow of September 11, 2001, which is widely viewed as a turning point in history. That it was, Noam Chomsky observes, insofar as the target on that terrible day was not "one of the . . . traditional victims of international terrorism"; to the contrary, the attacks showed that rich and powerful nations "no longer are assured the near monopoly of violence that has largely prevailed throughout history."[11] But the rhetoric that has saturated our airwaves since that day—of an endless war between good and evil, between the virtue of a free people and the dark forces arrayed against it—presumes the same ideological premise as the "end of history": There is no feasible alternative to "the freedom" that the United States represents and imposes.[12]

For the majority of the world's people, that date brought no fundamental change in circumstances, except that they now seem even more inexorable. "There exists only one lord and master, and only one system," theologian of liberation Franz Hinkelammert declared already in 1995. That system is the "wild" or "savage capitalism" that wreaks havoc throughout Latin America and beyond. "The empire," meaning the neocolonial empire of global capitalism, "is everywhere. It has total power and it knows it. . . . The consciousness that an alternative exists is lost. It seems there are no longer alternatives."[13] From the imperial center, the global struggle is perceived as a combat between good and evil, virtue and tyranny; but from other points of view, the line of demarcation seems clearly to follow the gradient of power. Outside of those centers, the drama remains one of exploitation and misery, and virtue does not appear to be the monopoly of the powerful.

An apocalyptic logic of dissent

We have seen in earlier chapters that the truths proclaimed by Roman imperial ideology were not universally recognized. Not all Judeans shared Josephus's perception of Roman virtue. Perhaps a century earlier, the author of the Habakkuk Pesher had detected in the first encounters with Roman intervention nothing but arrogance, brutality, and limitless greed. Nor did he feel any need to justify Roman domination theologically. It was enough to know that God would at last condemn the conquerors, and to describe the unexpected prolongation of that final accounting as a matter of divine "mysteries" (*razim*).[14]

It is tempting to regard Josephus, by comparison, as a rank and cynical opportunist, an apostate, even as a traitor.[15] But rather than inquire as to Josephus's psychology or level of patriotic feeling, we might as reasonably ask how the author of the Habakkuk Pesher managed to avoid what to many of his contemporaries must have seemed self-evident. Claiming to present, on the strength of inspired interpretation, the true meaning of ancient Scripture, the pesharist declared the true destiny of peoples. The present was only a historical aberration, of necessarily limited duration. Apocalyptic rhetoric provided a strategy of containment that allowed the pesharist and his community to perceive present circumstances not as determinative of the future, but as a temporary deviation from God's ultimate disposition of human affairs.

If history had indeed reached its end, then that end meant, for the poor, unrequited heartbreak. Philo described feeling that heartbreak when his delegation stood before the dismissive and contemptuous emperor Gaius, aware that his policies toward the Judeans of Alexandria and Judea itself would bring swift and utter ruin to his people everywhere. It would have seemed natural for Paul to feel it as he contemplated the status of the Judean community of Rome, broken and defamed as the miserable and unworthy recipients of Nero's pity. In Roman eyes—and (I have argued in earlier chapters) in the eyes of some of the non-Judean members of the *ekklēsia* to whom he addressed this letter—the Judeans were to be numbered among the vanquished. If history had reached its end, as imperial ideology proclaimed, then the "mysteries" of which the author of the Habakkuk Pesher spoke were nothing else but the inscrutable *mysterium iniquitatis.*[16]

But both Judeans—Paul and the author of the Habakkuk Pesher—relied upon apocalyptic *topoi* to insist that history had *not* reached its end. Mystery was the apocalyptic category to which Paul, too, resorted at the climax of his letter:[17] "So that you may not claim to be wiser than you are, brothers and sisters, I want you to understand this mystery" (11:25). This *mystērion* concerns the *true* meaning of present circumstances, a meaning not available to observation but only as it is Paul's to reveal: "a hardening has come upon a part of Israel."

As we saw in chapter three, a dissociative logic shapes Paul's discussion of Israel's "stumbling" throughout Romans 9–11. His purpose there was to distinguish between *present appearances,* and the false conclusions to which they might lead, and *reality,* which will be fully manifest only in the future, but is already clear enough to those who (like Paul) understand Scripture and thus can discern history's paradoxical true meaning. As we also saw in chapter three, the failure to recognize the dissociative nature of Paul's argument in Romans 9–11 has often led to an erroneous, and historically disastrous, typological reading, according to which Paul here explains the logic of election (or exclusion) by which God has indeed allowed the majority of Israel to "stumble so as to fall." Israel's history, on this reading, has already run its course.

I referred in the Introduction to the "apodeictic" character of Paul's rhetoric, meaning his appeal to what Aristotle called inartificial proofs (such as laws, testimonies, and oracles: for Paul, Scripture). Paul appeals to the Spirit's witness to the truth he seeks to reveal—

I am speaking the truth in Christ. I am not lying; my conscience confirms it by the Holy Spirit.... (9:1)

—and invokes scriptural "promises" as more real than mere historical circumstance:

It is not the children of flesh who are the children of God, but the children of the promise are counted as descendants.... (9:8)

He calls his hearers to abandon what seems obvious and to understand instead that God is revealing a paradoxical and counterintuitive reality:

But if God, desiring to demonstrate [*endeixasthai*] his wrath and to make known [*gnōrisai*] his power, has endured with great patience the vessels of wrath that are made for destruction; and has done so in order to make known the riches of his glory for the vessels of mercy...? (9:22-23, italics added)

Opposing visions of the destinies of peoples. Left: *The goddess Venus appearing to Aeneas. Illustrated manuscript of Virgil's* Aeneid *(Biblioteca Apostolica Vaticana, Vatican Museums, Vatican State; photo © Snark/Art Resource, N.Y.).* Right: *The prophet Ezekiel receives revelation from God; fresco, ca. 239 C.E., from the synagogue in Dura Europos, Syria (photo © Art Resource, N.Y.).*

The manifest character of this reality—its being shown, that is, "made known"—clearly remains in the future. For now, appearances can be deceiving. Those who have been "endured with much patience"—that is, *the disobedient among the nations*—might appear, through the lens of imperial ideology, to be heaven's favorites. Those who have not yet been revealed as the "objects of mercy"—that is, those who are called, including Judeans and obedient men and women from the nations (9:24)—might appear at present to be history's God-forsaken victims.

But Paul reveals, through a mystery, the actual state of affairs. God had imposed a temporary hardening upon Israel in order to bring about a breathtaking alternative future that would include the nations and a restored Israel together. Paul cannot refer his hearers to what appears self-evident, but must appeal instead to the clear testimonies of Scripture and the Spirit, which witness that "the gifts and calling of God are irrevocable" (11:29). He calls his audience to resist the mind-set of the present age and contemplate the "the mercies of God" (12:1-2), which as he has just demonstrated (11:25-36) are not what they might seem. He bids them offer themselves to God in a "reasonable worship" (*logikē latreia*), being enabled by the renewing of their minds to perceive God's will (12:1-2).

Other Judeans in Paul's day made similar appeals, in similar terms, urging their hearers (or readers) not to confuse present circumstances with God's providential will. The martyrs under Antiochus were able to defy the tyrant, the author of *4 Maccabees* explained, because the law had already instructed their minds. Reason—*logos*—ruled over their senses. Their knowledge—despite the evidence around them—that their defiance would be rewarded, and the tyrant's oppression punished eternally, empowered them to endure his tortures without yielding. It bears notice that the *logos* that the martyrs exhibited was completely *alogos,* irrational, by the standards of the Greek king. This was a contested *logos:* The martyrs could demonstrate that this *logos* reigned in their minds only by their submission to torture and death. The tyrant and his officers "marveled" as the Judeans refused perfectly reasonable and sympathetic appeals for them to consider their own persons, their family, and their community. Despite the author's use of the vocabulary of Greek philosophy, the "logic" of the defiance ascribed to the martyrs is premised on an apocalyptic vision of a coming reversal of fortunes. Their deaths will be avenged, and they will live in eternal blessedness.

Only at the end of a "most philosophical" discussion does the author betray the ferocity that occasioned his writing, very probably in the wake of the pogrom in Alexandria in 38–41 C.E. (see chapter three). "For these crimes"—ostensibly, the deaths by torture of Judeans on a "bitter day" during the reign of Antiochus IV, *in the second century B.C.E.*—the author declares that "divine justice pursued, *and will pursue* the accursed tyrant."[18] The tyrant to be pursued in the future tense can only be a Roman.

Philo similarly challenged his readers not to perceive with the bodily senses, which "discern [only] what is manifest and close at hand." Doing so, they might draw from the enormity of recent events the wrong conclusions, and end up miserably "ruled by the present." Rather he calls on them to perceive with reason, *to logismos,* which will reveal to them that "the Deity takes thought for human affairs," and especially for Israel.[19]

For Paul, as for these Hellenistic Judeans who are his closest literary contemporaries known to us, the "reasoned" discernment to which he calls his hearers is informed by an apocalyptic logic. The exhortation in Romans 12–15 depends upon the argumentation in earlier chapters, especially the climactic chapters 9–11. But despite the keen interest of Christian interpreters in elaborating the relationship of "indicative and imperative" at this argumentative hinge,[20] the rhetorical connection here is not a theological abstraction. It has a situational *and ideological* specificity, as do the comparable dissociative gestures made by Philo and the author of *4 Maccabees.* The mercies of God (*tōn oiktirmōn tou theou,* 12:1) are specifically the strategic mercies whereby (according to Paul) God has maneuvered Israel out of position in order to bring about the inclusion of the nations (9:32-33; 11:22-23).[21]

The exhortation in Romans 12–15 is grounded in the dissociative argumentation that has preceded it. In Romans, as for Paul's Judean contemporaries, the appeal to apocalyptic categories of revelation and mystery served as an ideological strategy of containment that effectively represses "the unthinkable."[22] The notion that God had actually abandoned Israel was beyond contemplation for Paul (*mē genoito!* 11:1). But closing off that prospect—which seemed evident enough to some among Paul's hearers—required closing off the apparent course of history itself, so to speak, so that present circumstances could *not* be read as indicators of the course of the future. "God has imprisoned all in disobedience," Paul declared (11:32). The present is not the inevitable result of some process in which heaven has let history run its course (as it was for Virgil). Rather, the present is the result of God's arbitrary, paradoxical, and decisive intervention. God has *interrupted* the course of history so as to suspend it; and God as abruptly will bring about the long-promised fulfillment of God's own purposes ("showing mercy to all," 11:32) in a break with the present as sharp as the raising of Jesus from the dead. It is not an accident that Paul praises God's inscrutable mystery in a quotation from Second Isaiah. There is a dramatic analogy between the assertion, on the part of the apostle and the prophet, of a future wholly discontinuous with the present.[23]

An ethic of solidarity

If we failed to recognize the dissociative argumentation that informs Paul's exhortation, we might regard the appeals in Romans 12 as private, appropriate to "the 'inner room' of the transformed, . . . the cult room and its atmosphere of 'brotherly love'":[24] so writer Halvor Moxnes. Moxnes recognizes that Paul shares with others a critique of the competitive honor-and-shame system of Roman culture, opposing *sōphrosynē* to *hyperphronein* and urging his hearers not to think of themselves more highly than they ought to think (12:3). But Moxnes limits that exhortation to the sphere of the congregation; it is an ethic "primarily addressed to internal relations within groups of Christians."[25] Necessarily so, for Moxnes reads the subsequent exhortation to be subject to the governing authorities (13:1-7) as straightforward evidence of "Paul's acceptance of the system of honor" that played out on the public square in Roman society, "with the emperor at the top, followed by his representatives and city officials." On Moxnes's reading, Paul accepted in the public sphere the same system that he repudiated in the private sphere of the church because his church was "in a dependent situation"; his critique of the honor culture "therefore had certain given limits," and "could only be expressed within the area of self-determination."[26] But the apocalyptic logic that shapes Romans 1–11 precludes so static a reading of the exhortation in 12–15. The coolly balanced acceptance of "private" and "public" spheres is exactly what the apocalyptic strategy of containment renders unthinkable.

Similarly, if we discounted or ignored the apocalyptic texture of Paul's argumentation, we might compare Paul's statements about the governing authorities (13:1-7) in a flatly literal way with the tradition of popular Hellenistic philosophy on kingship. Thus Bruno Blumenfeld has compared "the political Paul" with a supposed "'standard' political doctrine" in the Hellenistic and Roman eras, which he draws from a tradition of Hellenistic treatises among the philosophical schools, all heavily dependent upon Plato and Aristotle (and all easily aligned with what we should call—though Blumenfeld does not—the "public transcript" in the Hellenistic and Roman periods).[27] Blumenfeld himself acknowledges the rigidly hidebound character of this tradition,[28] but does not explain why anyone should look to so moribund and intellectually isolated a tradition, "a small heap of miserable scraps—a defunct collection of boring or trivial cogitation of only archival interest,"[29] to illuminate actual political and ideological realities in Paul's world, let alone the thought of the apostle himself.[30] Observing that within the "increasingly artificial and incongruous" tradition of Hellenistic treatises on kingship—

the narrow vein of material to which he has restricted himself—"the intellectual critique of the empire" was "feeble," and that there "really [was] the feeling that there [was] no substitute for Rome," Blumenfeld makes the same generalization for the wider political landscape in Paul's day. But as we have seen, that statement is easily falsified by observing oblique expressions of defiance among Paul's Judean contemporaries. By comparing isolated phrases in Paul's letters with phrases in a tightly circumscribed body of materials, Blumenfeld concludes that "Paul loves Rome" and belongs to a tradition of "apologetics for Roman power." In a flagrant anachronism, he characterizes Paul as "the ideological guardian of the processes and structures of imperial power" on the basis of the way Rom 13:1-7 was later appropriated by the Christian Byzantine empire.[31] But Blumenfeld provides only a particular egregious example of the common modern temptation: to project onto Paul the perfect hindsight we enjoy at a safe distance from the crisis of his time,[32] and thereby to derive from Paul a "Christian theology of the state."

If we failed to acknowledge the apocalyptic coordinates of Paul's exhortation in 14:1—15:13, we might read this part of the letter as Paul's answer to a flatly halakic question about the status of foods. His verdict "in the Lord Jesus" that "nothing is unclean in itself; but it is unclean to anyone who thinks it unclean" (14:14, 20) certainly sufficed for the Gentile Christianity that believed it had achieved unity through Christ's cancellation of the law (either by his word, Mark 7:19, or through his death, Eph 2:11-16). But as Mark D. Nanos rightly protests, if we read Romans in this way, we stigmatize the Torah-observant Judean as "weak in faith" by virtue of their scrupulosity—something Paul himself warns "the strong" *not* to do (in 14:1-4).[33] Interpreters who characterize "the weak" as "over-sensitive Jews" with "'hyper-halakhic' anxieties," who because of their "narrow-minded cowardliness" "fail to trust God completely and without qualification," have fallen into what Nanos calls "Luther's trap": they perpetuate, and attribute to Paul, the very attitude Paul seeks to oppose.[34]

The issue between "weak" and "strong" was much more than halakic, though it clearly sprang from Judean observance of the food regulations of the Torah. There is ample evidence to suggest that at least in some quarters of the Rome to which Claudius's exiles returned, observance of *kashrut* would have required Judeans to practice a de facto vegetarianism.[35] Roman satirists mocked Judean observances, including vegetarianism and the observance of days, and associated them with "weakness."[36] Mark Reasoner has shown that the label "weak" in Romans 14 was a contemptuous term wielded in the larger status-conscious Roman society against those who displayed excessive scrupulosity, especially if they belonged to a foreign cult. "It appears that the 'strong' applied the Roman society's evaluation of superstition on this group within their community."[37] Paul never contrasts "weak in faith" (*ton asthenounta tē pistei*, 14:1) with "strong in faith" (as if the disparity was a matter of the measure of faith). Rather "the strong," or "the powerful" (*hoi dynatoi*), is the self-perception of those able, by position and privilege, to distinguish themselves from the "weak" (or "sickly"), upon whom they could look down disparagingly. The "weakness" of "the weak" is due to their observance of kosher laws, but Paul never describes that observance as a matter of inadequate response to God and forbids "the strong" from doing so.[38] Indeed, Paul takes the side of "the weak" and prohibits the powerful from disputing over opinions (14:1), showing disdain for those who abstain from food (14:3, 10), or scandalizing the abstaining brother or sister (14:13). Paul does not congratulate the "powerful" but instead admonishes them to practice an abstinence of their own, holding back from any food that would scandalize their neighbor at a common meal.

Unity at the common meal is not the horizon of his exhortation, however. That horizon is the moment of judgment when the one who eats and the one who abstains must both stand before their Lord (14:4, 10-12). Paul looks to an eschatological horizon when the Judeans and the nations will stand together in praise of God, and this is why they must "welcome one another" now (15:7-12).

That eschatological horizon is fundamentally at odds with the Roman vision of the nations united in offering tribute to Caesar. Paul's exhortations throughout 12–15 are grounded in his concern to incorporate the Roman congregations in his own priestly service, the "offering of the nations" that he has collected from other congregations in Macedonia and Achaia and that he now prepares to take to Jerusalem (15:14-29). But that priestly service clashes inevitably with the cultic performances meant to unite all peoples in worshipful subservience to Rome.

The exhortation in Romans 12–15 goes far beyond the goal of ethnic unity in the Roman church. Paul confronts the ideological construction of a hierarchy of peoples, the discrimination of "powerful" and "weak," peoples "honorable" and "put to shame," that was daily ritualized in the Roman cult. Though the admonition to "not think of yourself more highly than you ought to think but to think with sober judgment" (12:3) was of immediate relevance within the congregations, it necessarily clashed with the values of Roman public life that were at play in those same congregations. Contributing to "the needs of the saints," that is, through Paul's collection, and extending hospitality to strangers (12:13) required opening up the social circles of the household and the tenement-assembly to others, not only in the city but internationally. The exhortation, usually translated "associate with the lowly" (12:16), speaks in Greek of "making one's way with the oppressed": the noun *tapeinoi* is routinely translated as if it were a category of social status in other literature, including the Septuagint.[39] This is a solidarity not easily confined to the house-church. Necessarily, these exhortations led to the contemplation of opposition from others, even to suffering evil from enemies (12:17-21), and then in turn to the contemplation of confrontation with the representatives of Roman power (13:1-7).

The force of ideological constraint in Romans 13:1-7

Just here, Paul draws back—fatefully, as far as the history of interpretation is concerned—from offering advice for the inevitable confrontation with Roman authority, or even from offering criticism of their conduct of office. The exhortation in 13:1-7 is an infamous *crux interpretum,* not least because of the instrumental role to which it has been put in neutralizing Christian dissent to unjust policies.[40] Despite the occasional interpreter who simply accepts these lines as an uncomplicated endorsement of state authority,[41] it is widely recognized now that what Paul says here is an abrupt transition from what has preceded it.

As Jewett remarks, Paul's statements here clash with the "apocalyptic hostility" he shows elsewhere "against the old age and its institutions." "While Paul speaks of the 'rulers of this age' with bitter resistance in 1 Cor 2:8 and views the 'principalities and powers' as opponents in Rom 8:38, this passage seems to reflect a time when the church has made peace with the world."[42] We may further observe that this is the only point in the letter where Paul declares that his hearers' obedience to God will require their *submission*: "every soul" is to be subject to governing authorities (*pasa psychē exousiais hyperechousais hypotassesthō*, 13:1). This language strikes echoes of his earlier reference to the involuntary subjection (*hypetagē*) of creation to "futility" and "corruption" (8:20-21), but there he speaks of the Spirit's groaning within the children of God as they await deliverance from the subjected order. The characterization of ruling authorities as "ministers of God," rewarding those who do good and bringing wrath against evildoers (13:3-4), is difficult to reconcile with the earlier assignment of just those activities to God alone (2:6-11), nor does it offer any hint of the eschatological tone that immediately follows in Paul's cryptic assurance that "the hour" and "the day" are near (13:12-13). This is the only point where Paul suggests—in a telling inconsistency—that those who are in Christ owe "fear" to their rulers (*phobon*, 13:7; contrast 13:3-4).[43] The language of submission and fear that appears here is a startling exception to the rhetoric of the rest of the letter; more typical is the declaration to which it immediately gives way, that obedience to God can be summed up in a single obligation, "to love one another, for the one who loves the neighbor has fulfilled the law" (13:8-11).

James Kallas sums up the disparities between these verses and the rest of Paul's corpus by declaring that "Paul could not have ascribed such an exalted status to Rome without being not only hypocritical and servile, but untrue to his whole theological position." Kallas, like a few others, concludes that the passage is an interpolation into Paul's letter.[44] In the absence of corroborating textual variants, most scholars have rejected that interpretive option—though Ernst Käsemann declared that even if the passage is genuine, the notion "that the authorities constantly seek to be God's servants" is "obviously exaggerated if not wholly incredible"; it did not reflect Paul's own thinking but was a stock piece of traditional material that Paul appealed to in a "forced" and unpersuasive way.[45] Leander E. Keck suggested posting a warning to any interpreter essaying to make sense of the passage as it stands: "Danger: Thin Ice."[46]

The warning has not deterred skaters. I will not try to survey all the attempts to account for Paul's disturbingly uncharacteristic language here, but three avenues of interpretation bear particular note. One, which I continue to find compelling, appeals to recent disturbances, including Suetonius's report of "tumults" in 49 C.E. (sometimes read as "riots"), the account of a recent tax protest in nearby Puteoli that was suppressed by deadly force, and popular resentment of new taxes in Rome itself, as indications that the situation in Rome was volatile.[47] This situation is sometimes described as one in which Jewish agitation has created problems for the Christian congregation. Given the vulnerability of the Judean population throughout the Diaspora, however, I consider it much more likely that Paul was concerned to ward off any civil disturbances on the part of his *non-Judean hearers* that might easily have gone the way of previous disturbances in Alexandria and elsewhere, that is, by injuring a proxy target, the local Judeans.[48]

Another approach, represented most recently by Robert Jewett, finds in Paul's language a subtle, but nonetheless recognizable critique of Roman rule. After all, Paul does not distinguish citizens from non-citizens or persons of higher from lower rank, but calls on *all* to be subject to the authorities. The participle *tetagmenai*, mistranslated "instituted" (NRSV) or "established," has rather the stronger sense that the authorities have been "put in their place." Further, Jewett and others (notably John Howard Yoder) have argued that by calling for a *willing* subordination, Paul makes his hearers active agents rather than the passive subjects of Roman rule, something "far removed from an authoritarian ethic of obedience." Certainly the exhortation to *everyone* to be subject would have struck a jarring note if heard by Roman citizens accustomed to thinking of their own compliance not as "subjection," but as willing consent (see chapter one). But were there citizens in Paul's audience? Jewett concludes that, "if the Roman authorities had understood this argument, it would have been viewed as thoroughly subversive."[49] But that is an enormous *if.* The argument Jewett describes would have been too subtle to have provoked the average magistrate, who at any rate would have found the net result—the compliance of Paul's hearers—congenial enough to his purposes. The nuances that Jewett and others have identified point us to the constraints that make a whole-hearted endorsement of Roman rule impossible for Paul; but they hardly constitute a clear and unambiguous critique.

A third approach is represented by T. L. Carter's recent proposal that Paul intentionally characterizes the Roman authorities in such slavishly deferential terms that his audience must have recognized his remarks as ironic.[50] "When the straightforward meaning of a text is recognizably implausible or unacceptable," Carter writes, "that is one of the signals that may alert the reader or audience to the presence of irony."

> If the letter's original readers shared with the author an experience of oppression at the hands of the authorities, that shared experience would have paved the way for the readers' understanding of Paul's use of irony, by rendering the surface meaning of Paul's commendation of the authorities blatantly implausible to them.[51]

Carter argues that despite the subsequent characterization of the early years of Nero's rule as good years, Paul and his hearers would have known better. The eschatological references to "this age" (12:2) and to the coming "hour" and "day" of reversal (13:11-14) inevitably would have subverted the "apparent" commendation of the authorities in 13:1-7: "Paul only *seems* to grant the authorities an unconditional status: in reality they belong to the present age of darkness which is passing away."[52]

I agree with Carter's suggestion that aspects of Paul's language militate against hearing this passage as an unambiguous endorsement of Roman rule. Indeed, in an earlier essay, I argued that specific aspects of this passage would have struck Paul's hearers as explicitly contravening aspects of imperial propaganda; but I am not convinced that these aspects—significant as they are—allow us to read the whole passage as intentionally ironic or subversive. The exhortation to *every soul* to "be subject" and to show "fear" to the authorities flew in the face of the imperial claim that some peoples experienced the "good faith" and "friendship" of Rome, and that for those peoples "fear" and the threat of force was unnecessary (see chapter one). More dramatically, Paul's comment that the authority "does not bear the sword idly" (13:4) not only strikes an echo with his earlier reference to "the sword" as one of the perils faced by the faithful in the present age (8:35-36); it also directly contradicts one of the central themes of Neronian propaganda, that in contrast to his predecessors Nero did not resort to the sword:

- Calpurnius Siculus presented a prophecy that described Nero's accession as the dawning of a golden age in which no one could remember the use of the sword. The goddess of war would turn upon herself the weapons that had previously been deployed in warfare; "fair peace" would come; "clemency . . . has broken every maddened sword-blade. . . . Peace in her fullness shall come; knowing not the drawn sword, she shall renew once more the reign of Saturn in Latium" (*Eclogue* 1.45–60).
- The first Einsiedeln *Eclogue* described a paradise inaugurated by Nero: "We reap with no sword, nor do towns in fast-closed walls prepare unutterable war." No woman anywhere gave birth to a future enemy of Rome; "unarmed, our youth can dig the fields, and the boy, trained to the slow-moving plow, marvels at the sword hanging in the abode of his fathers" (25–31).
- In the speech he presented to Nero, Seneca put into the emperor's mouth the boast that he had surpassed even his ancestor Augustus, who had come to power only through warfare: "With all things at my disposal, I have been moved neither by anger nor youthful impulse to unjust punishment. . . . With me the sword is hidden, nay, is sheathed; I am sparing to the utmost of even the meanest blood; no man fails to find favor at my hands though he lack all else but the name of man" (*Clem.* 1.2–4).
- Seneca continued by flattering the emperor that his gift to the world was "a state unstained by blood, and your prideful boast that in the whole world you have shed not a drop of human blood is the more significant and wonderful

because no one ever had the sword put into his hands at an earlier age" (11.3). Nero would so excel among the Caesars that he would need no bodyguard for his protection; "the arms he wears are for adornment only" (13.5).

The criteria of "intertextuality" discussed in the Introduction apply here. The consistent theme expressed in three different imperial sources shows that the "idle sword" was a mainstay of Neronian propaganda. That claim would also have struck anyone living in the capital as spurious. (One even can imagine an audience hearing an unintended joke in the imperial claim; after all, Nero himself repeatedly quipped that his stepfather had been "made a god" by eating a mushroom. The sword was hardly his preferred weapon.) Paul cannot have declared that the authority "does not bear the sword idly" without his audience hearing a pointed refutation of a central theme in Nero's propaganda.[53]

But recognizing that Paul says things in clear tension with imperial claims does not yet mean that we must read the whole of 13:1-7 as deliberate and sustained irony. Carter finds Paul's reference to the authorities as "priests of God" (*leitourgoi theou*) so blatantly unrealistic that it must have been meant to guide his hearers to an ironic understanding of his words. Carter argues that Paul did not mean all that he said, but he does not tell us what Paul meant his audience to understand instead. He cannot; for it remains the case that to whatever extent Paul may regard Roman officials as a hostile and powerful danger, *he still enjoins subjection and compliance to the authorities.* As Carter admits, much of what Paul says in these verses can be read straightforwardly as the basis for that appeal.[54]

It is impossible to read a single coherent posture in Rom 13:1-7. The text is an instance neither of straightforward endorsement of Roman power nor of an ironic subversion of imperial claims. Rather, as argued in chapter one, we are in touch here with the constraining force of ideology, with "voice under domination." Given the constraining power of ideology, we must do more than ask what Paul meant; we must ask, What *larger forces* were at work to shape, and to inhibit, his response?

I have characterized Paul's rhetoric in Romans as *dissociative argumentation,* achieved by the assertion of an alternative reality through the *topoi* of apocalypticism. I do not mean that Paul has self-consciously selected certain rhetorical techniques in order to achieve desired effects. We have seen contradictions on the surface of Romans that reveal tensions beneath the surface: for example, God is the one who subjects the world to futility, *yet* God's Spirit groans for deliverance from that bondage (8:18–25). God calls human beings to free and willing obedience, not to slavery, *yet* this obedience also requires submission to God (8:7; 10:3) and, improbably, subjection to the governing authorities (13:1). And we have seen that these tensions arise, not from an idiosyncratic incoherence on Paul's part, but from fundamentally irresolvable contradictions in the material and ideological conditions in which the letter was written and which the letter was an attempt to resolve.

———————————— **Living at the End of History** ————————————

Fredric Jameson proposes that we read texts, not only as expressions of the thoughts of individuals or the values of communities, but also as occasions for the emergence of the aspirations of collectives, especially social classes. That approach is not new to biblical studies. Norman Gottwald has taught us to understand the writings of the Hebrew Bible as the artifacts of a great struggle in ancient Israel between, on the one hand, a communitarian mode of production, inaugurated as a cultural revolution in the villages and cities of Canaan, and on the other hand, the "tributary" economy of the city-states that resisted or were overthrown by that revolution, of the subsequent Israelite monarchy, and at last of "colonial Judah" under Persian rule.[55]

In the Roman era, the ideological requirements of the tributary mode of production generated a fundamental tension between the coercive force that was necessary, but not sufficient, to hold the system together, and the ideological representation of justice, expressed in codes of reciprocity, of "faithfulness" and "friendship," that functioned to elicit the consent of the governed. We have seen that the figure of the emperor, the "sole ruler" (*autokratōr*), was a crucial central symbol within Roman imperial ideology, simultaneously representing the force necessary to maintain order and the justice necessary to win consent. Both values were sublimated in the symbolization of the Augusti at the heart of the imperial cult, which represented the emperor as the embodiment of piety and allowed the incorporation of those who participated in sacrifice into the destiny of the Roman people to rule the other peoples of the earth.[56]

In Romans we can see Paul appealing to the values appropriate to a communitarian mode of production. Those values include the mutual regard, deference, and generosity that will enable economic mutualism within the Roman assembly and among assemblies in other cities, but also the regard for "the weak" and for Israel that will guarantee the "sanctity" of the "offering" he takes to Jerusalem.[57] These resemble the values that in our day Jesuit theologian and martyr Ignacio Ellacuría has described as the "civilization of poverty," which is also the "civilization of solidarity."[58] But Paul, like others of his Judean contemporaries, lives within the constraining power of the Roman tributary mode of production; and like them, he confronts the dismaying reality of his people's decline and subjugation, made notoriously evident in recent events. Given the ideological tension generated by this situation, and given the constraining force of Roman ideology, Paul can imagine a resolution only in terms of an inversion of the present state of affairs. That is, he expects the advent of a superior "sole ruler," a *kyrios* who will rule the nations instead of Caesar, and who will receive the tribute of the nations—but will rule as "servant of the circumcised," that is, those who are perceived by Roman ideology as "the weak" and contemptible (15:8-9). Paul understands himself as that lord's emissary, working to prepare the assemblies in Rome (and elsewhere) to welcome that lord at his arrival.

Non-Judean members of the Christ assemblies in Rome have begun to adopt the ideological perspective of the Roman Empire, particularly regarding the "weak"—meaning, in particular, displaced Judeans—among them. They have collapsed the imperial perception of a hierarchy of peoples into an *ecclesial* perception of Israel's "stumbling so as to fall." They have taken in the values of what Ellacuría called the "civilization of wealth" (which in our own day is the civilization of capital).[59] Such a civilization regards the future as a further continuation of the process of accumulation of power and prestige that is its basis. In such a civilization in our own day, Jon Sobrino writes, expectations of the future are based on "calculations" extrapolated from the present, and so "there is not a radical break between the present and the future." In Paul's day, the non-Judeans in his audience also have begun to confuse their own status "in Christ" with the status that imperial ideology promised them as participants in the civilization of wealth. They should expect to be included among "the powerful," enjoying the impunity of victors who stand at the effective end of history.

Romans is Paul's attempt to counteract the effects of imperial ideology within the Roman congregations. He seeks to reorient their perceptions around a more authentically Judean scriptural perspective, which in this case means (as Gottwald has shown) a more communitarian perspective appropriate to the practice of a "civilization of solidarity."

Because his own perspective is in the precise ideological sense "kyriarchal," it is inconceivable to Paul that human affairs are beyond the control of the *kyrios*; yet at present they clearly contradict what Scripture reveals about the "irrevocable" gifts and calling of God. It must therefore be the case, given his kyriarchal premises, that present circumstances are, paradoxically, the result of the action of God to bring the world under subjection (*hypetagē*, 8:20) and that similarly, the governing authorities have been ordered by God (*tetagmenai*, 13:1). All that Paul says about the ruling authorities flows from the constraints of his own kyriarchal perspective: it is inconceivable that it should be otherwise—that is, that the authorities should have a free hand. The same justice that has been manifested in "wrath" against the unjust (1:18-32) will inevitably be manifest on the great and coming "day" (13:11-12); it is inconceivable that it should be otherwise. To remove Rom 13:1-7 from the eschatological context of the letter is to utterly misunderstand that passage and the letter.

Because the resolution achieved in Romans is a *kyriarchal* resolution (involving a very particular *kyrios,* as we have seen), history must be seen as the arena in which God has now "imprisoned everyone in disobedience," so that God might bring about the final redemption of creation and of the children of God alike. This history has in effect been put in suspense until God should release it. History as the continuing process of accumulation and reward for the virtuous is, for Paul, *unthinkable,* and so must be suspended, brought to a halt so that another history, the history of the revelation of God's mercy "to all" (11:30-32), may commence. In these terms, Sobrino's decisive formulation is glimpsed already in Paul: *ex pauperes nulla salus,* "no salvation outside [or: apart from] the poor."

Because Paul's theology is kyriarchal, the possibility that "the weak," meaning Israel in its historical experience of subjection to foreign powers, might serve a redemptive role is obscured. Israel has been "hardened" for the sake of the nations (11:7, 11-12, 25, 28), specifically the nations as they perceive themselves as having arrived at history's culmination (9:30). But Paul does not offer or invite further reflection on the historical experience of subjected Israel; nor is there any role for the *ekklēsiai* other than waiting, with patience, endurance, and eager anticipation, for the coming redemption.

Nevertheless, the letter is driven by the longing of the earth's peoples for their liberation from bondage and entry into their proper destiny as the children of God (8:18-25). At just this point, we see the compelling power for Paul of those collective aspirations that Fredric Jameson has termed the "political unconscious," temporarily repressed from the public sphere by the pressures of hegemony but ultimately irrepressible. It is the work of an energizing Spirit that brings these aspirations to expression in "sighs too deep for words." Alongside the kyriarchal representation of God as the lord subjecting the world to bondage, Paul also—simultaneously—speaks of the activity of the Spirit in the longings of the oppressed world.

Just here we confront the central irony of this letter's legacy down to the present. The apocalyptic logic of Romans was a necessary attempt to close off a particular way of construing the present that was current in imperial ideology. Paul's apocalyptic logic depended for its force on the imminent realization of an alternative kyriarchy, the coming "day" of the Messiah. Centuries later, we who live in the "civilization of wealth" are accustomed to read Paul with perfect hindsight: we know that he was *not* living on the threshold of the end of history. To the contrary, history—the history of continuing accumulation—continues. It has proven far easier for us to assimilate Romans to that history, *our* history, and to perceive Paul's alternative history as apocalyptic fantasy. Removed from the context of its apocalyptic coordinates, the Spirit's voice in the "groaning of creation" is readily ignored as we live "as if the poor did not exist," or else it is heard only as the cry of the wretched asking for our magnanimity.[60] The kyriarchy of Paul's rhetoric is all too easily aligned with the very ideology of empire that Paul sought to oppose.

The ghosts in Romans

"Only the Messiah himself consummates all history," wrote Marxist literary critic Walter Benjamin, "in the sense that he alone redeems, completes, creates its relation to the Messianic. For this reason, nothing historical can relate itself on its own account to anything Messianic."[61] The thought, though modern, was first Paul's.[62] As Slavoj Žižek elaborates,

The past is not simply past, but bears within it its proper utopian promise of a future Redemption; in order to understand a past epoch properly, it is not sufficient to take into account the historical conditions out of which it grew—one also has to take into account the utopian hopes of a Future that were betrayed and crushed by it—that which was "negated," that which did not happen—so that the past historical reality was the way it was. . . . [W]hat the proper *historical* stance "relativizes" is not the past . . . but, paradoxically, *the present itself*—our present can be conceived only as the outcome (not of what actually happened in the past, but also) of the crushed potentials for the future that were contained in the past.[63]

Just so Paul resisted the perception of the present as the latest stage in a continuous history of accumulation, the inevitable unfolding of destiny and crowning of virtue (as history appears to the victors in the "civilization of wealth" at any particular historical moment—including our own). Rather, ancient promises given to Israel, and long delayed, remained determinative of the future and, for Paul, of the present as well. From an ideological-critical perspective, this is what Paul means in Romans when he speaks of *the world being "subjected" to God in the present*. It is to affirm that the present is not, so to speak, self-sufficient, but is determined by "the crushed potentials for the future that were contained in the past" but that continue, for Paul, in the urgent groaning of a creation in travail. Those heretofore "crushed potentials" are the seed of the future, for as Paul put it, the "gifts and calling of God are irrevocable." From this perspective, we may understand that the reason Paul does not regard the *ekklēsia* as the agent of history (as the rather flamboyant language of Paul founding "an alternative society" might otherwise imply)[64] is that the *ekklēsiai* in Rome (and elsewhere) had not yet adequately lived into their role of embodying the past.

I quote Žižek again:

We, the "actual" present historical agents, have to conceive of *ourselves* as the materialization of the ghosts of past generations, as the stage in which these past generations retroactively resolve their deadlocks,[65]

—though this formulation does not yet identify the ghosts of the past with sufficient specificity. The "ghosts" haunting Paul's letter are, in the first place, the "branches broken off," who remain Israel's future, and because they are the focus of God's eternal purposes, the future of the world as well. An imagination—such as the imperial imagination—that the past is truly dead, that the vanquished have no future, is to Paul's mind unthinkable. It is not some "ethnic prejudice" on Paul's part that drives him to defend the future of a vanquished Israel: it is the (fundamentally Israelite) vision that because the future belongs to the God who can raise the dead and bring into being what did not exist, it does not in any way depend upon the present.

In a larger perspective this letter is haunted by the "groaning in labor" of creation itself (8:22-23). The "spectrality" that haunts Paul's thought is the unfulfilled destiny of the world's liberation. That liberation cannot emerge organically out of the present, which God has (necessarily) subjected to bondage, corruption, and futility, but it is nevertheless inevitable.[66]

There are ghosts enough to haunt us today, not least in the social sites where the interpretation of Paul is at a premium—the churches above all. Responding in astonishment to the meeting of the Latin American Bishops' Conference in Santo Domingo in 1992, theologian Jon Sobrino decried the "incredible silence" of the proceedings "on the martyrs":

> In Latin America martyrdom is not anecdotal or exceptional, but a massive and indisguisable reality: it is the new thing, the grace, the credential and seal of the most genuine evangelization that has occurred between Medellín and Santo Domingo. . . . To ignore the martyrs really means ignoring the signs of the times.

The words of judgment are not reserved for Latin American bishops alone. "Ignoring the martyrs" is just what is done, lamentably but apparently not to Sobrino's surprise, in "the world of the North": a world he describes as "sinful and hypocritical, never expecting to ask forgiveness of anyone" for those killed in wars from Vietnam to Iraq, "nor for the slow death of the Southern half of the planet."[67] From within the civilization of wealth, a future such as Paul projects is strictly utopian—"the (impossible) ideal of social and political perfection, conceived out of abundance" by the non-poor. But to the wretched of the earth, "'utopia' means a dignified and just life for the majorities"; it is *eu-topia,* that 'good place' that must exist."[68]

It is no clearer for us today than it was in Paul's day just what the agency is that might bring in the world to come. Paul could assign to the assembly the role of expectant waiting because the agitation of the Spirit within and around the assembly convinced him that the waiting would not be long. We who live in the global North today stand in a very different situation, inescapably caught up in the instrumentality of empire, and readily seduced by it. Our responsiveness to the impulses of the Spirit who groans around us may require our own refusal to be conformed to the present age—to the civilization of capital—but to seek our salvation precisely among the poor, as Sobrino writes; or as Paul put it, by "making our way with the oppressed" (12:16).

The apostle Paul. Byzantine fresco from a monastery in Sopocani, Serbia. Photo ©
Scala/Art Resource, N.Y.

Epilogue

Paul and the Horizon of the Possible

I began this book by describing an encounter in Port-au-Prince, a city in which one finds concentrated the crushing misery to which the Haitian people have been subjected for the last century and more. In the year 2000, the United Nations Food and Agriculture Organization declared Haiti the country with the highest index for "depth of hunger" in the western hemisphere, the third highest in the world.[1] That is a measure of a country's per capita deficit of calorie intake to calorie expenditure, or more prosaically, of the rate at which its people are slowly starving to death.

The statistics with which Mike Davis begins his own recent book, *Planet of Slums,* suggest that the plight of millions of men and women, massed in the desperate slums of Port-au-Prince, is increasingly the planetary norm. We probably already have passed the moment when more human beings on Earth live in cities—the vast majority in slums—than outside of them. Davis asks whether this unprecedented development in human evolution will be ecologically sustainable. The answer, of course, is that for untold millions of human beings, it long has been too late.[2] The problem is not simply one of mass, as we in the privileged global North are tempted to imagine—as if there were simply too many people *elsewhere*. Davis describes the sordid patterns by which the poor have been betrayed, not only by foreign empires and their own governments alike, but also by the international institutions ostensibly established to help them. The poor have been offered patronizing platitudes about self-help that no one would dream of directing to the international corporations that extract their natural resources and exploit their labor. Meanwhile, the strict disciplines of economic austerity are imposed on their governments, requiring the abandonment of programs that might lift their people—to quote deposed Haitian President Jean-Bertrand Aristide—"from misery to poverty with dignity." They are after all a "surplus humanity," virtually "disappeared" from the awareness of the prosperous center.[3]

Michael Hardt and Antonio Negri have argued that, given the subtlety and texture of the globalized economy today, "Empire" is a reality that reaches beyond centralized state control and makes it largely irrelevant. The "multitude" of the wretched of the earth will be the agents of countless spontaneous micro-revolts, and given the global saturation of an instantaneous electronic media, these micro-revolts *will* be televised.[4] But critics object that Hardt and Negri have dismissed the global significance of the exertion of U.S. military force and the severity of economic exploitation throughout the world. As Gopal Balakrishnan writes in protest, any vision of another world must first "take stock of the remorseless realities of this one, without recourse to theoretical ecstasy."[5]

As we saw in chapter five, Salvadoran theologian and martyr Ignacio Ellacuría insisted that the global poor must be at the center of any just future order. Jon Sobrino formulated that insistence in the theological principle *ex pauperes nulla salus*, "there is no salvation outside [or without] the poor." Ellacuría insisted further that the world's poor were the agents of that future order, because only their civilization of poverty and of solidarity—not the civilization of capital—could achieve it.[6] Sobrino appealed to the apostle Paul in his critique of the hubris of the civilization of capital. But as we also saw, Paul's confidence in the inevitability of a just future, the future of the Messiah, was constrained by the kyriarchal ideology of the Roman tributary order, and these constraints prevented him from assigning a significant historical agency to the poor.

Any interpretation of Paul today is necessarily a gesture within an ideological field of forces. Given the realities of our world, I submit that the kyriarchal constraints on Paul's thinking are constraints we cannot afford to perpetuate. I read the ideological closure achieved in Romans as Paul's preemptive strike against the arrogant presumption, fueled by imperial ideology, of standing at the "end of history." His appeals to the Roman congregations to "make their way with the oppressed" and to participate in an international campaign of economic mutualism, his collection for "the poor among the saints," point in the direction of an alternative civilization. These are important gestures on which we do well to reflect as we examine our own complicity in the ideology and instrumentality of empire in our own day. But because of the kyriarchal constraints on his thinking, Paul never ascribed to these efforts the power to bring about another world.

An uncritical appropriation of Paul today too readily reinforces tropes of subordination and a pious political quietism. Within North American churches, perhaps the closest correlate to Ellacuría's and Sobrino's vision of a civilization of solidarity was the impulse of the Central American solidarity and sanctuary movements of the late 1970s and 1980s; but much of that energy has left the churches, forced out by ferocious federal harassment and selective prosecutions, congregational timidity, and conservative takeovers of denominational jurisdictions.[7] Ideologically, a popular version of Reinhold Niebuhr's Christian realism retains a more powerful hold in mainstream churches, invoking the name of Paul to express pessimism about collective action in the public sphere and portraying the distant horizon of the "kingdom of God" as an "impossible ideal." The constraints of our own ideological environment are such that debate over Niebuhr's legacy involves less frank talk about the merits of socialism than Niebuhr's own writings did.[8] Meanwhile, the enthusiasm for Paul among postliberal theologians offers a bracing corrective to the domestication of the apostle with its insistence that a political theology based on distinctive ecclesial practices is in continuity with his legacy.[9] On the U.S.

scene, however, the presumption that the distinctiveness of these countercultural practices inheres *within* the church, and that those practices have only an indirect relevance for public life, runs the risk of reinforcing the isolation of the congregation as a spiritual enclave removed from the public arena.[10] Further, as Elisabeth Schüssler Fiorenza warns, the trope of recovering "the voice of Paul" can simply reinforce a biblicism that allows us to evade more challenging assessments of our own responsibilities.[11]

But our situation is even more constrained. Within the congregational orientation of most U.S. churches, it is a routine expectation that biblical interpretation will bear practical fruit primarily in the sermon. From an ideological-critical viewpoint, however, other questions must precede—and relativize—the rush to determine "what we can preach":

- In what ways have U.S. churches been shaped by the ideological pressures of a globalizing capitalist culture?
- To what extent have churches incorporated the values of the "civilization of wealth"?
- How do the churches function within a larger ideological system to channel the potentially volatile energy of religious symbols away from conflict with the mechanisms of power?
- How do the privatization of the churches, their co-optation into the routines of the civil religion, and their careful maintenance of the boundaries assigned to them by the dominant capitalist order (for example, the scrupulous avoidance of speaking against one or another war from the pulpit) effectively domesticate those symbols?
- How do these considerations determine the scope of any preaching to effect needed change in perceptions, attitudes, and practices?[12]

In chapter one I noted the tremendous effect to which Paul's voice can be deployed to serve ideological ends in U.S. culture. Though I consider it a matter of urgency to contest that deployment, that contestation plays only a very subordinate role in the greater public responsibilities we must exercise today. Fredric Jameson's program for ideological criticism points at last *beyond* the text to the larger currents of hegemony and resistance that shape our own history, as well as that of the past. But at just this point the question of *agency*—not only of *what* must be done, but of *who* has the power to do what must be done to achieve a more just world—becomes as problematic as it is urgent. World-systems theorist Immanuel Wallerstein has written that we stand in a "period of systemic transition," a time of "deep uncertainty, in which it is impossible to know what the outcome will be. History is on no one's side. Each of us can affect the future, but we do not and cannot know how others will act to affect it, too."[13]

Given the complexity of our global situation, the most adequate intellectual stance may be "a certain *defiant humility*," as social theorist Göran Therborn writes: "defiance before the forces of capital and empire, however powerful.

Humility before the coming new world and the learning and unlearning that it will call for."[14] Those can appear maddeningly vague counsels, but they address a situation in which the unprecedented complexity and reach of the global capitalist order make the modest appeal of the World Social Forum, that "another world is possible," seem to many quixotically utopian.[15]

No reading of Romans will mitigate the complexity of the challenges before us. The purpose of my analogical reading—offered in terms of Marxist analysis rather than more conventionally theological categories—is to heighten awareness of the seductive hazard of the ideological air we breathe. But such a reading cannot reveal our responsibility for action. I have argued that Paul's messianic convictions precluded just the sort of reflection on historical agency that is needed today.

That realization may cause greatest dissatisfaction to those of us in the prosperous global north who are used to imagining ourselves the shapers and bearers of historical destiny. Perhaps the most important lesson we should draw from Paul's apocalypticism is the intuition that the world's true future will not emerge from the designs and instruments of the present order. But we should not need the "haunting" of Paul to tell us that.

The Gospel of Luke provides a parable for our situation vis-à-vis Paul. Jesus tells the story of a rich man who ignored a miserable human being lying on his doorstep. Dying, he abruptly finds himself in Hades. From a great distance, the nameless man who had been rich sees Lazarus—who *is* named—lying in the consolation of Abraham's bosom. Still presuming the privileges of his class, he pleads with Abraham to send Lazarus with the sparse relief of a few drops of water, but his request is impossible. "A great chasm" stands between them—as great as the social gulf that separated the two men in their earthly lives. The man who had been rich makes a final request: Send the now blessed Lazarus to earth, to warn his brothers so that they can avoid the hell awaiting them because of their indifference. But Abraham replies, "They have Moses and the prophets; they should listen to them. . . . If they do not listen to Moses and the prophets, neither will they be convinced even if someone rises from the dead" (16:19-31).

Rather like the rich man's brothers, we have the prophets in our own day, not least among them martyrs like Ellacuría and the "voice of the voiceless," Archbishop Oscar Romero.[16] We have available to us all the information we need to understand the brutal dynamics of global capitalism and the military power that enforces its demands. None of us can pretend ignorance of the misery that results. None of us can pretend not to know of the many organizations and movements, including some of the national structures of the churches to which many of us belong, who advocate and militate for the sort of structural change that is so urgently needed. If we continue nevertheless to find the present order congenial enough, we are unlikely to be troubled by the "ghost" of a long-dead Judean.

Abbreviations

ABD	*Anchor Bible Dictionary*
Aen.	*Aeneid*
Ag. Ap.	*Against Apion*
Agr.	*Agricola*
A. J.	*Antiquitates judaicae*
Ann.	*Annales*
Ant.	*Jewish Antiquities*
Ant. rom.	*Antiquitates romana*
Ap.	*Apologia*
Apoc.	*The Apocolocyntosis*
art. cit.	article cited
Aug.	*Augustus*
AV	Authorized Version
BDAG	Danker, F. W., W. Bauer, W. E. Arndt, and F. W. Gingrich (*Greek-English Lexicon of the New Testament and Other Early Christian Literature*. 3rd ed. Chicago, 2000)
Bell. gall.	*Bellum Gallicum*
BibInt	*Biblical Interpretation*
BJRL	*Bulletin of the John Rylands University Library of Manchester*
BR	*Biblical Research*
Caes.	*Caesar*
chap(s).	chapter(s)
Clem.	*De clementia*
1–2 Cor	1–2 Corinthians
CPJ	*Corpus Papyrorum Judaicarum*
Dan	Daniel
Deut	Deuteronomy
Div. inst.	*Divinae institutiones*
Dreams	*On Dreams*
Embassy	*On the Embassy to Gaius*
Ep.	*Epistulae*
Eph	Ephesians

Epit.	*Epitome of Pompeius Trogus*
Epon.	*Eponymous (Ab urbe condita)*
Esth	Esther
Exod	Exodus
Ex ponto	*Epistulae ex Ponto*
Ezek	Ezekiel
Fin.	*De finibus*
Flacc.	*In Flaccum*
Gen	Genesis
Hist.	*Historiae*
Hist. rom.	*Historia romana*
Hos	Hosea
ICC	International Critical Commentary
IG	*Inscriptiones graecae*
Isa	Isaiah
Iug.	*Bellum Iugurthinum*
JBL	*Journal of Biblical Literature*
Jdt	Judith
Jer	Jeremiah
JSNT	*Journal for the Study of the New Testament*
JSNTSup	Journal for the Study of the New Testament: Supplement Series
JSOT	*Journal for the Study of the Old Testament*
JSOTSup	Journal for the Study of the Old Testament: Supplement Series
JTS	*Journal of Theological Studies*
J.W.	*Jewish War*
LCL	Loeb Classical Library
Life	*The Life*
LXX	Septuagint
Macc.	*Maccabees*
Mos.	*De vita Mosis*
NF	Neue Folge
NovT	*Novum Testamentum*
NRSV	New Revised Standard Version
NTS	*New Testament Studies*
OCD	*Oxford Classical Dictionary*
OJRS	*Ohio Journal of Religious Studies*
Panegyric.	*Panegyricus*
Pol.	*Politica*
Prov. cons.	*De provinciis consularibus*
PssSol	*Psalms of Solomo*n
1QH	*Hodayot* or *Thanksgiving Hymns*
4QMMT	*Miqsat Ma'ase ha-Torah* [or the Halakic Letter]
1QpHab	*Pesher Habakkuk*

1QS	*Serek Hayahad* or *Rule of the Community*
REB	Revised English Bible
Rep.	*De republica*
Rom	Romans
RSV	Revised Standard Version
Sat.	*Satirae*
SBL	Society of Biblical Literature
SBLDS	Society of Biblical Literature Dissertation Series
SE 4/TU	*Studia evangelica /[Theologische Untersuchungen]*
Sest.	*Pro Sestio*
SNTSMS	Society for New Testament Studies Monograph Series
Spec. Laws	*Special Laws*
s.v.	*sub verbo*, under the word
TDNT	*Theological Dictionary of the New Testament*
1–2 Thess	1–2 Thessalonians
Ti. C. Gracch.	*Tiberius et Caius Gracchus*
Virt.	*De virtutibus*
WUNT	Wissenschaftliche Untersuchungen zum Neuen Testament
ZNW	*Zeitschrift für die neutestamentliche Wissenschaft und die Kunde der älteren Kirche*
ZTK	*Zeitschrift für Theologie und Kirche*

Notes

Epigrams (p. v) are from Karl Barth, *The Epistle to the Romans,* 2nd English ed., trans. from the 6th German edition by Edwyn C. Hoskyns (London: Oxford University Press, 1933), 7–9; Fredric Jameson, *The Political Unconscious: Narrative as a Socially Symbolic Act* (Ithaca: Cornell University Press, 1981), 18, 19; and John B. Cobb Jr. and David J. Lull, *Romans,* Chalice Commentaries for Today (St. Louis: Chalice, 2005), 21, 27.

Introduction

1. Christian Parenti, *The Freedom: Shadows and Hallucinations in Occupied Iraq* (New York: New, 2004), 42–44.

2. The human rights report on the 1993–94 terror campaign against women in Port-au-Prince was published as *Another Violence against Women: The Challenge of Accountability in Haiti* (Minneapolis: Minnesota Advocates for Human Rights, 1995). Victims of the same violence still awaited redress a decade later, in the terrifying aftermath of another U.S.-sponsored coup d'état: DeNeen Brown, "'Political Rapes' of 1991 Still Haunt Haitian Democracy Activists," *Washington Post,* March 20, 2004.

3. The office to which President Aristide was restored remained very tightly constricted by U.S. and World Bank policies until the coup d'état of 2004 removed him from power. In 1994 the United States secured safe passage out of the country and a $5,000-a-month pension for coup mastermind (and former CIA "asset") Lt. General Raoul Cedras and whisked his confederates safely abroad as well. The flamboyant Emmanuel "Toto" Constant, who told journalist Allan Nairn about the CIA agent who recruited him to organize FRAPH, found his way through U.S. Customs to Brooklyn, where he worked for years as a real estate agent; the State Department initially refused to extradite him, on the pretext that a trial in Haitian courts would be "destabilizing." In January 2008, Constant faced charges of mortgage fraud in a Brooklyn court but denied liability in a civil suit brought by three of FRAPH's former victims: *Haiti Libète* 1:26 (Jan 16–22, 2008). As a first order of business, the U.S. military confiscated at least 60,000 pages of files from FRAPH headquarters and refuses to release them to Haitian prosecutors. Haitian activists reported that U.S. Embassy personnel spirited the accused murderer of Haitian justice minister Guy Malary out of Haitian custody to freedom. On the 1915 U.S. invasion of Haiti and subsequent Congressional and military investigations, see Noam Chomsky, *Year 501: The Conquest Continues* (Boston: South End, 1993), 201–3. On U.S. complicity in the bloody Haitian coup d'état of 1991, see James Ridgeway, ed., *The Haiti Files: Decoding the Crisis* (East Haven: Essential Books, 1994); on the 2004 coup, see Noam Chomsky, Paul Farmer, and Amy Goodman, *Getting Haiti Right This Time: The U.S. and the Coup* (Monroe: Common Courage, 2004), and Paul Farmer, *The Uses of Haiti,* 3rd ed., with an Introduction by Noam Chomsky (Monroe: Common Courage, 2006). It is important to note that the facts described previously were given coverage—albeit scanty—in the Associated Press and reported by reputable human rights groups at the time.

4. Noam Chomsky, *Year 501,* 201–3.

5. Personal interview at the U.S. embassy, Aug. 1995; quoted from notes.

6. Fredric Jameson, *The Political Unconscious: Narrative as a Socially Symbolic Act* (Ithaca: Cornell University Press, 1981), 19–20. The language of "wresting a realm of Freedom from a realm of Necessity" comes from Karl Marx, *Capital* (German original 1867; New York: International, 1977), III, 820.

7. José Porfirio Miranda, *Marx and the Bible: A Critique of the Philosophy of Oppression,* trans. John Eagleson (Maryknoll: Orbis, 1974; Spanish original 1971), 152, 160.

8. Elsa Tamez, *The Amnesty of Grace: Justification by Faith from a Latin American Perspective,* trans. Sharon H. Ringe (Nashville: Abingdon, 1991), 20–22.

9. Neil Elliott, *Liberating Paul: The Justice of God and the Politics of the Apostle* (Maryknoll: Orbis, 1994; Minneapolis: Fortress Press, 2005), esp. 72–75; see also my essay, "Paul's Letter to the Romans," in *A Postcolonial New Testament Commentary,* eds. R. S. Sugirtharajah and F. S. Segovia (New York: Continuum, 2007).

10. Theodore W. Jennings Jr., *Reading Derrida/Thinking Paul: On Justice* (Stanford: Stanford University Press, 2006), 1, 157.

11. John B. Cobb Jr. and David J. Lull, *Romans,* Chalice Commentaries for Today (St. Louis: Chalice, 2005), 4, 22.

12. Robert Jewett, *Romans*; assisted by Roy D. Kotansky; edited by Eldon Jay Epp; Hermeneia (Minneapolis: Fortress Press, 2007), 49; see also Elliott, "Paul's Letter to the Romans."

13. Helmut Koester, "Paul's Proclamation of God's Justice for the Nations," *Paul and His World: Interpreting the New Testament in Its Context* (Minneapolis: Fortress Press, 2007), 3–4.

14. Adam Hochschild, *King Leopold's Ghosts: A Story of Greed, Terror, and Heroism in Colonial Africa* (New York: Houghton Mifflin, 1999).

15. Mark Twain inscribed *The War Prayer* in 1904, but no publisher would accept the manuscript until after his death. The work is in the public domain.

16. Fernando F. Segovia, "Biblical Criticism and Postcolonial Studies: Toward a Postcolonial Optic," in *The Postcolonial Bible,* ed. R. S. Sugirtharajah (Sheffield: Sheffield Academic, 1998), 48–65; quotation from p. 56.

17. G. E. M. de Ste. Croix, *The Class Struggle in the Ancient Greek World: From the Archaic Age to the Arab Conquests* (Ithaca: Cornell University Press, 1980), chaps. 6 and 7; I have quoted from pp. 374 and 382–3. Peter Garnsey and Richard Saller characterized the Roman economy as fundamentally "parasitic": *The Roman Empire: Economy, Society, and Culture* (Los Angeles: University of California Press, 1987), 8.

18. See Fredric Jameson, *Postmodernism: or the Cultural Logic of Late Capitalism* (Durham: Duke University Press, 1991), and Göran Therborn's critique in "After Dialectics: Radical Social Theory in a Post-Communist World," *New Left Review* 43 (Jan.–Feb. 2007), 63–114, esp. 70–73.

19. The literature on U.S. imperial ambitions is vast and growing. Global military supremacy is the explicit goal of *The National Security Strategy of the United States of America* (Washington, D.C.: The White House, 2002). See also Andrew J. Bacevich, *American Empire: The Realities and Consequences of U.S. Diplomacy* (Cambridge: Harvard University Press, 2002), and among the many works by Noam Chomsky detailing the logic of capitalism's domination of U.S. military and foreign policy, see *Hegemony or Survival: America's Quest for Global Dominance,* The American Empire Project (New York: Henry Holt, 2003). For critical theological responses to empire see Michael L. Budde and Robert W. Brimlow, eds., *The Church as Counterculture* (Albany: SUNY Press, 2000); Sharon D. Welch, *After Empire: The Art and Ethos of Enduring Peace* (Minneapolis: Fortress Press, 2004); Wes Avram, ed., *Anxious about Empire: Theological Essays on the New Global Realities* (Grand Rapids: Brazos, 2004); Jack Nelson-Pallmeyer, *Saving Christianity from Empire* (New York: Continuum, 2005); Mark Lewis Taylor, *Religion, Politics, and the Christian Right: Post-9/11 Powers and American Empire* (Minneapolis: Fortress Press, 2005); and David Ray Griffin and others, *The American Empire and the Commonwealth of God: A Political, Economic, and Religious Statement* (Louisville: Westminster John Knox, 2006).

20. Terry Eagleton provides a clear and accessible survey of modern thinking on ideology and ideological criticism: *Ideology,* 2nd ed. (London and New York: Verso, 2007). On the rhetorical-critical

investigation of ideology in the New Testament texts and in their modern interpretation, see Elisabeth Schüssler Fiorenza, *Rhetoric and Ethic: The Politics of Biblical Studies* (Minneapolis: Fortress Press, 1999), and *The Power of the Word: Scripture and the Rhetoric of Empire* (Minneapolis: Fortress Press, 2007).

21. Edward W. Said, *Culture and Imperialism* (New York: Knopf, 1993), xvii.

22. Papers presented to the Paul and Politics Section have subsequently been published in volumes edited by Richard A. Horsley: *Paul and Politics: Ekklesia, Israel, Imperium, Interpretation* (Harrisburg: Trinity International, 2000), and *Paul and the Roman Imperial Order* (Harrisburg: Trinity International, 2004). Earlier discussions of Paul in the context of Roman imperialism include my own *Liberating Paul* and Richard A. Horsley, *Paul and Empire: Religion and Power in Roman Imperial Society* (Harrisburg: Trinity Press International, 1997); most recently see John Dominic Crossan and Jonathan L. Reed, *In Search of Paul: How Jesus' Apostle Opposed Rome's Empire with God's Kingdom: A New Vision of Paul's Words and World* (San Francisco: HarperSanFrancisco, 2004). This field of scholarship relies on important studies of Roman imperial society, including P. D. A. Garnsey and C. R. Whittaker, eds., *Imperialism in the Ancient World* (Cambridge: Cambridge University Press, 1978); G. E. M. de Ste. Croix, *Class Struggle in the Ancient Near East* (New York: Columbia University Press, 1980); S. R. F. Price, *Rituals and Power: The Roman Imperial Cult in Asia Minor* (Cambridge: Cambridge University Press, 1984); Peter Garnsey and Richard Saller, *The Roman Empire: Economy, Society, and Culture* (Los Angeles: University of California Press, 1987); Paul Zanker, *The Power of Images in the Age of Augustus* (Ann Arbor: University of Michigan Press, 1988); and Karl Galinsky, *Augustan Culture: An Interpretive Introduction* (Princeton: Princeton University Press, 1996).

23. On "people's history" or "history from below" in the Roman republic and early empire, see recently Michael Parenti, *The Assassination of Julius Caesar: A People's History of Ancient Rome* (New York: New, 2003), and now Richard A. Horsley, ed., *Christian Origins*, vol. 1 in *A People's History of Christianity*, gen. ed. Denis R. Janz (Minneapolis: Fortress Press, 2005). On "hidden transcripts" among the oppressed, see James C. Scott, *Weapons of the Weak: Everyday Forms of Peasant Resistance* (New Haven: Yale University Press, 1985); Scott, *Domination and the Arts of Resistance: Hidden Transcripts* (New Haven: Yale University Press, 1990); and Richard A. Horsley, ed., *Hidden Transcripts and the Arts of Resistance: Applying the Work of James C. Scott to Jesus and Paul,* Semeia Studies 48 (Atlanta: Scholars, 2004).

24. Neil Elliott, *The Rhetoric of Romans: Argumentative Constraint and Strategy and Paul's Dialogue with Judaism* (JSNTSup 45; Sheffield: JSOT, 1990; reprinted with a new preface, Minneapolis: Fortress Press, 2006); Stanley K. Stowers: *A Rereading of Romans: Gentiles, Jews, Justice* (New Haven: Yale University Press, 1994); Ben Witherington III, *Paul's Letter to the Romans: A Socio-Rhetorical Commentary* (Grand Rapids: Eerdmans, 2004).

25. Krister Stendahl repeatedly asserted, but offered no argument to support the assertion, that Paul's arguments regarding justification by faith were not anti-Jewish polemic, but "apologetic as he defends the right of Gentile converts to be full members of the people of God" (*Paul among Jews and Gentiles* [Philadelphia: Fortress Press, 1976], 130; similarly in *Final Account: Paul's Letter to the Romans* [Minneapolis: Fortress Press, 1995], ix).

26. On this point, see Neil Elliott, "Paul's Letters: God's Justice against Empire," in *The New Testament: Introducing the Way of Discipleship,* eds. Wes Howard-Brook and Sharon H. Ringe (Maryknoll: Orbis, 2002), 122–47.

27. Karl Barth, *The Epistle to the Romans*, trans. Edwyn C. Hoskyns (New York: Oxford, 1933), 9, 11.

28. José Comblin, *The Church and the National Security State* (Maryknoll: Orbis, 1979), 64.

29. Ignacio Ellacuría, "Uncovering a Civilization of Capital, Discovering a Civilization of Work," in *New Visions for the Americas: Religious Engagement and Social Transformation,* ed. David Batstone (Minneapolis: Augsburg Fortress Press, 1993), 74; "Utopia and Prophecy in Latin America,"

in *Mysterium Liberationis: Fundamental Concepts of Liberation Theology*, eds. Ignacio Ellacuría and Jon Sobrino (Maryknoll: Orbis, 1993), 298.

30. "Message to the Black Church and Community," presented at the Black Theology Conference in Atlanta, 1977; in *Black Theology: A Documentary History, 1966–1979*, eds. Gayraud S. Wilmore and James H. Cone (Maryknoll: Orbis, 1979), 348. See Cornel West's discussion in *Prophesy Deliverance! An Afro-American Revolutionary Christianity*, Anniversary Edition (Louisville and London: Westminster John Knox, 2002), 95–127.

31. For a theological critique of the disciplines of capitalist culture, see Daniel M. Bell, Jr., *Liberation Theology after the End of History*, and Michael Budde, *The (Magic) Kingdom of God: Christianity and Global Culture Industries* (Boulder: Westview, 1997).

32. Jameson, *The Political Unconscious*, 19–20.

33. Ibid., 47–58.

34. Parenti uses the language of reading "against the grain": *The Assassination of Julius Caesar*, 10–11.

35. I've argued this case in *Liberating Paul*, 154–6.

36. Cobb and Lull point out that Paul's audience could hardly be expected to take direct political action aimed at changing or "reforming" the Roman Empire (*Romans*, 27). They insist nevertheless that his insistence on loyalty ("faithfulness") to Christ alone would have been a powerful implicit challenge to imperial claims on the allegiance of individuals.

37. Jameson, *The Political Unconscious*, 75–77.

38. Ibid., 84–85.

39. See Norman K. Gottwald, *The Hebrew Bible: A Socio-Literary Introduction with CD-ROM* (Minneapolis: Fortress Press, 2002); Gottwald, "Sociology of Ancient Israel," *ABD* 6:79–89. Jameson discusses the necessary revision of an early Marxist "sequence" of modes of production to recognize the simultaneity of incompatible modes of production, some ascendant, some vestigial, and others only anticipated: *The Political Unconscious*, 89–102; see now Roland Boer's excellent discussion of "the question of mode of production" in *Marxist Criticism of the Bible* (London and New York: Sheffield Academic, 2003), 229–46.

40. Miguel De La Torre speaks of "unmasking" racism and sexism in biblical interpretation: *Reading the Bible from the Margins* (Maryknoll: Orbis, 2002), chaps. 3–4. Much to the same point, Ignacio Ellacuría has written of "uncovering a civilization of capital," which is "the most basic form of structural violence" Ellacuría, "Uncovering a Civilization of Capital"; Cornel West, of "unmasking falsehoods" (*Prophesy Deliverance!* 108–11). See now Fernando Segovia, *Decolonizing Biblical Interpretation* (Maryknoll: Orbis, 2002).

41. Galinsky, *Augustan Culture*, 3–9.

42. Ibid., 12, quoting J. Hellegouarch, *Le vocabulaire latin des relations et des partis politiques sous la République*, 2nd ed. (Paris: PUB, 1972), 312; and J. Béranger, *Recherches sur l'aspect idéologique du principat* (Basel: PUB, 1953), 115.

43. Cobb and Lull set the resemblance between Roman and American imperialism at the foreground of their commentary of the letter: *Romans*, 25–27. Gary Dorrien responds theologically to different meanings of empire current in U.S. discourse in "Consolidating the Empire: Neoconservatism and the Politics of American Dominion," *Political Theology* 6, no. 4 (2005): 409–28.

44. See Elliott, *Liberating Paul*, 230 (Paul as "apostle of liberation for the First World"), and passim (chap. 4 was reprinted in revised form as "The Anti-Imperial Message of the Cross" in Horsley, *Paul and Empire*, 167–83); Horsley, "Paul and Politics: Problems and Prospects," in Horsley, *Paul and Politics*, 39 (Romans provides "a direct challenge to the ritual and ceremony of empire"). John W. Marshall has provided an insightful critique of such language, for which I am grateful: "'Hybridity': A Postcolonial Interpretive Approach to Romans 13" (paper presented at the Paul and Politics Section of the SBL, Philadelphia, November 2005).

45. Schüssler Fiorenza, *The Power of the Word*, 13 and passim.

46. See most recently Schüssler Fiorenza, *Rhetoric and Ethic*.

47. Shaye D. Cohen, *The Beginnings of Jewishness: Boundaries, Varieties, Uncertainties* (Berkeley and Los Angeles: University of California Press, 1999), 104–5.

48. Philip F. Esler, *Conflict and Identity in Romans: The Social Setting of Paul's Letter* (Minneapolis: Fortress Press, 2003), 62–74.

49. Bruce J. Malina and John J. Pilch have argued that observations about first-century Judeans "have little if anything to do" with modern Jews, the "vast majority" of whom are genetically descended from "non-Semitic," physiognomically "northern" ninth-century Central Asian converts, the Khazars (*Social-Scientific Commentary on Paul's Letters* [Minneapolis: Fortress Press, 2005], 365). The peculiar terms in which this argument is made suggest that it is Malina and Pilch, far more than most modern Jews, who are obsessed with a racial understanding of ethnicity. I endorse Amy-Jill Levine's urgent protest that in the hands of some interpreters, translating *Ioudaios* as Judean can mean sundering the connection between ancient *Ioudaioi* and modern Jews: see *The Misunderstood Jew: The Church and the Scandal of the Jewish Jesus* (San Francisco: HarperSanFrancisco, 2006), 164–65 and specifically eschew those implications of the word *Judean* here.

50. This was the burden of my argument in *The Rhetoric of Romans*.

51. I have quoted George A. Kennedy, *New Testament Interpretation through Rhetorical Criticism* (Chapel Hill: University of North Carolina Press, 1984), 152; David Aune, *The New Testament in Its Literary Environment* (Philadelphia: Westminster, 1987), 219; Stanley K. Stowers, *Letter Writing in Greco-Roman Antiquity* (Philadelphia: Westminster, 1986), 114 (but compare his characterization of the letter in *A Rereading of Romans*, 36–41); Jewett, *Romans*, 44; Cobb and Lull, *Romans*, 5–6; and Krister Stendahl, *Final Account*, 5.

52. Some measure of the breadth of this perception is the diversity of interpreters who profess it: I have quoted from Rudolf Bultmann, *The Theology of the New Testament*, vol. 1 (trans. Kendrick Grobel; New York: Charles Scribner's Sons, 1950), 190; Juan Luis Segundo, *The Humanist Christology of Paul*, Jesus of Nazareth Yesterday and Today, vol. 3, trans. John Drury (Maryknoll: Orbis, 1986), 9; and James D. G. Dunn, *The Theology of Paul the Apostle* (Grand Rapids: Eerdmans, 1998), 25–26.

53. The clear subordination of 1:16 to 1:15 (*gar*) and of 1:18 to 1:17 (*gar*) and the absence of any conventional indication that Paul is introducing a theme make this reading impossible: see Elliott, *Rhetoric of Romans*, 62–63; 82–83. Jewett declares as "fully justified" the consensus that 1:16–17 mark the "thesis of the letter (*Romans*, 43) but offers no exegetical substantiation of that judgment.

54. K. P. Donfried included Martin Luther Stirewalt's essay, "The Form and Function of the Greek Letter-Essay," in *The Romans Debate*, 2nd ed. (Peabody: Hendrickson, 1991), 147–71, in the conviction that it illuminated the character of Romans as a letter-essay (see Donfried's own essay, "False Presuppositions in the Study of Romans," ibid., 123–25). But precisely the key indicators of the genre that Stirewalt discusses—a statement of topic (usually with the prepositional phrase *peri* . . . , "concerning . . .") and of the author's purpose in expounding his or her thought on the topic (usually, in response to a direct question)—are missing from Romans.

55. Thus, for example, George A. Kennedy described the letter as "more epideictic" than 1 Thessalonians because he presumed that in Romans, Paul wished to show the Romans "in advance what his gospel [would] be," and thus offered them "an example of the kind of preaching or teaching he [would] practice when among them"—a characterization of the letter in the subjunctive mood that Kennedy did not bother to defend, perhaps because he, like many other interpreters, regarded it as self-evident (Kennedy, *New Testament Interpretation*, 152, 156; similarly Aune, *The New Testament in Its Literary Environment*, 219). Klaus Berger, on the other hand, labeled the letter an example of "protreptic" rhetoric, a subcategory of deliberative rhetoric concerned with showing the advantages of adopting a particular way of life, because (like Kennedy) he read Romans as a treatise on the superiority of the Christian "way" to Judaism (Klaus Berger, *Formgeschichte des Neuen Testaments* [Heidelberg: Quelle & Meyer, 1984]), 217–18. David Aune seeks to split the difference: "Romans incorporates protreptic discourse into an epideictic letter" (*The New Testament in Its Literary Environment*, 203). Robert Jewett regards the letter as epideictic because it exhibits aspects of parenetic and hortatory speeches (although these are regarded by other scholars as subcategories of deliberative

rhetoric!) but subordinates these aspects to his characterization of Romans as an "ambassadorial" letter (*Romans*, 42–46), even though he recognizes that "diplomatic" rhetoric was a common mode for issuing commands in Roman discourse (726, on the *parakalō* clause at 12:1-2).

56. Kennedy makes the point (regarding what he calls "radical Christian rhetoric") in *New Testament Interpretation*, 6–8; see also Amos Wilder, *Early Christian Rhetoric: The Language of the Gospel* (London: SCM, 1964).

57. Aristotle, *Rhetoric* 1375a–77b.

58. Philo similarly described the "signs and wonders" that Moses displayed to Pharaoh's court as the *apodeixis* confirming the words of God to the Egyptians (*On the Life of Moses* 1.95); see BDAG s.v. Aristotle names oracles as a sort of inartificial proof (*Rhetoric* 1375b–76a), but shows no comparable sense of the active power of the god in the oracle; the oracle's meaning remains completely at the disposal of the speaker.

59. Compare J. Louis Martyn's characterization of Paul's rhetoric in Galatians as a rhetoric of power: Paul wrote "in the confidence that *God* intended to cause a certain event *to occur*" when his letter was read. Paul "*does* theology by writing in such a way as *to anticipate* a theological *event*"; he is the herald of a divine word "that is at its heart *invasive* rather than responsive" ("Events in Galatia: Modified Covenantal Nomism versus God's Invasion of the Cosmos in the Singular Gospel: A Response to J. D. G. Gaventa and B. R. Gaventa," in *Pauline Theology I: Thessalonians, Philippians, Galatians, Philemon* [ed. Jouette M. Bassler; Minneapolis: Fortress Press, 1991], 161, 163) (emphasis in original). J. P. Sampley similarly observes that Romans is not about mission, "*it is mission* at work," an "assertive intervention" in Rome ("Romans in a Different Light: A Response to Robert Jewett," 109–30, in *Pauline Theology III: Romans*, 115, 129) (emphasis in original).

60. Mark Reasoner, *The Strong and the Weak: Romans 14.1—15.13 in Context*, SNTSMS 103 (Cambridge: Cambridge University Press, 1999), chap. 3; Jewett, *Romans*, 46 and passim, relying on J. E. Lendon, *Empire of Honour: The Art of Government in the Roman World* (Oxford: Oxford University Press, 1997).

61. Cicero, *De republica* 3.41.

62. Aristotle, *Rhetoric* 1376b–77a.

63. The genre of the admonitory letter was well established in Paul's day. Here is the description attributed to Demetrius of Phalerum (first century B.C.E.): "The admonishing type [of letter: *nouthetikē*] is one which indicates through its name what its character is. For admonition is the instilling of sense [*noun tithein*] in the person who is being admonished, and teaching him what should and should not be done" (Pseudo-Demetrius, *Epistolary Types*). See Abraham Malherbe's translation, "Ancient Epistolary Theorists," *OJRS* 5 (1977): 3–77; Malherbe, *Moral Exhortation: A Greco-Roman Sourcebook* (Philadelphia: Westminster, 1986), 81, and Stowers, *Letter Writing*, 125–26. Stowers points out that Paul's expression of confidence in the Romans is "a rather typical . . . assertion of the audience's lack of need for admonition which reflects the kinship between paraenesis and admonition" (128).

64. On the genre of paraenetic letter, see Abraham Malherbe, "Exhortation in First Thessalonians," *Novum Testamentum* 25 (1983), 238–56. On the phenomenon of paraenesis and paraenetic style, see Aune, *Literary Environment of the New Testament*, 191.

65. V. P. Furnish, *Theology and Ethics in Paul* (Nashville: Abingdon, 1968), 103, 105–6. See also Nils Dahl, "Missionary Theology in the Epistle to the Romans," in *Studies in Paul: Theology for the Early Christian Mission* (Minneapolis: Augsburg Press, 1977), 70–94.

66. Rudolf Bultmann, *Theology of the New Testament*, trans. Kendrick Grobel (New York: Charles Scribner's Sons, 1950), 1:105–6; Nils Dahl, "Form-Critical Observations on Early Christian Preaching," in *Jesus in the Memory of the Early Church: Essays* (Minneapolis: Augsburg Press, 1976), 33–34. See my further discussion in *Rhetoric of Romans*, 94–103. Dahl finds in Rom 15:16, discussed above, a clear indication that Romans conforms to the wider pattern of Christian preaching, and of Paul's apostolic endeavor in general: "he is the intercessor on behalf of his congregations who pleads

their cause before God and he is the advisor who counsels them, in order to be able to present them to Christ at his coming, which Paul expected in the near future" ("Missionary Theology," 73).

67. In *The Rhetoric of Romans* I followed Johannes Munck, Lloyd Gaston, and John G. Gager in arguing that Romans must be interpreted as an argument directed to the explicit addressees, non-Judeans (I wrote "Gentiles"). Both Stanley K. Stowers and Ben Witherington III subsequently made the same argument. Of course, this does not mean that there are no Judeans (Jews) in Paul's audience: the contrary is obviously the case, as the greetings in Romans 16 show. But Stowers insists that "because Paul begins by explicitly describing his readers as gentiles, the interpreter can go step by step asking at what point the text introduces a new audience or subverts the explicit one"; as he shows, there is in fact no such point in the letter. Stowers characterizes the contrary tendency among most interpreters, to insist that a Jewish-Christian minority is the direct target of much of the letter's argument, as an "obsession" that leads interpreters to "erase the gentile audience and replace it with 'Christians, both Jews and gentiles.'" See Johannes Munck, *Paul and the Salvation of Mankind* (London: SCM, 1959); Lloyd Gaston, *Paul and the Torah* (Vancouver: University of British Columbia Press, 1987); John G. Gager, *The Origins of Antisemitism* (New York: Oxford University Press, 1985); Stanley K. Stowers, *A Rereading of Romans,* 29–36; Ben Witherington III, *Paul's Letter to the Romans,* 1–8.

Indeed, so powerful is this "obsession" that a few interpreters find it inconceivable that the letter should be read as it is addressed, that is, to non-Judeans. "How," Philip F. Esler asks, "can one seriously maintain that the letter was not addressed to . . . Judeans? . . . Are we to suppose that very early in the reading . . . these Judeans must have realized, and Paul intended them to realize, that he only had non-Judean Christ-followers within the scope of his discourse and not them? . . . Did they then sit or stand patiently for over an hour while the letter was read, all the while saying to themselves something like 'Very interesting, but of course Paul did not intend this teaching for us'?" (Esler, *Conflict and Identity in Romans,* 119). Similarly, Steve Mason has written that it "strains the imagination" that Paul would have intended the letter's discussion of "typically Judaean questions" to find "any resonance with Gentile readers" (Steve Mason, "'For I Am Not Ashamed of the Gospel' [Rom 1:16]: The Gospel and the First Readers of Romans," 254–87, in *Gospel in Paul: Studies on Corinthians, Galatians, and Romans for Richard N. Longenecker,* ed. L. Ann Jervis and Peter Richardson; JSNT-Sup 108 [Sheffield: Sheffield Academic, 1994], 258–59). To the contrary, what strains the imagination is the suggestion that Paul would have expected the *explicitly named addressees* to sit out major sections of the letter without explaining that, or why, he was narrowing his focus to Judeans.

68. Elliott, *The Rhetoric of Romans.*

69. Nils Dahl, "The Future of Israel," in *Studies in Paul,* 139–42. Esler makes similar observations: *Conflict and Identity in Romans,* 270–73.

70. In Romans 1–8, Witherington writes, Paul "treads carefully through what could be called common ground" before he "comes to grips with a major issue" in 9–11, "following which in chaps. 12–15 he must deal with the ethical fallout in Rome of the bad theology he has confronted." The heart of the letter is long delayed because Paul does not enjoy the clout in Rome that he had in his own churches; he "must therefore follow the method known as *insinuatio,* not dealing at first with what most disturbs him but building rapport with his audience" (Witherington, *Paul's Letter to the Romans,* 17).

71. W. S. Campbell, "The Rule of Faith in Romans 12:1—15:13: The Obligation of Humble Obedience to Christ as the Only Adequate Response to the Mercies of God," in *Pauline Theology III: Romans,* 260–61; N. T. Wright, "Romans and the Theology of Paul," ibid., 35.

72. I will presume here many of the close rhetorical-critical arguments that I made in *The Rhetoric of Romans.*

73. Jewett refers to a "consensus" regarding the historical situation of the letter (*Romans,* 3, 18–19).

74. See Wilhelm Wuellner, "Toposforschung und Torahinterpretation bei Paulus und Jesus," *NTS* 24 (1978): 463–83.

178

Notes to Introduction

75. P. A. Brunt, *Roman Imperial Themes*; Paul Zanker, *The Power of Images in the Age of Augustus*; S. R. F. Price, *Ritual and Power*; Karl Galinsky, *Augustan Culture*. The first three works are excerpted in Horsley, *Paul and Empire*.

76. Scott, *Domination,* 138.

77. Ibid., 2.

78. Ibid., 12.

79. In his many writings, Noam Chomsky has analyzed the gap between actual U.S. foreign policy as described in internal government documents and the rhetoric offered for public consumption; see for example *Deterring Democracy* (New York: Verso, 1991). Norman Solomon offers an analysis of "the disconnect between public opinion," where mainstream media dangle "illusionary references" to the "withdrawal" of U.S. troops from Iraq, and "elite opinion," where it is frankly acknowledged that a substantial force will continue to occupy Iraq indefinitely "to protect America's most vital interests" ("Media Spin on Iraq: We're Leaving (Sort of)," *ZNet* Sept. 1, 2007, available online at www.zmag.org). Other examples of "hidden transcripts" of the powerful include the boast of former U.S. Ambassador to the United Nations, Daniel Patrick Moynihan, long after the fact, of having carried out secret instructions to render the U.N. Security Council "utterly ineffective" in sanctioning the genocidal invasion of East Timor by Indonesia (Chomsky, *Deterring Democracy,* 199–201); the admission by U.S. political and military strategists, similarly made public much later, that their chief goals in the Middle East are to maintain "our access to [their] vital economic and military resources," and to counter with force the "underdeveloped world's growing dissatisfaction over the gap between rich and poor nations" that jeopardizes that access (30–31); and so on. Gilbert Achcar observes (in *The Class of Barbarisms: Sept. 11 and the Making of a New World Disorder* [New York: Monthly Review Press, 2002], 7–11) that President George H. W. Bush acknowledged candidly enough that war against Iraq was motivated by "vital economic interests," including control of a tenth of the world's oil supply, but that such frankness has been abandoned by his successors. Other examples of the phenomenon within the administration of George W. Bush would include the claims of executive privilege for the vice president's consultation with CEOs of energy corporations regarding governmental energy policy, internal administration memos regarding exemption from international conventions against torture, the "Downing Street memos" regarding administration plans to invade Iraq long before allegations, later shown to be false, of weapons of mass destruction in that country, and plans to circumvent legislative restrictions on the warrantless wiretapping of U.S. citizens. The distinction of hidden and public transcripts is illustrated in presentations that L. Paul Bremer III, later the chief of the U.S. "Coalition Provisional Authority" in Iraq, made to international corporations in his role as head of "terrorism risk insurance" for the insurance firm Marsh & McLennan. Journalist Naomi Klein observed that in order to sell such insurance to corporations, Bremer "had to make the kinds of frank links between terrorism and the failing global economy that activists are called lunatics for articulating" ("Downsizing in Disguise," *The Nation,* June 23, 2003). Only in the hidden transcript of corporate boardrooms can it be frankly acknowledged that so-called free-trade policies devastate regional economies, producing the economic misery, desperation, and resentment that fuel anti-corporate and anti-U.S. terrorism.

80. The George W. Bush administration has generated an unprecedented number of former insiders producing damning exposés of previously secret internal discussions (in Scott's term, the hidden transcript): see especially Ron Suskind, *The Price of Loyalty: George W. Bush, the White House, and the Education of Paul O'Neill* (New York: Simon & Schuster, 2004), and Joseph Wilson, *The Politics of Truth: Inside the Lies That Led to War and Betrayed My Wife's CIA Identity* (New York: Carroll & Graf, 2004). Even current officials have off-handedly described internal decisions to manipulate information available to the public (the public transcript), as when unnamed U.S. officials admitted, after the fact, that allegations that Iraqi weapons of mass destruction were an imminent threat were never "the primary reason we went to war. We emphasized the danger of Saddam's weapons . . . in order to gain legal justification for war from the United Nations and to emphasize the danger here at home to our own people. We were not lying. . . . It was just a matter of emphasis"; as a Defense Department official explained, the campaign "had a lot to do with the U.S. government bureaucracy,

we settled on the one issue that everyone could agree on" (ABC News, Nightline, April 22, 2003; see Paul Krugman, "Does It Matter We Were Misled into War?" *New York Times,* April 30, 2003; David Corn, "Now They Tell Us: Postwar Truths and Consequences," *The Nation,* May 19, 2003; Jonathan Schell, "No Doubt," *The Nation,* June 30, 2003). The president himself revealed to reporters that he had given false information to a press conference in advance of the 2006 midterm elections to avoid a difficult line of questioning (White House transcript of the Nov. 8, 2006, press conference at www .whitehouse.gov/news/releases/2006/11/20061108-2.html) (accessed Oct. 1, 2007).

81. Martin Goodman, *The Roman World 44 BC–AD 180,* Routledge History of the Ancient World (New York and London: Routledge, 1997), 86, 83 (emphasis added).

82. Parenti, *The Assassination of Julius Caesar,* 36.

83. Jameson, *The Political Unconscious,* 85.

84. The point-counterpoint staged at the 2007 Society of Biblical Literature Annual Meeting between John M. G. Barclay, arguing "Why the Roman Empire Was Insignificant for Paul," and N. T. Wright, arguing for its centrality to Paul's gospel, hinged on the question of criteria. Barclay rightly (and archly) pointed out that much of the discussion of Paul's attitude toward empire has relied on assertion and declaration; Wright's counter reasserted the claim that the totality of Paul's theological claim left no room for a rival allegiance such as the emperor claimed. Missing from the debate (and from much of the discussion heretofore) have been the sort of criteria that might offer a measure of falsifiability to the "counter-imperial Paul" hypothesis. Part of my intention here is to identify such criteria.

Robert C. Tannehill suggests that different readings of Paul result from interpreters' different presuppositions regarding Paul's social location and reliability ("Paul as Liberator and Oppressor: How Should We Evaluate Diverse Views of First Corinthians?" in *The Meaning We Choose: Hermeneutical Ethics, Indeterminacy and the Conflict of Intepretations,* ed. Charles H. Cosgrove, JSOT-Sup 411 [London: T&T Clark, 2004], 122–37); similarly, N. T. Wright contrasts the "contextual and cultural agendas," corresponding to the different social locations of interpreters, that by "no accident" generate different readings of Paul (*Paul in Fresh Perspective* [Minneapolis: Fortress Press, 2005], 13–20). Over against the implication that Paul's social location, like beauty, is in the eye of the beholder, see Justin J. Meggitt's careful work in *Paul, Poverty, and Survival,* Studies of the New Testament and Its Social World (Edinburgh: T&T Clark, 1998); Steven L. Friesen, "Poverty in Pauline Studies: Beyond the So-called New Consensus," *JSNT* 26, no. 3 (2004): 323–61; and Elisabeth Schüssler Fiorenza's plea for an integrated critical liberationist approach, *The Power of the Word,* 90–93.

1. IMPERIVM

1. Fredric Jameson, "On Interpretation," in *The Political Unconscious: Narrative as a Socially Symbolic Act* (Ithaca: Cornell University Press, 1981), 17–102, esp. 52–53.

2. Edward W. Said, *Culture and Imperialism* (New York: Knopf, 1993), 8–9.

3. Twentieth-century Christian realist Reinhold Niebuhr gained a formidable reputation, in part, by his reflections on the "irony of American history" (*The Irony of American History: The Position of America in the World Community in Light of Her History* [New York: Charles Scribner's Sons, 1952]). In a critical review of Niebuhr's works, Noam Chomsky observed that elementary aspects of the historical record escaped Niebuhr's attention, and concluded that much of Niebuhr's prestige resulted from his solemn expositions on "the inescapable 'taint of sin on all historical achievements,' the necessity to make 'conscious choices of evil for the sake of good,' . . . soothing doctrines" for American policy makers "preparing to 'face the responsibilities of power'" ("Reinhold Niebuhr," *Grand Street* [Winter, 1987], 197–212). Niebuhr's legacy remains the subject of tremendous and weighty controversy today, with policy makers and theologians on the left and right alike claiming him as their inspiration. See the critical essays in a special issue of *The Journal of Religion* 54:4 (Oct. 1974); John C. Bennett, "Niebuhr's Ethic: The Later Years," *Christianity and Crisis* 42, no. 6 (1982),

91–95; R. Fox, *Reinhold Niebuhr: A Biography* (New York: Pantheon, 1985); Robert McAfee Brown, "Reinhold Niebuhr: His Theology in the 1980s," *Christian Century* 103, no. 3 Jan. 22, 1986, 66–68; Michael Novak, "Reinhold Niebuhr: Model for Neoconservatives," *Christian Century* 103, no. 3 Jan. 22, 1986, 69–71; Novak, "Father of Neoconservatives," *National Review*, May 11, 1992, 39–42; Bill Wylie-Kellerman, "Apologist of Power: The Long Shadow of Reinhold Niebuhr's Christian Realism," *Sojourners* (March 1987): 14–20; Larry Rasmussen, "Reinhold Niebuhr: Public Theologian," *Cross Currents* (Summer 1988): 198–210; Rasmussen, *Reinhold Niebuhr: Theologian of Public Life*, The Making of Modern Theology (Minneapolis: Fortress Press, 1991); Rasmussen, "Was Reinhold Niebuhr Wrong about Socialism?" *Political Theology* 6, no. 4 (2005): 429–57; and G. Dorrien, *The Making of American Liberal Theology: Idealism, Realism, and Modernity 1900–1950* (Louisville: Westminister John Knox, 2003).

4. Robert S. McNamara, comments at Harvard University on the "lessons of Vietnam," reported by Eric Black, "The Big Question: A Post to Ponder," *Star Tribune* (Minneapolis and St. Paul), Nov. 23, 2006; comments adapted from McNamara's memoir, *In Retrospect: The Tragedy and Lessons of Vietnam* (New York: Times Publishing, 1995).

5. The fullest statement of the legitimacy of U.S. military supremacy and the unquestioned responsibilities it involves is given in the *National Security Strategy of the United States* (Washington, D.C.: The White House, 2002). For salutary misgivings and dissent from the implicit theology of the *Strategy*, see Sharon D. Welch, *After Empire: The Art and Ethos of Enduring Peace* (Minneapolis: Fortress Press, 2004); and Wes Avram, ed., *Anxious about Empire: Theological Essays on the New Global Realities* (Grand Rapids: Brazos, 2004).

6. Thomas L. Friedman, "A Manifesto for the Fast World," *New York Times Magazine*, March 28, 1999, 40; at greater length, *The Lexus and the Olive Tree: Understanding Globalization* (New York: Farrar Straus Giroux, 1999), 373 and passim. For critiques, see Jack Nelson-Pallmeyer, *Saving Christianity from Empire* (New York and London: Continuum, 2005), chap. 6; Andrew J. Bacevich, *American Empire: The Realities and Consequences of U.S. Diplomacy* (Cambridge: Harvard University Press, 2002), passim.

7. The recent revision of the U.S. Army's manual on "Operations" includes instructions on counterinsurgency tactics that, according to its authors, seek "to move from high-intensity offensive to low-intensity security and stability operations—from creating shock and awe to winning hearts and minds. The new doctrine will emphasize that, where possible, *the two levels should co-exist*," something the policy-makers believe is possible so long as the occupying force strives to "avoid upsetting civilians," at least intentionally. See "How to Do Better," *The Economist*, Dec. 17, 2005, 21–23 (emphasis added).

8. In 2007, the U.S. Joint Forces Command commissioned a Rand Corporation study on "The Marketing Approach to Earning Popular Support in Theaters of Operation." "While not abandoning the more aggressive elements of warfare," the *Washington Post* reported, the study suggested "a more attractive brand for the Iraqi people might have been 'We will help you'" (Karen DeYoung, "$400,000 Buys Pitch for New Brand of Iraq" War," *Washington Post*, July 22, 2007; accessed online). Whether the rebranding campaign will win the hearts and minds of the Iraqi people remains unclear; the record of human history casts the prospect in a certain shadow of doubt.

9. Jonathan Schell, "What Happened to Hearts?" Letter from Ground Zero, *The Nation*, Dec. 6, 2004; accessed online. As it happened, the subsequent election in January 2005, warmly celebrated in mainstream U.S. media, was in fact won by a party that had campaigned for an immediate withdrawal of U.S. troops—a fact generally suppressed in the U.S. media. A rare exception, London-based journalist Naomi Klein, observed that the party winning a solid majority, the United Iraqi Alliance, had called for "a timetable for the withdrawal of the multinational forces from Iraq" and other economic policies that constituted a repudiation of "the free-market policies imposed" by the United States and the International Monetary Fund. President George W. Bush rejected a timetable for withdrawal out of hand, however, "four days after the Iraqis voted for exactly that." The vote, Klein concluded, "was not about what Iraqis were voting for, it was about the fact of their voting and, more important, how their plucky courage made Americans feel about their war. Apparently, the election's true purpose was to prove to Americans that, as George Bush put it, 'the Iraqi people

valued their own liberty.' Stunningly, this appears to come as news" ("Getting the Purple Finger," *The Nation*, Feb. 28, 2005; accessed online). Similarly, Patrick Cockburn observes that in 2005, "the Shia—who make up 60 per cent of the Iraqi population—won two elections, but the U.S. has fought to deny them complete control of the Iraqi state" ("What the Neighbours Are Up To," *London Review of Books*, June 8, 2006, 7).

10. James E. Pinkerton endorsed Secretary of Defense Donald Rumsfeld's view that unwarranted anti-American prejudice warped news reporting from Iraq: "We're being outwitted in the global war of words," *Newsday*, Feb. 28, 2006, accessed online.

11. Philosophers Chaim Perelman and L. Olbrechts-Tyteca discussed the inverse relationship between "Argumentation and Violence" in *The New Rhetoric: A Treatise on Argumentation*, trans. John Wilkinson and Purcell Weaver (Notre Dame: University of Notre Dame Press, 1969), 55.

12. Antonio Gramsci, *Selections from the Prison Notebooks,* ed. Quentin Hoare and G. Nowell Smith (London: Lawrence & Wishart, 1971), passim; see Terry Eagleton, *Ideology: An Introduction* (London, Verso, 1991), chap. 4 ("From Lukácz to Gramsci"); Noam Chomsky, on official and semi-official representations of the inferiority of subject peoples as "the common coin of modern political and intellectual discourse" in the United States, in *Deterring Democracy* (New York: Hill and Wang, 1992), chapter 12 ("Force and Opinion": quote from 361). Leela Gandhi discusses the complex "double representation" of power, the paradoxical interplay of its "fundamentally coercive" logic with its "frequently seductive" appearance to the colonized, in *Postcolonial Theory: A Critical Introduction* (New York: Columbia University Press, 1998), 9–16.

13. Clifford Ando, *Imperial Ideology and Provincial Loyalty in the Roman Empire* (Berkeley and Los Angeles: University of California Press, 2000), 67.

14. Ibid.; the rhetorical question is a quotation from J. Béranger, *Principatus* (Geneva: Droz, 1975), 166.

15. Richard Gordon, "From Republic to Principate: Priesthood, Religion, and Ideology," in *Pagan Priests: Religion and Power in the Ancient World,* eds. Mary Beard and John North (Ithaca: Cornell University Press, 1990), 192.

16. Walter Wink, *Engaging the Powers: Discernment and Resistance in a World of Domination* (Minneapolis: Fortress Press, 1992), 93.

17. Here the work of P. A. Brunt is indispensable: *Roman Imperial Themes* (Oxford: Clarendon, 1990).

18. See Gerhard E. Lenski's extended discussion of agrarian empires in *Power and Privilege: A Theory of Social Stratification* (New York: McGraw-Hill, 1966), chaps. 8 and 9. Roland Boer argues for shifting analysis away from Marx's category of "mode of production" to the more flexible concept of "regimes of allocation," distinguishing tribute, "war machine," corvée labor, slavery, and patron-client regimes of allocation and identifying the last two especially with the Roman world (*Marxist Criticism of the Bible* [Sheffield: Sheffield Academic, 2003], 244–45). G. E. M. de Ste. Croix observes that while slavery was an indispensable component of the Roman economy, it was only one form of unfree labor. The Roman economy depended on both the ownership of land and the control of unfree labor: "it was these assets above all which enabled the propertied class to exploit the rest of the population" (*Class Struggle in the Ancient Greek World: From the Archaic Age to the Arab Conquests* [Ithaca: Cornell University Press, 1980], 33; 133–34); Garnsey and Saller offer a very similar assessment (*The Roman Empire,* chaps. 3–5).

19. Ste. Croix, *Class Struggle in the Ancient Greek World,* 409.

20. Ibid., 409–11. V. Nutton remarks that by emphasizing the "concord" enjoyed by all in their cities, provincial elites could "announce to the governor and the emperor that police action [was] unnecessary" ("The Beneficial Ideology," in *Imperialism in the Ancient World,* eds. Peter Garnsey and C. R. Whittaker [Cambridge: Cambridge University Press, 1978], 212); see also M. H. Crawford, "Greek Intellectuals and the Roman Aristocracy," in Garnsey and Whittaker, 193–207.

21. Said, *Culture and Imperialism,* xvii. The characterization of the Roman economy as parasitic is that of Peter Garnsey and Richard Saller, *The Roman Empire: Economy, Society, and Culture* (Berkeley and Los Angeles: University of California Press, 1987), 8.

22. John H. Kautsky observes that "the aristocrat's claim to provide benefits to the peasant probably serves the function of making the peasant's exploitation more acceptable to him so that he will pay his dues and perform his labor services more willingly and cause less trouble for his lord"; but the relationship is not really reciprocal: "whereas the aristocrat is free to take or not to take the peasant's taxes, the peasant is not free to accept or reject the aristocrat's protection" (*The Politics of Aristocratic Empires* (Chapel Hill: University of North Carolina Press, 1982), 111–14; the same non-reciprocal dynamic applied between patron and client in an urban setting. On the prevalence of the rhetoric of benefaction see Frederick Danker, *Benefactor: Epigraphic Study of a Greco-Roman and New Testament Semantic Field* (St. Louis: Clayton, 1982); on its ideological aspect, V. Nutton, "The Beneficial Ideology," in *Imperialism in the Ancient World*, ed. Garnsey and Whittaker, 338–43; on its close symbolic connection with priesthood and sacrificial ceremony, see Richard Gordon, "The Veil of Power: Emperors, Sacrificers, and Benefactors," in *Pagan Priests: Religion and Power in the Ancient World*, ed. Beard and North, 199–234.

23. Ste. Croix, *Class Struggle*, 370–71; 360. Martin Goodman observes that "it was patent to all that [Octavian's] success was due to the ruthless manipulation of a huge fighting machine"; nevertheless, Augustan propaganda avoided "the crudity of the power struggle," choosing "not to mask power, but to legitimize it" (*The Roman World, 44 BC–AD 180* [London and New York: Routledge, 1997], 123–34).

24. Though modern historians often have hailed the "revolution" achieved by Augustus's "restoration" of republican values (due to their taking his propaganda claims at face value), Ste. Croix contends that the governing class accorded unprecedented power to Augustus precisely to avoid continuing and destructive struggles for dominance (*Class Struggle*, 362–63). The principate "was supremely successful in maintaining social stability, in the sense of the dominance of the Roman propertied classes" (360); its introduction occasioned "very little change in the economic system and not much in the social complexion of Italy" (370). Although he acknowledges that the people "saw in the emperors a restraint on the rapacity of the Senate . . . and for themselves a refuge" (362), he demonstrates that in reality "the very existence of the poorer classes, as a potential reservoir of unrest," helped to induce the upper classes "to accept as supreme ruler a man they knew to be by inclination entirely on their side against any conceivable kind of revolution from below" (371). Indeed, Ste. Croix argues, it was Augustus's own conservatism that secured his position (371). On the emperors' self-representation as champions of the people against the elite, see also Michael Parenti, *The Assassination of Julius Caesar: A People's History of Ancient Rome* (New York: Free Press, 2004), chap. 8 (on Caesar). P. A. Brunt observes that once empowered, regional aristocracies exploited the local peasantry on Rome's behalf: "the masses could not look to Rome for effective protection against their local masters" ("Romanization of the Local Ruling Classes," in *Roman Imperial Themes*, 271).

25. Augustus, *Res gestae* 32 (Greek and Latin texts in *Velleius Paterculus: Compendium of Roman History; Res gestae Divi Augusti*, with an English translation by Frederick W. Shipley (LCL).

26. On the essential interchangeability of emperors, see Ste. Croix, *Class Struggle*, 380–81.

27. *Aeneid* 1.263; 6.851–53.

28. Cicero, *De provinciis consularibus* 10. Seneca refers to the Judeans in Rome as *victi*, "the defeated" (*On Superstition*, according to Augustine, *City of God* 6.10); Tacitus declares that in pre-Hellenistic times, Judeans "were slaves regarded as the lowest of the low," a nation too "degraded" to be properly Hellenized by Antiochus (*Hist.* 5.9).

29. James C. Scott, *Domination and the Arts of Resistance: Hidden Transcripts* (New Haven: Yale University Press, 1990), 5.

30. Ibid., 28.

31. Historian P. A. Brunt makes the point when he observes that Cicero's "own personal opinions can only be properly elicited from his intimate letters," when he had no particular reason to "veil or distort his real views" ("*Laus Imperii*," in *Roman Imperial Themes*, 288–89).

32. "It is obvious that conquests proved immensely profitable both to the state and to innumerable individuals" (Brunt, "Roman Imperial Illusions," 440). One rival challenged the Romans to

admit that "if we are to say what is true rather than what is plausible, it is lust for empire that rouses two kindred and neighboring peoples to arms"; but from the Roman point of view, it was rather a contest to determine who would rule, and who would serve (Livy, *History* 1.23.7; 1.25.3). Suetonius accused Julius Caesar of having gone to war in Gaul out of greed (*Caesar*, passim). Lactantius later could concede that it was by "inflicting injuries under cover of law and unceasingly coveting and carrying off what belonged to others that Rome obtained possession of the world" (*de div. inst.* 6.9.4; Brunt, "*Laus imperii*," 307). Ste. Croix similarly discusses the "enormous wealth" that came to Rome as the result of its wars: "There is more than enough contemporary evidence to convict the Romans— or rather, their propertied class . . . of plundering the provinces on a vast scale" (*Class Struggle,* 355).

33. Ste. Croix, *Class Struggle,* 347–48.

34. The Roman system of "deficit spending . . . amounted to an upward redistribution of income, much like the kind practiced by indebted governments today, including our own" (Parenti, *The Assassination of Julius Caesar,* 52–53). Ste. Croix, *Class Struggle,* cites an analysis by Karl Marx regarding the British subjugation of India and the profits that advanced to individual Englishmen. A similar case is ready at hand in contemporary newspapers, where headlines detail the costs to the American public of the most recent wars, alongside the schedule of federal contracts with corporations closely tied to the White House for rebuilding shattered nations. (The costs to be borne by the conquered peoples do not seem to merit calculation.) Although we heard fervent denials in advance that the most recent war on Iraq involved any desire to control Iraqi oil, because the costs of war would be prohibitive to the interested oil companies, the aftermath of the war has shown what those with eyes could have seen from the beginning: that profits could safely accrue to a tiny few after costs had been imposed on the vast majority.

35. In a Syrian market, Apollonius of Tyana found nothing but animal fodder on sale, "and the citizens were feeding on this and on anything else they could get; for the rich had shut up all the grain and were holding it for export from the country." The second-century physician Galen makes a similar observation regarding the peasant class "among many of the peoples subject to the Romans," who (after exactions by the Roman cities) are reduced to making do with "an unwholesome diet," "shoots and suckers of trees and bushes, and bulbs and roots of unwholesome plants": Ramsay MacMullen, *Roman Social Relations, 50 B.C. to A.D. 284* (New Haven: Yale University, 1974), 33.

36. The phrase comes from the later emperor Julian, *Epistle* 89; cited by MacMullen, *Roman Social Relations,* 158 n. 25; on terms of elite contempt especially for the rural poor; ibid., 28–31.

37. Plutarch, *Moralia* 47.1.

38. Ste. Croix, *Class Struggle,* 355.

39. Dio Cassius, *History of Rome* 57.10 (quoted by Ste. Croix, *Class Struggle*, 363).

40. As Josephus quotes him, Tiberius told a group of dinner guests, "If. . .those appointed kept their posts longer, they would be gorged with their robberies and would by the very bulk of them be more sluggish in pursuit of further gain," thus very helpfully allowing the poor on whom they fed to replenish themselves for the next round of extortion. Just so, the emperor elaborated, a man bleeding from grievous injuries prefers not to swat away a swarm of flies, for once they begin to get "their fill of blood," they feed more slowly; while a new swarm of hungrier flies would promptly "be the death" of him (Josephus, *A. J.* 18.172–75).

41. Juvenal, *Sat.* 8.87–90.

42. Suetonius *Nero* 32. Nero thus fulfilled what an earlier Greek observer, Diodorus Siculus, had described as the unique character of the Roman people, a "genius for leaving nothing for anybody else" (*Hist.* 5.38.3).

43. Gaius Cassius, quoted by Tacitus (*Ann.* 14.42–45); Ste. Croix, *Class Struggle,* 409.

44. Pliny, *Ep.* 3.14.5; Ste. Croix, *Class Struggle,* 409.

45. Cicero, *Pro Flaccum* 1–16; *Rep.* 3.45; 5.6, 9–11; 6.9; 3.37.

46. Josephus, *J.W.* 2.345–404; 5.368.

47. P. A. Brunt, "*Laus Imperii*," in Garnsey and Whittaker, *Imperialism in the Ancient World*, 160.

48. Livy, *Ab urbe condita* 37.3.15–17.

49. Cicero, *De republica*, 5.6.

50. Velleius Paterculus, *History of Rome*, 2.126 (Latin text in *Velleius Paterculus: Compendium of Roman History; Res gestae Divi Augusti*, with an English translation by Frederick W. Shipley (LCL).

51. *The Fortunes of the Romans*, 318. See my comments on "Contextualizing Paul's Rhetoric within Empire," in "Paul and the Politics of Empire: Problems and Prospects," pp. 27–33 in *Paul and Politics: Ekklesia, Israel, Imperium, Interpretation*, ed. Richard A. Horsley (Harrisburg: Trinity Press International, 2000).

52. Susan E. Alcock, *Graecia Capta: The Landscapes of Roman Greece* (Cambridge: Cambridge University Press, 1993), 132, 144.

53. Ste. Croix, *Class Struggle*, 344.

54. Friedman, *The Lexus and the Olive Tree*, 8.

55. Ignácio Martín-Baró described (before he was murdered, with his fellow Jesuits, by a U.S.-armed death squad) how a campaign of state terrorism in El Salvador achieved the "internalized acceptance of terror" on the part of the subjugated and thus served a larger "government-imposed socio-political project" that secured the needs of the privileged (Ignácio Martín-Baró, transcript of comments at a symposium in Berkeley, California, January 17, 1989; cited by Noam Chomsky, *Deterring Democracy* [New York: Hill and Wang, 1992], 386–87; see ibid., chap. 12, "Force and Opinion," and Martín-Baró, *Writings for a Liberation Psychology*, eds. Adrianne Aron and Shawn Corne [Cambridge: Harvard University Press, 1994]). Fanon's searing anti-colonial writings include his correlation of mental disorders among the Algerian populace with the effects of French occupation: *The Wretched of the Earth*, trans. Constance Farrington (New York: Grove, 1963). The lesson can readily be generalized to Guatemala, Haiti, Algeria, and many other places around the world and is occasionally admitted by the colonial power itself. Declassified CIA documents characterized the CIA-organized "Front for the Advancement of the Haitian People" as "a sort of Mafia," "gun-carrying crazies" whose "use of force to intimidate and coerce is sanctioned by the local military" (Farhan Haq, "Haiti: Rights Groups Disclose U.S. Support for Extremists," InterPress Service, Feb. 7, 1996). A French Defense Ministry delegation described the counterinsurgency program in post-colonial Algeria as "the fairly simple technique of terrorizing the population" (*Los Angeles Times*, June 30, 1996). And so on.

56. Scott, *Domination*, 137; 138.

57. Scott, *Domination*, 8 (emphasis added).

58. "If their enemy has wealth, they have greed; if he is poor, they are ambitious. . . . To plunder, butcher, steal, these things they misname empire; they make a desolation and call it peace. . . . [Our children] are swept away from us by conscription to be slaves in other lands; our wives and sisters, even when they escape a soldier's lust, are debauched by self-styled friends and guests; our goods and chattels go for tribute; our lands and harvests, in requisitions of grain; life and limb themselves are used up in leveling marsh and forest to the accompaniment of gibes and blows. Slaves born to slavery are sold once for all and are fed by their masters free of cost; but Britain pays a daily price for her own enslavement, and feeds the slavers."

So Calgacus as quoted by Tacitus, *Agr.* 30.3—31.2; excerpted in Klaus Wengst, *Pax Romana and the Peace of Jesus Christ*, trans. John Bowden (Philadelphia: Fortress Press, 1987), 52–53. Wengst also cites the speeches of the Gaul Critognatus in Caesar's *Bell. gall.* 7.77.14–16, and the Parthian Mithridates in *Pompeius Trogus* 38.6, 7 (ibid. 194 n. 327); so also Parenti, *The Assassination of Julius Caesar*, 16–17; and compare Ste. Croix, *Class Struggle*, 441–45.

59. "I am not fighting for my kingdom and wealth. I am fighting as an ordinary person for my lost freedom, my bruised body, and my outraged daughters. Nowadays Roman rapacity does not even spare our bodies. Old people are killed, virgins raped. But the gods will grant us the vengeance we deserve! . . . Consider how many of you are fighting, and why. Then you will win this battle, or perish. That is what I, a woman, plan to do! Let the men live in slavery if they will."

So Boudicca, according to Tacitus, *Ann.* 14.35. Tacitus then recites the speech in which the Roman commander urged his soldiers to massacre the "unwarlike, unarmed" Britons, who offered defiance, killing some 80,000 people, not sparing "even the women"; in Tacitus's eyes, the massacre was "a glorious victory."

60. See further Ste. Croix, *Class Struggle,* 441–45.

61. See *J. A.* 18.9, Tessa Rajak, *Josephus: The Historian and His Society* (Philadelphia: Fortress Press, 1983); John M. G. Barclay, *Jews in the Mediterranean Diaspora from Alexander to Trajan (323 BCE–117 CE)* (Edinburgh: T&T Clark, 1996), 346–51.

62. Josephus, *J. W.* 2.348–49. Josephus explains that since the stubbornness of the rebels "is universally known and evident, I shall refrain from reporting it in greater detail" (*Ant.* 18.23–25). On the anti-Roman cause, see Martin Hengel, *The Zealots: Investigations into the Jewish Freedom Movement in the Period from Herod I until 70 A.D.,* trans. David Smith (Edinburgh: T&T Clark, 1980), and Richard A. Horsley, *Jesus and the Spiral of Violence: Popular Jewish Resistance in Roman Palestine* (San Francisco: Harper and Row, 1987). I have tried to reconstruct aspects of the anti-Roman position from the attitudes that Josephus caricatures (in *J. W.* 3.348–401) and to compare the results with the "philosophy" of the anonymous author of *4 Macc.* (Neil Elliott, *Liberating Paul* [Minneapolis: Fortress Press 2006], 149–67.)

63. Ste. Croix, *Class Struggle,* 352–53. Michael Parenti provides a vivid history of the brutal class warfare inflicted by the self-styled "best men" of republican Rome, the *optimates,* who used private armies to slaughter thousands and thus to destroy popular movements for even modest democracy and land reform. He notes that the three largest slave rebellions, occurring in the last two centuries of the Republic, "reached the level of open warfare. . . . All were mercilessly crushed. There were numerous other slave uprisings but they were small-scale, short-lived, and unsuccessful. . . ." Even among slaves who held back from rising up, Parenti suggests we can safely assume the same level of "hidden 'ingratitude'" that so inflamed former slaveholders in the South following the U.S. Civil War: *The Assassination of Julius Caesar,* 38, 42, 59–83.

64. Parenti (*The Assassination of Julius Caesar,* 117–18) quotes Plutarch, *Caesar* 6.1–4: "it was incredible how numerous" the supporters of a slain popular leader, Marius, proved to be, "and what a multitude of them appeared came shouting into the Capitol," on the subsequent occasion of his widow's death.

65. Scott, *Domination,* 36–37; 136; 150–51, 14. On the Roman "mob," see Ste. Croix, *Class Struggle,* 357, 361.

66. On graffiti as an important source for non-elite perceptions, see Justin J. Meggitt, *Paul, Poverty, and Survival;* Studies of the New Testament and Its World (Edinburgh: T&T Clark, 1998), 34–35. Edward Champlin, *Nero* (Cambridge: Harvard University Press, 2003) discusses anonymous expressions of disdain for the emperor (*Nero,* 91).

67. Scott, *Domination and the Arts of Resistance,* 136–52, 20–22; Meggitt, *Paul, Poverty, and Survival,* 34–35. The movement surrounding the populist land reformer Tiberius Gracchus relied on mass action and graffiti alike. See Plutarch, *Ti. C. Gracch.* 21.2–3; Parenti, *The Assassination of Julius Caesar,* 217.

68. Scott, *Domination,* chap. 6.

69. Tacitus, *Ann.* 12.64; 13.48; 14.42–45; Parenti, *The Assassination of Julius Caesar,* 215–16.

70. Ste. Croix, *Class Struggle,* 362.

71. On the corruption and avarice of the empire under Nero, see esp. Brunt, *Roman Imperial Themes,* 28–31.

72. Tacitus, *Ann.* 13.50–51; on the *portoria,* see Goodman, *The Roman World,* 100–101; Brunt, *Roman Imperial Themes,* 354–432. Ste. Croix points out that "an emperor could express solicitude for taxpayers on the ground that they needed to be protected against greedy officials, *in order to be able to pay their taxes in full*" (*Class Struggle,* 383).

73. See Meggitt's discussion of the dole in *Paul, Poverty, and Survival,* 51–53. Women, children, slaves, and non-citizens were excluded. The dole would have provided "a guarantee against starvation

for the recipient and one dependent," but their situation would nonetheless have been "precarious" (ibid., n. 53).

74. *Natural History* 18.35. Philo of Alexandria reported that a few rich individuals in Rome had amassed more wealth than was to be found in the rest of the empire: *Embassy* 108.

75. Suetonius, *Nero* 30–32; 45; Tacitus, *Ann.* 13.50–51.

76. In graffiti, Romans scorned the pretension that the emperor bore Apollo's image, comparing him instead to an official enemy:

> Though Nero may pluck the chords of a lyre
> And the Parthian King the string of a bow,
> He who chants to the lyre with heavenly fire
> Is Apollo as much as his far-darting foe.

Graffiti accused the arrogant emperor of provoking the rebels in Gaul—

> Nero's crowing has awakened the *galli*—

using a Latin pun meaning both "roosters" and "Gauls." After 59 C.E. they accused Nero of murdering his mother:

> Aeneas the Trojan hero
> Carried off his aged father;
> His remote descendant Nero
> Likewise carried off his mother;
> Heroes worthy of each other.

These are Robert Graves's translations of Suetonius, *Nero* 39 (*The Twelve Caesars*, ed. Michael Grant [New York: Penguin, 1957], 236–37). Champlin discusses these and other anonymous messages ("pasquinades"): *Nero*, 91–92.

77. See Champlin, *Nero*, chap. 4.

78. Robert Jewett (*Romans*; assisted by Roy D. Kotansky; ed. Eldon Jay Epp; Hermeneia [Minneapolis: Fortress Press, 2007]), 47–48, citing Miriam T. Griffin, *Nero: The End of a Dynasty* (London and New York: Routledge, 2000), 111; but Griffin herself discusses how artificial are various scenarios of "descent" from supposed "good years" to bad (ibid., 83–99). None of the sources "yields anything so definite and crude as a neat Quinquennium"; examples of commendable and shameful acts "come from all periods of Nero's reign" (83).

79. Champlin, *Nero*, chap. 1.

80. Ibid., 52; on the "disgraceful" aspects of Nero's public performances as seen by the aristocracy (and his consequent popularity among lower-class audiences), 65–68. Champlin's own view is that on balance, Nero was in fact "a bad man and a bad ruler" (52). My point is that Nero's *posthumous* popularity need not depend on actual memories of Nero as a good ruler, but rather as a capricious, powerful, and violent one; he was therefore a fitting target for fantasies of vengeance in later generations.

81. Martial, *Epigram* 7.34; Champlin, *Nero*, 25.

82. Scott, *Domination*, 14.

83. Philo, *On Dreams* 2.92. On the significance of this passage for an appropriate understanding of Philo's politics, see E. R. Goodenough, *An Introduction to Philo Judaeus*, 2nd ed. (Oxford: Basil Blackwell, 1962), 55–62; on its relevance for an adequate understanding of rhetoric in the Roman period, see my essay, "Romans 13:1-7 in the Context of Imperial Propaganda," in *Paul and Empire: Religion and Power in Roman Imperial Society*, ed. Richard A. Horsley (Harrisburg: Trinity Press International, 1997), 196–204; on these texts as examples of hidden transcripts, see my essays, "The 'Patience of the Jews': Strategies of Resistance and Accommodation to Imperial Cultures," in *Pauline Conversations in Context: Essays in Honor of Calvin J. Roetzel,* ed. Janice Capel Anderson, Philip Sellew, and Claudia Setzer, JSNTSup 221 (Sheffield: Sheffield Academic, 2002), 32–42, and "Strategies of Resistance and Hidden Transcripts in the Pauline Communities," in *Hidden Transcripts and*

the Arts of Resistance, ed. Richard Horsley (Atlanta: Society of Biblical Literature, 2004), 97–122. Scott's term for what Philo calls "caution" (*eulabeia*) is "tactical prudence" (*Domination,* 15).

84. The indispensable modern works are S. R. F. Price, *Rituals and Power: The Roman Imperial Cult in Asia Minor* (Cambridge: Cambridge University Press, 1984); Paul Zanker, *The Power of Images in the Age of Augustus* (Ann Arbor: University of Michigan Press, 1988); and Brunt, *Roman Imperial Themes.* These are helpfully excerpted, and their relevance for the study of Paul is discussed, in Horsley, ed., *Paul and Empire.* See also V. Nutton, "The Beneficial Ideology," especially 210–11, in Garnsey and Whittaker, *Imperialism in the Ancient World.*

85. Brunt, *"Laus Imperii,"* 160.

86. *Rep.* 3.15.

87. Aristotle, *Pol.* 1254a 22–24; Dionysius of Halicarnassus, *Ant. Rom.* 5.2; Appian, preface to the *Roman History* 30–31; Herodian, *History of the Empire* 3.2.8. Ando (*Imperial Ideology and Provincial Loyalty,* 55–56 and n. 30) cites P. A. Brunt (*Roman Imperial Themes,* 79) on the mutual rivalry of Greek cities, which in Ando's estimation speaks to "the value of the Roman Empire"; but Brunt himself recognizes that the glories of empire as described, for example, by Cicero "can have had no appeal to the poor" in Rome, or, we may infer, elsewhere; that argument is the burden of Ste. Croix's magisterial work *Class Struggle in the Ancient Greek World.*

88. Brunt, *"Laus imperii"*; "Roman Imperial Illusions," in *Roman Imperial Themes,* 433–80.

89. Brunt, *"Laus imperii,"* 309–14.

90. *Paul and Empire,* Richard A. Horsley; Karl Galinksy, *Augustan Culture* (Princeton: Princeton University Press, 1998) 60–61.

91. Sallust quotes Sulla in *Iug.* 102.6; Clifford Ando, who is at pains to emphasize the "sincerity" of the Roman sources (*Imperial Ideology,* 67), nevertheless finds Sallust's quotation "laden with irony" (58–59).

92. Livy, *Ab urbe condita* 37.3.15–17; Ste. Croix, *Class Struggle,* 342.

93. Ando reads these sources as "sincere" evidence that the Romans sought "to invite the cooperation of their subjects": *Imperial Ideology and Provincial Loyalty,* 58–59.

94. Horace, *Carmen Saeculare* 57–59.

95. *Res gestae* preface; 5.26, 29, 30, 32.

96. Ramsey MacMullen, *Roman Social Relations,* 44–45; on the humiliations accompanying patronage, 114; on patronage as a regimen allowing impunity to the aggressor, 8.

97. Ibid., 10–11. On the fabulous fortunes individual Romans were able to extract through legal and illegal means, see Ste. Croix, *Class Struggle,* 346–47.

98. Ando, *Imperial Ideology,* 5–7 and passim.

99. *Mos.* 2.49–51.

100. Josephus is "the most forthright example of Jewish-Roman political accommodation known to us" (John M. G. Barclay, *Jews in the Mediterranean Diaspora from Alexander to Trajan (323 B.C.E.–117 C.E.)* [Edinburgh: T&T Clark, 1996], 356).

101. Josephus, *Ag. Ap.* 2.164–67. The consequence, Josephus wrote, was that each Judean "is firmly persuaded" personally to be willing to face any coercive violence, even to the point of death, "rather than to utter a single word against the Law" (2.218–19, 232–35).

102. *PssSol* 1:4-8; 2:1-2; 1QpHab, passim; Philo, *On Dreams* 2.89–90 (Abraham and the sons of Cheth), 2.78–80 (on Joseph as a figure of the tyrant). For a fuller discussion of these texts in terms of Scott's hidden transcripts, see Elliott, "The 'Patience of the Jews'" (art. cit.). The political approach to Philo's allegorical biblical interpretation owes much to E. R. Goodenough, *The Politics of Philo Judaeus* (New Haven: Yale University Press, 1938); see also Dieter Georgi, *The Opponents of Paul in Second Corinthians* (Philadelphia: Fortress Press, 1986), 183–85.

103. *Spec. Laws* 3.159–62. On the regular coercion of the tax gatherers, see MacMullen, *Roman Social Relations,* 36–37; from Palestine we hear protests that "before the grain-tax is delivered, the poll-tax is due" and that "the cities are set up by the state in order . . . to extort and oppress" (ibid., 34, and references there).

104. For example, the Apocalypse to John or *4 Ezra* (2 Esdras), where Rome is represented as an eagle that has "held sway over the world with great terror, and over all the earth with grievous oppression" (*4 Ezra* 11:37-46); see Wengst, *Pax Romana*, 53–54.

105. Cynthia Briggs Kittredge, "Reconstructing 'Resistance' or Reading to Resist: James C. Scott and the Politics of Interpretation," in Horsley, *Hidden Transcripts and the Arts of Resistance*, 145–55.

106. Champlin, *Nero*, 94.

107. *Clem.* 1.1.1–2; 1.3.5–1.4.3.

108. Champlin, *Nero*, 63, quoting Cicero, *Pro Sestio*, 106.

109. Ibid., 63–64. Champlin means by his extended discussion of this political aspect of the games (63–68) to demonstrate that Nero was in earnest as a performer; his discussion also demonstrates that the very theatricality of the games ensured that the central message conveyed by the medium was that of the emperor's attentiveness to "his" people. Similarly, Miriam Griffin observes that "with the end of free political activity, only the games were left as a regular place where popular enthusiasms and grievances could be aired without counting as civic disorder," and that the games functioned to allow the emperor a public venue for displaying his civic virtues (*Nero*, 110–11).

110. Champlin, *Nero*, 66–67; on the relation between ostentatious benefactions (the games, the corn dole) and popularity, see Griffin, *Nero*, 104–12. On the heavily scripted theatricality of the "conversation" between emperor and people at the games, I note Scott's suggestion that the greater the pressure exerted by a disparity in power, the more ritualized the public discourse will be (*Domination and the Arts of Resistance*, 3).

111. Champlin, *Nero*, 95.

112. Ibid., 96; 103. N. T. Wright cites Champlin's work to support his contention that Paul's audience would have picked up the "counter-imperial signals" in Romans "loud and clear" (*Paul in Fresh Perspective* [Minneapolis: Fortress Press, 2005], 10).

113. On the oral performance of ancient letters, see Joanna Dewey, "Textuality in an Oral Culture: A Survey of the Pauline Traditions," *Semeia* 65 (1994): 37–65; Antoinette Clark Wire, "Performance, Politics, and Power: A Response," *Semeia* 65 (1994): 129.

114. Richard B. Hays, *Echoes of Scripture in the Letters of Paul* (New Haven: Yale University Press, 1989), 29–33.

115. Richard B. Hays, *The Faith of Jesus Christ: The Narrative Substructure of Galatians 3:1—4:11*; 2nd ed. (Grand Rapids: Eerdmans, 2002), xl–xlii.

116. N. T. Wright notes that imperial themes were "almost entirely screened out" in the work of the Pauline Theology Section of the SBL through the 1980s and early 1990s: "Paul's Gospel and Caesar's Empire," in *Paul and Politics: Ekklesia, Israel, Imperium, Interpretation*, ed. R. A. Horsley (Philadelphia: Trinity Press International, 2000), 162.

117. For Paul, "Christ" means fully *messiah*, the anointed king of Jewish scripture, destined to rule Israel and in fact the whole world, as N. T. Wright has shown conclusively (*The Climax of the Covenant: Christ and the Law in Pauline Theology* [Minneapolis: Fortress Press, 1991], chaps. 2, 3; Wright, "Paul's Gospel," 166–67). *Kyrios* was the title claimed by successive Caesars as a divine prerogative; in official inscriptions, each is *Kyrios Kaisaros*, "Lord" Caesar. Wright concludes that the gospel Paul proclaims is "a royal proclamation aimed at challenging other royal proclamations," at once fulfilling the prophecies of Jewish scripture and "subverting the imperial gospel of Caesar" ("Paul's Gospel," 168).

118. Ernst Käsemann rightly objected to efforts to derive the term *euangelion* solely from Second Isaiah (*Commentary on Romans*, trans. G. W. Bromiley [Grand Rapids: Eerdmans, 1980], 7). A famous inscription from Priene indicates that *euangelion* was "a technical term for 'news of victory,'" connoting the wonderful benefits bestowed by Caesar's triumphant accession to power (see G. Friedrich, "*euangelion*," *TDNT* 2:722–25, and now Dieter Georgi, *Theocracy in Paul's Praxis and Theology*, trans. David E. Green (Minneapolis: Fortress Press, 1991), 83. The inscription reads, in part:

The providence which has ordered the whole of our life, showing concern and zeal, has ordained the most perfect consummation for human life by giving it to Augustus, by filling him with virtue for doing the work of a benefactor among men, and by sending in him, as it were, a savior for us and those who come after us, to make war to cease, to create order everywhere.... The birthday of the god [Augustus] was the beginning for the world of the glad tidings that have come to men through him.

The inscription, dated to 9 B.C.E., is published in Wilhelm Dittenberger, ed., *Sylloge Inscriptionum Graecarum,* 3rd ed. (Leipzig: Hirzel, 1915–24), 458.

119. Käsemann, *Commentary,* 19–20; 391–92.

120. Robert Jewett observes that polite requests (like the *parakalō*-clause in 12:1) were regularly used in Roman diplomatic correspondence "in place of commands" that might have offended the sensibilities of subordinates (Jewett, *Romans,* 725–27). Jewett rightly refers to the parallel use of "diplomatic" language in Philemon 8-10: "though I am bold enough in Christ to command you to do your duty [*epitassein soi to anēkon*], yet for love's sake I prefer to exhort you [*parakalō*]—I, Paul, an ambassador and now a prisoner for Christ Jesus as well." These observations militate against Jewett's own identification of Romans as an "ambassadorial" letter (42–46).

121. The genre of the admonitory letter was well established in Paul's day. Here is the description attributed to Demetrius of Phalerum (first century B.C.E.): "The admonishing type [of letter: *nouthetikē*] is one which indicates through its name what its character is. For admonition is the instilling of sense [*noun tithein*] in the person who is being admonished, and teaching him what should and should not be done" (Pseudo-Demetrius, *Epistolary Types*). See Abraham Malherbe's translation, "Ancient Epistolary Theorists," *OJRS* 5 (1977): 3–77; Malherbe, *Moral Exhortation: A Greco-Roman Sourcebook* (Philadelphia: Westminster, 1986), 81; and Stanley K. Stowers, *Letter Writing in Greco-Roman Antiquity* (Philadelphia: Westminster, 1986), 125–26. Stowers points out that Paul's expression of confidence in the Romans is "a rather typical . . . assertion of the audience's lack of need for admonition which reflects the kinship between paraenesis and admonition" (128).

122. "The preferred way of instructing was through speech. Writers like Seneca regarded letters as the next best" (Malherbe, *Moral Exhortation,* 68). On the role of Paul's letters as surrogates for Paul's apostolic presence, see Robert W. Funk, "The Apostolic Parousia: Form and Significance," in *Christian History and Interpretation: Studies Presented to John Knox,* ed. W. R. Farmer, C. F. D. Moule, and R. R. Niebuhr (Cambridge: Cambridge University Press, 1967), 249–68. On the equal importance of Paul's coworkers who were prepared in person, by the apostle, to read the letters aloud and thus to embody his apostolic presence among the recipients, see Joanna Dewey, "Textuality in an Oral Culture: A Survey of the Pauline Traditions," *Semeia* 65 (1994): 37–65; Richard Ward, "Pauline Voice and Presence as Strategic Communication," *Semeia* 65, 102–3; and Antoinette Clark Wire, "Performance, Politics, and Power: A Response," *Semeia* 65, 129.

123. J. Paul Sampley insists, *"Rom 15:15 must be seen as a key to understanding (a) in what spirit and (b) why he has written* because there Paul *says how and why he wrote."* Romans "is not merely or even primarily written 'for the sake of mission': *it is mission* at work!" "Romans in a Different Light," in *Pauline Theology,* vol. 3: *Romans,* ed. David M. Hay and E. Elizabeth Johnson (Minneapolis: Fortress Press, 1993), 129; 115. As I made the point in *The Rhetoric of Romans* (Sheffield: JSOT, 1990), 87, "Rom 1:15 describes the visit Paul would like to have made, *but cannot;* Rom 15:24 refers to the visit he *will* be able to make after delivering the collection to Jerusalem (15:25-29). 'Evangelizing' the Romans is absent from Paul's future plans, not because that was never really his intention, but because that intention *has been achieved* between chaps. 1 and 15, that is, *by the letter itself.* Romans is written as a surrogate for the visit Paul has long desired to make (1:10–15) under the constraint of his obligation as apostle to *all* [the nations, including the churches in Rome]. The letter *is* Paul's *euangelisasthai.*" (Emphasis in original.)

124. James C. Miller, *The Obedience of Faith, the Eschatological People of God, and the Purpose of Romans* (Atlanta: Scholars, 2000), esp. 17–21; Don B. Garlington, *The 'Obedience of Faith,'* WUNT n.f. 38 (Tübingen: Mohr [Siebeck], 1991), 1.

125. Compare "your faithfulness," *hē pistis hymōn*, 1:8, with "your obedience," *hē . . . hymōn hypakoē*, 16:19; "the obedience of faithfulness among the nations," *hypoakoēn pisteōs en pasin tois ethnesin*, 1:5, with "the obedience of the nations," *hypakoēn ethnōn*, 15:18). See Käsemann, *Commentary on Romans*, 14–15. Regarding *hypakoēn pisteōs* in 1:5, Karl Barth wrote of the "fidelity towards God" that is the response to God's faithfulness; that faithfulness "is itself the demand for obedience" (*Commentary on Romans*, 31); Victor Paul Furnish discusses "the obedience character of faith" (*Theology and Ethics in Paul* [Nashville: Abingdon, 1968], 187, 226, 202–3). C. E. B. Cranfield translates the phrase "the obedience which consists in faith," though he cautions that he does not mean to collapse obedience into faith as assent (*The Epistle to the Romans*, ICC [Edinburgh: T&T Clark, 1975], 1:66). Similarly K. L. Schmidt argued that the response of the person "called by God can only be *pisteuein* in the sense of *hypakouein*" ("*kaleō*," *TDNT* 3:489). On this question, Richard B. Hays's narrative argument for understanding *pistis* as faithfulness, i.e., obedience, has proven decisive for many interpreters (*The Faith of Jesus Christ: An Investigation into the Narrative Substructures of Galatians 3:11—4:11*, 2nd ed. [Grand Rapids: Eerdmans, 2002]). Douglas Harink refers to Protestant interpretation before Hays as the "history of a bad translation" (*Paul among the Postliberals: Pauline Theology beyond Christendom and Modernity* [Grand Rapids, Mich.: Brazos, 2003], 26–30); see also Theodore W. Jennings, *Reading Derrida/Thinking Paul on Justice* (Palo Alto: Stanford University Press, 1980), 1–4.

126. Jewett interprets the genitive *pisteōs* as limiting the meaning of *hypakoē*: Paul speaks of the "special sort of obedience produced by the gospel," qualifying obedience in order to remove "the stigma of slavishness," which obedience held in the Roman world (*Romans*, 10–11). Similarly, John B. Cobb Jr. and David J. Lull translate "obedience defined as faithfulness" (*Romans* [St. Louis: Chalice, 2005], 30).

127. On paraenetic or exhortative letters, see Stowers, *Letter-Writing in Greco-Roman Antiquity*, 94–106; on the distinction between letters of advice and letters that command, 108.

128. So, rightly, Ernst Käsemann: "when the revelation of Christ is accepted, the rebellious world submits again to its Lord" (*Commentary on Romans*, 15). Similarly, Dieter Georgi hears in Paul's language of the "offering of the nations" (15:16) a clear indication that for Paul "the subjection of the cosmos has already begun" (*Remembering the Poor: The History of Paul's Collection for Jerusalem* [Nashville: Abingdon, 1992], 106).

129. See Georgi, *Remembering the Poor*; Sze-Kar Wan, "Collection for the Saints as Anti-Colonial Act: Implications of Paul's Ethnic Reconstruction," in *Paul and Politics*, Horsley, 206–10.

130. Christopher D. Stanley, "'Neither Jew nor Greek': Ethnic Conflict in Graeco-Roman Society," *JSNT* 64 (1996): 101–24 (emphasis added). Philip F. Esler makes much the same point: no "ethnic" group ever identified themselves as *ethnē*, "Gentiles," and therefore he declares that translation an "indefensible anachronism" (*Conflict and Identity in Romans: The Social Setting of Paul's Letter* [Minneapolis: Fortress Press, 2003], 12; see also 75, 113).

131. See James M. Scott, *Paul and the Nations: The Old Testament and Jewish Background of Paul's Mission to the Nations with Special Reference to the Destination of Galatians*, WUNT 84 (Tübingen: Mohr [Siebeck], 1995). Paul speaks in Romans of *ta ethnē*, meaning "the nations," when he cited prophecies in Israel's scriptures that the nations would at last join with Israel in the worship of Israel's God, and so the NRSV properly translates the Greek term at Rom 4:17-18 (citing Gen 17:5 and 15:5) and 10:19 (citing Deut 32:21). Elsewhere in Romans, however, the NRSV has, without explanation, turned "nations" into "Gentiles" in quotations of Jewish scripture (Rom 15:9-12, quoting Ps 18:49; Deut 32:43; Ps 117:1; and Isa 11:10), or replaced the AV and RSV "nations" with "Gentiles" (Rom 1:5; 16:26). On the unwarranted tendency to translate *ethnē* with "Gentiles," see James LaGrand, "Proliferation of the 'Gentile' in the NRSV," *Biblical Research* 41 (1996): 77–87; see also *BDAG*, under the entry *ethnē*.

132. Johannes Munck, *Paul and the Salvation of Mankind* (London: SCM, 1959), 52–54; 200–202; Dieter Georgi, *Remembering the Poor,* 102.

133. See John L. White, *The Apostle of God: Paul and the Promise of Abraham* (Peabody: Hendrickson, 1999), chap. 5: "The Roman Empire and God's Empire," esp. 130–32. White's language suggests that Paul's understanding of Christ was "influenced" by the popular image of Augustus. I would put the matter more sharply to emphasize the incompatibility of the two "lordships."

134. *Aen.* 8.720–23; the scene is depicted in the wondrous shield Vulcan has prepared for Aeneas.

135. As John Dominic Crossan puts it, Paul's "was a radically divergent, but equally global theology" (Crossan and Jonathan L. Reed, *In Search of Paul* [San Francisco: HarperSanFrancisco, 2004], 10). Crossan reminds us that these insights are a century old: Adolf Deissman already spoke of the "polemical parallelism" between the "cult of Christ" and the worship of the Caesars (*Light from the Ancient East*, trans. Lionel R. M. Strachan [Grand Rapids: Baker, 1965], 342); William Mitchell Ramsay considered it "inconceivable" that Paul could have been "insensible of the nature of the Imperial system" (*The Cities of Paul* [New York: Hodder & Stoughton, 1907]).

136. The term *New Perspective* is now used to describe a broad range of interpretations that hang together around specific judgments inspired by the works of E. P. Sanders and Krister Stendahl, as well as J. D. G. Dunn's seminal article. As the popular Web site "The Paul Page" defines the New Perspective,

> At its core is the recognition that Judaism is not a religion of self-righteousness whereby humankind seeks to merit salvation before God. Paul's argument with the Judaizers was not about Christian grace versus Jewish legalism. His argument was rather about the status of Gentiles in the church. Paul's doctrine of justification, therefore, had far more to do with Jewish-Gentile issues than with questions of the individual's status before God. (www.thePaulPage.com; accessed September 1, 2007)

137. Bruce J. Malina and John J. Pilch, *Social-Scientific Commentary on the Letters of Paul* (Minneapolis: Fortress Press, 2006), 371–74.

138. Ibid., 226.

139. Ibid., 17–20. "Paul's message was meant exclusively for Israelites" (20).

140. Ibid., 287.

141. Malina and Pilch are aware of the passage, of course, but do their best to minimize its significance. It is "the first time" Paul takes any account of non-Judeans in the Roman community, and "as a rule, Paul ignores the presence of such non-Israelite 'brothers,' since, it seems, he never recruited any"; ibid., (272–73). This is tortuous special pleading.

142. Esler, *Conflict and Identity in Romans,* 54–61.

143. Esler appeals to the "mutual hostility between Judeans and Greeks" played out in Syrian Antioch, Alexandria, and elsewhere, without any reference to the larger context of imperial policy that helped to shape or exacerbate those tensions (ibid., 74–75). Instead, he implies that ethnic tensions arise spontaneously whenever different groups are set side by side. The mere visibility and prominence of synagogue architecture in Rome would have been enough to exacerbate ethnic tensions between Judean and Greek Christ-followers (106–7); "the default position" among different house-churches would have been "one of competition, even conflict." The tensions between Judeans and Greeks in other cities would have meant that "their representatives in Rome cultivated toward one another attitudes that were similarly stereotyped and negative" (120–24).

144. Esler objects, "are we to suppose that very early in the reading . . . Judeans [in the audience] must have realized, and Paul intended them to realize, that he only had non-Judean Christ-followers within the scope of his discourse and not them? . . . Did they then sit or stand patiently for over an hour while the letter was read, all the while saying to themselves something like 'Very interesting, but of course Paul did not intend this teaching for us' . . . ?" (Ibid., 119). I consider it even more difficult to identify a place in the letter's rhetoric where the *explicitly named* audience is cued that they are no

longer being addressed. That is the methodological principle on which both Stanley K. Stowers and I based our earlier rhetorical-critical readings of Romans, and I do not understand Esler's remark that Stowers's work is "singularly unhelpful" (110).

145. Esler, *Conflict and Identity in Romans*, 138–39; from a Greek point of view, Judeans counted as barbarians, "even if Paul is mentally excluding Judeans from the ranks of the *barbaroi*."

146. See, for example, John M. G. Barclay's otherwise excellent work, *Jews in the Mediterranean Diaspora: From Alexander to Trajan (323 B.C.E.–117 C.E.)* (Edinburgh: T&T Clark, 1996).

147. Denise Kimber Buell and Caroline Johnson Hodge, "The Politics of Interpretation: The Rhetoric of Race and Ethnicity in Paul," *JBL* 123, no. 2 (2004): 235–51; see also Hodge's essay, "Apostle to the Gentiles: Constructions of Paul's Identity," in *Paul between Jews and Christians,* ed. Mark Nanos, *BibInt* 13, no. 3 (2005): 270–88.

148. Pamela Eisenbaum, "Paul, Polemics, and the Problem of Essentialism," in *Paul between Jews and Christians*, 224–38.

149. Esler, *Conflict and Identity in Romans*, 145–48.

150. Ibid., 152.

151. Tat-Siong Benny Liew, "Margins and (Cutting-) Edges: On the (Il)legitimacy and Intersections of Race, Ethnicity, and (Post)Colonialism," in *Postcolonial Biblical Criticism: Interdisciplinary Intersections,* ed. Stephen D. Moore and Fernando F. Segovia (London and New York: T&T Clark, 2005), 114–65.

152. Esler, *Conflict and Identity in Romans*, 50–51, citing D. L. Horowitz, *Ethnic Groups in Conflict* (Berkeley: University of California Press, 1985).

153. Ibid., 10; cf. 42, 52.

154. Leon V. Rutgers, "Roman Policy toward the Jews," in *Judaism and Christianity in First-Century Rome,* ed. Karl P. Donfried and Peter Richardson (Grand Rapids: Eerdmans, 1998), 98–103.

155. Esler, *Conflict and Identity in Romans*, 53–74.

156. Ibid., 102, 74–75.

157. Ibid., 10 (emphasis added).

158. Ibid.

159. Samantha Powers discussed the history of "missed opportunities" in Rwanda ("Bystanders to Genocide," *Atlantic Monthly,* Sept. 2001); a better description might have been "active efforts by the U.S. to suppress all initiatives to intervene," since she observes that American leadership was "devoted primarily to suppressing public outrage and thwarting U.N. initiatives" to intervene. Wayne Madsen discussed indications that the Halliburton corporation and its subsidiary military contractor, Root & Brown, were implicated in arming the Rwandan government in the 1990s ("Cheney at the Helm," *The Progressive,* Sept. 2000). On the political forces shaping "ethnic" conflict in the former Yugoslavia, see Noam Chomsky, *A New Generation Draws the Line: Kosovo, East Timor, and the Standards of the West* (New York: Verso, 2000), 112–14.

160. Mahmood Mamdani discusses the penchant in the United States to perceive "Muslim" or "Arab" violence, but not the violence of colonialism and imperialism and their role in creating "bad Muslims": *Good Muslim, Bad Muslim: America, the Cold War, and the Roots of Terror* (New York: Pantheon, 2004). See, as an example of the obscurantist viewpoint that Mamdani criticizes, Bernard Lewis's now infamous essay, "The Roots of Muslim Rage," *Atlantic Monthly,* Sept. 1990 (accessed online). For critiques of Lewis, see Edward Said: "The Clash of Ignorance," *The Nation,* Oct. 22, 2001 (accessed online), and "Impossible Histories: Why the Many Islams Cannot Be Simplified," *Harper's,* July 2002 (accessed online). On the Western colonial powers' creation of the "Middle East," see David Fromkin, *A Peace to End All Peace: The Fall of the Ottoman Empire and the Creation of the Modern Middle East* (New York: Avon, 1989); on the U.S. role in recruiting, arming, and training a desperate class of radical Islamists as a terror army in Afghanistan, see John K. Cooley, *Unholy Wars: Afghanistan, America, and International Terrorism,* new ed. (Sterling: Pluto, 1999), and Michael Griffin, *Reaping the Whirlwind: The Taliban Movement in Afghanistan* (Sterling: Pluto,

2001). Jameson writes that contemporary liberal ideologies of pluralism work to "forestall" more systematic analyses that would lead to "embarrassing questions" about their own political serviceability (*The Political Unconscious*, 32). See also Terry Eagleton's discussion of the limits of the multicultural perspective regnant in liberal humanities education in *Literary Theory: An Introduction* (Minneapolis: University of Minnesota Press, 1983), 169–89. Noting that "multicultural" analyses often "bypass power," Chandra Talpade Mohanty calls for a "fundamental reconceptualization of our categories of analysis so that [ethnic] differences can be historically specified and understood as part of larger political processes and systems" (*Feminism without Borders: Decolonizing Theory, Practicing Solidarity* [Durham, N.C., and London: Duke University Press, 2003], 193. In Chiapas, the rebel leader Subcomandante Marcos repudiates the colonial representation of "universalism" as a tool of oppression against the lower classes: *Our Word Is Our Weapon* (New York: Seven Stories, 2001), xx.

161. Käsemann, *Commentary on Romans*, 23; Hans Windisch, "*barbaros ktl*," *TDNT* 1:546–53.

162. See Windisch, "*barbaros ktl*." Already Cicero spoke of Roman influence "not only over Greece and Italy, but all the barbarian [nations]" (*Fin.* 2:49). Philo could flatter Augustus as the savior who had "healed the wars common to Greeks and barbarians" alike, the "barbarian" being the "unsociable and brutish nations" (*Embassy*,145–47; compare 8). It had been an important part of Philo's comprehensive apologetic campaign that Israel alone (or "the nation of the Jews," *to Ioudaiōn ethnos*) could offer the constitution that would unite all peoples, "Greeks and barbarians" alike (*Spec. Laws* 2:165f.; *Life of Moses* 2:19f.). As late as the second century C.E., Aelius Aristides could praise Rome as having "surpassed the Hellenes in wisdom and restraint, while outdoing the barbarians in riches and in might" (*Panegyric on Rome*, 41); it is some measure of Rome's achievement that "the categories into which you now divide the world are not Hellenes and barbarians, but Romans and non-Romans" (63).

163. On the social function of shame see Bruce J. Malina, *The New Testament World: Insights from Cultural Anthropology* (Atlanta: John Knox, 1981), 44; Rudolf Bultmann, "*aidōs*," *TDNT* 1:169–71; Jewett, *Romans*, 136–39. On the positive role of shame in world construction, see Peter Berger and Thomas Luckmann, *The Social Construction of Reality* (New York: Doubleday, 1967), 159–60; on its role in early Christian paraenesis, Leo Perdue, "Paraenesis and the Epistle of James" *ZNW* 72 (1981): 248–50; Abraham Malherbe, *Moral Exhortation*, 48–67.

164. Correctly emphasized by Halvor Moxnes, who cites Brunt's work explicitly: "Honor and Shame," in *The Social Sciences and New Testament Interpretation*, ed. Richard Rohrbaugh (Peabody: Hendrickson, 1996), 26–27.

165. See Fanon, *The Wretched of the Earth*, and Martín-Baró, *Writings for a Liberation Psychology*, previously cited. On the role of shame in producing submission in women trapped in the international sex trade, see Rita Nakashima Brock and Susan Brooks Thistlethwaite, *Casting Stones: Prostitution and Liberation in Asia and the United States* (Minneapolis: Fortress Press, 1996).

166. On Plato's account, he protested at last that he had been convicted on account of "lack of shamelessness" (*anaischyntia*: *Apology* 38D).

167. So a Roman general informs Gauls contemplating resistance that "it is for you that I feel shame and pity, for you are facing... war with Rome" (Tacitus, *Hist.* 4.58).

168. The pious elder, Eleazar, refuses to let his people or the Torah be put to shame (*kataischynein*, *4 Macc.* 5:34–38) and renounces the shame (*aischron*) of submitting to the king (6:20); the youths who follow him to their own deaths refuse to put their ancestors to shame (*aischynomesthai*, 9:2), insisting instead that the shame falls upon the Greek king (12:11). On *4 Maccabees* as a representation of the defiant posture that Josephus labeled the "fourth philosophy," see my *Liberating Paul*, 154–56.

169. See Luise Schottroff, "'Give to Caesar What Belongs to Caesar and to God What Belongs to God,'" in *The Love of Enemy and Nonretaliation in the New Testament*, ed. Willard Swartley (Louisville: Westminster/John Knox, 1992), 223–57.

170. Calvin J. Roetzel, "*Oikoumenē* and the Limit of Pluralism in Alexandrian Judaism and Paul," in *Diaspora Jews and Judaism: Essays in Honor of, and in Dialogue with, A. Thomas Kraabel*, ed. J. Andrew Overman and Robert S. MacLellan (Atlanta: Scholars, 1992), 163–82.

171. John White observes that "the physical specificity of [Paul's] obligation as Christ's ambassador was probably inspired by the boundaries of the Roman Empire" (*Apostle of God,* 132); curiously, he concludes that Paul's understanding of Christ was "clearly influenced by the image of Augustus" (133).

172. *Res gestae* 12–13; Suetonius, *Nero* 13 (on securing the submission of Tiridates of Armenia).

173. *Embassy* 17.

174. On *eritheia* in Rom 2:8, see *BDAG* s.v.

175. *Moralia* 814F.

176. Paul's ambiguous phrase "dead to that which held us captive" (*en hō kateichometha*, 7:6) is often taken to refer directly to the *law,* but I take his discussion of a widow's lack of obligation to her dead husband as a precise analogy: see Elliott, *The Rhetoric of Romans,* 244.

177. Jameson, *The Political Unconscious,* 46–49; 166–69; 254–57.

178. Compare 1 Corinthians 7, where Paul's attempt to resolve a similar tension in the social context is to urge the Corinthians to live "as though not" constrained by social roles (*hōs mē*); see Vincent Wimbush, *Paul the Worldly Ascetic: Responses to the World and Self-Understanding according to 1 Corinthians 7* (Macon: Mercer University Press, 1987).

179. Originally suggested by J. Friedrich, W. Pöhlmann, and P. Stuhlmacher ("Zur historischen Situation und Intention von Röm 13:1-7," *ZTK* 73 [1976]: 131–66), this possibility has gained wide acceptance as at least a partial explanation of the exhortation to "be subject to the governing authorities" and to pay taxes in Rom 13:1-7. See further chap. 5.

180. Rom 2:7; 5:3, 4; 8:25; and 15:4-5. See further chapter 5.

181. The most egregious example is surely Bruno Blumenfeld's assertion that his view that "Paul loves Rome" finds "confirmation" in a Byzantine mosaic (!), laid under a Christian emperor, encouraging Christian citizens to pay taxes (*The Political Paul: Justice, Democracy, and Kingship in a Hellenistic Framework,* JSNTSup 210 [Sheffield: Sheffield Academic, 2001], 282–83).

182. Scott, *Domination,* 79 (emphasis added).

2. IVSTITIA

1. See, for example, human rights reports by Human Rights Watch (www.hrw.org).

2. Jonathan Schell, "Empire without Law," Letter from Ground Zero [column], *The Nation* (May 31, 2004), 7.

3. As Noam Chomsky explains the logic: "the economic doctrines preached by the rulers are instruments of power, intended for others, so that they can be more efficiently robbed and exploited. No wealthy society accepts these conditions for itself" (*Year 501: The Conquest Continues* [Boston: South End, 1993], 99–117); see also Chomsky, *World Orders Old and New* [New York: Verso, 2001]). Others have similarly observed that the United States, and U.S.-dominated institutions like the World Bank and International Monetary Fund, routinely impose on developing nations free market practices that the United States has no intention of observing: see William Finnegan, "The Economics of Empire: The Washington Consensus," *Harper's,* April 2003. It is instructive that before he was appointed governor of U.S.-occupied Iraq, Paul Bremer explained, to clients of his security company, that U.S.-imposed free-trade policies would put "enormous pressure" on a country's labor and retail sectors, leading to "growing income gaps and social tensions." These would mean "immediate negative consequences for many," he admitted, but an opportunity for "the creation of unprecedented wealth" for companies like his. "New Risks in International Business," Nov. 2001 policy paper for the insurance company Marsh & McLennan, discussed by Naomi Klein, "Downsizing in Disguise," *The Nation,* June 23, 2003.

4. In the 1990s, American pundits celebrated the indictment and conviction of a Serbian soldier, Dusko Tadic, for crimes including the rape, torture, and murder of eight women in a concentration camp in Bosnia. That Emmanuel Constant, a Haitian "asset" working with an American CIA agent, had organized a terror campaign in which thousands of women were raped and brutalized, during the same years, did not prevent the State Department from granting Constant de facto immunity as he settled in Brooklyn, a notorious case that won only a fraction of the coverage in the American press. The juxtaposition is noted in Human Rights Watch's report for the year 1996, available on the Web at www.hrc.org/1997. Noam Chomsky and Edward Herman compared U.S. media coverage of contemporary crimes by "official enemies" and others in *Manufacturing Consent: The Political Economy of the Mass Media* (New York: Pantheon, 1988); the 2002 edition includes a substantially updated survey of examples.

5. Richard Hughes, *Myths America Lives By* (Urbana and Chicago: University of Illinois Press, 2003).

6. Jonathan Schell, "Empire without Law," Letter from Ground Zero [column], *The Nation* (May 31, 2004), 7.

7. G. E. M. de Ste. Croix, *Class Struggle in the Ancient Greek World: From the Archaic Age to the Arab Conquests* (Ithaca: Cornell University Press, 1980), 330.

8. P. A. Brunt, "Roman Imperial Illusions," citing the *Res gestae Divi Augusti* 438–39, in *Roman Imperial Themes* (Oxford: Clarendon, 1990); Ste. Croix, *Class Struggle,* 331.

9. 1QpHab, cols. III–VII, passim. Translation by Michael Wise, Martin Abegg Jr., and Edward Cook, *The Dead Sea Scrolls: A New Translation* (San Francisco: HarperSanFrancisco, 1996), 115–19.

10. Martin Goodman, *The Ruling Class in Judaea: The Origins of the Jewish Revolt against Rome A.D. 66–70* (Cambridge: Cambridge University Press, 1987).

11. Jacob Taubes, *The Political Theology of Paul,* trans. Dana Hollander, Cultural Memory in the Present (Stanford: Stanford University Press, 2004), 13–16; on the "messianic logic" of the letter, 1–11.

12. Neil Elliott, *Liberating Paul* (Minneapolis: Fortress Press, 2006), 215.

13. Richard Horsley, ed., *Paul and Empire: Religion and Power in Roman Imperial Society* (Harrisburg: Trinity Press International, 1997), 146.

14. In Augustus, Virgil found fulfilled the destiny of the Roman people to bring "peace crowned with justice" to the world (*Aen.* 6.853); the Senate agreed, awarding Augustus a ceremonial golden shield celebrating his justice, among other virtues (*Res gestae* 34). Under various names, the poets declared that the goddess of Justice had returned to earth under the Principate. At the consecration of a temple to *Iustitia,* Ovid exclaimed that she already was "enshrined in the temple of his [Augustus's] mind." Upon Nero's accession as well, Calpurnius Siculus exulted that a "Golden Age" had come into being, "kindly Themis" (*Iustitia* under her ancient Greek name) returning to the earth; "laws shall be restored; right [*ius*] will come in fullest force" (*Eclogue* 1.42–45, 71–73); and Seneca flatters the emperor that the absolute power he holds in his hands already has issued in "justice" among other blessings for all his subjects (*Clem.* 1.1.9). See Karl Galinsky, *Augustan Culture* (Princeton: Princeton University Press, 1998), 80–90.

15. Dieter Georgi, *Theocracy in Paul's Praxis and Theology* (Minneapolis: Fortress Press, 1991), 86–87.

16. Richard Hays writes that Georgi's essays, "epigrammatic in their brevity, fall far short of proving his case," but that Georgi "has gestured provocatively in the direction of issues that demand more careful investigation" (*The Faith of Jesus Christ: The Narrative Substructure of Galatians 3:1—4:11,* 2nd ed. [Grand Rapids: Eerdmans, 2002], xli–xlii).

17. Georgi, *Theocracy,* 86. Ben Witherington III cites Georgi in describing Paul's language here as "an implicit anti-imperial sort of rhetoric," but does not explain the point (*Paul's Letter to the Romans: A Socio-Rhetorical Commentary,* with Darlene Hyatt [Grand Rapids: Eerdmans, 2004], 31–32). Erik Heen cites Georgi as providing insight into the political environment of Paul's theology

but makes no explicit connection with Romans ("The Role of Symbolic Inversion in Utopian Discourse: Apocalyptic Reversal in Paul and in the Festival of the Saturnalia/Kronia," in *Hidden Transcripts and the Arts of Resistance,* ed. Horsley, 141–42). John B. Cobb Jr. and David J. Lull, *Romans* (St. Louis: Chalice, 2005), 28, cite Georgi in their discussion of Romans 1:3 but go no further than the suggestion that a "contrast with imperial ideology is understandable *if* [Paul's] intention was to contrast Jesus with the Roman Emperor" (emphasis added). On Robert Jewett's invocation of Georgi's work, see below.

18. Elliott, *Liberating Paul,* 184–85. Karl Galinsky offers an important qualification: the Golden Age ideology expressed the aspirations of Augustus's reforms, not a presumption of fruition (*Augustan Culture,* 90–106).

19. N. T. Wright, *The Climax of the Covenant: Christ and the Law in Pauline Theology* (Minneapolis: Fortress Press, 1991), chaps. 2, 3; Wright, "Paul's Gospel and Caesar's Empire," in *Paul and Politics: Ekklesia, Israel, Imperium, Interpretation,* ed. R. A. Horsley (Philadelphia: Trinity Press International, 2000), 166–67.

20. Wright, "Paul's Gospel," 168; compare Elliott, *Liberating Paul,* 184–89, and Elliott, "Paul and the Politics of Empire: Problems and Prospects," 24–26, in *Paul and Politics,* ed. Horsley.

21. The prophets were the servants of God, a stereotyped phrase in Roman-era Judean literature (e.g., 1QpHab 2:8-9; 7:5; 1QH 1:3; *4 Ezra* 1:32; 2:1, 18, etc.). The prophets are "sent" (*apestalmenos,* Isa 6:8; Jer 1:7; Ezek 2:3, etc.). But Jewett emphasizes that the closest analogies to the structure and vocabulary of Paul's self-presentation come from Roman diplomatic sources, in which Caesar's representatives could identify themselves as his slaves (*Romans,* Hermeneia [Minneapolis: Fortress Press, 2007], 96–97; 100–101).

22. See p. 188, n. 118.

23. Jewett, *Romans,* 48; on Rom 1:3-4, 96–108.

24. "The holy spirit" translates *to pneuma to hagion*; the Greek phrase here is *to pneuma tēs hagiosynēs,* more reminiscent of the Hebrew phrase occurring in Isa 63:10; Ps 51:11; and the Dead Sea Scrolls: 1QS 4:21; 8:16; 9:3, etc. Jewett adduces Greek parallels in Hellenistic Jewish literature, as well; see *Romans,* 97.

25. Ernst Käsemann declared that Paul quoted the creed to show "that he shared the same basis of faith as the Christians in Rome" (*Commentary on Romans,* trans. G. W. Bromiley [Grand Rapids: Eerdmans, 1980], 10–13). Calvin Roetzel characterized the verses as Paul's attempt to "establish the 'orthodoxy' of his gospel" against the suspicions of Jewish-Christians in Rome (*The Letters of Paul: Conversations in Context,* 4th ed. [Louisville: Westminster/John Knox, 1988], 20).

26. Chaim Perelman and L. Olbrechts-Tyteca, *The New Rhetoric: A Treatise on Argumentation,* trans. John Wilkinson and Purcell Weaver (Notre Dame: University of Notre Dame Press, 1969), 120–21.

27. As Edward Champlin observes, all three of the historians whose discussions of Claudius's death have come down to us—Suetonius, Tacitus, and Dio Cassius—depended in turn on three other sources, contemporaries of Nero, whose works are now lost. All these sources "agree without a doubt . . . that Agrippina was behind the murder of her husband. . . . But the variations in their accounts of the deed are not petty details: they betray the simple fact that no one *really* knew what happened, who did it, where it was done, or how it was done" (*Nero* [Cambridge: Harvard University Press, 2003], 46).

28. To be sure, Nero himself "did not stress his status as *divi filius,*" since this would have associated him too closely with Claudius (Goodman, *The Roman World, 44 BC–AD 180* [London and New York: Routledge, 1997], 55); rather, he emphasized his (distant) descent from Augustus. He was content to allow his poets to hail him as "himself God" (*ipse deus*: Calpurnius Piso).

29. Calpurnius Siculus, *Eclogue* 1.84–88 (in *Minor Latin Poets,* vol. 1, trans. J. Wight Duff and Arnold M. Duff, LCL [Cambridge: Harvard University Press, 1935], 224–25).

30. As Martin Goodman observes, "it was patent to all that [Octavian's] success was due to the ruthless manipulation of a huge fighting machine"; nevertheless, Augustan propaganda avoided

"the crudity of the power struggle," choosing "not to mask power, but to legitimize it." Augustus "established a new image for himself in which no hint of violence, or any need for violence, could be glimpsed" ("The Image of the Emperor," in *The Roman World,* 123–34). See also Paul Zanker, *The Power of Images in the Age of Augustus* (Ann Arbor: University of Michigan Press, 1988), esp. chaps. 5, 6; Galinsky, *Augustan Culture,* esp. chaps. 3, 4; Ste. Croix, *Class Struggle,* 363–71; and Richard Gordon, "The Veil of Power: Emperors, Sacrificers, and Benefactors," in *Pagan Priests: Religion and Power in the Ancient World,* ed. Mary Beard and John North (Ithaca: Cornell University Press, 1990).

31. Seneca strikes what would become the dominant tone of Neronian propaganda as he addresses the young emperor in *De clementia*: "no one today talks of the deified Augustus or the early years of Tiberius Caesar, or seeks for any model he would have you copy other than yourself" (1.1.6).

32. Text of the Einsiedeln Eclogues in *Minor Latin Poets* (see n. 29), 319–35; quote from 333.

33. Mercury advises the Fates to shorten Claudius's life: "Let him [Claudius] be slain, that he who best deserves [Nero] alone may reign" (*Apoc.* 3).

34. *Apoc.* 4; J. P. Sullivan's translation in *Petronius: The Satyricon; Seneca: The Apocolocyntosis,* rev. ed. (New York: Penguin, 1986), 223.

35. A less buoyant view of the period is provided by Ste. Croix, *Class Struggle*, 350–78.

36. See esp., Zanker, *The Power of Images.* The Augustan altar of the Lares from ca. 7 B.C.E. depicts the apotheosis of the god Julius (Caesar), being drawn toward heaven on a chariot pulled by winged horses; the Gemma Augustea, ca. 10 C.E., depicts Augustus enthroned in heaven beside Roma in the guise of Jupiter.

37. Suetonius acknowledges rumors that Agrippina committed incest with her son whenever they rode in the same litter but prefers to believe that her enemies prevented any consummation of a sexual relationship, fearing that "she would become even more powerful and ruthless" if she held such power over her son (*Nero* 28).

38. Tacitus, *Annales,* 12.69; 13.4; Dio Cassius, *History of Rome* 60.35.

39. Dio Cassius, *History of Rome* 59.11.

40. *Apoc.* 1 (trans. J. P. Sullivan).

41. Tiberius's deification was later rescinded by the Senate: Goodman, *The Roman World,* 132–33.

42. At one point Janus objects that Claudius has no rightful place among the gods: "Once . . . it was a great thing to become a god. Now you've made it a farce—not worth a bean." Later, the motion to deify appears about to carry the day because of some shrewd politicking by Hercules, but then the Divine Augustus rises to express his "pain" and "indignation" at the occasion. Augustus challenges Claudius with a long list of murders, including those of his descendants, members of Claudius's own family. He protests to his divine colleagues, "Who's going to worship him as a god? Who'll believe in him? While you create such gods, no one will believe that you yourselves are gods" (*Apocolocyntosis* 11).

43. Suetonius, *Nero* 33. On Nero's hostility to Claudius, see Griffin, *Nero,* 96.

44. Griffin, *Nero,* 97–98.

45. S. R. F. Price cautions against anachronistic perceptions of the Roman imperial cult as a crude political stratagem, devoid of "religious content" (*Rituals and Power: The Roman Imperial Cult in Asia Minor* [Cambridge: Cambridge University Press, 1984], 15–16). Price observes the (apparently sincere) enthusiasm with which provincials participated in the cult and presses for an understanding of the imperial cult as "a public cognitive system," through which Rome's subjects sought "to represent to themselves the ruling power" (p. 1). Much the same point is made by Richard Gordon ("The Veil of Power," 199–234) and by James C. Scott, "Protest and Profanation: Agrarian Revolt and the Little Tradition," *Theory and Society* 3 (1977), 1–38; 211–46.

On the other hand, as Michael Parenti observes, members of the Roman aristocracy could betray a wonderfully selective insight into the "superstitions" of the lower classes; Cicero, for example, was happy enough to use augury, though he disbelieved it, so long as it served to thwart "the unjust impetuosity of the people" (*The Assassination of Julius Caesar: A People's History of Ancient Rome* [New York: Free Press, 2004], 121–22, citing Cicero, *Laws* 3.27; *Pro Sestio* 46.98). Cicero is also G. E. M. de Ste. Croix's primary example of "the manipulation of the Roman state religion by the ruling class in such a way as to procure political advantage" (*Class Struggle*, 343–44). Perhaps the point made by Price and Gordon should be modified: the imperial cult was the means by which provincials who stood to gain most by cooperation with Roman power sought to represent that power to themselves and their subjects.

46. Griffin, *Nero*, 95–96. Griffin observes that Nero's appeal to his genealogy, "attested at various dates throughout his reign, combines both claims" consistently (97). She cites a number of inscriptions from 58 through 67 C.E. (258 n. 70); I have quoted *IG* 5.1.1450: (ΝΕΡΩΝΑ ΚΛΑΥΔΙΟΝ ΘΕΟΥ ΚΛΑΥ– | ΔΙΟΥ ΥΙΟΝ ΤΙΒΕΡΙΟΥ ΚΑΙΣΑΡΟΣ | ΣΕΒΑΣΤΟΥ ΚΑΙ ΓΕΡΜΑΝΙΚΟΥ | ΚΑΙΣΑΡΟΣ ΕΓΓΟΝΟΝ ΘΕΟΥ ΣΕ– | ΒΑΣΤΟΥ ΥΙΩΝ. . .).

47. As Jewett notes, the Greco-Roman parallels to *horisthentos* appear "in a political context" referring to things "decreed" by Roman officials. Jewett prefers to interpret the term as deriving from "the Aramaic-speaking primitive church," however, obviously out of theological, not linguistic, considerations (*Romans*, 104).

48. Ste. Croix, *Class Struggle*, 360. The establishment of the principate was "the completion of a pyramid of power and patronage, involving the placing of a coping stone, admittedly a very large and heavy one, on top of the whole oppressive edifice" (370–71).

49. Ovid, *Ex Ponto* 3.6.23–29; Georgi, *Theocracy*, 84. In Augustus, Virgil found fulfilled the destiny of the Roman people, to bring "peace crowned with justice" to the world (*Aen.* 6.853). Under various names, the poets declared that the goddess of Justice had returned to earth under the Principate: thus, at the consecration of a temple to *Iustitia*, Ovid exclaimed that she already was "enshrined in the temple of his [Augustus's] mind." Upon Nero's accession as well, Calpurnius Siculus exulted that a "Golden Age" had come into being, "kindly Themis" (*Iustitia* under her ancient Greek name) returning to the earth; "laws shall be restored; right [*ius*] will come in fullest force" (*Eclogue* 1.42–45, 71–73). Recalling the pretensions of the Augustan age, the meditation that Seneca puts onto the emperor Nero's lips similarly insists that the absolute power he holds in his hands (*in hac tanta facultate rerum*) has already issued in "security," "justice," "liberty," and "mercy" for all his subjects (*securitas, ius, libertas, clementia*: *De clementia* 1.1.9).

50. Jewett, *Romans*, 49.

51. William Sanday and Arthur C. Headlam, *The Epistle to the Romans*, ICC (Edinburgh: T&T Clark, 1902), 40.

52. Ernst Käsemann, *Commentary on Romans*, 29.

53. Jewett, *Romans*, 140.

54. Günther Bornkamm, "The Revelation of God's Wrath," *Early Christian Experience* (New York: Harper, 1970), 47–48, emphasis added.

55. José Porfirio Miranda, *Marx and the Bible: A Critique of the Philosophy of Oppression*, trans. John Eagleson (Maryknoll: Orbis, 1974), 160–92; Elsa Tamez, *The Amnesty of Grace: Justification by Faith from a Latin American Perspective*, trans. Sharon Ringe (Nashville: Abingdon, 1991), esp. 19–36 ("Perspectives on Justification by Faith from Latin America").

56. Precisely the careful literary observations of L. Stirewalt in his essay on "The Form and Function of the Greek Letter-Essay" (in *The Romans Debate*, 2nd ed. [Peabody: Hendrickson, 1991], 147–71) show how irrelevant the category is for the study of Romans, which actually bears none of the characteristics of the genre. See Elliott, *The Rhetoric of Romans* (Sheffield: JSOT, 1990), 69–86, esp. 84 n. 1; against K. P. Donfried, "False Presuppositions in the Study of Romans," in *Romans Debate*, 121–25.

57. Douglas Harink, *Paul among the Postliberals: Pauline Theology beyond Christendom and Modernity* (Grand Rapids: Brazos, 2003), chap. 1. Harink's work marks an important theological reorientation of Paul's theology.

58. See especially Ernst Käsemann, "The Righteousness of God," in *Perspectives on Paul*, trans. Margaret Kohl (Philadelphia: Fortress Press, 1977); this insight is carried through Käsemann's *Commentary on Romans* and shapes J. Christiaan Beker's portrait of Paul (*Paul, the Apostle: The Triumph of God in Life and Thought* [Philadelphia: Fortress Press, 1980]).

59. Baur complained that among his Protestant contemporaries, "the dogmatic view is not to yield one step to the historical, lest the position [of Romans] should be impaired, and the Lutheran forensic process of justification, which it is of such moment to maintain in its integrity, suffer from the shaking of its great buttress" (*Paul the Apostle of Jesus Christ*, vol. 1, trans. Eduard Zeller [London and Edinburgh: Williams & Norgate, 1876)], 308–13). More than a century later, Krister Stendahl (*Paul among Jews and Gentiles* [Philadelphia: Fortress Press, 1976), Walter Schmithals (*Römerbrief* [Gütersloh: Gütersloher, 1988], 7–8), and Stanley K. Stowers (*A Rereading of Romans: Gentiles, Jews, Justice* [New Haven: Yale University Press, 1994], passim) have raised the same protest, providing an index of the tremendous inertia imposed by the weight of one set of theological interests.

60. Note that Stowers must devote the first 82 pages of his important work, *A Rereading of Romans*, to simultaneously arguing against the conventional, theological reading and arguing for his more contextually nuanced "thick description" of Romans.

61. Harink, *Paul among the Postliberals*, 32.

62. Thus, C. E. B. Cranfield notes that commentators usually fail to give *gar* the normal sense, i.e., "for," preferring to read it in an adversative sense instead *(The Epistle to the Romans*, ICC, vol. 1 (Edinburgh: T&T Clark, 1975), 106–7.

63. So Cranfield: "The two revelations . . . are then really two aspects of the same process. The preaching of Christ . . . is at the same time both the offer . . . of a status of righteousness before God and the revelation of God's wrath against their sin. . . . We do *not* see the full meaning of the wrath of God in the disasters befalling [the sinful] in the course of history: the reality of the wrath of God is only truly known when it is seen in its revelation in Gethsemane and on Golgotha" (*Epistle to the Romans*, 110). Similarly, Käsemann asserts that "the need for the righteousness of God," i.e., the standing under God's wrath, "comes to light simultaneously with its actualization" (*Commentary on Romans*, 35).

64. C. H. Dodd, *The Epistle of Paul to the Romans* (London: Fontana Books, 1959), 49–50.

65. According to James Dunn, "an analysis of Paul's theology following the outline he himself provided"—i.e., in Dunn's view, Romans—"has little choice on where to begin. For the first main section of his exposition quickly unfolds as *an indictment of humankind* (Rom 1:18—3:20)" (*The Theology of Paul the Apostle* [Grand Rapids: Eerdmans, 1998], 79). Dunn refers repeatedly to the sin of Adam in his discussion of Romans 1. Similarly Richard B. Hays has described Romans 1 as describing the fallenness of "the human race in general": "Relations Natural and Unnatural," *Journal of Christian Ethics* 14 (1986): 184–215.

66. Dale B. Martin, "Heterosexism and the Interpretation of Romans 1:18-32," in *Biblical Interpretation* 3, no. 3 (1995), 334; Stowers, *A Rereading of Romans*, 86–94.

67. Käsemann refers to "the merciless accusation" that Paul levels here (*Commentary on Romans*, 40); he acknowledges that Paul's rhetoric is "one-sided" and "radical" but attributes this to Paul's penetratingly "eschatological" perspective. Cranfield recognizes that as a generalization about his epoch, the language is "thoroughly unfair" to Paul's contemporaries (*Epistle to the Romans*, 1:104), but argues that it is accurate regarding "the innermost truth of all of us, as we are in ourselves."

68. See Dunn, *Theology of Paul the Apostle*, 85, 91; Käsemann, *Commentary on Romans*, 45–52, for discussions of possible Jewish parallels. The reliance on Wisdom of Solomon 15 goes back to Hans Lietzmann, *An die Römer*, 3rd ed. (Tübingen: Mohr [Siebeck], 1928), 38–39; and especially Anders Nygren, *Commentary on Romans*, trans. Carl Rasmussen (Philadelphia: Muhlenberg, 1949), 114–17.

69. See Stowers, *A Rereading of Romans*, 88–93.

70. Ibid., 94–100.

71. Calpurnius Siculus, *Eclogue* 1.42–44; Einsiedeln Eclogue 2.21–22.

72. A convenient introduction to the controversy is available in Jeffrey S. Siker, ed., *Homosexuality in the Church: Both Sides of the Debate* (Louisville: Westminster/John Knox, 1994).

73. As Martin observes, the common search for a theological "explanation" of homosexuality is itself the result of heterosexism ("Heterosexism," 339). Surprisingly, Martin himself refers to Paul's "comments about the origins of homosexuality" (336), or his "etiology of homosexuality" (338); and at length declares that "Paul considers *any* homosexual activity necessarily to spring from lust in general" (347 n. 37). I do not see anything in Paul's rhetoric to justify these characterizations.

74. As Martin shows, the phrase *para physin* was normally used by Paul's contemporaries to refer, not to an "unnatural" direction of desire, but to an excessive indulgence of desire, an indulgence "beyond" the natural (ibid., 341–47).

75. Grammatically, I am taking the participial phrase in 1:18 (*anthrōpōn tōn tēn alētheian en adikia katechontōn*) in a restrictive sense; not "the impiety and injustice of human beings, who (by the way) suppress the truth in their injustice," but "the impiety and injustice of those human beings who suppress the truth in their injustice." On the participial construction's equivalence to a relative clause, see F. Blass and A. DeBrunner, *A Greek Grammar of the New Testament and Other Early Christian Literature,* trans. and rev. by Robert W. Funk (Chicago: University of Chicago Press, 1961), 212; Nigel Turner, *A Grammar of New Testament Greek,* vol. 3: *Syntax* (Edinburgh: T&T Clark, 1963), 152.

76. I first explored this line of interpretation in *Liberating Paul,* 192–95. Elsa Tamez briefly comments that this passage reflects Paul's perception that "in the imperial Greco-Roman society, injustice had usurped the place of truth. . . . For that reason, the empire's rallying cry of 'peace and security!' meant for the poor and oppressed only a lie intended to cover up injustice." When he spoke of idolatry, "very probably Paul also had in mind the divinization of Caesar, something that was abominable to him" (*The Amnesty of Grace: Justification by Faith from a Latin American Perspective* [Nashville: Abingdon, 1993], 98–99).

77. Philo, *Embassy* 14–15; 89–90; 97; 107; 118.

78. Philo, *In Flaccum* 102; 116–24; 146.

79. *Embassy* 3: *pronoiein to theion anthrōpōn.*

80. Philo occasionally, and Josephus consistently, represents "bad" Roman rule as the unfortunate deviation from the Augustan ideal, thus sharing in the dominant tropes of imperial ideology. Thus Philo's *Embassy to Gaius* begins with the wistful hope of peoples throughout the world that Gaius would continue to be, as he appeared, as benevolent and just a ruler as his ancestor Augustus.

81. Thomas Schmeller argued at some length that the target of Paul's rhetorical apostrophe at 2:1 should be read as "the Jew" who had just voiced the judgment of 1:18-32 (*Paulus und die "Diatribe"* [Münster: Aschendorff, 1987]). Although that argument is implicit in much Protestant commentary on the passage, Schmeller makes the surprising claim that Paul's text offered *explicit* rhetorical signals that the voice in 1:18-32 was not Paul's own. I find this argument rhetorically baseless, and consider its desperation a sign of how untenable the theological reading it is meant to prop up. See my discussion in *The Rhetoric of Romans,* 182–86.

82. Stanley K. Stowers, *A Rereading of Romans,* chaps. 2 and 3; I have quoted from p. 117. This study builds on Stowers's earlier work *The Diatribe and Paul's Letter to the Romans,* SBLDS 57 (Chico: Scholars, 1981).

83. Stowers, *A Rereading of Romans,* 37.

84. Ibid., 100–104.

85. I gave extended scrutiny to the rhetorical incoherence of the "trap for the Jew" reading in *The Rhetoric of Romans,* 167–90, and rely on those arguments here.

86. Wayne A. Meeks, "Judgement and the Brother: Romans 14.1—15.13," in *Tradition and Interpretation in the New Testament: Essays in Honor of E. Earle Ellis,* ed. G. F. Hawthorne and O. Betz (Grand Rapids: Eerdmans, 1987), 290–97.

87. See Perelman and Olbrechts-Tyteca's discussion of dissociative argumentation, especially concerning the distinction of appearance and reality (*The New Rhetoric,* 411–59, esp. 415–16). Elizabeth

A. Castelli characterizes the dominant rhetoric in Romans as "dualistic discourses" ("Romans," 272–300, in *Searching the Scriptures: A Feminist Commentary,* ed. Elisabeth Schüssler Fiorenza [New York: Crossroad, 1994], 285–86) but does not elaborate on the argumentative effect. See Antoinette Clark Wire's superb application of Perelman and Olbrechts-Tyteca's categories in *The Corinthian Women Prophets: A Reconstruction through Paul's Rhetoric* (Minneapolis: Fortress Press, 1990); on dissociation of concepts, 12–23.

3. CLEMENTIA

1. Slavoj Žižek describes the "logic of victimization" in Western journalism, represented in a *New York Times* article in which the subject to be protected by NATO intervention was "identified from the outset as a powerless victim of circumstances, deprived of all political identity, reduced to stark suffering," "beyond any political recrimination." Here Žižek finds "the ideological construction of the ideal subject-victim in aid of whom NATO intervenes: not a political subject with a clear agenda, but a subject of helpless suffering . . . caught up in the madness of a local clash that can be pacified only by the intervention of a benevolent foreign power . . ." ("Victims, Victims Everywhere," in *The Fragile Absolute: Or, Why Is the Christian Legacy Worth Fighting For?* [New York: Verso, 2000], 54–63).

2. Gilbert Achcar, *The Clash of Barbarisms: The Making of a New World Disorder,* expanded and updated ed. (London: Paradigm, 2006), 23; 65.

3. For sources and discussion, see Noam Chomsky, "The New Era of Enlightenment," *Hegemony or Survival: America's Quest for Global Dominance,* The American Empire Project (New York: Henry Holt/Metropolitan Books, 2003), chap. 3; and *A New Generation Draws the Line: Kosovo, East Timor, and the Standards of the West* (New York: Verso, 2000).

4. After the 1983 attacks, the U.S. Secretary of State invited Iraq's foreign affairs minister to Washington to warn that further massacres might make it "very difficult" for the Reagan administration to continue its "good relationship" with Hussein. The following year, George H. W. Bush sent his Assistant Secretary of State, Donald Rumsfeld, to Baghdad to assure Hussein that the U.S. considered him a "force for moderation in the region," with whom the United States wished to "broaden its relationship." A 1992 Congressional inquiry found that President George H. W. Bush and his top advisers covered up the extent of their support for Hussein and for illegal arms shipments to him from other countries and that Bush's CIA issued false reports blaming the Halabja massacre on Iran. A 1994 Senate report documented the transfer to Iraq of biological weapons elements, including botulism toxin and anthrax, in transactions approved by Bush's State Department. As Congressman Henry Gonzales summarized the Congressional inquiry, "Bush and his advisers financed, equipped, and succored the monster they later set out to slay, and they were now burying the evidence." See Anthony Arnove, "Convenient and Not So Convenient Massacres," *Z Magazine*, April 23, 2002; John Pilger, *The New Rulers of the World* (New York: Verso, 2002), 66–70.

5. Seymour Hersh, *Chain of Command: The Road from 9/11 to Abu Ghraib* (New York: Harper Collins, 2004), 5.

6. Cicero, *De republica* 3.15; Virgil, *Aen.* 6.851–53.

7. Karl Galinsky, *Augustan Culture* (Princeton: Princeton University Press, 1998), 82–85.

8. For contemporary analogies, alongside the delineation of America's vocation to bring democracy to the world in "The National Security Strategy of the United States of America" (Washington, D.C.: The White House, 2002), we may set the president's repeated statements that no people on earth could object to the United States' pursuit of its own interests, unless it is because "they hate our freedoms." But against these we might also set Achcar's insightful critique in *The Clash of Barbarisms.* The saturation of U.S. media with "iconic pictures"—scenes of grateful Iraqi crowds welcoming U.S. troops and cheering as statues of Saddam Hussein were toppled—was occasionally criticized even before "postwar" demonstrations by "ungrateful" Iraqis began.

9. Galinsky, *Augustan Culture,* 82–85.

10. P. A. Brunt, "Roman Imperial Illusions," 438–39, in *Roman Imperial Themes* (Oxford: Clarendon, 1990), 331; Brunt, *"Laus imperii,"* 288–89 in *Roman Imperial Themes*, p. 307.

11. In the 70s, the Roman general Cerialis declares to the Gauls that "the occupation of your land . . . was not prompted by [Roman] self-interest but happened at the invitation of your forefathers," to settle allegedly intractable internal warfare among the Gauls. He acknowledges that "lust, greed, and roving spirit," along with appreciation of rich soil and a new potential labor force, motivate conquest—on the part of others; however, the Romans imposed, "by right of conquest, only such additional burdens as were necessary for preserving peace." He declares that the Germans have used "liberty" as a pretext for conquest, but admits tellingly that "no one has ever aimed at enslaving others and making himself their master without using this very same language." At length cajolery gives way to outright threat: "Learn from your experience of the two alternatives not to choose insubordination and ruin in preference to obedience and security" (*Histories* 4.73–74).

12. For Cicero, it was only in the cause of "defending their allies" that the Romans had become "masters of all lands" (*Rep.* 3.23, 35). Suetonius insisted that Augustus never warred on any people "without just and necessary reasons" (*Augustus* 21).

13. Chomsky, *Deterring Democracy* (New York: Hill and Wang, 1992), 283–301.

14. Brunt, "Roman Imperial Illusions," 438–39, citing the *Res gestae Divi Augusti*; Ste. Croix, *Class Struggle in the Ancient Greek World: From the Archaic Age to the Arab Conquests* (Ithaca: Cornell University Press, 1980), 331.

15. The cup is damaged; the description depends on photographs and records of Baron Edouard Rothschild, who took possession of the cups after their excavation in 1895, and whose heirs eventually donated the cups to the Louvre in 1991. See Zanker, *The Power of Images,* 228, Fig. 180b.

16. Tacitus, *Ann.* 12.12–13.

17. Suetonius, *Nero* 10; Tacitus, *Ann.* 13.4.

18. *Clem.* 1.1.1–2; 1.4.2; 1.1.6; 1.11.3.

19. Ibid., 1.2.1–2; 1.4.2; 1.12.4; 2.2.2; see Griffin, *Nero,* 104.

20. Ramsay MacMullen, *Roman Social Relations 50 B.C. to A.D. 284* (New Haven: Yale University Press, 1974), 36; 10.

21. Ibid., 10, citing *Michigan Papyri VI: Papyri and Ostraca from Karanis,* ed. H. C. Youtie and O. M. Pearl (Ann Arbor: University of Michigan Press, 1944), numbers 422 and 424f.

22. Ibid., 44–45, citing *Papyri russischer und georgischer Sammlungen,* vol. 3: *Spätromische und byzantinische Texte* (ed. G. Zereteli and P. Jernstedt [Tiflits: n.p., 1930]), number 8.

23. Ibid., 11.

24. Ibid., 17; 35.

25. Philo, *Spec. Laws* 2.92–94; 3.158–62.

26. John G. Gager, *The Origins of Anti-Semitism: Attitudes toward Judaism in Pagan and Christian Antiquity* (New York: Oxford University Press, 1983), 43.

27. For what follows, see ibid., 43–54; Peter Schäfer, *Judeophobia: Attitudes toward the Jews in the Ancient World* (Cambridge: Harvard University Press, 1997); Emil Schürer, *The History of the Jewish People in the Age of Jesus Christ: A New English Edition,* vol. 3:1, rev. and ed. by Geza Vermes, Fergus Millar, and Martin Goodman (Edinburgh: T&T Clark, 1986), 38–60; 46–137; 594–616; John M. G. Barclay, *Jews in the Mediterranean Diaspora: From Alexander to Trajan (323 B.C.E.–117 C.E.)* (Edinburgh: T&T Clark, 1996), 19–228.

28. Our chief source is Philo, *In Flaccum.* Mary Smallwood characterized the relocation as "the first known ghetto in the world" (*The Jews under Roman Rule,* 240). The overcrowding produced disease and starvation; many Judeans tried to escape the ghetto and were killed, justifying Schäfer's characterization of "this first pogrom in Jewish history" (*Judeophobia,* 140).

29. Our sources for the anti-Judean tradition in Egypt include Josephus, *Against Apion*; Philo, *In Flaccum*; *Embassy to Gaius*; and the *Acts of the Alexandrian Martyrs.*

30. Josephus, *Ant.* 19.278; Gager, *The Origins of Anti-Semitism,* 51.

31. According to Josephus, Claudius recognized that "from earliest times" Judeans had enjoyed "equal civic rights" (*isēs politeias*) with Alexandrians (*Ant.* 19.278). Schäfer attributes the favorable

or ambiguous aspects of Josephus's version of the decree to his "wishful thinking"; the more likely authentic version is that in *CPJ* (see the next note): *Judeophobia,* 137–38.

32. Text and discussion in A. Fuks, V. Tcherikover, and M. Stern, eds., *Corpus Papyrorum Judaicarum,* 3 vols. (Cambridge: Harvard University Press, 1957–64), 2:36–55.

33. Schäfer observes the one-sidedness of the decree: *Judeophobia,* 147–51.

34. Greg Woolf, "Becoming Roman, Staying Greek: Culture, Identity, and the Civilizing Process in the Roman East," *Proceedings of the Cambridge Philological Society,* 40 (1994): 116–43; "Beyond Romans and Natives," *World Archaeology* 28, no. 3 (1995): 339–50.

35. Shaye J. D. Cohen, *The Beginnings of Jewishness: Boundaries, Varieties, Uncertainties* (Berkeley and Los Angeles: University of California Press, 1999), 67.

36. Gager, *The Origins of Anti-Semitism,* 45–46.

37. Schäfer emphasizes that the conflict was "first and foremost a political drama in the triangle of Flaccus, Gaius Caligula, and the Alexandrians. The Jews are the innocent victims of a political conflict of interests" (*Judeophobia,* 143).

38. Josephus, *Ant.* 18.3, 5; see Schürer, *History of the Jewish People,* 3.1: 75–76.

39. Philo, *Embassy,* 159–61.

40. Leonard Victor Rutgers, "Roman Policy toward the Jews: Expulsions from the City of Rome during the First Century C.E.," in *Judaism and Christianity in First-Century Rome,* ed. Karl P. Donfried and Peter Richardson (Grand Rapids: Eerdmans, 1998), 93–116, esp. 98–105.

41. H. Dixon Slingerland, *Claudian Policymaking and the Early Imperial Repression of Judaism at Rome* (Atlanta: Scholars, 1997). Slingerland opposes what he describes as an *interpretatio Christiana.*

42. For example, Mary Smallwood, *The Jews under Roman Rule,* 211; Peter Lampe, *From Paul to Valentinus: Christians at Rome in the First Two Centuries,* trans. Michael Steinhauser, ed. Marshall D. Johnson (Minneapolis: Fortress Press, 2003), 11–12.

43. For example, James C. Walters, "Romans, Jews, and Christians: The Impact of the Romans on Jewish/Christian Relations in First-Century Rome," in Donfried and Richardson, eds., *Judaism and Christianity in First-Century Rome,* 177.

44. James C. Walters, *Ethnic Issues in Paul's Letter to the Romans: Changing Self-Definitions in Earliest Roman Christianity* (Valley Forge: Trinity, 1993), 61.

45. In addition to Slingerland's critique (*Claudian Policymaking,* chap. 1), see Neil Elliott, "Disciplining the Hope of the Poor in Ancient Rome," in *Christian Origins,* vol. 1 of A People's History of Christianity (Minneapolis: Fortress Press, 2005), 177–97, esp. 178–80.

46. Lampe stresses that "Jewish *Christians* were actually involved in the unrest" (*From Paul to Valentinus,* 5).

47. Mark D. Nanos argues that if the issue had been "Christian" agitation by Jews like Prisca and Aquila, we should expect to see evidence of a decisive split between non-Christian and Christian Jews soon after, and by the time of Luke-Acts at the latest (*The Mystery of Romans: The Jewish Context of Paul's Letter* [Minneapolis: Fortress Press, 1996], 372–87). Nanos does not recognize Luke's tendentiousness in offering a conciliatory conclusion in Acts 28; to the contrary, he expects Luke to portray unalloyed animosity between Jews and Christians (375). Nevertheless, I agree with his argument that "the edict of Claudius had nothing to do with a negative Jewish response to Christ or to the Christian message" (377).

48. Slingerland points out that the cognomen was relatively common in Rome (*Claudian Policymaking,* chap. 9). He discusses one particular Chrestus, a Gaius Iulius Chrestus who dedicated an honorary inscription to a *legatus* (probably a governor of Asia) whom he served as a mounted officer, probably during the reign of Claudius (195–200). Slingerland's point is not to identify this Chrestus, "who stood only a single person away from the innermost circles of the imperial family," as the one to whom Suetonius refers, but to point out how easily Suetonius might have expected his readers to recognize the name of a Roman official of whom we know nothing else.

49. Slingerland, *Claudian Policymaking,* 167.

50. Slingerland, *Claudian Policymaking,* chap. 1: "Historical Ramifications of the Tendentious Portrayal of Jews and Their Cult." Slingerland quotes (26–29) from a number of respected historians.

51. Rutgers, "Roman Policy toward the Jews," 104–8. On this point Rutgers offers an important corrective to Slingerland's study, which emphasizes antipathy toward non-Roman religion as the primary motive of Roman policy toward the Jews.

52. Jewett speaks of a consensus that Romans is an occasional letter, and relies on the date of the edict of Claudius for establishing the date of the letter (Hermeneia [Minneapolis: Fortress Press, 2007], 3, 18–20).

53. Wolfgang Wiefel, "The Jewish Community in Ancient Rome and the Origins of Roman Christianity," in *The Romans Debate,* rev. and exp. ed., ed. Karl P. Donfried (Peabody: Hendrickson, 1991), 85–101, esp. 96–101. On Judean beggars in public: Martial, *Epigram* 10.57.13; Juvenal, *Sat.* 2.11; 6.541–44. On diet, see Juvenal's third *Satire,* which ridicules the figure of a Judean beggar who subsists on beans, leeks, vinegar, and boiled leather. Josephus tells of priests from Judea who, while awaiting a hearing with Nero in Rome, could maintain their diet only by subsisting on figs and nuts (*Life* 3). Hans-Werner Bartsch attributes the conflict between "weak" and "strong" over diet (Romans 14–15) to these circumstances: "Die antisemitischen Gegner des Paulus im Römerbrief," in *Antijudaismus im Neuen Testament?* ed. W. Eckert et al. (Munich: Kaiser, 1967), 27–43; idem, "Die historische Situation des Römerbriefes," *SE* 4/*TU* 102 (1968): 282–91.

54. Horace, *Sermones* 1.9.

55. Seneca, in a lost treatise, *De superstitione,* as quoted by Augustine, *City of God* 6.10.

56. Suetonius, *Nero* 10.

57. Ibid., 1.2.1–2; 1.4.2; 1.12.4; 2.2.2; see Griffin, *Nero,* 104.

58. On the hortatory thrust of this section, see Neil Elliott, *The Rhetoric of Romans* (Sheffield: JSOT, 1990; Minneapolis, Fortress Press edition, 2006), 146–52.

59. Ibid., 225–33.

60. "How characteristic 'boasting' is for the Jew, Rom. 3:27 shows": thus Rudolf Bultmann, without a shadow of doubt regarding the circularity of this assertion (*Theology of the New Testament,* vol. 1; trans. Kendrick Grobel [New York: Charles Scribner's Sons, 1951], 242); Ernst Käsemann, *Commentary on Romans* (trans. G. W. Bromiley [Grand Rapids: Eerdmans, 1980], 78) on "the demolition of Jewish privileges."

61. J. Christiaan Beker, *Paul, the Apostle: The Triumph of God in Life and Thought* (Philadelphia: Fortress Press, 1980), 80 (emphasis added); so also Käsemann, *Commentary on Romans,* trans. G. W. Bromiley (Grand Rapids: Eerdmans, 1980).

62. The strategic insertion of a comma in 3:19 in the Nestle-Aland 27th ed. and the NRSV produces three clauses:

(1) *hosa ho nomos legei*	whatever the law says,
(2) *tois en tō nomō lalei,*	to those who are under the law it speaks,
(3) *hina pan stoma phragē*	so that every mouth may be silenced,
kai hypodikos genētai	and the whole world
pas ho kosmos tō theō.	may be held accountable to God.

Removing the comma (after *lalei*) allows a more natural balance of verb phrases (*legei . . . lalei*) and changes the sense of the sentence dramatically:

hosa ho nomos	whatever the law
(1) *legei tois en tō nomō*	says to those who are in the law
(2) *lalei hina pan stoma phragē*	it speaks so that every mouth may be silenced
kai hypodikos genētai pas ho kosmos	and the whole world may be held accountable
tō theō.	to God.

See Elliott, *The Rhetoric of Romans,* 142–46.

63. I discuss this passage in greater detail in Elliott, *The Rhetoric of Romans,* 127–57.

64. Stanley K. Stowers, *The Diatribe and Paul's Letter to the Romans,* SBLDS 57 (Chico: Scholars, 1981), 110–12; so again in *A Rereading of Romans: Gentiles, Jews, Justice* (New Haven: Yale University Press, 1994), 153.

65. Stowers, *A Rereading of Romans,* 143–44.

66. A few of the scholars who read 2:17-29 as an indictment or critique of Jews in general concede that as such, it is empirically false, "not convincing," "internally inconsistent," and relies on the "exceptional" case and on "gross exaggeration." See my more extended discussion of the rhetorical inadequacy of this reading in *The Rhetoric of Romans,* 191–204.

67. Stowers, *Diatribe and Paul's Letter to the Romans,* 96, 112–13.

68. Elliott, *The Rhetoric of Romans,* 130–31.

69. "In the letter, Paul presents himself to the Romans as a teacher. . . . Paul uses the style of indictment and protreptic and presents himself to the Roman Christians not as a spiritual father and guide, but as a 'philosophical' or religious-ethical teacher. . . . [The letter] is the self-introduction of Paul as a teacher and preacher of the gospel. The body of Romans is written in the style *he would use in teaching a group of Christians.*" *Diatribe and Paul's Letter to the Romans,* 179–80, 182 (emphasis added). Similarly in his 1994 work, Stowers writes that "Romans allows gentile believers to overhear a discussion in which Paul argues for gentile justification through Christ against a Jew who opposes righteousness for gentiles apart from works of the law. In this way he can dramatically argue both for his own gospel and against its most threatening alternative" (*A Rereading of Romans,* 168).

70. In his 1994 work, Stowers identified the questions in 2:17-24 more precisely as "a polemical construction of 'missionary' opponents. This Jew is one of Paul's competitors for gentiles." Indeed, Stowers divines from the passage that the Jew against whom Paul inveighs represents "Jewish teachers [who] think that they can make gentiles righteous before God by teaching them to observe certain works from the law. . . . Paul's approach was utterly different" (*A Rereading of Romans,* 150–51).

71. Ibid., 152; 176–77.

72. Ibid., 182.

73. The point is obscured, unfortunately, in the Nestle-Aland 27th ed. Greek text, which ends all these phrases with a question mark except the last, which it ends with a semicolon (as if delivering an affirmative answer to the preceding questions). (The RSV and NRSV insert a question mark.) The earliest surviving manuscript of Romans to include punctuation marks, Codex Sinaiticus, has a question mark at the end of 2:23; see my *The Rhetoric of Romans,* 128–29.

74. The following table may help to represent the different ways of reading the diatribe here (adapted from Stowers, *Diatribe and Paul's Letter to the Romans,* 119–20; Elliott, *The Rhetoric of Romans,* 132–41; and Stowers, *A Rereading of Romans,* 165–66).

	Stowers 1981	Elliott 1990 (and now)	Stowers 1994
3:1	Objection (from the Jewish interlocutor)	Paul's leading question	Objection (from the Jewish interlocutor)
3:2	Paul's answer	Interlocutor's answer	Paul's answer
3:3	Objection	Paul's leading question	Paul's leading question
3:4	Paul's rejection of a false conclusion	Interlocutor's rejection of a false conclusion	Interlocutor's rejection of a false conclusion
3:5	Objection (or rhetorical question)	Paul's leading question	Paul's leading question
3:6	Paul's rejection of a false conclusion	Interlocutor's rejection of a false conclusion	Interlocutor's rejection of a false conclusion
3:7	Objection	Paul's leading question	Paul's leading question

	Stowers 1981	Elliott 1990 (and now)	Stowers 1994
3:8	Objection	Paul's leading question and interlocutor's answer (a true conclusion)	Paul's leading question and answer of his own question
3:9	Paul's rejection of a false conclusion	Paul's question and inter-locutor's rejection of a false conclusion	Interlocutor's question and Paul's rejection of a false conclusion

75. On the middle translation of *proechometha*, see Nils Dahl, "Romans 3:9: Text and Meaning," in *Paul and Paulinism: Essays in Honour of C. K. Barrett*, ed. M. D. Hooker and S. G. Wilson (London: SPCK, 1982), 184–204, here at 194; J. C. O'Neill, *Romans* (London: Penguin, 1975), 68; and Elliott, *The Rhetoric of Romans*, 132–33, 141.

76. Chaim Perelman and L. Olbrechts-Tyteca, *The New Rhetoric: A Treatise on Argumentation*, trans. John Wilkinson and Purcell Weaver (Notre Dame: University of Notre Dame Press, 1969), 411–50.

77. W. D. Davies, "Paul and the People of Israel," *NTS* 24 (1978): 4–39; reprinted in *Jewish and Pauline Studies* (Philadelphia: Fortress Press, 1984), here at 130–31. Beker declares that "Israel's tragedy is that it blindly claims what it has lost: it rejects the gospel" (*Paul the Apostle*, 88). Esler speaks of Israel's "failure to turn to Christ" (*Conflict and Identity in Romans: The Social Setting of Paul's Letter* [Minneapolis: Fortress Press, 2003], 275); Jewett, of "opposition to the gospel" and continued "unbelief" on the part of the Jews (*Romans*, 556–57 and passim).

78. E. Elizabeth Johnson, "Romans 9–11: The Faithfulness and Impartiality of God," in *Pauline Theology III: Romans*, ed. David M. Hay and E. Elizabeth Johnson (Minneapolis: Fortress Press, 1993), 215.

79. Peter Lampe argued that Aquila and Priscilla "had been expelled from Rome as *Christians*"; that the expulsion included only "the key figures of the conflict" like them (presumably, other Jewish Christians); and that the expulsion's chief effect was to impel Roman Christianity "*to separate from the synagogue*" (*From Paul to Valentinus*, 13–15, emphasis in original). Similarly, James C. Walters argued that "many if not most" of the "Christian Jews" of Rome were targeted for expulsion, resulting in a shift in the ethnic and socio-religious composition of the Christian assemblies. "The Claudian edict did not create the tensions between Christians and non-Christian Jews in Rome; however, it exacerbated them." After Nero rescinded the expulsion edict, *non*-Christian Jews would have concluded "that it would be in their best interests to go their separate ways" from the Christian assemblies; conversely, Gentile Christians were drawing the conclusion "that God had rejected Israel," a conclusion Paul is at pains to counteract in Romans 9–11. In this way "the expulsion played a decisive role in detaching Roman Christianity from synagogue communities in the capital" ("The Impact of the Romans on Jewish/Christian Relations," 177–79; Walters, *Ethnic Issues in Paul's Letter to the Romans*, 56–66). Rudolf Brändle and Ekkehard Stegemann go further, arguing that in impelling just this separation of Christ-believing non-Judeans from the synagogue, the Claudian edict "was the cause of the development of the 'Christ-faith' in Rome" ("Formation of the First 'Christian Congregations' in Rome in the Context of the Jewish Congregations," in *Judaism and Christianity in First-Century Rome*, ed. Donfried and Richardson, 125).

80. "The Christian congregation in Rome is surrounded by a society marked by its aversion and rejection of everything Jewish"; Wiefel, "The Jewish Community in Ancient Rome," 100.

81. Beker, *Paul the Apostle*, 77.

82. Richard B. Hays, *Echoes of Scripture in the Letters of Paul* (New Haven: Yale University Press, 1989), 52.

83. Johnson, "Romans 9–11," 220.

84. Representative of a widely held view, Richard B. Hays remarks on Paul's "scandalous inversions" that align Israel with Ishmael, Esau, and Pharaoh; Paul thus "deconstructs Scripture's witness to Israel's favored status" (*Echoes of Scripture*, 67). Similarly Nils Dahl, "The Future of Israel," *Studies in Paul: Theology for the Early Christian Mission* (Minneapolis: Augsburg, 1977), 144–47.

85. Hays observes that the restriction is without basis in the Greek text (*Echoes of Scripture*, 68).

86. Esler, *Conflict and Identity in Romans,* 278.

87. Johnson, "Romans 9–11," 220.

88. Ibid.

89. Esler ascribes the "passionate outbursts" in 9:1-5 and elsewhere to Paul's "reconnecting with the often dormant but nevertheless deeply rooted Israelite dimension of his self-concept" (*Conflict and Identity in Romans,* 272–73). Similarly, C. H. Dodd spoke of "the emotional interest in national hopes which [Paul's] estrangement from his nation had not destroyed": *The Epistle of St. Paul to the Romans* (New York: Harper & Row, 1932), 151; F. W. Beare, of the apostle "attempting to salvage some remnant of racial privilege for the historic Israel . . . in spite of his own fundamental position": *St. Paul and His Letters* (Nashville: Abingdon, 1962), 97. These are clear examples of what Pamela Eisenbaum has characterized as "*kata sarka*" scholarship, which attributes to Paul a *merely* ethnic Judaism.

90. Johnson, "Romans 9–11," 217–18. On Paul's fundamental inconsistency, see E. P. Sanders, *Paul, the Law, and the Jewish People* (Philadelphia: Fortress Press, 1983), 199; Heikki Räisänen, "Paul, God, and Israel: Romans 9–11 in Recent Research," in *The Social World of Formative Christianity and Judaism: Essays in Tribute to Howard Clark Kee,* ed. Jacob Neusner et al. (Philadelphia: Fortress Press, 1988), 178–206.

91. Hays, *Echoes of Scripture,* 225.

92. As Stowers phrases it, Romans 11 "treats the view that God has rejected Israel as a misunderstanding to be corrected." Paul's argument in 9–11 is, "Yes, God's way of acting is X and Israel is Y, while the Gentiles are X, *but do not conclude Z,*" that is, that God has rejected Israel (*A Rereading of Romans,* 298). I diverge from Stowers's understanding of chaps. 9 and 10, however, as the following argument will show.

93. Perelman and Olbrechts-Tyteca, *The New Rhetoric*; see chap. 2.

94. Here Ernst Käsemann's essay is of decisive importance: "The Cry for Liberty in the Worship of the Church," in *Perspectives on Paul,* trans. Margaret Kohl (Philadelphia: Fortress Press, 1971), 122–37. Unlike Käsemann, however, I understand Paul's rhetoric to be aimed not against "Palestinian" tradition but against the presumptions of the non-Judean congregation in Rome. I argued earlier that the object of Paul's argument beginning already in 8:17 was to warn against "boasting in *present* circumstances": *The Rhetoric of Romans,* 257.

95. I argued in *The Rhetoric of Romans* that 8:17—9:5 is a single rhetorical unit characterized by an appeal to the emotions (what Quintilian described as *excusitatio*), 261–64; so now Jewett, *Romans,* 556.

96. Johnson, "Romans 9–11," 226.

97. Stowers, *A Rereading of Romans,* 305; 316; similarly Johnson points out that it is *God's* action, not a failure on the part of the runner (Israel), that causes the downfall ("Romans 9–11," 226–27).

4. PIETAS

1. I rely here on Richard B. Hays's convincing arguments regarding the translation of Rom 4:1, "'Have We Found Abraham to Be Our Forefather according to the Flesh?': A Reconsideration of Rom. 4:1," *NovT* 27 (1985): 76–98.

2. This is the insight that governs Clifford Ando's argument in *Imperial Ideology and Provincial Loyalty in the Roman Empire* (Berkeley and Los Angeles: University of California Press, 2000). Ando explains the empire's stability as the result of genuine consensus: Rome's subjects indeed experienced the "good faith of the Roman people." That argument necessarily relies on minimizing the coercive aspects of Roman imperium and on taking elite sources at face value. In contrast, P. A. Brunt emphasizes the biases inherent in elite sources. Men of rank and wealth celebrated an empire "that maintained peace, peace which brought most benefits to those with most to lose, and secured them in their property and local dominance" ("The Romanization of the Local Ruling Classes in the Roman Empire," chap. 12 in *Roman Imperial Themes* [Oxford: Clarendon, 1990], 272–73).

3. S. R. F. Price, *Rituals and Power: The Roman Imperial Cult in Asia Minor* (Cambridge: Cambridge University Press, 1984), chap. 3 (quote from p. 52).

4. Richard Gordon, "From Republic to Principate: Priesthood, Religion and Ideology," chap. 7 in *Pagan Priests: Religion and Power in the Ancient World,* ed. Mary Beard and John North (Ithaca: Cornell University Press, 1990), 194.

5. Gordon, "The Veil of Power," chap. 8 in *Pagan Priests,* 207.

6. Brunt, "Romanization," 268, 269. "Everywhere it was the Roman policy to win over, and to enfranchise, the local leaders," and "enfranchisement implied . . . Romanization." See also Greg Woolf, "Beyond Romans and Natives," *World Archaeology* 28 (1995): 339–50, and "Becoming Roman, Staying Greek: Culture, Identity, and the Civilizing Process in the Roman East," 116–43.

7. Brunt observes (*"Laus imperii," Roman Imperial Themes,* 288) that one of Cicero's favorite themes is that Roman hegemony "was ordained by the gods, whose favor Rome had deserved by piety and justice"; Cicero writes that the gods had implanted in the Romans "a love of peace and tranquility which enable justice and good faith more easily to flourish" (*Rep.* 2.31).

8. G. E. M. de Ste. Croix, *Class Struggle in the Ancient Greek World: From the Archaic Age to the Arab Conquests* (Ithaca: Cornell University Press, 1980), 391–92; Goodman, *The Roman World, 44 BC–AD 180* (London and New York: Routledge, 1997), 123–25.

9. Gordon emphasizes the importance of this image and its function within an ideological system to normalize "uncontrolled imperialism": "From Republic to Principate," 191–93.

10. *Res gestae* 1.7 (LCL).

11. Gordon, "The Veil of Power," 219.

12. Paul Zanker, *The Power of Images in the Age of Augustus,* trans. Alan Shapiro (Ann Arbor: University of Michigan Press, 1988), 126–29.

13. Gordon remarks that the civil wars were "veiled," represented as the punishment of the Roman people for their lack of piety toward the gods, among other things. "The central cause, the competitive ethic of the elite, could not be admitted" ("From Republic to Principate," 192–93).

14. Gordon, "From Republic to Principate," 183–84.

15. Gordon, "The Veil of Power," 219; Frances V. Hickson, "Augustus *Triumphator*: Manipulation of the Triumphal Themes in the Political Program of Augustus," *Latomus* 50, no. 1 (1991): 124–38.

16. Karl Galinsky, *Augustan Culture: An Interpretive Introduction* (Princeton: Princeton University Press, 1996), 128–40.

17. So common was the *topos* that Philo could, in contrasting the reign of Augustus with that of Gaius, observe that the worldwide veneration of the former was a sign of his genuine superiority over the latter (*Embassy* 149–50). From the time of Nero, the theme appears in the Einsiedeln *Eclogue* 2.18–28.

18. Gordon discusses the iconography of sacrifice on Trajan's arch; I extend his discussion to include the *Ara Pacis* as well: "The Veil of Power," 202–7.

19. Gordon, "The Veil of Power," 207; see also John K. Chow's illuminating study, *Patronage and Power: A Study of Social Networks in Corinth,* JSNTSup 75 (Sheffield: JSOT, 1992).

20. As Martin Goodman observes, "it was patent to all that [Octavian's] success was due to the ruthless manipulation of a huge fighting machine"; nevertheless, Augustan propaganda avoided "the crudity of the power struggle," choosing "not to mask power, but to legitimize it." Augustus "established a new image for himself in which no hint of violence, or any need for violence, could be glimpsed" ("The Image of the Emperor," in *The Roman World,* 123–34). See also Zanker, *The Power of Images,* esp. chaps. 5, 6; Galinsky, *Augustan Culture,* esp. chaps. 3, 4; Ste. Croix, *The Class Struggle,* 363–71; and Gordon, "The Veil of Power" (art. cit.).

21. So Zanker, *The Power of Images,* 202–6.

22. *Aen.* 2.602–700, LCL.

23. *Iliad* 20.298, 347; 307.

24. Cyril Bailey and Charles Martin Robinson, "Aeneas," *OCD,* 14.

25. *Aen.* 1.33. Marianne Palmer Bonz characterizes the *Aeneid* as Rome's greatest salvation history in *The Past as Legacy: Luke-Acts and Ancient Epic* (Minneapolis: Fortress Press, 2000), 62.

26. Suetonius suggests that Virgil's father's estate was restored (*Life of Virgil* 20); but Colin Graham Hardie discusses indications in Virgil's own writings and other sources that the loss was permanent ("Virgil," *OCD,* 1123).

27. "Their task was to define Rome's moral and religious values and to inspire its people with a patriotic vision of a world where eschatological fulfillment was embodied in the Augustan identification with the return of the Golden Age" (Marianne Palmer Bonz, *The Past as Legacy: Luke-Acts as Ancient Epic* [Minneapolis: Fortress Press, 2000], 38). On Virgil as a "politically engaged writer," see R. J. Tarrant, "Poetry and Power: Virgil's Poetry in Contemporary Context," *The Cambridge Companion to Virgil,* ed. Charles Martindale (Cambridge: Cambridge University Press, 1997), 169–87.

28. Karl Galinsky contends that the auspicious child in the fourth *Eclogue* "is no more than a symbol or personification of the new age"; Virgil hardly expects that the golden age will depend on "a sole ruler" (*Augustan Culture,* 92).

29. Ibid., 91–93, citing *Georgics* 1.129–46.

30. *Aen.* 1.148–56. Seneca relied upon the same trope in *Clem.* 1.1.

31. *Aen.* 6.788–807.

32. *Aen.* 8.675–723.

33. This is R. J. Tarrant's argument for understanding the closing scene, "the focus of the sharpest disagreements in recent criticism." Tarrant observes that "where the imperial propagandist views crime, bloodshed, and violation of piety as exclusively the work of the enemy, while describing his own actions in antiseptically unemotive terms, such comforting polarities are pointedly denied the actors of Virgil's poem"—no doubt a literary effect that the agents of imperial policy would have appreciated. "Poetry and Power: Virgil's Poetry in Contemporary Context," pages 169–87 in *The Cambridge Companion to Virgil,* 181.

34. E. P. Sanders, *Paul and Palestinian Judaism* (Philadelphia: Fortress Press, 1977; Richard B. Hays, *Echoes of Scripture in the Letters of Paul* (New Haven: Yale University Press, 1989), 56–57.

35. Hays, *Echoes of Scripture,* 55, 59.

36. Ibid., 55 (emphasis added).

37. Ibid., 53.

38. Ibid., 35.

39. Ibid., 60.

40. Ibid., 34–35.

41. Paula Fredriksen, *From Jesus to Christ: The Origins of the New Testament Images of Jesus* (New Haven: Yale University Press, 1988), 142–53.

42. Ibid., 168.

43. Pamela Eisenbaum, "A Remedy for Having Been Born of Woman: Jesus, Gentiles, and Genealogy in Romans," *JBL* 123, no. 4 (2004): 670–702; quotations from 679, 680, 681; Eisenbaum, "Paul as the New Abraham," in *Paul and Politics: Ekklesia, Israel, Imperium, Interpretation,* ed. Richard A. Horsley (Harrisburg: Trinity Press International, 2000), 142–43 (emphasis added). Eisenbaum relies on Nancy Jay, *Throughout Your Generations Forever: Sacrifice, Religion, and Paternity* (Chicago: University of Chicago Press, 1992).

44. Eisenbaum, "A Remedy," 682, 683. Claiming to be the descendants of Abraham "was likely not taken as literally by the Jews of Paul's time as modern scholars often think." ("Paul as the New Abraham," 142–43).

45. Ibid., 688, 689.

46. Eisenbaum, "A Remedy," 689; "Paul as the New Abraham," 133–35, citing Philo, *Virt.* 39.212–17; Josephus, *Ant.* 1.7; 2.159–60.

47. Eisenbaum, "A Remedy," 691–92.

48. Denise Kimber Buell and Caroline Johnson Hodge, "The Politics of Interpretation: The Rhetoric of Race and Ethnicity in Paul," *JBL* 123, no. 2 (2004): 235–51, here 240–41.

49. Buell and Hodge, "The Politics of Interpretation," 236–37.

50. Hays denies the implication that he understands Paul to be "playing Christianity off against Judaism": "By no means!" (*Echoes of Scripture,* 59).

51. Pamela Eisenbaum, "Paul, Polemics, and the Problem of Essentialism," *BibInt* 13, no. 3 (2005): 224–38 (quote from 227–29).

52. Ibid., 224.

53. Terry Eagleton's discussion of the ideological limits of "liberal humanism" is a marvel of moral and conceptual clarity; see the conclusion, on political criticism, to *Literary Theory: An Introduction,* 2nd ed. (Minneapolis: University of Minnesota Press, 1996),169–89.

54. "Hear, O Israel! The Lord is our God, the Lord alone" (Deut 6:4, Jewish Publication Society translation).

55. Mark D. Nanos, *The Mystery of Romans: The Jewish Context of Paul's Letter* (Minneapolis: Fortress Press, 1996), 184.

56. Ibid., 693.

57. *4 Macc.* 6:17, 22; 7:19; 9:21; 13:17; 15:28; 16:20; 17:6; 18:23.

58. Nevertheless, that is just how Hays reads Paul's argument (*Echoes of Scripture,* 54–57). Ernst Käsemann seeks to set against Paul's statement a Jewish insistence that "grace can be imparted only to the pious," but to do so must explain away the evidence, for example, of the Dead Sea Scrolls (*Commentary on Romans,* 111). James D. G. Dunn finds Paul's doctrine of justification of the impious wholly without parallel in Judaism (*The Theology of Paul the Apostle* [Grand Rapids: Eerdmans, 1998], 367 n. 314).

59. Eisenbaum, "A Remedy," 696–97; "Paul as the New Abraham," 137.

60. Eisenbaum, "A Remedy," 694; "Paul as the New Abraham," 132–35.

61. Eisenbaum, "Paul as the New Abraham," 132–33; 144.

62. This is the heart of Eisenbaum's argument in "A Remedy."

63. The *Aeneid* was something of an instant classic. The ruins of Pompeii offer some twenty different inscriptions quoting the *Aeneid*; public and private recitations of it were popular entertainment; Tacitus shows that theater audiences quickly recognized even short quotations from it (see Bonz, *The Past as Legacy,* 61–65).

64. Craig A. Evans, "Paul and 'Works of Law' Language in Late Antiquity," in *Paul and His Opponents* (ed. S. E. Porter; Pauline Studies 2; Leiden: Brill, 2005), 201–26.

65. Evans ("Paul and 'Works of Law'") cites Rom 2:1-16, then immediately disqualifies it with the statement that Paul implies "that, of course, no one actually can do the law." That implication must be read into the text by those eager to sustain a Lutheran reading of the whole of the letter. Paul says nothing of the kind.

66. James D. G. Dunn, "The New Perspective on Paul," *BJRL* 65 (1983): 95–122; quotations from Dunn, *The Theology of Paul the Apostle,* 354–66.

67. Evans notes that there is considerable overlap of vocabulary between Romans and 4QMMT, but given the completely different settings (a letter from a Pharisee to an assembly of non-Judeans who believe Jesus is the Messiah; a letter from the leader of a proto-Sadducean sect to opponents—Pharisees?—regarding specific ritual practices in the Temple), I cannot agree with his verdict that 4QMMT is "an important parallel" to Paul's theology.

68. Gaston, *Paul and the Torah,* 25, 81, 100–106; Gager, *The Origins of Anti-Semitism,* chap. 8 and passim.

69. Jacob Taubes, *The Political Theology of Paul,* trans. Dana Hollander, ed. Aleida Assmann et al. (Stanford: Stanford University Press, 2004), 23–24.

70. John J. Collins, *Between Athens and Jerusalem: Jewish Identity in the Hellenistic Diaspora* (New York: Crossroad, 1983), 137.

71. The classic study is Fredrick Danker, *Benefactor: Epigraphic Study of a Greco-Roman and New Testament Semantic Field* (St. Louis; Clayton, 1980); *ergon* was "frequently used to describe people of exceptional merit, especially benefactors" (*BDAG* s.v.).

5. VIRTVS

1. On arguments "based on the structure of reality," see Chaim Perelman and L. Olbrechts-Tyteca, *The New Rhetoric: A Treatise on Argumentation,* trans. John Wilkinson and Purcell Weaver (Notre Dame: University of Notre Dame Press, 1969), 261–349.

2. Plutarch, *De Fortuna romanorum* 316C–317C (LCL).

3. Josephus, *War* 5.363–67; 372–76; 395–415.

4. Eagleton, *Ideology* (London: Verso, 1991), chap. 2.

5. *Aen.* 10.62–98; translation by Kevin Guinagh (New York: Holt, Rinehart & Winston, 1953), 249–50.

6. *Aen.* 10.100–114.

7. Fredric Jameson, *The Political Unconscious: Narrative as a Socially Symbolic Act* (Ithaca: Cornell University Press, 1981), 52–53.

8. Suetonius, *Nero* 46; see Davina C. Lopez, *Apostle to the Conquered: Reimagining Paul's Mission,* Paul and Critical Contexts Series (Minneapolis: Fortress Press, 2008), chap. 1.

9. On the pronounced "end of history," see Francis Fukuyama, *The End of History and the Last Man* (New York: Penguin, 1992).

10. Jean-Bertrand Aristide contrasts the actual "free markets" of the Haitian countryside with the global order imposed from Washington in *Eyes of the Heart: Seeking a Path for the Poor in the Age of Globalization,* ed. Laura Flynn (Monroe: Common Courage, 2000), 9–10. There is a rich literature available on the deleterious actual effects of the forcible expansion of a heralded free market: see Kevin Danaher, ed., *Fifty Years Is Enough: The Case against the World Bank and the International Monetary Fund* (Boston: South End, 1994); Doug Bandow and Ian Vásquez, ed., *Perpetuating Poverty: The World Bank, the IMF, and the Developing World* (Washington, D.C.: Cato Institute, 1994); John Isbister, *Promises Not Kept: The Betrayal of Social Change in the Third World,* 3rd ed. (West Hartford: Kumarian, 1995). Jim Yong Kim et al., ed., *Dying for Growth: Global Inequality and the Health of the Poor* (Monroe: Common Courage, 2000).

11. Noam Chomsky, *Hegemony or Survival: America's Quest for Global Dominance* (New York: Henry Holt & Co., 2003), 191.

12. The ironic lament of an Iraqi who, beholding the daily deprivations and outrages visited upon his people under U.S. occupation, declares that "this is the freedom" promised by the United States, inspired the title of journalist Christian Parenti's book *The Freedom: Shadows and Hallucinations in Occupied Iraq* (New York: New, 2004).

13. Franz J. Hinkelammert, "The Crisis of Socialism in the Third World," in *Cultura de la Esperanza y Sociedad sin Exclusión* (San José: DEI, 1995), 5–38; see also Daniel M. Bell Jr., *Liberation Theology after the End of History: The Refusal to Cease Suffering,* Radical Orthodoxy Series (London and New York: Routledge, 2001).

14. 1QpHab 7:7-8.

15. So he was regarded by his contemporaries (*Life* 140). John M. G. Barclay provides a judicious and sensitive portrait of Josephus's complex motivations, concluding that he offers "the most forthright expression of Jewish-Roman political accommodation known to us" (*Jews in the Mediterranean Diaspora from Alexander to Trajan (323 BCE–117 CE)* [Edinburgh: T&T Clark, 1996], 346–56; quotation from 356).

16. After writing this, I was surprised to find Jon Sobrino use the same phrase to describe the wickedness that takes place among the poor, reinforced by the deficiencies to which they are subjected: see *No Salvation Outside the Poor: Utopian-Prophetic Essays* (Maryknoll: Orbis, 2008), 72–73.

17. Raymond Brown, "The Semitic Background of the New Testament *mysterion,*" *Biblica* 39 (1958): 218–28; 40 (1959): 70–87.

18. *hē theia dikē metēlthen kai meteleusetai ton alastora tyrannon* (*4 Macc.* 18:22).

19. Philo, *Embassy to Gaius* 1–3; also 220 (on the *theou pronoia,* "providence of God").

20. See for example Rudolf Bultmann, "Das Problem der Ethik bei Paulus," *ZNW* 23 (1924): 123–40; Victor Paul Furnish, *Theology and Ethics in Paul* (Nashville: Abingdon, 1968), 224–27; Robert Jewett, *Romans,* Hermeneia (Minneapolis: Fortress Press, 2007), 725–26.

21. Jewett rightly refers to the "eschatological urgency" of Paul's exhortation in 12:1—15:13 (*Romans,* 724).

22. Jameson, *The Political Unconscious,* 52–53.

23. Isa 40:13 at Rom 11:34-35.

24. Halvor Moxnes, "The Quest for Honor and the Unity of the Community in Romans 12 and in the Orations of Dio Chrysostom," in *Paul in His Hellenistic Context,* ed. Troels Engberg-Pedersen

(Minneapolis: Fortress Press, 1995), 203–30; quotation from 214. To similar effect Robert Jewett observes that Paul's exhortation involves "nonconformity to the present world order" (*Romans*, 731; on the "Pyramid of Honor" in Roman culture, 49–51).

25. Moxnes, "The Quest for Honor," 228.

26. Ibid., 218, 229.

27. Indeed, Blumenfeld acknowledges that in his discussion, a perfectly plausible (and fairly obvious) alternative—situating Paul against "a Jewish conceptual background"—is "simply not addressed." He offers "only one option" for interpreting Paul, that of "a Greek perspective," in the conviction that it "is compelling in and of itself." His systematic neglect of a wealth of alternative data, the possible relevance of which he openly acknowledges, does little to inspire the same confidence in his readers: Bruno Blumenfeld, *The Political Paul: Justice, Democracy, and Kingship in a Hellenistic Framework* (JSNTSup 210; Sheffield: Sheffield Academic, 2001), 26.

28. Between Aristotle and Paul, Blumenfeld remarks (ibid., 15–16), "practically no new political theory was elaborated. The same old teachings were used, tirelessly and uncritically.... In the process, political thought became increasingly artificial and incongruous, deplorably inadequate and woefully inappropriate to describe or explain, much less to stimulate and improve, political structures and proceedings."

29. Ibid., 288 (on the Hellenistic Pythagorean tradition, which Blumenfeld argues is "brought back to life" by Paul).

30. Ibid., 26.

31. Ibid., 282–83. Blumenfeld declares his view of Paul's "love" for Rome confirmed by a Byzantine-era mosaic, on the floor of the taxation office, quoting Rom 13:3. Blumenfeld is surely right that "by the time this floor was laid, Paul was firmly embedded in the structure of Christian imperial power" (283). He offers no explanation whatever for what this has to do with the apostle himself.

32. Indeed, Blumenfeld cannot at last let Paul remain the uncritical apologist for empire that he has portrayed and ascribes to the apostle an irony so sublime as to be undetectable (ibid., 391–92, n. 273).

33. Mark D. Nanos, *The Mystery of Romans: The Jewish Context of Paul's Letter* (Minneapolis: Fortress Press, 1996), chap. 3.

34. Ibid., 88–95.

35. Robert Karris dismissed attempts to identify the particular orientation of the ascetics in Rom 14: "Romans 14:1—15:13 and the Occasion of Romans," in *The Romans Debate*, ed. Karl P. Donfried, 2nd ed. (Peabody: Hendrickson, 1991), 66–70. Ernst Käsemann denied that the asceticism was Judean because it included abstinence from wine (*Commentary on Romans* [Grand Rapids: Eerdmans, 1980], 367). But writings from the Hellenistic Diaspora show that abstinence from meat and wine routinely expressed Judean observance (Dan 1:3-16; Esth 3:28; 4:16; Jdt 12:1-2). Josephus shows that securing civic permission for acquiring, preparing, and selling kosher foods was an ongoing concern in the diaspora communities (*Ant.* 14.185–267); he also tells the story of "certain priests" who, being required to appear before Caesar, subsisted for months in Rome on a diet of "figs and nuts" (*Life* 3). See my discussion in "Asceticism in Romans 14–15," in *Asceticism and the New Testament*, ed. Leif E. Vaage and Vincent L. Wimbush (London: Routledge, 1999), 231–51, with further bibliography at 247 n. 19.

36. Juvenal describes the rough life of the Roman streets, where one daily risks mugging; he describes a particularly nasty thug who insults his victim, saying he smells like a Judean who has had to subsist on vinegar and beans (*Sat.* 3.278–301). Horace describes a friend who escapes an unwelcome conversation by pleading to be "one of the many weak," who must attend Sabbath services (*Sat.* 1.9.68–72).

37. Mark Reasoner, *The Strong and the Weak: Romans 14.1—15.13 in Context*, SNTSMS 103 (Cambridge: Cambridge University Press, 1999), 192.

38. See Robert Jewett's excellent discussion of the situation in *Romans*, 833–36. Jewett writes later that the "weaknesses" of the weak are probably "deficits that are perceived to be both theological and social" (ibid., 876); perceived, that is, by the Roman non-Judean majority, not by Paul.

39. Jewett translates the participle *synapagomenoi* "choosing to go along with others," and accepts the translation of *tapeinois* as "common, poor people," but inclines away from a social understanding of the noun: "if the argument of Romans is accepted, all persons are 'the lowly' because all have sinned and fallen short of the glory of God" (*Romans*, 769). He then interprets *tapeinois* as if it were the opposite of *hypsēla*, "exalted things," and concludes that Paul here opposes "an early form of Proto-Gnosticism" (770). I find no evidence in the letter for such a polemic and take the ordinary sense of *tapeinois*, referring to "being of low social status or to relative inability to cope" (*BDAG*), to be decisive.

40. See the example I give in the Introduction; for issues and bibliography, see Jewett, *Romans*, 780–803; Neil Elliott, *Liberating Paul* (Minneapolis: Fortress Press, 2006), 14–16, 19–20, and passim. I have discussed the passage at greater length in "Romans 13:1-7 in the Context of Imperial Propaganda," in *Paul and Empire: Religion and Power in Roman Imperial Society*, ed. Richard A. Horsley (Harrisburg: Trinity Press International, 1997), 184–204.

41. See my comments above on Bruno Blumenfeld's reading of Paul in *The Political Paul*. F. Gerald Dowling finds the "optimism" regarding the conduct of magistrates and the attitude of "compliance" toward them to be uncharacteristic of Jewish thought, but more at home in Stoicism; he argues that "the later Paul" has moved toward a more conservative Stoic ethic in which "public conventions are much more widely maintained" (*Cynics, Paul and the Pauline Churches*, Cynics and Christian Origins 2 [London and New York: Routledge, 1998], 280–81).

42. Jewett, *Romans*, 783.

43. The NRSV translates the second occurrence of *phobos* with "respect," and Jewett offers a sustained argument for this translation (*Romans*, 802–3). But Paul has already referred to "honor" (*timē*); his use of *phobos* in a way that jars with his previous usage is peculiar, to say the least.

44. James Kallas, "Romans XIII:1-7: An Interpolation," *NTS* 11 (1964–65): 365–74; so also J. C. O'Neill, *Paul's Letter to the Romans* (London: Penguin, 1975), 207–10; Winsome Munro, *Authority in Paul and Peter*, SNTSMS 45 (Cambridge: Cambridge University Press, 1983), 79.

45. Ernst Käsemann, *Commentary on Romans*, 357–59; Käsemann, "Principles in the Interpretation of Romans 13," in *New Testament Questions of Today*, trans. W. J. Montague (Philadelphia: Fortress Press, 1969), 200.

46. Leander E. Keck, "What Makes Romans Tick?" in *Pauline Theology III: Romans*, ed. David M. Hay and E. Elizabeth Johnson (Minneapolis: Fortress Press, 1993), 16.

47. Tacitus reports that a Roman cohort could only restore order in Puteoli through "a few executions" (*Ann.* 13.48). This line of argument depends upon J. Friedrich, W. Pöhlmann, and P. Stuhlmacher, "Zur historischen Situation und Intention von Röm 13,1-7," *ZTK* 73 (1976): 131–66.

48. See Elliott, "Romans 13:1-7," 191–92. Relevant factors here are (a) resentment on the part of their neighbors of the Judean practice of sending money to Jerusalem; there is no evidence that this ever involved Judeans being relieved of local tax obligations, but the practice was chronically perceived as removing wealth from the city (see James D. G. Dunn, "Romans 13:1-7—A Charter for Political Quietism?" *Ex Auditu* 2 [1986]: 60); (b) the perception that Judeans enjoyed a privileged position as clients of the Caesars, which while precarious (see above, chapter three), also inspired resentment (see Paula Fredriksen, "Judaism, the Circumcision of Gentiles, and Apocalyptic Hope," *JTS* 42, no. 2 [1991], 556–58; Christopher Stanley, "'Neither Jew nor Greek': Ethnic Conflict in Graeco-Roman Society," *JSNT* 64 [1996]: 101–24; and (c) a general Roman policy of suppressing or removing "foreign" populations in the event of civil disturbance, in effect "rounding up the usual suspects" (see Leonard V. Rutgers, "Roman Policy toward the Jews: Expulsions from the City of Rome during the First Century C.E.," in *Judaism and Christianity in First-Century Rome*, ed. Karl P. Donfried and Peter Richardson [Grand Rapids: Eerdmans, 1998], 93–116). Jewett declares this scenario unlikely but does not address any of the arguments named (*Romans*, 785). On the other hand, his reference to Nero's imposition of tribute upon recent immigrants, possibly including the returning Judean exiles, is quite consistent with the approach I take here (ibid., 799; see the literature cited there).

49. Jewett, *Romans*, 787–90.

50. T. L. Carter, "The Irony of Romans 13," *NovT* 46, no. 3 (2004): 209–28.

51. Ibid., 213, 215.

52. Ibid., 218.

53. Elliott, "Romans 13:1-7," 201–3.

54. Carter himself observes that "the text does not demand an ironic interpretation: it is perfectly possible to continue to understand it, in accordance with common opinion, as a straightforward injunction to submit to the governing authorities" ("The Irony of Romans 13," 227).

55. Norman Gottwald, *The Tribes of Yahweh: A Sociology of Liberated Israel 1050–1250* (Maryknoll: Orbis, 1979); Gottwald, *The Hebrew Bible: A Socio-Literary Introduction* (Philadelphia: Fortress Press, 1985).

56. On mode of production, and the importance of the sole-rule figure (the "oriental despot" at the center of Marx's "Asiatic" mode of production), see Roland Boer, "Conclusion: On the Question of Mode of Production," in *Marxist Criticism of the Bible* (Sheffield: Sheffield Academic, 2003), 229–46.

57. On economic mutualism as the "survival strategy" among the poor in Rome, see Justin J. Meggitt, *Paul, Poverty, and Survival* (Edinburgh: T&T Clark, 1998); on the economic and ideological significance of the collection, see Dieter Georgi, *Remembering the Poor: The History of Paul's Collection for Jerusalem* (Nashville: Abingdon, 1965), and Sze-Kar Wan, "Collection for the Saints as Anti-Colonial Act: Implications of Paul's Ethnic Reconstruction," in *Paul and Politics: Ekklesia, Israel, Imperium, Interpretation,* ed. Richard A. Horsley (Harrisburg: Trinity Press International, 2000), 191–215; see also Calvin Roetzel's response, "How Anti-Imperial Was the Collection and How Emancipatory Was Paul's Project?" ibid., 227–30. On the "civilization of poverty," see Jon Sobrino, "The Crucified People and the Civilization of Poverty: Ignacio Ellacuría's 'Taking Hold of Reality,'" chap. 1 in *No Salvation Outside the Poor.* I thank Robert Ellsberg of Orbis Books for his generous sharing of this manuscript with me before it went to press.

58. See Sobrino, *"Extra pauperes nulla salus*: A Short Utopian-Prophetic Essay," in *No Salvation Outside the Poor,* 51–53.

59. Sobrino, "The Crucified People and the Civilization of Poverty," 9–10.

60. Sobrino, *"Extra pauperes nulla salus,"* 48, 51.

61. Walter Benjamin, *Reflections: Essays, Aphorisms, Autobiographical Writings,* ed. and with an introduction by Peter Demetz (New York: Harcourt Brace Jovanovich, 1978), 312.

62. See further the discussion in Jacob Taubes, *The Political Theology of Paul,* trans. Dana Hollander (Stanford: Stanford University Press, 2004), 70–76.

63. Slavoj Žižek, *The Fragile Absolute; Or, Why Is the Christian Legacy Worth Fighting For?* (London: Verso, 2000), 89–90.

64. So, for example, Richard A. Horsley, Introduction to *Paul and Empire,* 3. Similarly, Robert Jewett suggests we understand Paul's language of "conquering evil with good" (12:21) "within a transformative framework that is universal in scope but local in operation. The thought of overcoming 'evil' through everyday acts of solidarity would be grandiose except for the framework of a global mission," which Jewett considers "the theme and purpose of Romans" (779). But I see no evidence that Paul attributes such globally "transformative" efficacy to the *ekklēsia.*

65. Žižek, *The Fragile Absolute,* 89–90.

66. On the notion of spectrality or the "haunting" by other histories that disrupt the dominant narrative in an imperial situation, see Laura Donaldson, "Gospel Hauntings: The Postcolonial Demons of New Testament Criticism," in *Postcolonial Biblical Criticism: Interdisciplinary Intersections,* ed. Stephen D. Moore and Fernando F. Segovia (London: T&T Clark, 2005), 97–113.

67. Jon Sobrino, S.J., "The Winds in Santo Domingo and the Evangelization of Culture," in *Santo Domingo and Beyond: Documents and Commentaries from the Historic Meeting of the Latin American Bishops' Conference,* ed. Alfred T. Hennelly, S.J. (Maryknoll: Orbis, 1993), 178–79; 172–73.

68. Sobrino, *"Ex pauperes nulla salus,"* 61.

Epilogue

1. *The State of Food Insecurity in the World* (New York: Food and Agriculture Organization of the United Nations, 2000), available at www.fao.org/DOCREP/004/X6727E/x6727e06.htm (accessed Oct. 1, 2007).

2. Mike Davis, *Planet of Slums* (London and New York: Verso, 2006).

3. Ibid., chap. 3, "The Treason of the State"; chap. 4, "Illusions of Self-Help"; chap. 8, "A Surplus Humanity." See Jon Sobrino, *No Salvation Outside the Poor: Utopian-Prophetic Essays* (Maryknoll: Orbis, 2008), 1–18.

4. Michael Hardt and Antonio Negri, *Empire* (Cambridge: Harvard University Press, 2000); their book has provoked important critical reviews, e.g., the essays gathered in Jodi Dean and Paul Passavant, eds., *Empire's New Clothes: Reading Hardt and Negri* (London: Routledge, 2003), and Atilio A. Boron, *Empire and Imperialism: A Critical Reading of Michael Hardt and Antonio Negri* (London: Zed Books, 2005); Hardt and Negri have responded in *Multitude: War and Democracy in the Age of Empire* (New York: Penguin, 2006).

5. Gopal Balakrishnan, "Virgilian Visions," *New Left Review* 5 (2000): 142–48; see also Malcolm Bull, "The Limits of Multitude," *New Left Review* 35 (2005): 19–39.

6. Jon Sobrino, *No Salvation Outside the Poor: Prophetic-Utopian Essays* (Maryknoll: Orbis, 2008).

7. See Hilary Cunningham, *God and Caesar at the Rio Grande: Sanctuary and the Politics of Religion* (Minneapolis: University of Minnesota Press, 1995).

8. See Bill Wylie-Kellerman, "Apologist of Power: The Long Shadow of Reinhold Niebuhr's Christian Realism," *Sojourners* (March 1987), 14–20; Theodore R. Weber described Christian realism from a Latin American perspective as "a religious ideology that serves to justify U.S. power, or the power of establishments in other countries in league with the United states, and the 'national security doctrine'": "Christian Realism, Power, and Peace," in *Theology, Politics, and Peace,* ed. Theodore Runyon (Maryknoll: Orbis, 1989), 59. Larry Rasmussen now offers a critically sensitive and insightful assessment of the reasons for Niebuhr's withdrawal from socialism: "Was Reinhold Niebuhr Wrong about Socialism?" *Political Theology* 6, no. 4 (2005): 429–57.

9. See Douglas Harink, *Paul among the Postliberals: Pauline Theology beyond Christendom and Modernity* (Grand Rapids: Eerdmans, 2003).

10. See a discussion of the issues by Kristin Heyer, "How Does Theology Go Public? Rethinking the Debate between David Tracy and George Lindbeck," *Political Theology* 5, no. 3 (2004), available at www.equinoxjournals.com/ojs/index.php/PT/index (accessed Oct. 1, 2007).

11. Elisabeth Schüssler Fiorenza, *The Power of the Word* (Minneapolis: Fortress Press, 2007).

12. See Noam Chomsky and Edward S. Herman, *Manufacturing Consent: The Political Economy of the Mass Media* (New York: Pantheon, 1988; with a new Introduction, 2002). I have adapted their model of a propaganda system for exploring the role of the congregational "production of the sacred" in "A Famine of the Word: A Stringfellowian Reflection on the U.S. Church Scene," in *The Bible in the Public Square: Reading the Signs of the Times,* eds. Ellen B. Aitken, Jonathan A. Draper, and Cynthia Briggs Kittredge (Minneapolis: Fortress Press, 2008), forthcoming.

13. Immanuel Wallerstein, "New Revolts against the System," *New Left Review* 18 (Nov.-Dec. 2002): 29–39; 38.

14. Göran Therborn, "After Dialectics: Radical Social Theory in a Post-Communist World," *New Left Review* 43 (Jan.-Feb. 2007): 63–114; 114.

15. See the Final Declaration of the World Social Forum in Porto Alegre (2000), online at www .forumsocialmundial.org.br.

16. See *Voice of the Voiceless: The Four Pastoral Letters and Other Statements of Archbishop Oscar Romero,* with introductory essays by Jon Sobrino and Ignacio Martín-Baró (Maryknoll: Orbis, 1985). After writing this, I was pleased to find Jon Sobrino make a similar point regarding the parable in Luke and the prophets of our own day, among whom he includes Monseñor Romero, Noam Chomsky, and others: *No Salvation Outside the Poor,* 47–48.

Indexes

Ancient Literature

Modern Authors

Selected Topics

PAUL IN CRITICAL CONTEXTS

Other Titles in the Series

Apostle to the Conquered
Reimagining Paul's Mission

Davina C. Lopez

ISBN 978-0-8006-6281-3

The Politics of Heaven
Women, Gender, and Empire in the Study of Paul

Joseph A. Marchal

ISBN 978-0-8006-6300-1

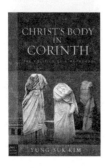

Christ's Body in Corinth
The Politics of a Metaphor

Yung Suk Kim

ISBN 978-0-8006-6285-1

call 800-328-4648
fortresspress.com